国家卫生和计划生育委员会"十三五"英文版规划教材
全国高等学校教材

供临床医学专业及来华留学生（MBBS）双语教学用

Medical Chinese
医学汉语

主　编　李　骢
Chief Editor　Cong Li

副主编　明珍平　　　李贡辉　　　孙　宏
Vice Chief Editor　Zhenping Ming　Gonghui Li　Hong Sun

人民卫生出版社
People's Medical Publishing House

图书在版编目（CIP）数据

医学汉语：英汉对照 / 李聪主编 . —北京：人民
卫生出版社，2018
全国高等学校临床医学专业第一轮英文版规划教材
ISBN 978–7–117–26577–5

I. ①医… Ⅱ. ①李… Ⅲ. ①医学 – 汉语 – 高等学校
– 教材 Ⅳ. ①H193

中国版本图书馆 CIP 数据核字（2018）第 129788 号

人卫智网	www.ipmph.com	医学教育、学术、考试、健康，
		购书智慧智能综合服务平台
人卫官网	www.pmph.com	人卫官方资讯发布平台

医 学 汉 语

主　　编：李　聪
出版发行：人民卫生出版社（中继线 010-59780011）
地　　址：北京市朝阳区潘家园南里 19 号
邮　　编：100021
E - mail: pmph @ pmph.com
购书热线：010-59787592　010-59787584　010-65264830
印　　刷：中国农业出版社印刷厂
经　　销：新华书店
开　　本：850×1168　1/16　印张：17
字　　数：527 千字
版　　次：2018 年 3 月第 1 版　2018 年 3 月第 1 版第 1 次印刷
标准书号：ISBN 978-7-117-26577-5
定　　价：53.00 元

打击盗版举报电话：010-59787491　E-mail: WQ @ pmph.com
（凡属印装质量问题请与本社市场营销中心联系退换）

编者（按姓氏笔画排序）

于澎涛　　　　郑州大学
Pengtao Yu　　Zhengzhou University

白　洋　　　　中国医科大学
Yang Bai　　　China Medical University

刘　兰　　　　安徽医科大学
Lan Liu　　　 Anhui Medical University

孙　宏　　　　牡丹江医学院
Hong Sun　　 Mudanjiang Medical University

刘婷雁　　　　福建医科大学
Tingyan Liu　 Fujian Medical University

杜幼芹　　　　三峡大学医学院
Youqin Du　　Medical College of China Three Gorges University

张庆富　　　　河北医科大学第一医院
Qingfu Zhang　The First Hospital of Hebei Medical University

李贡辉　　　　汕头大学·香港中文大学联合汕头国际眼科中心
Gonghui Li　　Shantou University. Chinese University of Hongkong Joint International Eye Center

汪　浩　　　　同济大学附属同济医院
Hao Wang　　Tongji Hospital, Tongji University

吴　涛　　　　昆明医科大学
Tao Wu　　　 Kunming Medical University

张彩华　　　　大连医科大学
Caihua Zhang　Dalian Medical University

李　骢　　　　大连医科大学
Cong Li　　　 Dalian Medical University

明珍平　　　　武汉大学
Zhenping Ming　Wuhan University

姜　安　　　　南京医科大学
An Jiang　　　Nanjing Medical University

贾月萍　　　　北京大学人民医院
Yueping Jia　 Peking University People's Hospital

徐　冬　　　　浙江大学医学院附属妇产科医院
Dong Xu　　　Women's Hospital School of Medicine Zhejiang University

曹秀平　　　　哈尔滨医科大学
Xiuping Cao　 Harbin Medical University

薛必成　　　　温州医科大学
BichengXue　 Wenzhou Medical University

1995 年,我国首次招收全英文授课医学留学生,到 2015 年,接收临床医学专业 MBBS (Bachelor of Medicine & Bachelor of Surgery)留学生的院校达到了 40 余家,MBBS 院校数量、规模不断扩张;同时,医学院校在临床医学专业五年制、长学制教学中陆续开展不同规模和范围的双语或全英文授课,使得对一套符合我国教学实际、成体系、高质量英文教材的需求日益增长。

为了满足教学需求,进一步落实教育部《关于加强高等学校本科教学工作提高教学质量的若干意见(教高[2001]4 号)》和《来华留学生医学本科教育(英文授课)质量控制标准暂行规定(教外来[2007]39 号)》等相关文件的要求,规范和提高我国高等医学院校临床医学专业五年制、长学制和来华留学生(MBBS)双语教学及全英文教学的质量,推进医学双语教学和留学生教育的健康有序发展,完善和规范临床医学专业英文版教材的体系,人民卫生出版社在充分调研的基础上,于 2015 年召开了全国高等学校临床医学专业英文版规划教材的编写论证会,经过会上及会后的反复论证,最终确定组织编写一套全国规划的、适合我国高等医学院校教学实际的临床医学专业英文版教材,并计划作为 2017 年春季和秋季教材在全国出版发行。

本套英文版教材的编写结合国家卫生和计划生育委员会、教育部的总体要求,坚持"三基、五性、三特定"的原则,组织全国各大医学院校、教学医院的专家编写,主要特点如下:

1. 教材编写应教学之需启动,在全国范围进行了广泛、深入调研和论证,借鉴国内外医学人才培养模式和教材建设经验,对主要读者对象、编写模式、编写科目、编者遴选条件等进行了科学设计。

2. 坚持"三基、五性、三特定"和"多级论证"的教材编写原则,组织全国各大医学院校及教学医院有丰富英语教学经验的专家一起编写,以保证高质量出版。

3. 为保证英语表达的准确性和规范性,大部分教材以国外英文原版教科书为蓝本,根据我国教学大纲和人民卫生出版社临床医学专业第八轮规划教材主要内容进行改编,充分体现科学性、权威性、适用性和实用性。

4. 教材内部各环节合理设置,根据读者对象的特点,在英文原版教材的基础上结合需要,增加本章小结、关键术语(英中对照)、思考题、推荐阅读等模块,促进学生自主学习。

本套临床医学专业英文版规划教材共 38 种,均为国家卫生和计划生育委员会"十三五"规划教材,计划于 2017 年全部出版发行。

In 1995, China recruited overseas medical students of full English teaching for the first time. Up to 2015, more than 40 institutions enrolled overseas MBBS (Bachelor of Medicine & Bachelor of Surgery) students. The number of MBBS institutions and overseas students are continuously increasing. At the meantime, medical colleges' application for bilingual or full English teaching in different size and range in five-year and long-term professional clinical medicine teaching results to increasingly demand for a set of practical, systematic and high-qualified English teaching material.

In order to meet the teaching needs and to implement the regulations of relevant documents issued by Ministry of Education including "Some Suggestions to Strengthen the Undergraduate Teaching and to Improve the Teaching Quality" and "Interim Provisions on Quality Control Standards of International Medical Undergraduate Education (English teaching)", as well as to standardize and improve the quality of the bilingual teaching and English teaching of the five-year, long-term and international students (MBBS) of clinical medicine in China's higher medical colleges so as to promote the healthy and orderly development of medical bilingual teaching and international students education and to improve and standardize the system of English clinical medicine textbooks, after full investigation, People's Medical Publishing House (PMPH) held the writing discussion meeting of English textbook for clinical medicine department of national colleges and universities in 2015. After the repeated demonstration in and after the meeting, PMPH ultimately determined to organize the compilation of a set of national planning English textbooks which are suitable for China's actual clinical medicine teaching of medical colleges and universities. This set will be published as spring and autumn textbooks of 2017.

This set of English textbooks meets the overall requirements of the Ministry of Education and National Health and Family Planning Commission, the editorial committee includes the experts from major medical colleges and universities as well as teaching hospitals, the main features are as follows:

1. Textbooks compilation is started to meet the teaching needs, extensive and deep research and demonstration are conducted across the country, the main target readers, the model and subject of compilation and selection conditions of authors are scientifically designed in accordance with the reference of domestic and foreign medical personnel training model and experience in teaching materials.

2. Adhere to the teaching materials compiling principles of "three foundations, five characteristics, and three specialties" and "multi-level demonstration", the organization of English teaching experts with rich experience from major medical schools and teaching hospitals ensures the high quality of publication.

3. In order to ensure the accuracy and standardization of English expression, most of the textbooks are modeled on original English textbooks, and adapted based on national syllabus and main content of the eighth round of clinical medicine textbooks which were published by PMPH, fully reflecting the scientificity, authority, applicability and practicality.

4. All aspects of teaching materials are arranged reasonably, based on original textbooks,the chapter summary, key terms (English and Chinese), review questions, and recommended readings are added to promote students' independent learning in accordance with teaching needs and the characteristics of the target readers.

This set of English textbooks for clinical medicine includes 38 species which are among "13th Five-Year" planning textbooks of National Health and Family Planning Commission, and will be all published in 2017.

全国高等学校临床医学专业第一轮英文版规划教材·教材目录

教材名称		主审	主编	
1 人体解剖学	Human Anatomy		刘学政	
2 生理学	Physiology		闫剑群	
3 医学免疫学	Medical Immunology		储以微	
4 生物化学	Biochemistry		张晓伟	
5 组织学与胚胎学	Histology and Embryology		李 和	
6 医学微生物学	Medical Microbiology		郭晓奎	
7 病理学	Pathology		陈 杰	
8 医学分子生物学	Medical Molecular Biology		吕社民	
9 医学遗传学	Medical Genetics		傅松滨	
10 医学细胞生物学	Medical Cell Biology		刘 佳	
11 病理生理学	Pathophysiology		王建枝	
12 药理学	Pharmacology		杨宝峰	
13 临床药理学	Clinical Pharmacology		李 俊	
14 人体寄生虫学	Human Parasitology		李学荣	
15 流行病学	Epidemiology		沈洪兵	
16 医学统计学	Medical Statistics		郝元涛	
17 核医学	Nuclear Medicine		黄 钢	李 方
18 医学影像学	Medical Imaging		申宝忠	龚启勇
19 临床诊断学	Clinical Diagnostics		万学红	
20 实验诊断学	Laboratory Diagnostics		胡翊群	王 琳
21 内科学	Internal Medicine		文富强	汪道文
22 外科学	Surgery		陈孝平	田 伟
23 妇产科学	Obstetrics and Gynaecology	郎景和	狄 文	曹云霞
24 儿科学	Pediatrics		黄国英	罗小平
25 神经病学	Neurology		张黎明	
26 精神病学	Psychiatry		赵靖平	
27 传染病学	Infectious Diseases		高志良	任 红

PREFACE

With the rapid development of China medical science, more and more international students come to China to study medical professional knowledge. Medical Chinese has become the basis for these students to study and live in China. At present, there are two kinds of medical Chinese teaching materials used by colleges and universities. One is a general Chinese textbook, which can only solve the general communication problems of foreign students entering undergraduate study and it is not enough for clinical medicine that requires a large number of specialized terms and terminology, then it may lead to a great deal of obstacles in understanding their professional knowledge, especially in clinical practice, and even their completion of studies. The other kind of medical Chinese teaching materials has a strong professionalism, which is too hard for the students at this stage, and is not suitable to be vigorously promoted.

Therefore, it is very necessary and urgent to write a Chinese teaching material that is really suitable for foreign students to solve the medical language problems. With the strong support of the People's Medical Publishing House, relying on the cooperation of the teachers from nearly 20 medical universities in different areas, who work in frontline of clinical and medical Chinese teaching, the book *Medical Chinese* is now presented to its readers.

The book is composed of 21 chapters, organized by six parts. The first part is common medical Chinese which includes one chapter: Hospital situation. This chapter provides a general description of the Chinese hospital. Subsequent chapters are present in the sequence of internal medicine, surgery, obstetrics and gynecology, pediatrics and stomatology. Every chapter is divided into sections emphasizing new words, text, and an introduction of disease, language points and exercises. Each text consists of two dialogues which are from the most common and typical medical cases in each clinical department. Listening script and more exercises are provided in the network of value-added part as materials for further studying. In fact, this book is not only applicable to foreign students studying medicine in China, but also for the domestic students in bilingual teaching and foreign medical staff working in China.

We are most grateful to all the contributors for their hard and efficient work to make this book available. We are thankful to the three vice chiefeditors: Zhenping Ming, Gonghui Li and Hong Sun. We thank Dr.Caihua Zhang for the industrious secretary work.

Cong Li

本书文中所提到的所有人物姓名纯属虚构，如有雷同，纯属巧合。

目 录
CONTENTS

第四篇　妇产科学
PART 4　Obstetrics and Gynecology

第五篇　儿科学
PART 5　Pediatrics

第六篇　口腔科学
PART 6　Stomatology

第一章	医 院 概 况

 **会话一** 　　医院各部门介绍

 词汇

医务处	yīwùchù	名	medical affairs office
护理部	hùlǐbù	名	nursing department
科研处	kēyánchù	名	scientific research department
人力资源处	rénlìzīyuánchù	名	human resources department
财务处	cáiwùchù	名	financial department
器械设备处	qìxièshèbèichù	名	instrument and equipment department
外科	wàikē	名	surgery department
内科	nèikē	名	internal medicine
门诊	ménzhěn	名	outpatient department
急诊	jízhěn	名	emergency department
骨科	gǔkē	名	orthopedic surgery
心脏外科	xīnzàngwàikē	名	cardiac surgery
妇产科	fùchǎnkē	名	obstetric and gynecologic department
眼科	yǎnkē	名	ophthalmic department
神经外科	shénjīngwàikē	名	neurosurgery
泌尿外科	mìniàowàikē	名	urinary surgery
肝胆外科	gāndǎnwàikē	名	hepatobiliary surgery
消化内科	xiāohuànèikē	名	gastroenterology department
呼吸内科	hūxīnèikē	名	respiratory medicine
心血管内科	xīnxuèguǎnnèikē	名	cardiovascular medicine
血液内科	xuèyènèikē	名	hematology department
内分泌科	nèifēnmìkē	名	endocrinology department
神经内科	shénjīngnèikē	名	neurology department
儿科	érkē	名	pediatrics
重症监护室	zhòngzhèngjiānhùshì	名	intensive care unit
超声医学科	chāoshēngyīxuékē	名	ultrasound department

检验科	jiǎnyànkē	名	clinical laboratory
病理科	bìnglǐkē	名	pathology department
放射科	fàngshèkē	名	radiology department

地点：医院
人物：菲利普（医生）
　　　格雷（实习医生）

格　雷　菲利普医生，早上好！我是实习医生格雷，很荣幸能到你们医院实习。

菲利普　格雷，你好！欢迎你来我们医院。我先带你参观一下我们医院，熟悉熟悉环境。

格　雷　好的，谢谢您！

菲利普　我们现在所在的这一层，主要都是医院的一些行政部门，主要有行政办公室、**医务处**、**护理部**、**教学处**、**科研处**、**人力资源处**、**财务处**、**器械设备处**等。

格　雷　请问哪个部门负责我的实习安排呢？

菲利普　就是我们医院的教学处啊！如果你在实习期间有什么问题都可以来找我们。

格　雷　请问，隔壁的医务处主要负责什么呢？

菲利普　医务处主要负责管理医疗相关的事务，像制订医疗管理制度、管理临床科室和检查科室什么的。

菲利普　现在，我带你去临床科室参观，走吧。你对临床科室了解吗？

格　雷　知道一些，以前见习的时候去过一些临床科室。

菲利普　我们医院临床科室主要在**外科大楼**、**内科大楼**，还有些在**门诊**和**急诊**。

格　雷　哦，这就是外科大楼吧？

菲利普　是的，外科大楼里有普通外科、**骨科**、**心脏外科**、**妇产科**、**眼科**、**神经外科**、**泌尿外科**、**肝胆外科**等。

格　雷　有这么多科室啊！

菲利普　是的，外科主要接收需要手术的病人，手术室和麻醉科也在这座大楼里。现在我们去内科大楼吧。

格　雷　好的。

菲利普　内科大楼主要接收各种内科住院病人，包括**消化内科**、**呼吸内科**、**心血管内科**、**血液内科**、中医科、**内分泌科**、**神经内科**、**儿科**、**重症监护室**等科室。

格　雷　菲利普医生，最前面的那栋大楼是什么地方？

菲利普　那是门诊和急诊科。门诊主要接收普通就诊的病人，急诊接收来医院看急诊的病人，也是抢救生命的重要场所。

格　雷　菲利普医生，请问如果病人发生了严重车祸，他应该去哪个科室呢？

菲利普　病人发生严重车祸后，应立即到急诊外科就诊，由护士根据病情分诊，然后由医生立即实施诊治。

菲利普　接下来，我再带你去看看临床辅助科室。我们医院的诊断科室包括**超声医学科**、**检验科**、**病理科**、**放射科**等。

格　雷　谢谢您，菲利普医生！我明天就可以来实习了，对吗？

菲利普　明天你还不用到临床科室去实习。从明天开始，老师会给你们做三天的实习前指导。然后，你们就可以根据实习安排到实习科室报到了。

格 雷 好的,谢谢您。

Hospital Department Introduction

SITE: Hospital

CHARACTERS: Philips (Physician)

Gary (Intern)

Gary: Good morning, Dr. Philips! I'm Gary, an intern. It's my honor to come to your hospital for practice.

Philips: Hi, Gary! Welcome to our hospital. Let me show you around our hospital and you'll be familiar with it.

Gary: Ok, thanks!

Philips: Now we'll visit the administrative department, including administrative office, medical affairs office, nursing department, teaching department, scientific research department, human resources department, financial department, instrument and equipment department, etc.

Gary: Which department will be responsible for my practice?

Philips: Our teaching department. Don't be hesitant to contact with us if you have any question.

Gary: What are the duties of the medical affairs department?

Philips: They are mainly responsible for the management of medical affairs such as institution of medical rules, management of clinical department and the diagnostic department.

Philips: We'll go and visit the clinical department now. Do you know anything about them?

Gary: Yes, but just a little. I've been to a few clinical department before.

Philips: The clinical department distribute in the surgical building, internal medical builing, outpatient department and emergency department, etc.

Gary: Is this the surgical building?

Philips: Yes, it is. It contains general surgery, orthopedic surgery, cardiac surgery, obstetrics and gynecology, ophthalmology, neurosurgery, urinary surgery, hepatobiliary surgery, etc.

Gary: Wow, so many department!

Philips: Yes, it's true. The surgical department receive patients for surgery. Anesthesia and operating theatre are both in this building. Now we are going to the internal medical building.

Gary: Ok.

Philips: There are digestive system department, respiratory medicine, cardiovascular medicine, hematology department, Chinese medicine, endocrinology department, neurology department, pediatrics, intensive care unit and other related sections in it.

Gary: What is the building over there, Doctor Philips?

Philips: The outpatient department and emergency department are in it. The former provides treatment for outpatient and the latter, a very important department for saving lives, serves the patients with emergent conditions.

Gary: Which department will treat the patient who is wounded in a serious accident, Doctor Philips?

Philips: It's the emergency department. The triage nurse will lead the patient to a certain department according to his/her condition and doctors will manage the patient immediately.

Philips: Then we will visit the diagnostic department, including ultrasound department, clinical laboratory, pathology department and radiology department.

Gary: Thanks for your tour guide. Can I come tomorrow?

Philips: You don't need to go to clinical department tomorrow. You will have the practice instruction for three days from tomorrow before you go to the department according to our arrangement.

Gary:　I see. Thanks!

三级 综合 医院 介绍

在 中国 ，医院 可 分为 综合 医院 与 专科 医院 。综合 医院 又 可 分 为 一 、二 、三级 医院 。这里 我们 简单 介绍 一下 三级 综合 公立 医院 。三级 综合 公立 医院 一般 是 集 医疗 、教学 、科研 于 一体 的 大型 医院 ，承担 政府 公益性 任务 ，以 学科 齐全 、技术 力量 雄厚 、特色 专科 突出 、多学科 综合 优势 强 著称 。

首先 ，三级 综合 公立 医院 主要 承担 服务 区域 内 急危 重症 和 疑难 疾病 的 诊疗 ，必须 具备 诊治 急危 重症 和 疑难 疾病 所 必需 的 设施 设备 、技术 梯队 与 处置 能力 ，医学 影像 与 介入 诊疗 部门 可 提供 24 小时 急诊 诊疗 服务 。临床 科室 一 、二级 诊疗 科目 设置 、人员 梯队 与 诊疗 技术 能力 符合 省级 卫生 行政 部门 规定 的 三级 标准 ，重点 科室 专业 技术 水平 与 质量 处于 本 区域 前列 。同时 ，三级 综合 公立 医院 还 承担 服务 区域 内 突发 公共 事件 的 紧急 医疗 救援 任务 和 配合 突发 公共 卫生 事件 防控 工作 ，必须 建立 院前 急救 与 院内 急诊 "绿色 通道" 有效 衔接 的 工作 流程 。

其次 ，三级 综合 公立 医院 必须 坚持 医院 的 公益性 ，推动 医疗 质量 持续 改进 。三级 综合 公立 医院 须 承担 公立 医院 与 基层 医疗 机构 对口 协作 等 政府 指令性 任务 。开展 健康 教育 、健康 咨询 等 多种 形式 的 公益性 社会活动 。同时 ，还须 承担 临床 医学 教育 和 科研 任务 ，包括 开展 本科 及 以上 医学生 的 临床 教学 和 实习 、住院 医师 规范化 培训 及 继续 医学 教育 ，承担 各级 各类 科研项目 ，开展 临床 与 基础 相 结合 的 研究 工作 等 。

Introduction to the Tertiary Public General Hospital

Hospitals are classified into general and specialized hospitals in China. There are three tiers in general hospitals: primary, secondary and tertiary. Here is a brief introduction to the tertiary public general hospitals which are generally large-scaled, provide integrating medical treatment and medical education, and carry out scientific research together and public mission mandated by the government. They are known for their comprehensive subjects, technical resources, distinctive specialties and multidisciplinary superiority.

First of all, the tertiary public general hospitals undertake the treatment of emergent, severe and complicated diseases; therefore they are equipped with all the necessary resources and equipment, medical echelon and responding capacity. Their departments of medical imaging and interventional therapy provide 24-hour emergency service. The clinical rooms have the necessary specialty assignments, medical personnel and techniques of diagnosis and treatment to satisfy the standard for the tertiary hospitals formulated by the provincial health departments. The technical level and professional quality of their key departments rank top of their regions. Meanwhile, the tertiary public general hospitals shoulder the responsibility of providing the medical service for the public emergencies and the prevention work for the health emergencies in their service regions. The procedures of linking prehospital care and the Green Channel of hospital emergency have been effectively established.

What's more, the tertiary public general hospitals adhere to their social functions and promote the continuous improvement of healthcare quality. They undertake the compulsory tasks from the government like cooperating with the basic medical institutions and launching various public activities like health education and health counseling. Meanwhile, the tertiary public general hospitals undertake both clinical education and scientific research, including the clinical education and internship for students at and above the collegiate level, standardized resident training and continuing medical education, various scientific projects and research work combining basic theories with clinical techniques.

1. 很荣幸……

"很荣幸"这是一种客套的说法，表示自谦和对对方的尊重。

In spoken English, this is a polite statement, represents modesty and respect for others, meaning "be honored", e.g. 我很荣幸在这里见到你。

2. 主要……

指事物中关系最大的，起决定作用的。

It means "main or mainly", e.g. 这堂课主要讲叙事医学。

3. 负责……

"负责"是动词，指担负责任。

It means "be responsible for or be in charge of", e.g. 医生对工作很负责。

 # 门诊就诊流程

流程	liúchéng	名	process
挂号处	guàhàochù	名	registration office
发烧	fāshāo	动	fever
感冒	gǎnmào	动	cold
喉咙	hóulóng	名	throat
咳嗽	késou	动	cough
量	liàng	动	measure
体温	tǐwēn	名	temperature
血常规	xuèchángguī	名	blood routine

胸部 X 片	xiōngbùXpiàn	名	chest X-ray
检查	jiǎnchá	动	check
抽血	chōuxuè	动	draw blood
肺炎	fèiyán	名	pneumonia
住院	zhùyuàn	动	hospitalize
治疗	zhìliáo	动	treatment
登记	dēngjì	动	register
病房	bìngfáng	名	ward

地点：医院门诊部
人物：菲利普（医生）
　　　玛丽（护士）
　　　大卫（病人，男，37 岁）

大　卫　打扰一下！护士，我不舒服，想找个医生给我看看。请问，我应该去哪儿找医生？

玛　丽　嗨，我是玛丽护士，您先别急，看病得先挂号。

大　卫　挂号？我要去哪儿挂号？

玛　丽　得去**挂号处**挂号。我带您去吧。

大　卫　好的。太感谢您了！

玛　丽　不客气！您告诉我您哪儿不舒服，这样我才知道您应该挂什么科？

大　卫　我从昨晚开始**发烧**，头疼，可能**感冒**了。

玛　丽　那我建议您挂呼吸内科。这儿就是挂号处。您在这儿排队挂号吧。您填一下个人信息，待会儿先办张就诊卡、买本病历，然后告诉他们，您要挂呼吸内科，就可以了。

大　卫　好的。挂好号，我就可以去找医生了，对吗？

玛　丽　对。挂号以后，您就可以到 16 号内科诊室外面排队候诊了。

大　卫　好的，谢谢您。

　　　　（大卫进入诊室。）

菲利普　您好！您怎么了？

大　卫　我昨晚开始觉得头疼，**喉咙**疼，还一直**咳嗽**、发烧。

菲利普　我先帮您量一下**体温**，给您做个体格检查吧。

菲利普　您现在的体温是 39.5℃，先去查一下**血常规**，拍个胸部 X 线片吧。

大　卫　好的。请问，我该去哪里做这些**检查**呢？

菲利普　请到一楼放射科拍胸部 X 线片，二楼检验科**抽血**检查。（30 分钟后，检查结果出来）

菲利普　根据您的检查结果，您很可能是**肺炎**，需要**住院治疗**一段时间。

大　卫　很严重吗？

菲利普　别担心，不是很严重，但是最好住院观察观察。

大　卫　好吧。住院的话，我要办什么手续吗？

菲利普　要。您要先去住院登记处**登记**，然后到六楼呼吸内科**病房**办理住院手续。

大　卫　好的，谢谢。

Outpatient Service Process

SITE:　Outpatient Department

CHARACTERS:　　Philips (Physician)

　　　　　　　　Mary (Nurse)

　　　　　　　　David (Patient, male, 37 years old)

David:　Excuse me, nurse. I've got ill and I want to go and see a doctor. Would you like to tell me the process?

Mary:　Hi, I am Mary. Don't worry. Register first, please.

David:　Register? Where should I register?

Mary:　Registration office. I will take you there.

David:　Thanks.

Mary:　You are welcome. Can you tell me what's wrong with you? Then I can decide which clinic is suitable for you.

David:　I've got a fever and headache since last night and I think I have got a cold.

Mary:　Oh, I see. I suggest you to go to the respiratory medicine. Here is the registration counter. Please get into the queue, fill your personal information, get a medical card and a case sheet, and then tell them you'll see a doctor of respiratory department.

David:　All right. Then I'll go and see a doctor?

Mary:　Yes. After that you can go to Room 16, waiting for your turn.

David:　Thanks.

　　　　(David enters the room.)

Philips:　Hello, what's wrong with you?

David:　I've got a sore throat, headache and fever since last night while coughing.

Philips:　Let me measure your temperature and do a physical examination first.

Philips:　Your body temperature is 39.5℃. You'd better go to take a routine blood test and a chest x-ray.

David:　Where shall I go for check?

Philips:　Please go to the radiology department on the 1st floor, and go to the second floor to take blood at the laboratory.

　　　　(After 30 minutes, the results come out)

Philips:　According to your results, you may have pneumonia and you need to be hospitalized for it.

David:　Is it severe?

Philips:　Don't worry, it's not serious. But you'd better be hospitalized.

David:　Ok. How do I deal with the procedures of hospitalization?

Philips:　First, you'll go to the in-patient department for registration, and then to the respiratory medical ward on the 6th floor.

David:　I see. Thank you.

门诊介绍

ménzhěn
门诊

ménzhěn shì yīyuàn jiēzhěn bìngrén de chǎngsuǒ　　tōngcháng jiēzhěn bìngqíng jiàoqīng de bìngrén　　jīngguò yìzhěngtào de zhěnduàn
门诊 是 医院 接诊 病人 的 场所 ，通常 接诊 病情 较轻 的 病人。 经过 一整套 的 诊断

shǒuduàn hé fǔzhù jiǎnchá děng　　gěi bìngrén zuòchū chūbù zhěnduàn bìng jìnxíng chūbù zhìliáo　　rúguǒ ménzhěn yīshēng duì bìngrén
手段 和辅助 检查 等，给 病人 做出 初步 诊断 并 进行 初步 治疗。 如果 门诊 医生 对 病人

bìngqíng yǒu yíwèn huòzhě rènwéi bìngqíng jiàozhòng huò jiàojí　　zé jiāng bìngrén shōurù zhùyuàn bìngfáng　　zài yīyuàn zuò jìnyíbù
病情 有 疑问 或者 认为 病情 较重 或 较急，则 将 病人 收入 住院 病房 ，在 医院 做 进一步

jiǎnchá huò zhìliáo
检查 或 治疗。

The Outpatient Department

The outpatient department is the setting where the hospital receives patients with relatively mild symptoms. After a set of diagnostic tests and auxiliary examinations, the clinician can give a primary diagnosis and initial treatment for the patient. If the clinician has doubts on patient's condition or considers it severe or acute, the patient may be admitted to the hospital for further examination or treatment.

语言点

1. 请问……
请教他人问题时的开头用词,表示客气,尊重对方。
It is used when you ask a question, similar to "excuse me", e.g. 请问,你叫什么名字?
2. 而且……
"而且"是连词,表示进一步,前面往往用"不但、不仅"等。
It is a conjunction, meaning "what's more" and "in addition", e.g. 我不仅头晕,而且肚子痛。
3. 怎么……
"怎么"常加动词,表示询问。
"怎么 +v." means how to do something, e.g. 这台机器怎么用?

➤ 听力练习

一、听录音,选择你听到的词语

(　)1. A. 办公室 　　B. 医务处 　　C. 护理部 　　D. 教学处
(　)2. A. 人力资源处 　B. 财务处 　　C. 器械设备处 　D. 信息管理处
(　)3. A. 检验科 　　B. 病理科 　　C. 放射科 　　D. 输血科
(　)4. A. 消化内科 　　B. 呼吸内科 　　C. 内分泌科 　　D. 肾脏内科
(　)5. A. 医院 　　B. 医疗 　　C. 医生 　　D. 医术
(　)6. A. 急诊 　　B. 门诊 　　C. 就诊 　　D. 诊室
(　)7. A. 发热 　　B. 发烧 　　C. 发病 　　D. 发哑
(　)8. A. 挂号 　　B. 挂牌 　　C. 挂失 　　D. 挂画
(　)9. A. 科室 　　B. 科学 　　C. 外科 　　D. 内科
(　)10. A. 入院 　　B. 住院 　　C. 出院 　　D. 转院

二、请选出与所听录音相符的答案

(　)1. A. 病人家 　　B. 彩超室 　　C. 护士家 　　D. 门诊部
(　)2. A. 咳嗽 　　B. 头晕 　　C. 恶心 　　D. 呕吐
(　)3. A. 急诊 　　B. 门诊 　　C. 药房 　　D. 检验科
(　)4. A. 手术室 　　B. 医务处 　　C. 心电图室 　　D. 皮肤科

三、听录音,完成下面的练习

1. 根据所听到的录音判断对错

1）这个病人在外科看病。（　　　）

2）这个病人得了肺炎。（　　　）

3）医生告诉病人拍胸部 X 片。（　　　）

4）负责实习生实习的是科研科。（　　　）

5）实习医生进入临床科室前进行 2 天实习前培训。（　　　）

6）病理科负责抽血。（　　　）

2. 听录音，选择正确答案回答问题

1）他们现在最可能在哪儿？（　　　）

  A. 住院病房   B. 门诊部   C. 内科   D. 外科

2）护士建议病人看什么科？（　　　）

  A. 呼吸内科   B. 普通外科   C. 血液科   D. 传染科

3）病人可能得了什么病？（　　　）

  A. 肝炎   B. 肺炎   C. 胃肠炎   D. 脑炎

➤ 词汇和语法练习

一、给下列词语标注拼音

1. 门诊＿＿＿＿＿＿＿＿＿＿＿　　2. 挂号处＿＿＿＿＿＿＿＿＿＿＿

3. 内科＿＿＿＿＿＿＿＿＿＿＿　　4. 胸片＿＿＿＿＿＿＿＿＿＿＿

5. 血常规＿＿＿＿＿＿＿＿＿＿＿　　6. 住院＿＿＿＿＿＿＿＿＿＿＿

7. 肺炎＿＿＿＿＿＿＿＿＿＿＿　　8. 骨科＿＿＿＿＿＿＿＿＿＿＿

9. 心脏外科＿＿＿＿＿＿＿＿＿＿＿　　10. 妇产科＿＿＿＿＿＿＿＿＿＿＿

11. 眼科＿＿＿＿＿＿＿＿＿＿＿　　12. 神经外科＿＿＿＿＿＿＿＿＿＿＿

13. 泌尿外科＿＿＿＿＿＿＿＿＿＿＿

二、选词填空

头痛　　内科　　肺炎　　胸部 X 线片　　发烧

1. 医生告诉我，我可能得了＿＿＿＿＿＿＿＿。

2. 护士让我去＿＿＿＿＿＿＿＿病房找菲利普医生。

3. 病人体温 38.5℃，＿＿＿＿＿＿＿＿了。

4. 请问，我应该去哪里拍＿＿＿＿＿＿＿＿？

5. 您怎么了？我觉得＿＿＿＿＿＿＿＿。

三、用指定的词语或结构完成句子或对话

1. 我感觉头晕，＿＿＿＿＿＿＿＿。（而且……）

2. ＿＿＿＿＿＿＿＿？直走就是了。（怎么）

四、把下列词语排列成句子

1. 哪里　在　请问　门诊

2. 六楼　在　病房　内科

3. 去　请　查　二楼　胸部 X 线片

4. 医务处　医疗相关事务　主要负责　管理

5. 主要　病人　接收　普通　门诊

6. 根据　开一些　病人病情　相关检查　医生

➢ 阅读与应用练习

一、根据课文内容补全对话

会 话 一

医　　　生：首先我们到医院行政部门参观。行政部门在行政大楼,主要包括___1___、___2___、___3___、
　　　　　　___4___、___5___、___6___、___7___器械设备处等,教学处主要负责你的___8___安排,你在实习
　　　　　　期间有什么问题可以找教学处老师。

实习医生：请问医务处主要负责什么呢?

医　　　生：医务处主要负责___9___,如制订___10___、临床科室与诊断相关科室的管理等。

会 话 二

病　　　人：护士,我最近感觉___11___。

护　　　士：建议您挂___12___。

病　　　人：好的。

医　　　生：您有可能得了___13___。

病　　　人：很严重吗?

医　　　生：您要先做一个___14___和___15___。可能需要___16___一段时间。

护　　　士：请去___17___办理住院手续。

病　　　人：好的,谢谢!

二、根据课文内容回答问题

1. 护士玛丽建议大卫看什么科?

2. 医生菲利普诊断大卫得了什么病?

3. 大卫应该做什么检查? 去哪里检查?

4. 大卫要不要住院?

5. 菲利普医生带格雷医生去了哪些部门参观?

6. 格雷医生问了菲利普医生关于病人遇到意外车祸后该去哪个部门看医生,请问菲利普医生怎么
回答?

第二章 呼 吸 内 科

 会话一

急性上呼吸道感染

词汇

急性	jíxìng	形	acute
上呼吸道	shànghūxīdào	名	upper respiratory tract
感染	gǎnrǎn	动	infect
症状	zhèngzhuàng	名	symptom
咽痛	yāntòng	动	have a sore throat
鼻涕	bítì	名	nasal discharge
脓	nóng	形	purulent
退烧药	tuìshāoyào	名	antipyretic
胸痛	xiōngtòng	动	have chest pain
肌肉	jīròu	名	muscle
心悸	xīnjì	动	palpitate
胸闷	xiōngmèn	动	chest distress
病毒	bìngdú	名	virus
细菌	xìjūn	名	bacteria
X线	Xxiàn	名	X-rays
排除	páichú	动	exclude
听诊器	tīngzhěnqì	名	stethoscope
啰音	luōyīn	名	rales
抗生素	kàngshēngsù	名	antibiotics
镇咳	zhènhāi	动	relieve cough
鼻黏膜	bíniánmó	名	nasal mucosa
充血	chōngxuè	名	congestion
控制	kòngzhì	动	control
副作用	fùzuòyòng	名	side effect
嗜睡	shìshuì	名	somnolence
腹泻	fùxiè	名	diarrhea
复诊	fùzhěn	动	return visit

地点:呼吸内科门诊

人物:周医生(主治医师)

赵振(病人,男,31 岁)

赵　振　周医生,我前几天感冒了,现在咳嗽得厉害。

周医生　是受凉引起的吗?

赵　振　可能是。四天前我去爬山,爬得满身大汗,到了山顶,风嗖嗖地刮,凉快极了,结果回家我就发烧了。

周医生　当时体温多少度?

赵　振　我去诊所量了一下,大约 39℃左右。

周医生　除了发烧,还有其他什么**症状**吗?

赵　振　有,头痛、**咽痛**、咳嗽,还流**鼻涕**。

周医生　鼻涕是什么颜色?

赵　振　开始是清鼻涕,后来变成黄色的**脓鼻涕**。

周医生　诊所医生给您开药了吗?

赵　振　嗯,开了些**退烧药**。

周医生　用药后好一点儿了吗?

赵　振　用药后体温降下来了,但是咳嗽还是很厉害,咽部很痒,总觉得有痰咳不干净,鼻涕很多,还有点头痛。

周医生　您是不是觉得鼻子里有东西往咽喉部流?

赵　振　对,太对了,就是觉得鼻子里有东西往咽喉部流,特别是晚上躺在那里睡觉时,感觉很明显。

周医生　痰多不多? 什么颜色?

赵　振　痰比较多,是黄色的,与鼻涕一模一样。

周医生　有没有**胸痛**或呼吸困难?

赵　振　没有。

周医生　有没有全身**肌肉酸痛**?

赵　振　没有。

周医生　有没有**心悸**或者胸闷?

赵　振　这些症状我都没有。

周医生　由此看来,这是**病毒**引起的感冒,继发上呼吸道感染。发烧、头痛和鼻涕都是感冒引起的。感冒后流鼻涕,继发**细菌**感染,鼻涕滴到喉咙,导致咳嗽与黄脓痰。

赵　振　那该怎么治疗啊?

周医生　最好先做个胸部 X 线**检查,排除**一下肺炎,我再给您开点药。做胸部 X 线检查前,我先用**听诊器**给您听一下肺。

赵　振　好的。

　　　　　(听诊结束)

周医生　您的肺听起来没有什么问题,没有**啰音**,应该不会有肺炎。保险起见,您还是去查一下胸部 X 线。

　　　　　(30 分钟后,胸部 X 线检查结束。)

周医生　根据您的胸部 X 线检查结果,可以排除肺炎,所以您不用担心,只是急性上呼吸道感染。

赵　振　可是我老是这样咳嗽真是太难受了。

周医生　我给您开点儿止咳药和**抗生素**。

赵　振　这些药要怎么吃?

周医生　这种口服液包含右美沙芬、马来酸氯苯那敏、盐酸伪麻黄碱三种成分,具有**镇咳**、抗过敏和减少**鼻黏膜充血**作用,可以止咳并减少鼻涕,是对症治疗的药物。一次口服 10ml,一天三次。

赵　振　太好了,我就是咳嗽得厉害,而且鼻涕很多。

周医生　阿奇霉素是**控制**细菌感染的抗生素,服药后黄脓痰就会消失。一天一次,一次两片,服用三天就可以了。

赵　振　好的。请问这些药有什么**副作用**吗?

周医生　口服液可能会引起**嗜睡**,阿奇霉素可能会引起**腹泻**。

赵　振　哦,我什么时候来**复诊**?

周医生　看情况吧。一般来说,这些药吃完了,您就会好的,不用来复诊。

赵　振　谢谢周医生!

Acute Upper Respiratory Tract Infection

SITE:　Respiratory Department

CHARACTERS:　Doctor Zhou (Attending physician)

Zhao Zhen (Patient, male, 31 years old)

Zhao Zhen:　Dr. Zhou, I caught a cold a few days ago, and have a bad cough now.

Dr. Zhou:　Is it caused by cold?

Zhao Zhen:　It might be. I was sweating all over when I climbed the mountain four days ago. Reaching the summit, I enjoyed the cool breezes blowing repeatedly, but I had a fever after I got home.

Dr. Zhou:　What was your temperature then?

Zhao Zhen:　I visited a clinic and my temperature was 39℃.

Dr. Zhou:　Did the fever occur with any other symptoms?

Zhao Zhen:　Yes, headache, sore throat, cough and nasal discharge follow.

Dr. Zhou:　What is the color of your nasal discharge?

Zhao Zhen:　It was colorless watery and became yellow purulent later.

Dr. Zhou:　Did the doctor give you any medicine in the clinic?

Zhao Zhen:　Yes, I was given some antipyretics.

Dr. Zhou:　Did you feel a little better after medication?

Zhao Zhen:　My temperature was down, but I still had a serious cough with sputum, an itchy throat, a lot of nasal discharge and a little headache.

Dr. Zhou:　Do you get a sense of postnasal dripping?

Zhao Zhen:　Yeah, I feel something flowing from my nose to my throat, especially at night when lying on my bed.

Dr. Zhou:　How much is the sputum and what's its color?

Zhao Zhen:　There are a lot of sputa that look yellow just like the color in nasal discharge.

Dr. Zhou:　Do you have any dyspnea or experience chest pain?

Zhao Zhen:　No, I don't.

Dr. Zhou:　Do you have muscle soreness?

Zhao Zhen:　No, I don't either.

Dr. Zhou:　Do you have palpitations or chest tightness?

Zhao Zhen:　No, I don't have them either.

Dr. Zhou:　Well, your problem is a common cold caused by viral infection and upper respiratory tract infection follows. Your fever, headache and nasal discharge are caused by your common cold. A running nose results in bacterial infection, therefore you've coughed with purulent sputum after nasal discharge dropping into your throat.

Zhao Zhen:　How do we treat it?

Dr. Zhou:　You'd better take a chest X-ray to make sure you've got pneumonia or not and then I'll prescribe some medication for you. Let me listen to your lungs with my stethoscope before the chest X-ray examination.

Zhao Zhen:　Ok.

　　　　　(After auscultation)

Dr. Zhou:　There isn't any problem in your lungs and there are no rales either, so we can exclude pneumonia but you'll have to take an X-ray examination to confirm it.

　　　　　(After 30 minutes, the chest X-ray examination finished.)

Dr. Zhou:　Don't worry. Your chest X-ray result shows it is merely an acute upper respiratory infection so that pneumonia can be excluded.

Zhao Zhen:　I feel very embarrassed when coughing.

Dr. Zhou:　I will prescribe you some cough medicine and antibiotics.

Zhao Zhen:　How do I take these drugs?

Dr. Zhou:　This oral liquid contains dextromethorphan, chlorpheni-ramine maleate and pseudoephedrine hydrochloride, which relieve cough and nasal congestion, respectively, with anti-allergic effect. It can also improve your cough and runny nose. You need to take 10ml each time, three times daily.

Zhao Zhen:　Great! I've been coughing terribly with a lot of nasal discharge.

Dr. Zhou:　Azithromycin is an antibiotic to control the bacterial infections and your yellow purulent sputum will disappear after taking this medicine. Have two tablets each time, once a day, for three days.

Zhao Zhen:　That sounds good. Are there any side effects when I take the medication prescribed?

Dr. Zhou:　The oral liquid may cause sleepiness and azithromycin may cause diarrhea.

Zhao Zhen:　Oh, when shall I return?

Dr. Zhou:　It depends. In general, you'll recover and needn't visit the hospital again after taking all the medicines.

Zhao Zhen:　I see. Thank you, Dr. Zhou.

疾病介绍

急性 上呼吸道 感染
jíxìng　shànghūxīdào　gǎnrǎn

急性 上呼吸道 感染 简称 上感 ，包括 普通 感冒 、急性 病毒性 咽炎 和 喉炎 、急性 疱疹性 咽峡炎 、急性 咽结膜炎 和 急性 咽扁桃体炎，为 外鼻孔 至 环状 软骨 下缘 包括 鼻腔 、咽 或 喉部 急性 炎症 的 总称 。主要 病原体 是 病毒，少数 是 细菌。发病 不 分 年龄 、性别 、职业 和 地区，免疫 功能 低下 者 易感 。 通常 病情 较轻 ，病程 短 ，可 自愈，预后 良好 ，但 由于 发病率 高 ，不仅 影响 工作 和 生活 ，有时 还 伴有 严重 并发症 ，而且 有 一定 的 传染 性 ，应 积极 防治 。

Acute Upper Respiratory Tract Infection

　　Acute upper respiratory tract infection or acute UTI is a general term of the acute inflammation of the nasal cavity, pharynx or larynx from the nostril to the edge of cricoid cartilage, including common cold, acute viral pharyngitis, laryngitis, acute herpangina, acute pharyngeal conjunctivitis and acute pharyngeal tonsil inflammation. The main pathogens are virus and a few of them are bacteria. People with low immune function are susceptible to the disease regardless of age, sex, occupation, region, featuring mild condition, short duration, self-healing and favorable prognosis. With high incidence and infectiousness, it may not only influence our life and work but also bring about serious complications, hence it should be actively prevented and treated.

语言点

1. 除了……，还有……
排除……在外，还有别的。
It means "besides", e.g. 他除了哮喘病，还有心血管病。

2. 只是……
仅仅是……，表示强调。
It means "merely", e.g. 你只是太劳累了，注意休息。

支气管哮喘

支气管哮喘	zhīqìguǎnxiāochuǎn	名	bronchial asthma
花粉	huāfěn	名	pollen
喷嚏	pēntì	名	sneeze
气喘	qìchuǎn	名	breathlessness
诊所	zhěnsuǒ	名	clinic
打点滴	dǎdiǎndī	名	intravenous drip
哮鸣音	xiāomíngyīn	名	wheezing rale
肺功能	fèigōngnéng	名	lung function
舒张	shūzhāng	动	relax
提示	tíshì	动	reveal
阻塞性	zǔsèxìng	形	obstructive
通气功能障碍	tōngqìgōngnéngzhàngài	名	ventilation dysfunction
根治	gēnzhì	名	radical cure
预防	yùfáng	动	prevent
过敏原	guòmǐnyuán	名	allergen
痉挛	jìngluán	动	spasm

定期	dìngqī	副	regularly
随访	suífǎng	动	follow up
气雾剂	qìwùjì	名	aerosol
吸入剂	xīrùjì	名	inhalation
支气管扩张剂	zhīqìguǎnkuòzhāngjì	名	bronchodilators
平滑肌	pínghuájī	名	smooth muscle

地点:呼吸内科门诊
人物:江医生(主治医师)
      赵易伟(病人,男,31岁)

江医生　请坐,您觉得哪儿不舒服?

赵易伟　江医生,我这两天呼吸很困难。

江医生　您的呼吸困难是怎么开始的?

赵易伟　昨天我闻到**花粉**气味,先是鼻子痒、打**喷嚏**、咳嗽,后来就觉得胸闷、**气喘**。

江医生　晚上感觉怎么样?

赵易伟　昨天晚上气喘得厉害,根本没有办法睡觉。

江医生　您以前有过类似的情况吗?

赵易伟　有过。15岁以前我经常咳嗽,有时候也会气急,后来就好了。3年前我搬到新的小区,这里种了好多花儿,每年6月份闻到小区里的花粉气味就会发作。

江医生　通常是怎样好起来的呢?

赵易伟　有时候持续几天,自己就好了;有时候去**诊所**打几天**点滴**就好了。不过,这次特别严重,呼吸比前几次要困难得多。

江医生　诊所给您用的什么药,知道吗?

赵易伟　我想不起来了,不过有一种药好像是地塞米松。

江医生　您的胸痛不?

赵易伟　不痛。

江医生　有没有脓痰或发烧?

赵易伟　没有。

江医生　走路吃力吗?

赵易伟　有点儿吃力,刚才爬三层楼梯就感觉有点儿累。

江医生　我先用听诊器给您听一听吧。

赵易伟　好的。

　　　　(听诊结束)

江医生　您的肺部**哮鸣音**很明显。

赵易伟　我得的是什么疾病?

江医生　依据您的病史、症状与体征,应该是支气管哮喘。为了进一步确诊,还要检查一下**肺功能**并做一下支气管**舒张**试验。

　　　　(30分钟后,检查结束。)

江医生　您的肺功能检查结果**提示阻塞性通气功能障碍**,支气管舒张试验阳性。可以断定,您得的是典型的支气管哮喘。

赵易伟　支气管哮喘是不是很严重的疾病?

江医生　不要紧张。虽然支气管哮喘急性发作很严重,不能**根治**,但是哮喘是可以**预防**、可以控制的疾病。

赵易伟 那支气管哮喘是怎么发生的?

江医生 因为有些人对环境中的一些**过敏原**敏感,接触这些过敏原后就会引起支气管**痉挛**,导致支气管哮喘发作和呼吸困难。您的过敏原就是花粉。

赵易伟 那我应该怎么预防?

江医生 首先您要尽量避免接触花粉,其次要按时用药并**定期随访**就诊。

赵易伟 那麻烦医生给我开些药吧。

江医生 好的。我先给您开三种药,一个是沙丁胺醇**气雾剂**,是在支气管哮喘急性发作时用的,您现在就可以用。还有一种是布地奈德福莫特罗粉**吸入剂**。其中的成分布地奈德是一种激素,可以预防支气管哮喘的发作,而另一成分福莫特罗是**支气管扩张剂**,可以解除支气管痉挛。这个药需要长期使用,每天两次,每次吸一下。

赵易伟 另外一个药呢?

江医生 另外一个药叫孟鲁司特。每天晚上睡前吃一颗,可以预防控制哮喘,特别是对于控制您晚上的症状,效果很好。

赵易伟 太好了。我用了这三种药之后,呼吸困难就可以控制吗?

江医生 基本上是可以得到很好控制的。

赵易伟 那我需要来复诊吗?

江医生 下周要来复诊,看看用药后的效果。康复后最好每个月都来复诊。

赵易伟 还有什么要注意的吗?

江医生 您最好远离有花粉的环境。万一出现呼吸特别困难的情况,要先吸入沙丁胺醇气雾剂,舒张支气管**平滑肌**,然后立即到医院急诊室就诊,因为支气管哮喘急性发作是很危险的。

赵易伟 我明白了。谢谢您,江医生。

Bronchial Asthma

SITE: Respiratory Outpatient Department

CHARACTERS: Dr. Jiang (Attending physician)

Zhao Yiwei (Patient, male, 31 years old)

Dr. Jiang: Sit down, please. What's wrong with you?

Zhao Yiwei: Dr. Jiang, I have been suffering from dyspnea for two days.

Dr. Jiang: How did it start?

Zhao Yiwei: I have been feeling an itch in my nose coupled with sneezing and coughing, and then having chest tightness with breathlessness since I smelled the pollen yesterday.

Dr. Jiang: How about your feelings at night?

Zhao Yiwei: Last night I was severely breathlessness and could not sleep all night.

Dr. Jiang: Were you in such situations before?

Zhao Yiwei: Yes, I was. I remember I coughed and sometimes breathlessness but I would be fine afterwards before the age of 15. Three years ago I moved to a new house, where many flowers are planted every year, and I'll start wheezing in every June when I smell the taste of the pollen near my house.

Dr. Jiang: And how did the wheezing subside before?

Zhao Yiwei: Sometimes I would be fine without medication after a few days or I had intravenous drip at clinic for days. This time, however, it is very severe and worse than the previous occurrences.

Dr. Jiang: What medicines were you given at clinic for treatment previously?

Zhao Yiwei: I can't recall it, but one of the medicines might well be dexamethasone.

Dr. Jiang: Do you have any chest pain?

Zhao Yiwei: No, I haven't got it.

Dr. Jiang: Do you have purulent sputum or fever?

Zhao Yiwei: No, I have none of them.

Dr. Jiang: Do you feel tired when you walk?

Zhao Yiwei: Yes, a little bit. I felt a bit tired just now when I went up three flights of stairs.

Dr. Jiang: I see. Let me auscultate your lungs with a stethoscope now.

Zhao Yiwei: Ok.

(After auscultation)

Dr. Jiang: There is obvious wheezing rale in your lungs.

Zhao Yiwei: What disease do I have?

Dr. Jiang: It looks like bronchial asthma based on your medical history, symptoms and signs. You'll have to do a lung function test and bronchial dilation test for a confirmed diagnosis

(After 30 minutes, examination finished)

Dr. Jiang: Your lung function test reveals obstructive ventilator dysfunction and bronchial dilation test is positive, which shows typical bronchial asthma.

Zhao Yiwei: Is it a very serious disease?

Dr. Jiang: Take it easy. Although acute attack of bronchial asthma is very serious and cannot be cured, bronchial asthma is preventable and controllable.

Zhao Yiwei: What causes it?

Dr. Jiang: Some people are sensitive to environmental allergen and exposure to these allergens can cause bronchial spasms, which lead them to bronchial asthma attacks and present with symptoms such as dyspnea. In your case, your allergen is pollen.

Zhao Yiwei: What shall I do to prevent it?

Dr. Jiang: First, you should try your best to avoid exposure to pollen and then you have to take medication and follow up regularly.

Zhao Yiwei: Could you prescribe me medicines?

Dr. Jiang: Yes, I will prescribe 3 kinds of drugs for you. The first is salbutamol aerosol that'll be used at the onset of acute bronchial asthma, and you can take it now. The second is budesonide formoterol powder inhalation. The former is a type of hormone that can prevent an attack of asthma and the latter is a bronchodilator relieving bronchial spasm. This drug will be taken twice a day on a long-term basis.

Zhao Yiwei: What is the last drug?

Dr. Jiang: It is montelukast. Take one tablet each night before going to bed. It can prevent and control asthma, especially effective for your symptoms at night.

Zhao Yiwei: Great! Do you think my dyspnea will be controlled after I take these three drugs?

Dr. Jiang: Normally, these symptoms can be well controlled.

Zhao Yiwei: Shall I return?

Dr. Jiang: You need to return next week to evaluate the efficiency of the medication, and preferably check up once a month.

Zhao Yiwei: What else shall I pay attention to?

Dr. Jiang: You'd better stay away from the environment with pollen, and in case of severe dyspnea, you inhale salbutamol aerosol first, which will help relax the bronchial smooth muscle, and then come to the emergency room immediately, because acute attack of asthma is very dangerous.

Zhao Yiwei:　I see. Thank you, Dr. Jiang.

支气管哮喘

支气管 哮喘 简称 哮喘，是 由 多种 细胞（如 嗜酸性 粒细胞、肥大 细胞、T 淋巴 细胞、中性 粒细胞、平滑肌 细胞、气道 上皮 细胞 等）和 细胞组分 参与 的 气道 慢性 炎症 性 疾病。主要 特征 包括 气道 慢性 炎症，气道 对 多种 刺激 因素 呈现 的 高反应性，广泛 多变 的 可逆性 气流 受限 以及 随 病程 延长 而 导致 的 一系列 气道 结构 的 改变，即 气道 重构。临床 表现 为反复 发作 的 喘息、气急、胸闷 或 咳嗽 等 症状，常 在 夜间 及 凌晨 发作 或 加重，多数 病人 可 自行 缓解 或 经 治疗 后 缓解。根据 全球 和 中国 哮喘 防治 指南 提供 的 资料，经过 长期 规范化 治疗 和 管理，80% 以上 的 病人 可以 达到 哮喘 的 临床 控制。

Bronchial Asthma

Bronchial asthma or asthma is a chronic inflammatory disease of the airway caused by a variety of cells (acidophilic granulocyte, mast cells, T-lymphocytes, neutrophils, smooth muscle cells airway epithelial cells, etc.)and cellular components. Its main characteristics include chronic inflammation of the airway, the airway's hyper responsiveness to various stimulus, wide range of reversible airflow limitation and airway remodeling, the alterations in the airway structure resulting from the duration of the disease. Clinical manifestations are such symptoms as recurrent wheezing, shortness of breath, chest tightness and cough, attacking or worsening often during the night or in the early morning. Most symptoms can be relieved or eased through proper treatment. The data collected from all over the world, including China, suggest that long term of standard treatment and management can help more than 80% of the patients control their clinical symptoms.

1. 然后
一件事之后,接着又发生另一件事。
It means "then" or "afterwards", e.g. 我们应该先调查研究,然后再下结论。

2. 根据
论断或言行的依据。
It means "based on", e.g. 用药量要根据病人的病情而定。

➤ **听力练习**

一、听录音, 选择你听到的词语

(　　) 1. A. 感冒　　　　　B. 感动　　　　　C. 感觉　　　　　D. 赶考
(　　) 2. A. 咯血　　　　　B. 咳痰　　　　　C. 科室　　　　　D. 咳嗽
(　　) 3. A. 头痛　　　　　B. 头疼　　　　　C. 头晕　　　　　D. 疼痛
(　　) 4. A. 真假　　　　　B. 症状　　　　　C. 正当　　　　　D. 告状
(　　) 5. A. 鼻涕　　　　　B. 鼻子　　　　　C. 脓涕　　　　　D. 流涕
(　　) 6. A. 花粉　　　　　B. 花费　　　　　C. 花朵　　　　　D. 岩粉
(　　) 7. A. 发烧　　　　　B. 发热　　　　　C. 退烧　　　　　D. 高烧
(　　) 8. A. 心功能　　　　B. 肺功能　　　　C. 肺气肿　　　　D. 肾功能
(　　) 9. A. 笑场　　　　　B. 孝顺　　　　　C. 气喘　　　　　D. 哮喘
(　　) 10. A. 急救室　　　　B. 输液室　　　　C. 急诊室　　　　D. 化验室

二、请选出与所听录音相符的答案

(　　) 1. A. 咳嗽　　　　　B. 咳痰　　　　　C. 发烧　　　　　D. 流鼻涕
(　　) 2. A. 嗜睡　　　　　B. 失眠　　　　　C. 腹痛　　　　　D. 腹泻
(　　) 3. A. 已康复　　　　B. 好转　　　　　C. 无变化　　　　D. 加重
(　　) 4. A. 没有　　　　　B. 有但不重　　　C. 偶尔　　　　　D. 不清楚
(　　) 5. A. 有信心根治哮喘　　　　　　　B. 担心不能根治哮喘
　　　　　 C. 有信心控制哮喘　　　　　　　D. 担心不能控制哮喘

三、听录音, 完成下面的练习

1. 根据所听到的录音判断对错

1) 医生与患者在面对面交流。(　　　　)
2) 这个患者闻到花粉气味后哮喘复发了。(　　　　)
3) 这个患者 1 个月来每天坚持用药。(　　　　)
4) 这个患者刚才吸入沙丁胺醇后, 气喘没有好转。(　　　　)
5) 这个患者明天下午会来医院复诊。(　　　　)

2. 听录音, 选择正确答案回答问题

1) 小林**没有**下面哪种症状? (　　　　)
　　A. 咳嗽　　　　　B. 流鼻涕　　　　C. 发烧　　　　　D. 胸痛
2) 小林得的是什么病? (　　　　)
　　A. 急性上呼吸道感染　　B. 支气管哮喘　　C. 肺炎　　　　　D. 鼻炎
3) 小林吃的是什么抗生素? (　　　　)
　　A. 头孢他啶　　　　B. 阿奇霉素　　　C. 左氧氟沙星　　D. 阿莫西林

➤ **词汇和语法练习**

一、给下列词语标注拼音

1. 咳嗽＿＿＿＿＿＿＿＿＿＿　　　　2. 体温＿＿＿＿＿＿＿＿＿＿
3. 鼻涕＿＿＿＿＿＿＿＿＿＿　　　　4. 感染＿＿＿＿＿＿＿＿＿＿
5. 呼吸困难＿＿＿＿＿＿＿＿　　　　6. 打喷嚏＿＿＿＿＿＿＿＿
7. 气喘＿＿＿＿＿＿＿＿＿＿　　　　8. 哮鸣音＿＿＿＿＿＿＿＿

9. 发烧_____ 　　　　　10. 肺功能_____

二、选词填空

| 胸部 X 线　　阿奇霉素　　花粉　　预防　　复诊　　体温　　哮鸣音　　发烧 |

1. 昨天我_____了,到医院就诊,医生说我得了感冒。

2. 我昨天到医院,护士给我量了一下_____,大约 39℃左右。

3. 我咳脓痰,吃了_____后,脓痰就没有了。

4. 您的_____检查完全正常,肺炎可以排除了。

5. 我昨天闻到_____气味,一下子就气喘了。

6. 您两肺听诊_____很明显,应该是支气管哮喘发作了。

7. 医生,我下周要来_____吗?

8. 支气管哮喘是可以_____并可以控制的疾病。

三、用指定的词语或结构完成句子或对话

1. 我是急诊室护士,_____? (请问)

2. 不用紧张,您_____。(只是)

3. 请坐,您这次来就诊_____? (主要)

4. 您说您咳嗽,_____? (除了……,还有……)

5. _____,您得的是支气管哮喘。(根据……)

四、把下列词语排列成句子

1. 昨天　我　淋了雨　在　路上

2. 流　清鼻涕　感冒后　这次　总是

3. 一　花粉　闻到　就　气味　我　气喘

4. 开了　些　医生　药　给我

5. 病人　缓解　可以　多数　病情

➢ 阅读与应用练习

一、根据课文内容补全对话

病人：医生,我这几天感冒了,__1__得厉害。

医生：当时__2__多少度?

病人：我去诊所量了一下,__3__39℃。

医生：除了发烧,还有其他什么症状吗?

病人：还咳嗽、头痛、__4__,流鼻涕。

医生：哦,您应该是普通__5__后,继发细菌性上呼吸道感染。

病人：老是这样咳嗽真是太__6__了。

医生：我给您开两种药,您回去按时服用。一种是__7__,另一种是__8__。

二、根据课文内容回答问题

1. 急性上呼吸道感染都有哪些症状?

2. 医生给赵振开的抗生素阿奇霉素有什么副作用?

3. 赵易伟这次支气管哮喘急性发作,过敏原是什么?

4. 医生根据什么给赵易伟诊断为支气管哮喘?

5. 支气管哮喘可以根治吗? 可以预防吗? 可以控制吗?

三、写作练习

根据会话二,简单描述病人的主要临床表现。(不少于 50 字)

四、交际练习

参考括号里的词语进行情景对话。

情景:病人的检查报告出来了,医生和病人进行对话。

(支气管舒张试验阳性,支气管哮喘,花粉,过敏原,哮鸣音)

心血管内科

 会话一

高 血 压

词汇

高血压	gāoxuèyā	名	hypertension
头晕	tóuyūn	动	be dizzy
降压药	jiàngyāyào	名	antihypertensives
恶心	ěxīn	形	nauseous
状态	zhuàngtài	名	state
发作	fāzuò	动	break out
持续	chíxù	动	last
伴随	bànsuí	动	accompany
呕吐	ǒutù	动	vomit
眼花	yǎnhuā	形	giddy
肾病	shènbìng	名	kidney disease
甲状腺	jiǎzhuàngxiàn	名	thyroid gland
补充	bǔchōng	动	supplement
患病	huànbìng	动	be ill
遗传	yíchuán	动	inherit
眼底	yándǐ	名	fundus oculi
视网膜	shìwǎngmó	名	retina
病变	bìngbiàn	名	pathological changes
心律失常	xīnlùshīcháng	名	arrhythmia
清淡	qīngdàn	形	mild, light
钠盐	nàyán	名	sodium salt
脂肪	zhīfáng	名	fat
摄入	shèrù	动	intake
熬夜	áoyè	动	stay up
毒	dú	名	poison
肾脏	shènzàng	名	kidney

地点:心血管内科门诊
人物:张强(主治医师)
 刘阳(病人,男,46岁)

张医生　请坐！哪儿不舒服？具体说说,好吗？

刘 阳　从去年夏天开始,我劳累或情绪不好时就**头晕**或头痛,休息以后就好了,我也没当回事。三个月前体检时,我的血压有点高,高压(收缩压)140mmHg,低压(舒张压)90mmHg。医生要我注意休息,按时吃**降压药**。我没吃,因为平时没感觉,也不影响工作和生活。这些日子,我头晕、头痛得厉害,而且还有点儿**恶心**,休息后也没缓解。我量了血压,高压160mmHg,低压100mmHg。我吓坏了,就赶快来看病了。

张医生　这种**状态**有多长时间了？

刘 阳　大概三四天了。

张医生　这种情况以前发生过吗？

刘 阳　没有,以前偶尔有点儿难受,但没有这次这么严重。

张医生　一般什么时候出现这种症状,有规律吗？

刘 阳　没有太明显的规律,但晚上发生次数多一些。

张医生　每次**发作**大概**持续**多久？

刘 阳　以前每次都半天,而这次连续三四天了。

张医生　头晕时看东西是什么感觉？头痛有什么特点吗？

刘 阳　说不太清楚。因为头晕,看东西都在转,我总是闭着眼睛,不敢睁开。头痛起来像要炸开似的,躺着坐着都胀痛。

张医生　发作的时候还**伴随**其他症状吗？

刘 阳　还觉得恶心、**呕吐**和**眼花**,心跳得厉害。

张医生　您能想起来引起头晕和头痛的原因吗？

刘 阳　记得发病前一天,我和朋友喝了酒,回家就觉得不舒服。

张医生　来之前做过什么检查和治疗？用过什么药？

刘 阳　没有。我哪儿也没去,也没用过药。

张医生　大小便怎么样？尿少吗？

刘 阳　大小便正常,尿量和往常一样。

张医生　饮食正常吗？睡眠怎么样？

刘 阳　不爱吃饭,总是恶心,睡眠不好。

张医生　您做什么工作？平时抽烟喝酒吗？

刘 阳　我是会计,不抽烟,但喜欢喝酒。我每天晚上都得喝上半斤白酒,边看电视边喝,常常喝到后半夜。

张医生　过去得过什么病吗？比如说**肾病**、**甲状腺**疾病等等？

刘 阳　没有。

张医生　您家人身体状况怎么样？包括您的父母亲和兄弟姐妹。

刘 阳　我母亲有高血压二十多年了,我只有一个妹妹,父亲和妹妹身体都很好。

张医生　我知道了。您还有其他需要**补充**的吗？

刘 阳　没有了。

张医生　接下来需要给您做一下检查。

　　　　(检查结果出来后)

张医生　刘先生,检查结果显示您患的是高血压,这和您家族**遗传**以及不良生活习惯有关。您除了血压高以外,还**有眼底视网膜**的**病变**和**心律失常**。我给您开点降压药,每天早晨起来吃一片,两周后再来复诊。另外,平时注意**清淡饮食**,减少**钠盐**和**脂肪**的**摄入**,控制酒量,增加运动,不要**熬夜**。

刘　阳　张医生,我现在先不吃药可以吗?

张医生　您不仅血压高,而且眼底和心脏也出现问题了,所以必须要服用降压药。

刘　阳　可是"是药三分**毒**",这个药不会影响我的**肾脏**吧?

张医生　放心吧,这个药副作用很小。下周我们医院有关于高血压的健康知识讲座,欢迎您来参加。

Hypertension

SITE:　　　Cardiovascular Outpatient Department

CHARACTERS:　　Zhang Qiang (Attending physician)

　　　　　　　Liu Yang (Patient, male, 46 years old)

Dr. Zhang:　Sit down, please. What's the matter with you? Would you like to tell me whatever you think I should know about your condition?

Liu Yang:　Since last summer, I've been dizzy or had a headache when I was tired or in a bad mood, but I recovered soon after taking a rest. Therefore, I did not take it seriously. It was detected that my systolic pressure was 140mmHg and diastolic pressure 90mmHg when I had a routine checkup 3 months ago. My doctor told me to take a rest and medication on time, but I didn't, as it didn't have any effect on my life and work. Recently I've been feeling dizzy and headachy severely, even nauseous. Taking a rest didn't alleviate my symptoms. I came here because I was threatened that my systolic pressure was 160mmHg and diastolic pressure 100mmHg.

Dr. Zhang:　How long have you been like this?

Liu Yang:　About 3 or 4 days.

Dr. Zhang:　Did it happen before?

Liu Yang:　No, I feel a bit uncomfortable sometimes, but this time it is quite different from what took place before.

Dr. Zhang:　When did the symptom start approximately? Did it occur regularly?

Liu Yang:　There was no distinct regularity but it seemed a bit more at night.

Dr. Zhang:　How long did it last every time?

Liu Yang:　It was only half a day in the past, but it has lasted for 3 or 4 days this time.

Dr. Zhang:　What do you feel when you see something and have headache?

Liu Yang:　I'm not quite sure. I have to close my eyes when I feel dizzy, for what I see is spinning and I can barely keep my eyes open. I feel a swelling pain in my head as if my head would blow up whenever I sit or lie down.

Dr. Zhang:　Do you have any other symptoms during the attack?

Liu Yang:　Yes, nausea, vomit, dazzle and heart-throb occur.

Dr. Zhang:　Can you recall what caused your dazzle and headache?

Liu Yang:　I remember I didn't feel myself when I arrived at home after drinking with my friends on the day before they took place.

Dr. Zhang:　Have you been checked or treated or taken any medication before you came here?

Liu Yang:　No. I did not go to any hospital and took no medication.

Dr. Zhang:　What about your bowel movement and urine? Are you oliguric?

Liu Yang:　No, they are normal and my urine volume is the same as usual.

Dr. Zhang:	What about your diet and sleep?
Liu Yang:	I don't like to eat anything and always feel sick. What's more, I usually sleep poorly.
Dr. Zhang:	What do you do? Do you smoke and drink?
Liu Yang:	I'm an accountant. I like spirit but smoke. I drink about 250g liquor every night while watching TV. I don't stop drinking until midnight.
Dr. Zhang:	Have you got any illness such as kidney disease, thyroid problems or others?
Liu Yang:	No, I haven't.
Dr. Zhang:	What about the health of your family, including your parents and siblings?
Liu Yang:	My mother has got high blood pressure for over 20 years and nothing is going wrong with my father and younger sisters.
Dr. Zhang:	I see. Do you have any more to tell me?
Liu Yang:	No, I haven't.
Dr. Zhang:	And you need examinations next.
	(After the examinations)
Dr. Zhang:	Mr. Liu, the results show that you've got hypertension. It is associated with your family heredity and bad living habits. You've also developed retinal lesions and arrhythmia besides hypertension. I'll prescribe the medicine for you. Take one tablet when you get up in the morning. Come back for the re-examination in 2 weeks. In addition, you'd better have light diet, reduce the intake of salt and fat, cut down liquor, increase exercise, and not stay up.
Liu Yang:	Is there any way I can feel better without taking medication?
Dr. Zhang:	No, you have to take medicine because your fundus oculi and heart have got problems besides your high blood pressure.
Liu Yang:	As long as it is a medicine, there might be some poisonous components in it. It will not affect my kidneys, right?
Dr. Zhang:	Don't worry about it, as it has little side effect. Our hospital will hold a health knowledge lecture on high blood pressure next week. I hope you'll come.

疾病介绍

高血压
gāoxuèyā

高血压 是 一种 常见病，世界 上 很多人 患 这种 病。血压 过高 会 加重 心脏 负担，对 动脉 造成 严重 损害。随着 时间 的 推移，高血压 控制 不好 会 增加 心脏病 、脑卒中 及 肾病 的 风险 。如果 你 被 确诊 为 高血压，就要 改变 生活 方式，比如 睡眠 充足 、低盐 低脂 饮食 和 少 吃 带 糖 的 食物。除此之外，规律 地 锻炼 ，如 瑜伽、太极拳 和 深 呼吸 也 会 有助于 降压。用 药物 和 这些 方法 相 结合 来 治疗 高血压，比较 有效 。

Hypertension

Hypertension, also known as high blood pressure, is a common disease that affects many people across the world. When blood pressure is too high, it raises the heart's workload and can cause serious damage to the arteries. Over time, uncontrolled high blood pressure increases the risk of heart disease, stroke, and kidney disease. If you have been diagnosed with high blood pressure, you have to change your lifestyle, such as enough sleep, the diet low in salt and fat, and limited sugary foods. In addition, regular exercise, like yoga, tai chi, and deep breathing help lower blood pressure. It is effective to take medication coupled with these measures to treat hypertension.

语言点

1. 和……有关

与（同）……有关。

It means "be associated with", e.g. 她发病和她的生活习惯有关。

2. 也没……也没

既没有……又没有。

It means "neither…nor", e.g. 他也没去医院，也没吃药。

3. 边……边

形容同时做两件事，同"一边……一边"。

You do one thing while you do another at the same time, e.g. 他边工作边学习。

会话二　冠 心 病

词汇

冠心病	guānxīnbìng	名	coronary heart disease
浑身	húnshēn	名	whole body
缘故	yuángù	名	reason
虚汗	xūhàn	名	abnormal sweat
气短	qìduǎn	形	short of breath
心脏病	xīnzàngbìng	名	heart disease
维持	wéichí	动	maintain
体重	tǐzhòng	名	body weight
偏好	piānhào	动	prefer
咸菜	xiáncài	名	brined vegetable
供血	gòngxuè	动	supply blood
心肌	xīnjī	名	myocardium
心绞痛	xīnjiǎotòng	名	angina pectoris
狭窄	xiázhǎi	形	stenosis
抗凝	kàngníng	动	anticoagulate
血栓	xuèshuān	名	thrombosis
血脂	xuèzhī	名	blood lipid
服用（药物）	fúyòng（yàowù）	动	take (medicine)

反应	fǎnyìng	名	reaction
异常	yìcháng	形	abnormal

地点：急诊科
人物：周颖（主治医师）
　　　张兰（病人，女，63岁）

张　兰　周大夫，我喘气困难，胸闷得很，**浑身**没劲。

周医生　这种情况多长时间了？

张　兰　有一周了。前些天我在院子里种花，感觉很累，上气不接下气，以为是太累的**缘故**，没放心上。
　　　　这些日子感觉越来越严重，一活动就加重，但休息时症状会减轻点儿。我感觉平躺时，症状会
　　　　加重，坐着会好些。发病的时候，浑身一点儿力气都没有，心突突地跳，前胸后背都疼，有时疼
　　　　得我直冒**虚汗**。

周医生　您以前有过这种情况吗？

张　兰　没有。以前走路久了，会**气短**，休息一会儿就好。这次不知怎么了，难受死了。

周医生　以前去医院看过吗？有没有用过什么药？

张　兰　以前没觉得是多大的事，就没去看，也没吃过药。

周医生　您有没有什么病史？像高血压或是**心脏病**？

张　兰　我得高血压十多年了，我每天坚持吃降压片，血压基本**维持**在高压130mmHg，低压60mmHg。

周医生　您身高**体重**多少？做什么工作？

张　兰　我1.65米，体重有91公斤。我是作家，我喜欢晚上写作，常常写到天亮。

周医生　您家里人身体怎么样？您的父母亲、兄弟姐妹和您丈夫有没有类似的情况？

张　兰　我父亲十年前因冠心病突然发作去世了，母亲有高血压，我没有兄弟姐妹。我丈夫除了血压
　　　　高，没有其他毛病。

周医生　您平时锻炼身体吗？

张　兰　我每天散步二十分钟。自从感觉不舒服后，就不走了。

周医生　说说您的日常饮食情况吧？您和您的家人都有哪些饮食**偏好**？

张　兰　我们一家人都喜欢吃肉，特别喜欢吃红烧肉，每周都得烧一次，而且我们每顿饭都得配点儿**咸
　　　　菜**。大夫，您这一问，我想起来了，我这病是不是跟我高盐高脂的饮食有关？而且我还这么胖，
　　　　又总是熬夜。

周医生　是的。从您的描述和症状来看，您的情况很可能是冠状动脉粥样硬化性心脏病，也就是我们通
　　　　常所说的冠心病。冠心病主要是由于心脏冠状动脉**供血**不足引发的**心肌**急性暂时性的缺血缺
　　　　氧，常会有**心绞痛**。先给您做检查吧，根据检查结果，确定您属于哪种类型的冠心病，才能有针
　　　　对性地治疗。这是心电图、心脏超声和冠状动脉造影检查单。
　　　　（护士把病人的检查结果拿给医生）

张　兰　大夫，您快看看，报告上是怎么说的？

周医生　从检查结果看，这是冠心病引起的稳定型心绞痛。冠状动脉造影和心电图显示您的冠状动脉
　　　　狭窄，这会引起心肌缺血。我建议您吃一点儿改善心肌缺血的药——美托洛尔和硝酸甘油，用
　　　　阿司匹林来**抗凝**，防止**血栓**形成，同时还得用降脂药辛伐他汀来降**血脂**。在饮食上，注意不要
　　　　吃油脂多的食物。您有高血压，要严格限制盐的摄入量，改变作息时间，不要熬夜，保证充足的
　　　　睡眠，注意休息，保持心情愉快。我给您开了两周的药，回去按时**服用**，两周后再来复查。

张　兰　大夫，我同时服用好几种药，而且都是化学药品，会不会有药物**反应**或副作用啊？我有点儿
　　　　担心。

周医生　没问题,您放心服用。这都是临床常用药,副作用小,基本上没有药物反应。万一服药过程中出现**异常**情况,请立即来复诊。

Coronary Heart Disease

SITE:　Emergency Department

CHARACTERS:　Zhou Ying (Attending physician)

　　　　　　　Zhang Lan (Patient, female, 63 years old)

Zhang Lan:　Doctor Zhou, I have dyspnea and feel weak with chest tightness.

Dr. Zhou:　How long have the symptoms lasted?

Zhang Lan:　For a week. When I planted flowers in the yard a few days ago, I felt very tired and out of breath. I thought my symptoms had been caused by fatigue and I didn't care, but these days they have been deteriorating. Once I move, I feel worse, while I'm better at a rest. Furthermore, I feel more serious when I lie flat on my back and better when I sit up. I do not have any strength all over and my heart is beating very fast with chest pain and back pain, which sometimes lead me to abnormal sweating during the attack.

Dr. Zhou:　Did you feel bad before?

Zhang Lan:　No, I only panted for shortness of breath after walking for a while and recovered after taking a rest. I don't know what's wrong with me this time. I'm suffering from it too much.

Dr. Zhou:　Did you go and see any doctor or take any medication?

Zhang Lan:　I did not notice it, so I didn't see any doctor and took no medicine, either.

Dr. Zhou:　Have you ever had any history such as hypertension or heart disease?

Zhang Lan:　Yes, I've got hypertension for more than ten years. I keep taking antihypertensive tablets every day and my blood pressure always maintains systolic pressure 130mmHg and diastolic pressure 60mmHg.

Dr. Zhou:　Would you mind telling me your height and weight? And what do you do?

Zhang Lan:　I am 1.65m tall and weigh 91kg. I'm a writer. I like to write at night till dawn.

Dr. Zhou:　What about your family's condition? Do your parents, siblings and your husband have the same symptoms?

Zhang Lan:　My father died of a sudden attack of coronary heart disease. My mother has got high blood pressure. I have no siblings. My husband has no other diseases except hypertension.

Dr. Zhou:　Do you exercise regularly?

Zhang Lan:　I took a walk for 20 minutes every day, but I stopped due to illness.

Dr. Zhou:　What about your diet? And do your family and you have any dietary preferences?

Zhang Lan:　My family and I like meat, especially stewed meat in soy sauce, which we cook once a week and have it combined with salted vegetables that are our favorite. Doctor, your question recalls me that my condition is associated with my diet in high salt and fat, right? Also, I'm fat and usually stay up to write.

Dr. Zhou:　Yeah, you are right. Your symptoms suggest you might have developed coronary atherosclerotic heart disease, so-called coronary heart disease, which is acute myocardial transient ischemia and hypoxia caused by heart coronary artery insufficiency with angina. You need a physical examination to confirm which type it is. If results show it is coronary heart disease, let's have appropriate treatment for it. Take this check list to undergo ECG, echocardiography and coronary angiography, please. Let's discuss the treatment plan based on their results.

(The nurse takes the results to the doctor.)

Zhang Lan: Doctor, read the report, please. What is it?

Dr. Zhou: The results reflect that you've got stable angina pectoris caused by coronary heart disease. ECG and echocardiography show your coronary artery stenosis that leads to myocardial ischemia. I suggest you take metoprolol and nitroglycerin to improve myocardial ischemia. Also, you have to take aspirin and simvastatin. The former prevents thrombosis and the latter lowers blood lipid level. As for your diet, you should not have fatty foods and strictly limit intake of salt due to your high blood pressure. Moreover, you have to change your schedule of work and rest. Keep normal sleep without staying up. It is also very important for you to be in good mood and take a rest. I prescribed the medicines for 2 weeks. Please take them on time and come back to have a review in 2 weeks.

Zhang Lan: Doctor, I take several medicines at the same time and they are all chemicals. Will there be drug reactions or side effects, ah? I'm a little worried.

Dr. Zhou: No problem. You can rest assured, as they are the medicines we always use in clinical settings due to their few side effects and drug reactions. Please come and have a review as soon as possible in case of abnormal conditions.

疾病介绍

<ruby>冠心病<rt>guānxīnbìng</rt></ruby>

冠心病，又被称为冠状动脉粥样硬化性心脏病。由于给心脏供血和供氧的冠状动脉粥样硬化，造成血管腔狭窄或阻塞或冠状动脉痉挛，导致心肌缺血、缺氧或坏死。此病常见于欧美发达国家，而中国的发病率不像欧美国家那么高，但近年来呈增长趋势并成为导致人们死亡的主要因素。治疗方法依据症状和疾病的严重程度而定，用药要遵医嘱，没有经过医生同意，不可以擅自停药，否则会导致心绞痛加重及心肌梗死发作。

Coronary Heart Disease

Coronary heart disease (CHD) is also known as coronary atherosclerotic cardiopathy. The atherosclerosis of the coronary artery which supplies blood and oxygen to the heart results in the narrowing or clogging of the blood vessels or coronarospasm, which leads to the ischemia, hypoxia even necrosis of cardiac muscles. CHD takes place commonly in the developed countries like United States and some European countries. The incidence of this disease in China is not as high as that in Europe and the United States, but it is on the increase and becomes the leading cause of death. Treatment depends on its symptoms and severity. Medication should be based on the doctor's advice. Never stop the medication before talking to the doctor, otherwise, the angina would get worse and a myocardial infarction would attack.

语言点

1. 再加上

在原有的基础上,加上……。

It means "addition to", e.g. 玛丽掌握了英语和法语,再加上她的母语,她一共能讲三种语言。

2. 也就是

即……。

It means "that is…", e.g. 一般的体检,也就是做个血常规和胸透。

3. 从……来看

从某个角度、方面或观点看。

It means "from one's perspective", e.g. 从我个人观点来看,我不赞同你的做法。

4. 万一

表示极小的可能性。

It means "in case", e.g. 万一你这次没考过去,还得接着努力。

练习

➢ **听力练习**

一、听录音,选择你听到的词语

(　)1. A. 眼病　　　　　B. 眼底　　　　　C. 眼花　　　　　D. 眼光

(　)2. A. 发作　　　　　B. 发展　　　　　C. 发现　　　　　D. 发起

(　)3. A. 海盐　　　　　B. 咸盐　　　　　C. 竹盐　　　　　D. 钠盐

(　)4. A. 生病　　　　　B. 肾病　　　　　C. 心病　　　　　D. 疾病

(　)5. A. 心率　　　　　B. 心脏　　　　　C. 心理　　　　　D. 心血

(　)6. A. 维护　　　　　B. 维持　　　　　C. 维新　　　　　D. 维修

(　)7. A. 原油　　　　　B. 缘由　　　　　C. 远古　　　　　D. 缘故

(　)8. A. 线材　　　　　B. 鲜菜　　　　　C. 咸菜　　　　　D. 贤才

(　)9. A. 供销　　　　　B. 供血　　　　　C. 供需　　　　　D. 供认

(　)10. A. 血栓　　　　　B. 血压　　　　　C. 血脉　　　　　D. 血脂

二、请选出与所听录音相符的答案

(　)1. A. 170/100　　　B. 175/100　　　C. 180/100　　　D. 185/100

(　)2. A. 头晕　　　　　B. 头痛　　　　　C. 恶心　　　　　D. 呕吐

(　)3. A. 心脏病　　　　B. 肺源性心脏病　C. 糖尿病　　　　D. 高血压

(　)4. A. 什么也不干　　B. 什么都不能干　C. 不干什么　　　D. 干不了什么

(　)5. A. 改变生活习惯　B. 减少盐的摄入量　C. 睡眠充足　　　D. 减少降压药的剂量

三、听录音,完成下面的练习

1. 根据所听到的录音判断对错

1)人们已经了解冠心病的病因。(　　　)

2)血压高不是患冠心病的危险因素。(　　　)

3)随着年龄的增长,要预防冠心病。(　　　)

4)男性心血管发病率高于女性。(　　　)

5)吸烟与患冠心病无关。(　　　)

6) 如果体重超标,再加上有高血压,就得当心患冠心病。(   )

7) 心血管病家族史是患心血管病的危险因素之一。(   )

8) 如果有肾脏疾病史,也要注意预防心血管疾病。(   )

2. 听录音,选择正确答案回答问题

1) 下列哪一种饮食方式与高血压有关? (   )
    A. 高脂高盐　　　　B. 低脂低盐　　　　C. 多盐多糖　　　　D. 低盐低糖

2) 为什么肥胖是导致高血压的因素之一? (   )
    A. 身体血液量增加　B. 身体所需氧气增多　C. 血管压力升高　　D. ABC

3) 维生素 D 过剩产生的后果是什么? (   )
    A. 肝硬化　　　　　B. 肾钙化和大血管钙化　C. 动脉硬化　　　D. 腰椎间盘钙化

4) 下列哪一项与高血压的发生**无关**? (   )
    A. 肝肾综合征　　　B. 肾动脉狭窄　　　　C. 隐匿性肾炎　　　D. 肾盂肾炎

5) 下列哪一条**不**属于高血压预防范围? (   )
    A. 合理饮食　　　　　　　　　　　　B. 保持正常体重
    C. 利用学习时间　　　　　　　　　　D. 避免维生素 D 过剩

➢ 词汇和语法练习

一、给下列词语标注拼音

1. 高血压＿＿＿＿＿＿＿＿＿　　　2. 甲状腺＿＿＿＿＿＿＿＿＿

3. 视网膜＿＿＿＿＿＿＿＿＿　　　4. 心脏病＿＿＿＿＿＿＿＿＿

5. 心电图＿＿＿＿＿＿＿＿＿　　　6. 心绞痛＿＿＿＿＿＿＿＿＿

7. 钠盐＿＿＿＿＿＿＿＿＿　　　　8. 反应＿＿＿＿＿＿＿＿＿

9. 虚汗＿＿＿＿＿＿＿＿＿　　　　10. 偏好＿＿＿＿＿＿＿＿＿

二、选词填空

高血压	副作用	血压	降压片	血栓	症状	复诊	虚汗	狭窄	遗传

1. 我的＿＿＿＿＿＿＿有点儿高,医生让我按时吃药。

2. 这些＿＿＿＿＿＿＿一般出现在什么时候,有规律吗?

3. 检查结果显示您患的是高血压,这和您家族＿＿＿＿＿＿＿有关。

4. 这个药＿＿＿＿＿＿＿很小,您可以放心服用。

5. 病人发病时,前胸后背都疼,有时疼得直冒＿＿＿＿＿＿＿。

6. 我每天都吃＿＿＿＿＿＿＿,血压一直很平稳。

7. 病人除了＿＿＿＿＿＿＿,没有其他毛病。

8. 从冠状动脉造影和心电图可以看出病人是否存在冠状动脉＿＿＿＿＿＿＿。

9. 您需要吃点儿阿司匹林,预防＿＿＿＿＿＿＿。

10. 如果服药过程中出现异常,请立即来＿＿＿＿＿＿＿。

三、用指定的词语或结构完成句子或对话

1. 这位病人不仅头晕头痛,＿＿＿＿＿＿＿。(而且)

2. 他的血压总是降不下来,＿＿＿＿＿＿＿。(和……有关)

3. 他常常胸闷和心慌,可是他＿＿＿＿＿＿＿。(也没……没……)

4. 病人心绞痛还没有缓解,只好＿＿＿＿＿＿＿。(边……边……)

5. 大夫说我是＿＿＿＿＿＿＿才得高血压的。(因为……)

6. 病人＿＿＿＿＿＿＿,去年还患上了严重的肾病。(除了)

四、把下列词语排列成句子

1. 按时　高血压　要坚持　服药　病人
2. 疾病　肥胖　导致　心血管　容易
3. 常备　病人　药物　冠心病　应　急救
4. 建议　生活方式　医生　病人　改变
5. 高于　发病率　心血管病　男性　女性

➤ 阅读与应用练习

一、根据课文内容补全对话

医生：这种状态有多长时间了？

病人：大概有三四天了。

医生：这种情况以前___1___过吗？

病人：没有，有时___2___有点难受，但没有像这次这么难受。

医生：一般出现___3___的时候大约是什么时间，有规律吗？

病人：没有太___4___的规律，晚上好像多一点。

医生：每次发作大概持续多久？

病人：以前___5___都半天，而这次连续三四天了。

医生：头晕时和___6___睁开闭上有关系吗？看东西转不？头是怎么痛的？跟体位有什么关系吗？

病人：说不太___7___，因为头晕，我总是闭着眼睛，不敢睁眼，看东西都在转。头痛得像要炸了，___8___坐着都胀痛。

二、根据课文内容回答问题

1. 刘阳在患高血压初期为什么不服降压药？
2. 医生为什么说刘阳患高血压与家族遗传和不良生活习惯有关？
3. 张兰到医院之前都有哪些症状？
4. 医生根据什么给张兰确诊为冠心病？
5. 根据课文，谈一谈如何预防心血管疾病？

三、写作练习

根据课文中周医生给病人张兰的建议，写出一篇短文，要求字数不少于60个字。

四、交际练习

参考括号里的词语进行情景对话。

情景：一位老年病人前来就诊，医生和病人进行对话。

（眼底，高血压，血脂，心绞痛，药物治疗，血栓，血管狭窄）

消 化 内 科

会话一　消化性溃疡

词汇

消化性溃疡	xiāohuàxìngkuìyáng	名	peptic ulcer
反酸	fǎnsuān	名	acid reflux
嗳气	àiqì	名	belching
食欲	shíyù	名	appetite
腹胀	fùzhàng	名	abdominal distention
隐隐约约	yǐnyǐnyuēyuē	形	indistinct
黑便	hēibiàn	名	melena
呕血	ǒuxuè	名	hematemesis
上消化道	shàngxiāohuàdào	名	upper gastrointestinal tract
出血	chūxuè	名	hemorrhage
体格检查	tǐgéjiǎnchá	名	physical examination
胃镜	wèijìng	名	gastroscopy
幽门螺杆菌	yōuménluógǎnjūn	名	*Helicobacter pylori*
十二指肠	shíèrzhǐcháng	名	duodenum
奥美拉唑	àoměilāzuò	名	omeprazole
抑制	yìzhì	动	restrain
胃酸	wèisuān	名	gastric acid
分泌	fēnmì	动	secrete
阿莫西林	āmòxīlín	名	amoxicillin
克拉霉素	kèlāméisù	名	clarithromycin

 地点：消化内科门诊
人物：周医生（消化内科医生）
　　　赵哲（病人，男，31 岁）

周医生　请进！（起立，与病人握手。）赵先生，你好！我是周医生。请坐！你今天来是哪里不舒服啊？
赵　哲　大夫，我最近这几天胃疼得很厉害，还经常**反酸**，总是觉得肚子胀、**嗳气**，没有**食欲**。
周医生　那你胃疼、反酸、嗳气、**腹胀**有多长时间了？
赵　哲　我这可是老毛病了，少说也有十几年了吧。最近这一周又犯病了。
周医生　你感觉是什么原因引起的胃疼？

赵　哲　可能因为我是出租车司机,吃饭不太规律吧。另外我一喝完酒或茶呀、咖啡什么的也会胃疼。

周医生　那你这次胃疼加重有什么特殊原因吗?

赵　哲　有。一周前,我哥哥因为得了重病需要手术。我特别担心,所以就拼命抽烟,而且每天都要去医院照顾他,挺累的。这不,胃病就犯了,疼得要命。

周医生　是一种什么样的疼痛呢? 与吃饭有关吗?

赵　哲　是一种**隐隐约约**的疼痛,一般是饿了的时候疼,吃点东西就不疼了。不过,最近这几天无论是饿了还是吃饱了都疼。

周医生　能说一下具体是哪个位置疼吗?

赵　哲　也不是很确切,多数时间是这里疼(指上腹部),有时好像又是这里(指右上腹部)。

周医生　最近几天大便如何? 有排黑色大便吗?

赵　哲　大便正常,每天一次,是黄色的。

周医生　哦! 另外你觉得过去这十几年,你的胃疼与季节变化有关系吗?

赵　哲　有的。每到快入冬那段时间,总是觉得特别不舒服。

周医生　哦! 以前来医院看过吗?

赵　哲　看过一次。那次是因为和朋友喝酒喝多了,回家后胃就开始疼,还拉了一些**黑便**,家里人就把我送到了医院。

周医生　当时**呕血**了吗? 医生告诉你得了什么病吗?

赵　哲　没有呕血。医生说我得了**上消化道出血**,马上让我住进了急诊观察室。还给我输液了。

周医生　我明白了! 那现在我想给你做一下**体格检查**。请你躺到床上,露出肚子。

　　　　(10分钟后,体格检查结束。)

周医生　根据病史和体格检查,我考虑你可能是患了消化性溃疡,但你还需要做一个**胃镜**检查和**幽门螺杆菌**检测。这种菌是与消化性溃疡发生有密切关系的一种细菌。今天我先给你开检查单,等胃镜和其他检查结果出来后,你再来找我。你还有其他问题吗?

赵　哲　没有。谢谢医生!

周医生　不用谢!

　　　　(三天后,病人所有的检查都已经完成。)

周医生　赵先生,胃镜检查发现你的胃和**十二指肠**上都有溃疡,说明你确实是得了消化性溃疡。另外,幽门螺杆菌检测还证实你感染了幽门螺杆菌。

赵　哲　那该怎么治疗啊?

周医生　我建议你同时服用三种药物,总共需要两周左右的时间来治疗。

赵　哲　是哪三种药啊?

周医生　这三种药,一种叫**奥美拉唑**,是**抑制胃酸分泌**的。另外两种都是用来根除幽门螺杆菌的,一种叫**阿莫西林**,另一种叫**克拉霉素**。

赵　哲　医生,这些药是饭前吃还是饭后吃呢? 一天要吃几粒?

周医生　你先别急,等药取回来后,我再详细告诉你。

赵　哲　好的。谢谢周医生!

周医生　不用谢! 希望你早日康复!

Peptic Ulcer

SITE:　Gastroenterology Clinic

CHARACTERS:　Doctor Zhou (Attending physician)

　　　　　　　Zhao Zhe (Patient, male, 31 years old)

Dr. Zhou: Come in, please. (Stand up and shake hands with the patient) Hello, Mr. Zhao! I am Doctor Zhou. Sit down, please. What's the matter with you?

Zhao Zhe: Hello, doctor. I've got an awful stomachache recently with acid reflux. I always feel bloated in my abdominal area, belch and have no appetite.

Dr. Zhou: How long have you been like this?

Zhao Zhe: This is my old disease that I've got at least 10 years. I've been suffering from it again since last week.

Dr. Zhou: Do you know what triggers your stomachache?

Zhao Zhe: I'm a taxi driver and it might be caused by my irregular eating habit. Sometimes my stomach hurts after drinking alcohol, tea or coffee.

Dr. Zhou: What made your stomachache worse?

Zhao Zhe: A week ago, my elder brother had surgery because of his serious disease and I was so worried about it that I smoked heavily. What's more, I had to go to the hospital to take care of him every day. All these make my stomach ache very much.

Dr. Zhou: What is the pain like? Is it related to your eating?

Zhao Zhe: It is the dull pain and commonly occurs when I'm hungry. Then I feel better after eating. In addition, I always have heartburn. However, I've been feeling a pain whether I eat or not these days.

Dr. Zhou: Would you like to show me where it is?

Zhao Zhe: I'm not quite sure. Most of the time it is here (Point to the upper abdominal region), and sometimes it seems to be here (Point to the right upper abdominal region).

Dr. Zhou: How about the stools in recent days? Have you had dark stools?

Zhao Zhe: No, it is normal and yellow, once a day.

Dr. Zhou: Oh, do you think your stomachache was closely related to the seasonal changes in the past decade?

Zhao Zhe: Yes, it was. I always feel very uncomfortable in the beginning of winter.

Dr. Zhou: Oh, have you ever seen a doctor?

Zhao Zhe: Yes, I have. My family sent me to the hospital as my stomach began to ache and I passed some black stools after I drank too much with my friends.

Dr. Zhou: Did you have haematemesis at that time? What disease did your doctor tell you?

Zhao Zhe: No, I didn't. The doctor told me I had got upper gastro-intestinal hemorrhage. I was admitted to the emergency observation room immediately and was given fluid transfusion.

Dr. Zhou: I see. Now, I'll give you a physical examination. Please lie down on the bed and expose your abdomen.

(10 minutes later, the physical examination ended)

Dr. Zhou: According to the medical history and physical examination, you may have got peptic ulcer. You need a gastroscopy and the examination of *Helicobacter pylori* (Hp) that is a kind of bacteria correlated with peptic ulcer. Today, I'll prepare some application forms for you to be tested; you can come back to me after examination results come out. Do you have any more questions?

Zhao Zhe: No, I haven't. Thanks, doctor.

Dr. Zhou: You are welcome!

(All the tests were done 3 days later.)

Dr. Zhou: Mr. Zhao, the gastroscopy examination reveals that there are ulcers taking place both in your stomach and duodenum, which shows that you do have peptic ulcer. Besides, the *Helicobacter pylori* (Hp) examination confirms that you have got Hp infection.

Zhao Zhe: How to treat them?

Dr. Zhou:　I suggest that you take three drugs at the same time and the total treatment course needs about two weeks.

Zhao Zhe:　What are the three drugs?

Dr. Zhou:　One is omeprazole that can inhibit gastric acid secretion. The other two drugs are used to eradicate Hp. They are ampicillin and clarithromycin.

Zhao Zhe:　Doctor, when shall I take them, before or after meals? How many pills shall I have per day?

Dr. Zhou:　Take it easy. I'll tell you in detail after you take back the drugs.

Zhao Zhe:　Ok! Thank you, doctor.

Dr. Zhou:　You are welcome! Wish you get well soon!

疾病介绍

消化性 溃疡

消化性 溃疡 是 指 发生 于 胃 或 十二指肠 黏膜（起始于 小肠 ）的 慢性 侵蚀性 疾病。它 是 全球性 的 多发病，全球 约 10% 的 人口 患 该病。消化性 溃疡 最 常见 的 病因 是 幽门螺杆菌（HP）感染。许多 幼年 接触 幽门螺杆菌 的 人，成年 后 才 会 出现 症状。另 一个 主要 的 病因 是 非甾体 抗炎 药（NSAIDs）的 使用。其他 不太 常见 的 原因 包括 吸烟 或 严重 疾病引起 的 应激、白塞综合征、卓-艾综合征、克罗恩病 和 肝硬化 等。最 常见 的 症状 是 上腹痛，通常 被 描述 为 灼烧感 或 钝痛。其他 症状 包括 打嗝、呕吐、体重 减轻 或 食欲 缺乏。并发症 有 出血，穿孔，梗阻 或 癌变。消化性 溃疡 的 诊断，可以 根据 上消化道 一系列 的 症状 和 胃镜 检查 确定。消化性 溃疡 的 治疗，可以 使用 抗生素 联合 胃酸 抑制 药，根除 幽门螺杆菌 或 消除 诱发 因素。

Peptic Ulcer

Peptic ulcer is a chronic erosive disease that occurs in the stomach or duodenal mucosa from the beginning of the small intestine. It is the disease that approximately 10% of population suffers from in the world. The most common cause of peptic ulcer is a stomach infection associated with the *Helicobacter pylori* (*H. pylori*) bacteria. Many people contact *H. pylori* at a young age, but their symptoms most commonly occur in adulthood. Another major cause is the use of non-steroidal anti-inflammatory drugs (NSAIDs). Other less common causes include tobacco smoking, stress due to serious illness, Behcet syndrome, Zollinger-Ellison syndrome, Crohn disease and liver cirrhosis.

The most common symptom is upper abdominal pain that is often described as a burning or dull ache. Other symptoms include belching, vomiting, weight loss, or poor appetite. Complications may include bleeding, perforation, blockage of the stomach and canceration.

Diagnosis of ulcer can be made with an upper GI series symptoms or endoscopy. Treatment of ulcers involves the combinations of antibiotics with stomach acid suppression to eradicate *H. pylori*, or eliminate precipitating factors.

语言点

1. 那……

"那"在这里是连词,在口语中表示"那么",常用在句子的开头,起承上启下的作用,使内容自然过渡。

"那"is a conjunction here, it means "那么" in spoken Chinese. It is often used at the beginning of a sentence and serves as a connecting link between the preceding and the following, e.g. 既然这样做不行,那你打算怎么办呢?

2. 可……

"可"这里是副词,强调语气,常用在形容词或动词的前面。

"可"is an adverb here, used to emphasize sth. before an adjective or a verb, e.g. 今天医院里的病人可多了。

3. ……什么的

用在一个或多个并列成分之后,表示列举,相当于"之类"、"等等"。

It means "and so on" used after the things you enumerate, e.g. 不上班的时候,他就喜欢在家照顾他的花儿呀、草儿呀什么的。

4. adj. + 得 + 要命

"要命"通常表示极端的程度,用作补语。

It is used to express an extreme degree, e.g. 我的肚子疼得要命。

肝 硬 化

词汇

肝硬化	gānyìnghuà	名	cirrhosis
水肿	shuízhǒng	动	edema
腹水	fùshuǐ	名	ascites
乙型肝炎(乙肝)	yǐxínggānyán(yǐgān)	名	hepatitis B
牙龈	yáyín	名	gum
转氨酶	zhuǎn'ānméi	名	aminotransferase
少尿	shǎoniào	名	oliguria
巩膜黄染	gǒngmóhuángrǎn	名	icteric sclera
结膜	jiémó	名	conjunctiva
蜘蛛痣	zhīzhūzhì	名	spider nevus
肝掌	gānzhǎng	名	liver palms
静脉曲张	jìngmàiqūzhāng	名	vein varix
移动性浊音	yídòngxìngzhuóyīn	名	shifting dullness
肝功能失代偿	gāngōngnéngshīdàicháng	名	hepatic dysfunction
肝肾综合征	gānshènzōnghézhēng	名	hepatorenal syndrome

利尿药	lìniàoyào	名	diuretics
白蛋白	báidànbái	名	albumin
电解质紊乱	diànjiězhìwěnluàn	名	electrolyte disturbance
肝性脑病	gānxìngnǎobìng	名	hepatic encephalopathy
肾功能	shègōngnéng	名	renal function

地点：消化内科病房
人物：姜医生（主治医师）
　　　朱麦拉（住院医师）
　　　护士
　　　赵子宇（病人，男，43岁）

护　士　朱医生，刚才门诊收了一位新病人，住在4床，麻烦您去看一下！

朱麦拉　好的。
　　　　（朱麦拉查阅完赵子宇病人的门诊病例后，走向病人病房）

朱麦拉　赵先生，您好！我是您的管床医生朱麦拉。

赵子宇　您好！朱医生。

朱麦拉　这次是因为什么来医院的啊？

赵子宇　最近这一个星期我觉得肚子越来越胀，两条腿也有些**水肿**。去门诊部做了B超检查，医生发现有很多**腹水**，就收我住院了。

朱麦拉　除了腹胀和腿肿，还有别的症状吗？大小便怎么样？

赵子宇　大便没问题，都是正常的黄色大便，可是最近一周小便量却很少。

朱麦拉　您以前得过什么病吗？

赵子宇　嗯，得过。15年前单位组织体检，发现我得了**乙型肝炎**，当时也没太在意。

朱麦拉　那后来身体有什么感觉吗？

赵子宇　开始的时候都很好，可后来逐渐就觉得越来越没有力气了，吃东西也没有什么食欲。

朱麦拉　去医院检查了吗？

赵子宇　没有。一直到后来发现早上刷牙的时候，**牙龈**经常出血，还流鼻血，我老婆才硬把我拽到了医院。

朱麦拉　噢，那是哪一年？医生怎么说呢？

赵子宇　我想想，大概9年前，医生诊断为肝硬化，让我住院治疗，可我没同意。后来，医生就给我开了些药，拿回家吃。

朱麦拉　还记得是什么药吗？

赵子宇　具体的药名想不起来了，好像有保肝药。

朱麦拉　从那以后又去过医院吗？

赵子宇　经常去，还住过两次医院呢。一次是因为发现**转氨酶**有些高，医生就让我住院了；还有一次是因为我吃了一些生辣椒后吐血了，也住院治疗了一段时间。

朱麦拉　哦，知道了。您现在躺下，我帮您检查一下吧。
　　　　（30分钟后，朱麦拉回医生办公室向主治医师姜医生汇报病史。）

朱麦拉　姜医生，您好！4床收了一位新病人，我刚刚去看过。

姜医生　那你把他的病史简单汇报一下吧。

朱麦拉　好的！病人赵子宇，男，43岁。因腹胀伴**少尿**1周入院。病人有乙肝病史15年，肝硬化病史9年。

姜医生　体格检查发现有什么主要体征吗？

朱麦拉	病人面色晦暗，**巩膜黄染**，结膜苍白，可见**蜘蛛痣**及**肝掌**。
姜医生	腹部检查有什么发现吗？
朱麦拉	腹部膨隆，腹壁**静脉曲张**，**移动性浊音**阳性。另外，病人的双下肢有水肿。
姜医生	不错。你的初步诊断是什么？
朱麦拉	肝硬化，**肝功能失代偿期**。
姜医生	对。由于病人明显少尿，我们还要考虑**肝肾综合征**的可能性。下面我们来讨论一下赵先生的治疗方案及接下来的检查。
朱麦拉	我想我们需要为他排放腹水并适当应用**利尿药**，另外还要给他输注一些**白蛋白**。
姜医生	很好，但千万注意，排放腹水时，每次的排放量不能过大，以免引起**电解质紊乱**并诱发**肝性脑病**。同时，还要密切监测病人血清离子及**肾功能**的变化。
朱麦拉	明白了。我是不是还应该观察病人的尿量变化？
姜医生	是的，还要提醒病人的家属注意控制赵先生水和盐的摄入。下面我们给病人开药和化验申请单吧。

Cirrhosis

SITE:	The Ward of Digestive System Department
CHARACTERS:	Doctor Jiang (Attending physician)
	Zhu Maila (Resident)
	Nurse
	Zhao Ziyu (Patient, male, 43 years old)

Nurse: Dr. Zhu, the patient in bed No.4 was admitted from the outpatient department just now and you'd better see him first.

Zhu Maila: Ok.

(Zhu Maila went to Zhao Ziyu's ward after consulting his outpatient medical records.)

Zhu Maila: Hello, Mr. Zhao. I am a resident, Zhu Maila and responsible for you.

Zhao Ziyu: Hello, doctor.

Zhu Maila: What's wrong with you?

Zhao Ziyu: My belly has been distending since last week and my two legs have swelled up. I had a B ultrasound examination which found that there are a lot of ascites, so I was hospitalized.

Zhu Maila: Do you have any other symptoms besides abdominal distention and legs edema? How about your stools and urine?

Zhao Ziyu: My stools are normal and the color is yellow, but I've been oliguric since last week.

Zhu Maila: Did you have any disease in the past?

Zhao Ziyu: Yes, the physical checkup organized by our unit 15 year ago showed that I had hepatitis B, but I did not care too much at that time.

Zhu Maila: What did you feel after that?

Zhao Ziyu: Everything was okay at the beginning and then I felt weak and had no appetite.

Zhu Maila: Did you go to the hospital to have a check?

Zhao Ziyu: No, I didn't. Later I found that my gums bled when I brushed teeth in the morning and had nosebleeds, so my wife forced me to go to the hospital.

Zhu Maila: Oh. Which year it was and what was your doctor's diagnosis?

Zhao Ziyu: Let me think, about 9 years ago and the doctor diagnosed me as cirrhosis. I was suggested to be treated in hospital. But I didn't agree and asked the doctor to prescribe some pills for me to eat at home.

Zhu Maila: Can you remember what pills they are?

Zhao Ziyu: I can't recall their names clearly. One of them might be hepatic protector.

Zhu Maila: Did you go to the hospital again?

Zhao Ziyu: I've been to the hospital frequently since then and had inpatient treatment twice. The first time I was hospitalized due to elevated aminotransferase and the second time it was because I vomited blood after eating some raw chilli.

Zhu Maila: Oh, I see. Please lie down and let me examine you.

(30 minutes later, Zhu Maila comes back to the office and reports the condition of the patient to attending physician, Doctor Jiang.)

Zhu Maila: Hello, Doctor Jiang. There is a new patient in the No.4 bed and I have already interviewed him.

Dr. Jiang: Please tell me his history in brief.

Zhu Maila: Ok. The patient, Zhao Ziyu, male, 43 years old, is admitted to hospital due to abdominal distention with oliguria for a week. The patient has a history of hepatitis B for 15 years and cirrhosis for 9 years.

Dr. Jiang: Are there any main signs in physical examination?

Zhu Maila: The patient's face looks dark with icteric sclera, pale conjunctiva and spider nevus as well. Liver palm can be seen.

Dr. Jiang: What have you found in abdominal examination?

Zhu Maila: His abdomen has distended with abdominal wall varicosis and the shifting dullness is positive. What's more, his lower limbs are swollen.

Dr. Jiang: Good job. What is your diagnosis?

Zhu Maila: Cirrhosis, hepatic dysfunction.

Dr. Jiang: Right. Significant oliguria still exists in the patient, so we have to consider the possibility of hepatorenal syndrome. Now, let's make a treatment plan for Mr. Zhao and determine the next examination.

Zhu Maila: I think we should discharge ascites for him, treat with diuretic, and transfuse albumin.

Dr. Jiang: Ok. But most care must be taken not to discharge ascites too much one time, otherwise it will result in disorder of acid-base as well as electrolyte, and induce hepatic encephalopathy. Meanwhile we have to closely monitor the changes in serum ions and renal function.

Zhu Maila: I see. Should we observe the alteration of urine volume?

Dr. Jiang: Yes, you should. What's more, we have to remind his families of paying attention to him to limit the intake of water and salt, and then let's give him a prescription for medicines and application forms of laboratory examination.

疾病介绍

gānyìnghuà
肝硬化

gānyìnghuà shì línchuáng chángjiàn de mànxìng jìnxíngxìng gānbìng yóu yìzhǒng huò duōzhǒng bìngyīn chángqī huò fǎnfù zuòyòng
肝硬化 是 临床 常见 的 慢性 进行性 肝病 ， 由 一种 或 多种 病因 长期 或 反复 作用

xíngchéng de mímànxìng gān sǔnhài yánzhòng wēixié zhe rénlèi de shēntǐ jiànkāng zhèzhǒng bìng zǎoqī méiyou rènhé zhèngzhuàng   kě
形成 的 弥漫性 肝 损害 ， 严重 威胁 着 人类 的 身体 健康 。 这种 病 早期 没有 任何 症状 ，可

qiānyán shùyuè zhì shùnián　dào wǎnqī gāngōngnéng huì zhújiàn sàngshī　gān shuāijié　　suízhe bìngqíng de jiāzhòng　bìngrén huì biàn
迁延 数月 至 数年 ，到 晚期 肝功能 会 逐渐 丧失（肝 衰竭）。随着 病情 的 加重 ，病人 会 变

de fálì　 fùzhàng 　shíyù jiǎntuì huò yǒu chūxuè qīngxiàng děng　　bìngrén kě yǒu huángdǎn　 gānzhǎng jí zhīzhuzhì děng tǐzhēng
得 乏力 、腹胀 、食欲 减退 或 有 出血 倾向 等 。病人 可有 黄疸 、肝掌 及 蜘蛛痣 等 体征 ，

tóngshí bùfen bìngrén chūxiàn fùshuǐ huò bìngfā zìfāxìng xìjūnxìng fùmóyán　　qítā bìngfāzhèng hái bāokuò gānxìng nǎobìng　 shíguǎn
同时 部分 病人 出现 腹水 或 并发 自发性 细菌性 腹膜炎 。其他 并发症 还 包括 肝性 脑病 、食管

wèidǐ jìngmài pòliè chūxuè　 gānshèn zōnghézhèng hé gānái
胃底 静脉 破裂 出血 、肝肾 综合征 和 肝癌 。

yǐnqǐ gānyìnghuà de zhǔyào yuányīn shì yǐxínggānyán　　bǐngxínggānyán hé fēi jiǔjīngxìng zhīfánggān yǐjí　 chíxù de guòdù
引起 肝硬化 的 主要 原因 是 乙型肝炎 、丙型肝炎 和 非 酒精性 脂肪肝 以及 持续 的 过度

yǐnjiǔ　 gānyìnghuà de tèzhēng shì zhèngcháng de gān zǔzhī bèi bānhén zǔzhī suǒ tìdài　 zhèxiē biànhuà dǎozhì gāngōngnéng de
饮酒 。肝硬化 的 特征 是 正常 的 肝组织 被 瘢痕 组织 所 替代 ，这些 变化 导致 肝功能 的

sǔnshāng　 gāi bìng de zhěnduàn jīyú xuèyè cèshì　 yīxué yǐngxiàng huò gānzàng huójiǎn
损伤 。该 病 的 诊断 基于 血液 测试 、医学 影像 或 肝脏 活检 。

gānyìnghuà de zhìliáo mùbiāo tōngcháng shì fángzhǐ bìngqíng jìnyíbù　 èhuà hé bìngfāzhèng de fāshēng　 fángzhì yǐxínggānyán
肝硬化 的 治疗 目标 通常 是 防止 病情 进一步 恶化 和 并发症 的 发生 。防治 乙型肝炎 ，

kěyǐ cǎiyòng yìmiáo jiēzhòng hé kàng bìngdú yàowù　 jiànyì bìngrén jièjiǔ　　tíngyòng duì gānzàng yǒu sǔnhài de yàowù　 duìyú
可以 采用 疫苗 接种 和 抗 病毒 药物 ，建议 病人 戒酒 ，停用 对 肝脏 有 损害 的 药物 。对于

yánzhòng de gānyìnghuà　 gān yízhí kěnéng shì yìzhǒng xuǎnzé
严重 的 肝硬化 ，肝 移植 可能 是 一种 选择 。

Cirrhosis

Cirrhosis, a chronic progressive liver disease often found in clinical settings, means a diffusive damage to the liver resulting from long-term effect of one cause or more causes. It severely threatens people's health. There are no symptoms at the early stage of the disease and it develops slowly over months or years. Liver function decreases gradually in the terminal stage. As the disease worsens, the sick may feel weak, lose appetite, have abdominal distension and bleeding tendency, jaundice, liver palms, spider telangiectasia, etc. At the same time, some patients develop ascites or spontaneous bacterial peritonitis. Other complications include hepatic encephalopathy, bleeding from dilated veins in the esophagus or dilated stomach veins, hepatorenal syndrome and liver cancer.

Cirrhosis is commonly caused by hepatitis B, C, and non-alcoholic fatty liver disease and continuing excessive alcohol consumption, characterized by the replacement of normal liver tissue with scar tissue. These changes lead to damage of liver function. Diagnosis is based on blood test, medical imaging and liver biopsy.

The goal of the treatment is to prevent its progression and complications. Some causes of cirrhosis, such as hepatitis B, can be prevented by vaccination and antiviral medications. Avoiding alcohol is recommended. Stop the use of drugs that can induce liver damage. For severe cirrhosis, a liver transplant may be an option.

语言点

1. A 被诊断为 B

"A 被诊断为 B"，在这个结构中，A 表示病人；B 代表疾病。

"A 被诊断为 B" means "A is diagnosed B". "A" is a patient and "B" is a disease, e.g. 他被诊断为肝肾综合征。

2. 考虑……的可能性

"考虑……的可能性"通常用于医生给病人做初步诊断时，意思是"考虑可能得/患了…"。

The possibility is considered, e.g. 我们还要考虑上消化道出血的可能性。

3. ……，以免……

"以免"是连词，用来连接两个从句，意思是"为了避免"。前一个从句是采取的措施，后一个从句是想要尽力避免的结果。

It is a conjunction used to connect two clauses, means "in order to avoid…". The first clause is the measure taken, and the second clause is the consequences tried to avoid, e.g. 老师讲课时要记笔记,以免忘记。

➢ **听力练习**

一、听录音,选择你听到的词语

( ) 1. A. 腹水　　　　B. 腹部　　　　C. 腹壁　　　　D. 腹胀

( ) 2. A. 胃镜　　　　B. 胃酸　　　　C. 胃胀　　　　D. 胃痛

( ) 3. A. 输入　　　　B. 输出　　　　C. 输液　　　　D. 输氧

( ) 4. A. 秀发　　　　B. 黑发　　　　C. 开发　　　　D. 诱发

( ) 5. A. 浮水　　　　B. 浮肿　　　　C. 浮云　　　　D. 浮力

( ) 6. A. 巩膜　　　　B. 角膜　　　　C. 结膜　　　　D. 腹膜

( ) 7. A. 疲惫　　　　B. 疲倦　　　　C. 疲劳　　　　D. 疲乏

( ) 8. A. 保肝药　　　B. 止痛药　　　C. 利尿药　　　D. 退烧药

( ) 9. A. 肝功能　　　B. 肾功能　　　C. 胃肠功能　　D. 心脏功能

( ) 10. A. 静脉注射　　B. 静脉血栓　　C. 静脉输液　　D. 静脉曲张

二、请选出与所听录音相符的答案

( ) 1. A. 在病人的家里　　B. 在医院住院部　　C. 在医生家里　　D. 在医院门诊部

( ) 2. A. 喝酒　　　　　　B. 喝咖啡　　　　　C. 喝茶　　　　　D. 喝水

( ) 3. A. 病人先吃药止痛　　　　　　B. 现在没时间做胃镜检查
　　　　C. 方便时做胃镜检查　　　　D. 病人马上要做胃镜检查

( ) 4. A. 患者一好点儿就不服药了　　B. 患者一直不按时服药
　　　　C. 患者一开始没有按时服药　　D. 患者一开始不按时服药

( ) 5. A. 夏季　　　　B. 冬季　　　　C. 春季　　　　D. 秋季

三、听录音,完成下面的练习

1. 根据所听到的录音判断对错

1) 打电话的患者患有肝病。(　　　)

2) 这个患者喝完白酒以后胃痛。(　　　)

3) 这个患者的胃病和季节没有关系。(　　　)

4) 这个患者以前就有过胃痛。(　　　)

5) 医生建议患者戒酒并注意胃部保暖。(　　　)

2. 听录音,选择正确答案回答问题

1) 老王有什么病史?(　　　)
　　A. 肺炎　　　　B. 胃炎　　　　C. 乙肝　　　　D. 丙肝

2) 老王**没有**下面哪种症状?(　　　)
　　A. 呕吐　　　　B. 牙龈出血　　　C. 没胃口　　　D. 身体虚弱

3) 老王得了什么病?(　　　)
　　A. 肝癌　　　　B. 脂肪肝　　　C. 白血病　　　D. 肝硬化

➢ **词汇和语法练习**

一、给下列词语标注拼音

1. 输液_____　　　2. 食欲_____

3. 水肿_____　　　　4. 肾功能_____

5. 静脉曲张_____　　　6. 移动性浊音_____

7. 消化性溃疡_____　　8. 幽门螺杆菌_____

9. 蜘蛛痣_____　　　　10. 巩膜黄染_____

二、选词填空

| 排放腹水　　乙型肝炎　　胃镜　　诱发　　难受　　隐隐约约 |
| 消化道出血　　高热　　电解质　　挂号单 |

1. 昨天我排的是黑便,到医院一查,结果是_____。

2. 护士让我拿着_____去消化科看病。

3. 病人连续三天_____不退,已经处于昏迷状态。

4. 病人腹部膨隆并伴有双下肢水肿,要_____,适当用些利尿药。

5. 这位肝硬化病人有十五年的_____病史。

6. 我早上吃了冰激凌,_____感觉下腹部不舒服。

7. 病人面色晦暗,看上去很_____的样子。

8. 研究表明,饮食不规律是_____胃病的重要因素。

9. 你患了消化性溃疡,要做_____检查。

10. 一次不要排放腹水太多,以免引起_____紊乱。

三、用指定的词语或结构完成句子或对话

1. 现在他这样的情况比较危险,_____。(尽快)

2. 病人的家属担心手术可能会有危险,_____。(是否)

3. 出现这种情况,你要马上来医院,_____。(以免)

4. _____,但是他还继续抽烟、喝酒。(诊断为)

5. 从病人的体征来看,_____。(考虑……可能是……)

四、把下列词语排列成句子

1. 高　病人　的　有些　转氨酶

2. 有　五六颗　左手背上　病人的　蜘蛛痣

3. 考虑　的　还要　可能性　肝肾综合征

4. 让我　住进　医生　观察室　了　急诊

5. 效果　这种　通过　治疗感染　药物　很好

➤ 阅读与应用练习

一、根据课文内容补全对话

病人：大夫,我最近这几天＿＿1＿＿得很厉害。

医生：能说一下具体是＿＿2＿＿位置疼吗?

病人：也不是很确切,＿＿3＿＿是这里疼(指上腹部),有时好像又是这里(指右上腹部)。

医生：有多长时间了?

病人：我这可是老毛病了,少说＿＿4＿＿十几年了吧。

医生：还记得是什么＿＿5＿＿引起的胃疼吗?

病人：也没有＿＿6＿＿特殊的原因,可能是因为我是出租车司机,吃饭不太规律吧;再有就是我还＿＿7＿＿喝点酒,有时喝完酒后也会胃疼。

医生：我明白了,给你开三种＿＿8＿＿,总共需要两周左右的时间来治疗。

二、根据课文内容回答问题

1. 赵哲胃痛都有哪些症状?

2. 赵哲为什么胃痛？

3. 医生给赵哲的诊断是什么？如何治疗？

4. 赵子宇的乙型肝炎为什么不治疗？

5. 赵子宇病程经历是怎么样的？

三、写作练习

请简单描述会话二中病人赵子宇的主要临床表现。（不少于50字）

四、交际练习

参考括号里的词语进行情景对话。

情景：病人的检查报告出来了，医生和病人进行对话。

（胃镜，消化性溃疡，感染，幽门螺杆菌，药物治疗）

内 分 泌 科

 会话一

糖 尿 病

词汇

糖尿病	tángniàobìng	名	diabetes mellitus
小便	xiǎobiàn	名	urine
尿量	niàoliàng	名	urine volume
典型	diǎnxíng	名&形	typical case, typical
多饮	duōyǐn	名&动	polydipsia, drink more
多尿	duōniào	名	polyuria
多食	duōshí	名&动	polyphagia, eat more
消瘦	xiāoshòu	形	weight loss, emaciation
家族史	jiāzúshǐ	名	family history
确诊	quèzhěn	名&动	confirmed diagnosis, diagnose
糖耐量	tángnàiliàng	名	glucose tolerance
试验	shìyàn	名	test
胰岛素	yídǎosù	名	insulin
释放	shìfàng	动	release
C 肽	Ctài	名	C peptide
胰岛	yídǎo	名	pancreas islet
慢性	mànxìng	形	chronic
并发症	bìngfāzhèng	名	complication
尿常规	niàochángguī	名	urine routines
生化	shēnghuà	名	biochemistry
损害	sǔnhài	名&动	damage

地点:内分泌科门诊
人物:王小兵(主治医师)
    托马斯(实习医生)
    张仲光(病人,男,40岁)

王医生 您好,您哪儿不舒服?

张先生 医生,不知道什么原因,最近两个月我一下子瘦了将近7公斤,我担心身体出了什么大毛病,想
检查一下。

王医生　您这两个月吃饭怎么样？喝水多不多？

张先生　我胃口比以前好，每餐都吃很多；水也喝得多，一天可以喝掉 3 大壶开水，就是体重下降了！

王医生　**小便怎么样？尿量有变化吗？**

张先生　小便次数增多了，每天大概 10~12 次，而且每次量都很大。

王医生　除了体重减轻，您还有其他什么地方觉得不舒服吗？

张先生　没有，我身体一直很好，没有觉得哪里不舒服。

王医生　那您或者您家里有没有人患过糖尿病、高血压等慢性病？

张先生　我没有这些病，不过我父亲患糖尿病十多年了。

王医生　您今天吃早饭没有？

张先生　我想着可能要做检查，就没有吃早饭。

王医生　那好，您先去测一下指尖血糖，把结果拿回来给我看。这是检查单。

张先生　好的，谢谢。我等下回来找您。

（主治医师转向实习医生托马斯）

王医生　托马斯，根据刚才对这个病人的问诊，你的初步诊断是什么？

托马斯　老师，他有**典型**的"三多一少"，即**多饮、多尿、多食**和**消瘦**症状，还有糖尿病的**家族史**，初步诊断应该是糖尿病。

王医生　你说得很对，所以我让他先去检测一下空腹血糖。这个病人如果要进一步**确诊**，还需要进行哪些必要检查？

托马斯　嗯，他是第一次就诊，还需要做**糖耐量试验、胰岛素释放**试验和 C 肽释放试验，检查血糖情况和**胰岛**功能。老师，我说得对吗？

王医生　没错。此外，还要检查病人有没有合并糖尿病**慢性并发症**。

托马斯　知道了，还需要做**尿常规、血生化**和眼底检查等，这些检查可以帮助了解病人有没有合并肾脏、脑血管、心脏、眼部及神经系统**损害**。

Diabetes Mellitus

SITE:　Endocrinology Clinic

CHARACTERS:　Xiaobing Wang (Attending physician)

　　　　　　Thomas (Intern)

　　　　　　Zhongguang Zhang (Patient, male, 40 years old)

Dr. Wang:　Hello, how are you feeling today?

Mr. Zhang:　I've no idea about why I lost nearly 7kg in the last two months without any apparent reason. I am worried something might be wrong with me. I would like to have it checked out.

Dr. Wang:　What about your appetite in the recent two months? Have you drunk plenty of water?

Mr. Zhang:　My appetite has increased more than before so that I eat a lot at each meal and also drink plenty of water, up to three bottles of water a day, but I still have weight loss.

Dr. Wang:　How is your urination? Is there any change in urine volume?

Mr. Zhang:　The frequency of urination has increased to 10-12 times a day, each time with a large volume of urine.

Dr. Wang:　What else in addition to your weight loss?

Mr. Zhang:　No, there is not. I have always been in good condition without any discomfort.

Dr. Wang:　Do you or your family members have any chronic diseases such as diabetes or hypertension?

Mr. Zhang:　No, I don't, but my father has suffered from diabetes for more than ten years.

Dr. Wang: Did you have breakfast today?

Mr. Zhang: No, I didn't. I thought I might need a test.

Dr. Wang: That's right. Please go to do the fingertip blood sugar test, then take the results back to me. Here is the checklist.

Mr. Zhang: I see. Thank you. I'll be back soon.

(The attending physician turns to the intern)

Dr. Wang: What presumptive diagnosis do you give the patient based on your interview, Thomas?

Thomas: The patient has got diabetes due to his typical symptoms of polydipsia, polyuria, polyphagia and emaciation. Furthermore, he has a family history of diabetes.

Dr. Wang: You're quite right, and that's why I asked him to do the fasting plasma glucose test. What other examinations are necessary to confirm his diagnosis?

Thomas: It's his first visit, so he needs to undergo the glucose tolerance test, the insulin release test and the C peptide release test, which help examine his blood sugar level and also the function of his pancreas.

Dr. Wang: That's right. Other examinations that help evaluate whether or not the patient has diabetic chronic complications should be done too.

Thomas: I see. Other examinations such as routine urine tests, blood biochemical examinations and fundus oculi examinations are also needed. These tests can determine whether the patient has related damages in the kidney, brain, heart, eyes and nervous system.

疾病介绍

糖尿病

糖尿病 是 一种 以 高血糖 为 特征 的 代谢 性 疾病 ， 通常 由 胰岛素 分泌 缺陷 或 胰岛素 作用 障碍 所致 。 持续 的 高血糖 与 长期 的 代谢 紊乱 可 导致 眼 、 肾 、 心血管 及 神经 等 系统 出现 损害 和 功能 障碍 ，合并 糖尿病 慢性 并发症 。 严重者 可 导致 急性 代谢 紊乱 ， 并发 酮症酸中毒和高渗性 昏迷 。 糖尿病 的 主要 症状 有 多饮 、 多尿 、 多食 和 消瘦（ 三 多一 少） 。 糖尿病 的 临床 检查 包括 ： 血糖 测定（ 糖耐量 试验） 、胰岛 功能 检测（ 胰岛素 释放 试验 和 C 肽 释放 试验） 、尿液 检测（ 尿糖 和 尿酮体 、尿蛋白 测定 ）、 血生化 检测（ 血脂 、 甘油三酯 、胆固醇 测定 ）和 眼底 检查 。 糖尿病 的 临床 治疗 分 为 健康 教育 和 药物 治疗 。 健康 教育 主要 包括 饮食 控制 、加强 锻炼 和 血糖 监测；药物 治疗 主要 包括 降糖药 和 胰岛素 的 使用 以及 并发症 的 药物 治疗 。

Diabetes

Diabetes is a metabolic disease characterized by high blood sugar, usually caused by a defect in insulin secretion and/or insulin function. Sustained high blood sugar and long-term metabolic disorders can cause damage and dysfunction in the eyes, kidneys, cardiovascular and nervous system, and lead to diabetic chronic complications. Severe cases can lead to acute metabolic disorder, concurrent ketoacidosis and hypertonic coma.

The main symptoms of diabetes are polydipsia, polyuria, polyphagia and weight loss (three more one less). Clinical examination of diabetes include: determination of blood sugar (glucose tolerance test), islet function test (insulin and C peptide release test), urine test (urine sugar and urine ketone body, urine protein determination), blood biochemical tests (determination of blood lipids, triglycerides, and cholesterol), and fundus oculi examination. The clinical treatment of diabetes includes health education and drug treatment. Health education mainly includes diet control, more exercise and blood glucose monitoring. Drug treatment includes treatment with hypoglycemic drugs and insulin, and the treatment of chronic complications.

1. ……有变化吗?

临床常用问诊疑问句型。通常用在症状、体征或检查结果后面。

It is a commonly used interrogative term in clinics, usually used after describing the symptoms, physical signs or test results, e.g. 血糖水平有变化吗?

2. ……怎么样?

问诊常用疑问句式,可用来询问病人的感觉、检查结果等,放在句末。

It is a frequently used interrogative term used to ask about the patients' feelings, examination results etc. It is placed at the end of the sentence, e.g. 最近两天您感觉身体怎么样?

3. ……,就是……

"就是"是连接副词,表示转折,通常用在转折句的开始。

It is a conjunctive adverb indicating transition, usually used at the beginning of transitional sentences, e.g. 我每天都能吃能喝的,就是体重不断下降。

4. 有……,还有……,应该是……

这是临床上分析病情时常用的推测句式。通过"有……,还有……"并列句式的内容,推导出可能的结论"应该是……"。

It is a commonly-used sentence structure for diagnosis speculation in clinics. Based on the content of parallel structures of "有……,还有……", the possible conclusion may be deduced "应该是……", e.g. 她有消瘦、厌食油腻以及黄疸的临床症状,还有乙肝病史,应该是乙型肝炎急性发作。

甲状腺功能亢进

词汇

甲状腺功能亢进	jiǎzhuàngxiàngōngnéngkàngjìn	名	hyperthyroidism
多汗	duōhàn	形	excessive sweating, hyperhidrosis
眼球	yǎnqiú	名	eyeball
突出	tūchū	动	extrude, protrude
震颤	zhènchàn	名	tremor
听诊	tīngzhěn	名	auscultation
杂音	záyīn	名	murmur

甲状腺功能	jiǎzhuàngxiàngōngnéng	名	thyroid function
彩超	cǎichāo	名	color doppler ultrasound
免疫性	miǎnyìxìng	形	immunologic
病因	bìngyīn	名	pathogenesis
对症治疗	duìzhèngzhìliáo	名	symptomatic treatment
药物	yàowù	名	Medicine
放射性	fàngshèxìng	名	Radioactivity
碘	diǎn	名	Iodine
饮食禁忌	yǐnshíjìnjì	名	diet prohibition
甲亢性心脏病	jiǎkàngxìngxīnzàngbìng	名	hyperthyroid cardiopathy
甲亢危象	jiǎkàngwēixiàng	名	thyrotoxic crisis
甲亢性肌病	jiǎkàngxìngjībìng	名	hyperthyroid myopathy

地点：内分泌科医生办公室
人物：汤姆森（实习医生）
　　　托马斯（实习医生）

汤姆森　托马斯,6 床新来的病人有哪些临床表现?

托马斯　她说自己最近脾气很大,易激动,特别容易发火,而且非常怕热、**多汗**,饭吃得越来越多,人却越来越瘦。

汤姆森　这些症状听起来很像**甲状腺功能亢进**,我们一起去检查一下病人吧?

托马斯　好的,一起去吧。

　　　　（两人一起来到病房对病人进行体格检查）

托马斯　病人身高 160 厘米,体重 40 公斤;甲状腺呈弥漫性 II 度肿大,有轻微的**眼球突出**。

汤姆森　心率是 118 次 / 分钟,明显加快。双手**震颤**明显。

托马斯　是的,甲状腺**听诊**也有**杂音**。

　　　　（回到医生办公室）

汤姆森　病人的**甲状腺功能**检查结果出来了吗?

托马斯　出来了,你看她的甲状腺功能检查:FT_3 和 FT_4 升高,TSH 降低,是典型的甲状腺功能亢进。

汤姆森　是的,甲状腺**彩超**也提示双侧甲状腺弥漫性病变。

托马斯　引起甲亢的原因有很多,这位病人到底是哪一种病因呢?

汤姆森　她有甲亢的症状,血 FT_3 和 FT_4 升高,TSH 降低,同时甲状腺 B 超也显示弥漫性肿大。所以应该首先考虑 Graves 病。

托马斯　是甲亢中的 Graves 病呀,那应该怎么治疗?

汤姆森　老师说过,甲亢是一种自身**免疫性**疾病,目前**病因**不明确,只能采取**对症治疗**。

托马斯　我想起来了,甲亢的治疗方法有三种:**药物治疗**、**放射性碘**治疗和手术治疗,对吧?

汤姆森　是的。这个病人是初次发病,没有并发症,应该先采用药物治疗。

托马斯　除了药物治疗,还要交代病人放松心情,注意**饮食禁忌**,这些都有利于疾病的康复。

汤姆森　嗯。甲亢治疗不及时会导致**甲亢性心脏病**、**甲亢危象**和**甲亢性肌病**等严重并发症,一定要尽早治疗!

Hyperthyroidism

SITE: Endocrinologists Office
CHARACTERS: Thomson (Intern)
Thomas (Intern)

Thompson: What are the symptoms of the new patient in bed 6, Thomas?

Thomas: She said she has been ill-tempered, excitable and irritable recently. Furthermore, she has heat intolerance, sweats excessively and is becoming thinner, although she eats more than before.

Thompson: These symptoms sound like hyperthyroidism. Let's go and see the patient together.

Thomas: All right.

(They go to the ward and perform a physical examination on the patient.)

Thomas: The patient is 160cm high and weighs 40kg. Her thyroid diffusion exhibits Ⅱ degree swelling and both her eyeballs have slight exophthalmos.

Thompson: Her heart rate is 118/min, which is quicker than normal, and her hands have obvious tremors.

Thomas: That's right. Vascular murmurs could be heard on her thyroid as well.

(They go back to the doctor's office)

Thompson: Have the patient's thyroid function test results come out?

Thomas: Yes, they have. Look, it is a typical hyperthyroidism case because of increased FT_3 and FT_4 and decreased TSH.

Thompson: I agree. The color Doppler ultrasound also indicates diffuse lesions in the bilateral thyroid gland.

Thomas: There are many etiologies that can induce hyperthyroidism. Which etiology does the patient belong to?

Thompson: Her hyperthyroidism symptoms, increased blood FT_3 and FT_4 and decreased TSH, together with the diffuse enlargement of her thyroid suggest the prior diagnosis: Graves' disease.

Thomas: Ok. How do you treat the Graves' hyperthyroidism disease?

Thompson: My professor said that hyperthyroidism was an autoimmune disease and only symptomatic treatment could be given at this time because its etiology is unclear.

Thomas: Yes. Here are three kinds of treatments for hyperthyroidism: drug therapy, radioactive iodine therapy and surgical treatment, right?

Thompson: Yes, you are right. The patient is onset with hyperthyroidism for the first time without complications, so we should use the drug treatment first.

Thomas: The patient should also be told that a relaxed mood and diet prohibition will contribute much to her recovery in addition to drug treatment.

Thompson: If not treated in time, hyperthyroidism will lead to serious complications like hyperthyroid heart disease, hyperthyroid crisis and hyperthyroid myopathy. Be sure to treat it as soon as possible!

疾病介绍

jiǎzhuàngxiàngōngnéngkàngjìnzhèng
甲状腺功能亢进症

jiǎzhuàngxiàngōngnéngkàngjìnzhèng yòu chēng bìng huò dúxìng mímànxìng jiǎzhuàngxiànzhǒng shì yìzhǒng zìshēn miǎnyìxìng
甲状腺功能亢进症 又 称 Graves 病 或 毒性 弥漫性 甲状腺肿 。是 一种 自身 免疫性

<ruby>疾病<rt>jíbìng</rt></ruby>，<ruby>临床<rt>línchuáng</rt></ruby> <ruby>表现<rt>biǎoxiàn</rt></ruby> <ruby>并<rt>bìng</rt></ruby> <ruby>不<rt>bù</rt></ruby> <ruby>限于<rt>xiànyú</rt></ruby> <ruby>甲状腺<rt>jiǎzhuàngxiàn</rt></ruby>，<ruby>而是<rt>érshì</rt></ruby> <ruby>一种<rt>yìzhǒng</rt></ruby> <ruby>多<rt>duō</rt></ruby> <ruby>系统<rt>xìtǒng</rt></ruby> <ruby>的<rt>de</rt></ruby> <ruby>综合征<rt>zōnghézhēng</rt></ruby>，<ruby>包括<rt>bāokuò</rt></ruby>：<ruby>高代谢症群<rt>gāodàixièzhèngqún</rt></ruby>、<ruby>弥漫性<rt>mímànxìng</rt></ruby> <ruby>甲状腺<rt>jiǎzhuàngxiàn</rt></ruby> <ruby>肿<rt>zhǒng</rt></ruby>、<ruby>眼征<rt>yǎnzhēng</rt></ruby>、<ruby>皮损<rt>písǔn</rt></ruby> <ruby>和<rt>hé</rt></ruby> <ruby>甲状腺肢端病<rt>jiǎzhuàngxiànzhīduānbìng</rt></ruby>。<ruby>多数<rt>duōshù</rt></ruby> <ruby>病人<rt>bìngrén</rt></ruby> <ruby>同时<rt>tóngshí</rt></ruby> <ruby>有<rt>yǒu</rt></ruby> <ruby>高代谢症<rt>gāodàixièzhèng</rt></ruby> <ruby>和<rt>hé</rt></ruby> <ruby>甲状腺<rt>jiǎzhuàngxiàn</rt></ruby> <ruby>肿大<rt>zhǒngdà</rt></ruby>。<ruby>临床<rt>línchuáng</rt></ruby> <ruby>症状<rt>zhèngzhuàng</rt></ruby> <ruby>与<rt>yǔ</rt></ruby> <ruby>体征<rt>tǐzhēng</rt></ruby> <ruby>通常<rt>tōngcháng</rt></ruby> <ruby>表现<rt>biǎoxiàn</rt></ruby> <ruby>为<rt>wèi</rt></ruby> <ruby>怕热<rt>pàrè</rt></ruby>、<ruby>多汗<rt>duōhàn</rt></ruby>、<ruby>激动<rt>jīdòng</rt></ruby>、<ruby>纳亢<rt>nàkàng</rt></ruby> <ruby>伴<rt>bàn</rt></ruby> <ruby>消瘦<rt>xiāoshòu</rt></ruby>、<ruby>心率<rt>xīnlǜ</rt></ruby> <ruby>过速<rt>guòsù</rt></ruby>、<ruby>眼球突出<rt>yǎnqiú tūchū</rt></ruby>、<ruby>甲状腺<rt>jiǎzhuàngxiàn</rt></ruby> <ruby>肿大<rt>zhǒngdà</rt></ruby> <ruby>及<rt>jí</rt></ruby> <ruby>血管杂音<rt>xuèguǎn záyīn</rt></ruby>、<ruby>双手<rt>shuāngshǒu</rt></ruby> <ruby>震颤<rt>zhènchàn</rt></ruby> <ruby>等<rt>děng</rt></ruby>。<ruby>临床<rt>línchuáng</rt></ruby> <ruby>检查<rt>jiǎnchá</rt></ruby> <ruby>包括<rt>bāokuò</rt></ruby> <ruby>甲状腺<rt>jiǎzhuàngxiàn</rt></ruby> <ruby>功能<rt>gōngnéng</rt></ruby> <ruby>检查<rt>jiǎnchá</rt></ruby> <ruby>和<rt>hé</rt></ruby> <ruby>甲状腺<rt>jiǎzhuàngxiàn</rt></ruby> <ruby>彩超<rt>cǎichāo</rt></ruby>。<ruby>甲亢<rt>jiǎkàng</rt></ruby> <ruby>的<rt>de</rt></ruby> <ruby>并发症<rt>bìngfāzhèng</rt></ruby> <ruby>有<rt>yǒu</rt></ruby> <ruby>甲亢性<rt>jiǎkàngxìng</rt></ruby> <ruby>心脏病<rt>xīnzàngbìng</rt></ruby>、<ruby>甲亢<rt>jiǎkàng</rt></ruby> <ruby>危象<rt>wēixiàng</rt></ruby> <ruby>和<rt>hé</rt></ruby> <ruby>甲亢性<rt>jiǎkàngxìng</rt></ruby> <ruby>肌病<rt>jībìng</rt></ruby>。<ruby>甲亢<rt>jiǎkàng</rt></ruby> <ruby>病人<rt>bìngrén</rt></ruby> <ruby>要<rt>yào</rt></ruby> <ruby>注意<rt>zhùyì</rt></ruby> <ruby>情绪<rt>qíngxù</rt></ruby> <ruby>控制<rt>kòngzhì</rt></ruby> <ruby>和<rt>hé</rt></ruby> <ruby>饮食<rt>yǐnshí</rt></ruby> <ruby>禁忌<rt>jìnjì</rt></ruby>，<ruby>同时<rt>tóngshí</rt></ruby>，<ruby>可以<rt>kěyǐ</rt></ruby> <ruby>采取<rt>cǎiqǔ</rt></ruby> <ruby>药物<rt>yàowù</rt></ruby> <ruby>治疗<rt>zhìliáo</rt></ruby>、<ruby>放射性<rt>fàngshèxìng</rt></ruby> <ruby>碘<rt>diǎn</rt></ruby> <ruby>治疗<rt>zhìliáo</rt></ruby> <ruby>或<rt>huò</rt></ruby> <ruby>手术<rt>shǒushù</rt></ruby> <ruby>治疗<rt>zhìliáo</rt></ruby> <ruby>等<rt>děng</rt></ruby>。

Hyperthyroidism

Hyperthyroidism, also called Graves' disease or diffuse toxic goiter, is an autoimmune disease. Clinical manifestations of hyperthyroidism are not limited to the thyroid but a multisystem syndrome. Clinical manifestations include high metabolic disease group, diffuse goiter, ophthalmic symptom, skin lesions and thyroid acre disease. Most patients have high metabolic disease and thyroid enlargement at the same time. Clinical symptoms and signs include heat intolerance, increased sweating, irritability, weight loss while eating more, fast heart rate, exophthalmos, goiter and vascular murmur, hands tremor, etc. Clinical examination includes thyroid function test and thyroid color Doppler ultrasound. Its complications have hyperthyroid heart disease, hyperthyroid crisis and hyperthyroid myopathy. Treatment of hyperthyroidism includes emotional control and diet control combining with drug therapy, radioactive iodine therapy or surgical treatment.

语言点

1. ……提示……

这是在临床诊疗中常用的动词,通常用在临床症状、体征和检查等词后面,推测可能的结论。

This is a verb commonly used in clinical diagnosis and treatment, usually used after words like clinical symptoms, signs and examination, deducing possible conclusion, e.g. 临床症状和检查结果提示她是甲亢。

2. 只能……

副词,表示唯一的选择。

It is an adverb meaning the only option, e.g. 他是穿孔性阑尾炎,只能手术治疗。

➤ 听力练习

一、听录音,选择你听到的词语

( )1. A. 销量　　　　B. 消瘦　　　　C. 消息　　　　D. 小兽

( )2. A. 喝药　　　　B. 夺秒　　　　C. 多尿　　　　D. 少尿

( )3. A. 真短　　　　B. 审案　　　　C. 针对　　　　D. 诊断

( )4. A. 糖耐量　　　B. 太难了　　　C. 躺那里　　　D. 太牛了

( )5. A. 已到手　　　B. 已消瘦　　　C. 胰岛素　　　D. 要多少

( )6. A. 机动　　　　B. 激动　　　　C. 觉得　　　　D. 悸动

( )7. A. 突然　　　　B. 涂鸦　　　　C. 同意　　　　D. 突眼

（　　）8. A. 震撼　　　　B. 正常　　　　C. 震颤　　　　D. 镇山
（　　）9. A. 弥漫性　　　B. 明显性　　　C. 慢慢想　　　D. 迷茫性
（　　）10. A. 意思　　　　B. 饮食　　　　C. 有事　　　　D. 因素

二、请选出与所听录音相符的答案
（　　）1. A. 多食　　　　B. 多饮　　　　C. 少尿　　　　D. 体重减轻
（　　）2. A. 指尖血糖　　B. 糖耐量试验　C. 眼底检查　　D. 血生化检查
（　　）3. A. 脾气大　　　B. 饭量大　　　C. 尿量多　　　D. 出汗多
（　　）4. A. 甲状腺呈弥漫性Ⅰ度肿大　　　　B. 眼球突出
　　　　　 C. 双腿有震颤　　　　　　　　　 D. TSH 升高
（　　）5. A. 手术治疗　　B. 饮食控制　　C. 情绪控制　　D. 药物治疗

三、听录音，完成下面的练习
1. 根据所听到的录音判断对错
1）8 床的病人最近两个月饭吃得很多、水喝得也多，体重也明显增加。（　　）
2）8 床的病人每天小便的次数和量也明显增加。（　　）
3）医生对 8 床病人的初步诊断是糖尿病。（　　）
4）糖尿病的典型症状是多饮、多食、多尿和体重增加。（　　）
5）病人没有糖尿病的家族史。（　　）
6）病人还需要进一步检查血糖情况和胰岛功能才能确诊。（　　）
7）尿常规检查有助于了解病人的血糖水平。（　　）
8）糖尿病病人需要做尿常规、血生化和眼底检查。（　　）

2. 听录音，选择正确答案回答问题
1）下面哪项**不是** 6 床病人的临床症状？（　　）
　　A. 脾气很大、容易激动　　B. 怕热、出汗多　　C. 吃得多　　　D. 长得胖
2）下面哪项**不是** 6 床病人的检查结果？（　　）
　　A. 甲状腺呈弥漫性肿大　　B. 眼睑水肿　　　C. 双手震颤　　D. 甲状腺听诊有杂音
3）6 床病人的心率是：（　　）
　　A. 180 次 / 分钟　　　B. 188 次 / 分钟　　C. 118 次 / 分钟　　D. 108 次 / 分钟
4）病人的甲状腺功能检查结果正确的是：（　　）
　　A. FT$_3$ 和 FT$_4$ 升高，TSH 降低　　　　B. FT$_3$ 和 FT$_4$ 升高，TSH 升高
　　C. FT$_3$ 和 FT$_4$ 降低，TSH 降低　　　　D. FT$_3$ 和 FT$_4$ 降低，TSH 升高
5）下面哪一项**不是**病人目前的治疗方法？（　　）
　　A. 药物治疗　　　　B. 情绪控制　　　C. 注意饮食禁忌　　D. 放射性碘治疗

➤ **词汇和语法练习**

一、给下列词语标注拼音
1. 消瘦＿＿＿＿＿＿＿＿　　　　2. 多尿＿＿＿＿＿＿＿＿
3. 典型的＿＿＿＿＿＿＿＿　　　 4. 尿量＿＿＿＿＿＿＿＿
5. 眼底检查＿＿＿＿＿＿　　　　6. 甲状腺＿＿＿＿＿＿＿
7. 震颤＿＿＿＿＿＿＿＿　　　　8. 弥漫性病变＿＿＿＿＿
9. 药物治疗＿＿＿＿＿＿　　　　10. 禁忌＿＿＿＿＿＿＿

二、选词填空

并发症　　甲状腺功能亢进　　糖尿病　　临床表现　　还要　　怎么样　　确诊　　易激动

1. 您饭量＿＿＿＿＿＿＿？喝水多不多？

2. 您有＿＿＿＿＿＿＿＿或其他慢性疾病吗?

3. 这个病人还需要进行哪些必要检查进一步＿＿＿＿＿＿＿＿呢?

4. 此外,还要检查病人有没有合并糖尿病慢性＿＿＿＿＿＿＿＿。

5. 托马斯,6床新来的病人有哪些＿＿＿＿＿＿＿＿?

6. 这些症状听起来很像是＿＿＿＿＿＿＿＿呀,我们一起去检查一下病人吧?

7. 她说自己最近脾气很大,＿＿＿＿＿＿＿＿,特别容易发火,而且非常怕热、多汗,饭吃得越来越多,人却越来越瘦。

8. 除了药物治疗,＿＿＿＿＿＿＿＿交代病人放松心情、注意饮食禁忌,这些都有利于疾病的康复。

三、用指定的词语或结构完成句子或对话

1. 不知什么原因,＿＿＿＿＿＿＿＿。(最近)

2. 我胃口比以前好,每餐都吃很多,＿＿＿＿＿＿＿＿。(就是)

3. 情况怎么样?＿＿＿＿＿＿＿＿。(……有变化吗?)

4. 没有这些病史,＿＿＿＿＿＿＿＿。(但……有……很多年了)

5. 病人的检查结果出来了,她＿＿＿＿＿＿＿＿。(有……症状,初步诊断是……)

6. 这种疾病的病因不明确,＿＿＿＿＿＿＿＿。(只能)

7. 临床表现和体格检查,＿＿＿＿＿＿＿＿。(提示)

四、把下列词语排列成句子

1. 的 小便 增多 次数 了

2. 有没有 病人 糖尿病 慢性并发症 合并 检查

3. 很像 这些 听起来 甲状腺功能亢进 症状 是

4. 自身免疫性 一种 甲亢 是 疾病

5. 双侧 甲状腺彩超 提示 弥漫性病变 甲状腺

➤ 阅读与应用练习

一、根据课文内容补全对话

主治医师: 托马斯,你认为这个病人的＿1＿是什么?

实习医生: 老师,他有典型的"三多一少"即＿2＿,还有糖尿病的＿3＿,初步诊断应该就是糖尿病。

主治医师: 你说得很对,那么这个病人还需要进行哪些必要检查＿4＿呢?

实习医生: 他是第一次就诊,还需要做＿5＿、胰岛素释放试验和C肽释放试验,检查＿6＿。

主治医师: 没错。此外,还要检查病人有没有合并糖尿病＿7＿。

实习医生: 知道了,还有＿8＿等,可以了解病人有没有合并肾脏、脑血管、心脏、眼部及神经系统损害。

二、根据课文内容回答问题

1. 糖尿病的典型症状是什么?

2. 确诊糖尿病需要做哪些检查?

3. 糖尿病的慢性并发症有哪些?

4. Graves病有哪些诊断依据?

5. 甲亢应该如何治疗?

三、写作练习

请简单描述会话二中6床病人的主要临床表现、体征和检查结果。(不少于50字)

四、交际练习

参考括号里的词语进行情景对话。

情景:糖尿病病人问诊结束后,医生A指导实习生B如何进行初步诊断及下一步的临床检查。

(三多一少,糖尿病的家族史,血糖水平,胰岛功能,糖尿病慢性并发症,尿常规,血生化,眼底检查)

会话一 尿 路 感 染

词汇

血尿	xuèniào	名	hematuria
混浊	húnzhuó	形	cloudy
留意	liúyì	动	notice
尿频	niàopín	名	frequent urination
尿急	niàojí	名	urgent urination
尿痛	niàotòng	名	dysuria
精疲力尽	jīngpílìjìn	形	be completely exhausted
受凉	shòuliáng	动	have a cold
腰痛	yāotòng	名	low back pain
绞痛	jiǎotòng	名	angina; colicky pain
肾结石	shènjiéshí	名	kidney stone
单位	dānwèi	名	company
泌尿道	mìniàodào	名	urinary tract
中段尿培养	zhōngduànniàopéiyǎng	名	midstream urine culture
输尿管	shūniàoguǎn	名	ureter
膀胱	pángguāng	名	bladder
白细胞	báixìbāo	名	white cell
红细胞	hóngxìbāo	名	red cell
膀胱炎	pángguāngyán	名	cystitis
下尿路	xiàniàolù	名	lower urinary tract
过敏	guòmǐn	形	be allergic to
大肠埃希菌	dàchángāixījūn	名	*Escherichia coli*
敏感	mǐngǎn	形	sensitive
改善	gǎishàn	动	improve

地点：肾脏内科门诊

人物：王医生（主治医师）

张丽（病人，女，30 岁）

王医生　张女士，您好！我是王医生。请坐！请问您哪儿不舒服？

张　丽　王医生,我今天早上发现小便颜色是鲜红的。

王医生　哦,那有可能是**血尿**,也就是尿中带血。还有其他什么发现吗?

张　丽　小便看起来很**混浊**,几次都是这样的。

王医生　您有没有**留意**过,您的小便次数跟以前有什么不同?

张　丽　这几天小便次数明显增多了,大概一天十几次,而且每次小便都很急,感觉憋不住,小便时还很痛。

王医生　这是**尿频**、**尿急**、**尿痛**的典型表现,还有其他症状吗?

张　丽　我想想看啊……哦,对了。我最近几天下班后感觉**精疲力尽**。有时候还有点儿发热,不过没有量体温。

王医生　大概什么时候开始的? 当时有**受凉**或者感冒吗?

张　丽　大概 3 天前吧。好像没有明显受凉和感冒。但是之前两天工作很忙,天天加班,水都来不及喝一口,每天都感觉很累。

王医生　明白了。有没有感觉**腰痛**?

张　丽　没有。

王医生　那有过腹部或肾部**绞痛**吗?

张　丽　也没有。

王医生　以前小便有没有异常情况?

张　丽　从来没有过。

王医生　体检过吗? 有没有发现什么问题? 比如**肾结石**之类的?

张　丽　每年**单位**都组织体检,但是检查结果没问题,没发现有肾结石。

王医生　服用过什么药物吗?

张　丽　没用过。

王医生　现在我给您检查一下。请您脱下衣服,躺在床上。

　　　　(10 分钟后,体格检查结束。)

王医生　您现在可以穿好衣服了。我想您的问题可能是**泌尿道**感染。我希望您做一下血常规、尿常规、肾功能、**中段尿培养**以及肾、**输尿管**和**膀胱**的超声检查。然后我们就可以根据检查结果判断感染的部位以及是否存在尿路结石。

　　　　(3 小时后,病人部分检查完成)

张　丽　医生,我的检查结果怎么样?

王医生　您的血常规、肾功能都是正常的。尿常规提示**白细胞** 3526/μl,**红细胞** 2585/μl。泌尿系 B 超提示急性膀胱炎。这些结果显示您得了急性**膀胱炎**,也叫**下尿路**感染。

张　丽　严重吗?

王医生　不是很严重,请不要担心。您只要保证好好休息,多喝水,每天至少喝 2 升水,吃一些抗生素就可以了。您有药物**过敏**史吗?

张　丽　没有。我大概需要吃多长时间药?

王医生　10 天左右。这种抗生素叫左氧氟沙星,每天一次,每次一粒,0.5g,饭后半小时服用。等中段尿培养结果出来,再来复诊。

　　　　(5 天后,病人检查全部完成)

王医生　请坐! 张女士,这几天感觉如何?

张　丽　感觉好多了! 小便颜色正常了,次数也不多了。王医生,我的尿培养结果怎么样?

王医生　您的中段尿培养提示您感染的是**大肠埃希菌**,它对左氧氟沙星是**敏感**的。您的症状改善也提示治疗是有效的。您再继续服药 5 天就可以了。记得要多喝水,不要憋尿。

张　丽　好的,知道了,非常感谢!

Urinary Tract Infection

SITE:　　Nephrology Clinic

CHARACTERS:　　Doctor Wang (Attending physician)

　　　　　　　　　Zhang Li (Patient, female, 30 years old)

Dr. Wang:　Hello, Miss Zhang. I am Dr. Wang. Take your seat, please. What's the trouble with you?

Zhang Li:　Dr. Wang. My urine looked bright red this morning.

Dr. Wang:　Well, it might be hematuria, i.e. blood in your urine. Did you have any more abnormalities?

Zhang Li:　My urine was very cloudy for several times.

Dr. Wang:　Have you noticed any changes in your urination frequency?

Zhang Li:　Yes, it has increased more than 10 times a day. And I always feel urgent to pee and painful when I pass water.

Dr. Wang:　They are typical symptoms of urgent urination, frequent urination and pain during urination. Have you noticed anything else?

Zhang Li:　Let me see. Yes, I've felt completely exhausted after work for a few days. Maybe I've had a fever, but I did not take temperature.

Dr. Wang:　When did they occur? Did you have a cold then?

Zhang Li:　About 3 days ago. I didn't catch a cold. I had a lot of work to do and worked overtime every day. I was so busy that there was not enough time to drink a cup of water. I really felt tired out.

Dr. Wang:　Oh, I see. Have you felt flank pain?

Zhang Li:　No.

Dr. Wang:　Have you felt renal or abdominal colic?

Zhang Li:　No.

Dr. Wang:　Did you have the trouble with your urine before?

Zhang Li:　No, never.

Dr. Wang:　Have you ever had physical examination? Have you been found any problem, such as renal stone?

Zhang Li:　Yes, I have, but I had no problem. My company organized us to have the routine checkup every year.

Dr. Wang:　Have you taken any drug at home?

Zhang Li:　No.

Dr. Wang:　Well, I'd like to examine you. Please take off your clothes and lie on the bed.

　　　　　(10 minutes later, the physical examination done)

Dr. Wang:　You can get dressed now. I think that, you have got urinary tract infection. You need to take routine blood test, urine test, kidney function test, midstream urine culture and ultrasound examination of your kidneys, ureter and bladder. Based on the outcomes, we'll determine the infection site and if there is stone in your urinary tract.

　　　　　(3 hours later, some of the tests finished)

Zhang Li:　What about my test results, Dr. Wang ?

Dr. Wang:　Well, your routine blood test and kidney function are normal. Your routine urine test shows that white cells are 3526/μl and red cells are 2585/μl. Urinary tract ultrasonography demonstrates acute cystitis. All the results show that you are in a condition called acute cystitis, also called lower urinary tract infection.

Zhang Li:　Is the acute cystitis severe?

Dr. Wang:　No, it is not very severe. Don't worry. You just need a good rest and drink a lot of water at least 2L one day. Then take antibiotics. Are you allergic to any drugs?

Zhang Li:　No, I've never been allergic to any drugs. How long shall I take drugs?

Dr. Wang:　For about 10 days. This antibiotic is called levofloxacin. You'd better take the drug half an hour after meals once a day and 1 tablet (0.5g) each time. You should return visit after the result of midstream urine culture is out.

(5 days later, all of the tests finished)

Dr. Wang:　Sit down, please! Are you feeling better these days?

Zhang Li:　Yes, I am. The color and frequency of my urine are all normal. What about my test result of midstream urine culture, Dr. Wang?

Dr. Wang:　It shows that you have been infected with *Escherichia coli* sensitive to levofloxacin. The improving of your symptoms also shows the treatment is effective. You can continue taking the medicine for 5 days. Be sure to drink more water and not to hold back make water.

Zhang Li:　I see. Thank you, doctor.

疾病介绍

niàolùgǎnrǎn

尿路感染

尿路感染是泌尿系统的一种感染性疾病，分为上尿路感染和下尿路感染。前者为肾盂肾炎，后者主要为膀胱炎。女性发生尿路感染的风险高，是因为女性的尿道比男性短，来自于粪便或阴道的细菌很容易转移到尿道。其他致病因素包括妨碍尿液排泄的因素，如男性的前列腺增生或肾结石等，糖尿病以及其他可能影响免疫系统的慢性疾病，某些引起免疫力下降的药物或长期使用导尿管。

不是所有尿路感染病人均有明显的症状和体征，但是大部分病人会表现出其中的一种或几种，包括排尿烧灼感、排尿频繁、尿急、排尿困难、尿液混浊（有时伴有难闻的异味）、尿中带血。感染累及肾脏时，会出现发烧、呕吐或侧腹部痛。

Urinary Tract Infection

Urinary tract infection (UTI) is an infection that begins in urinary system, which can be divided into upper urinary tract infection and lower urinary tract infection. The former usually manifests as nephropyelitis and the latter mainly manifests as urocystitis. Women are highly at risk of developing UTI because female's anatomic feature of urethra is shorter than that of men. It is easy for bacteria from fecal matter or vagina to be transferred to the urethra.

Other risks include such factors impeding the flow of urine as an enlarged prostate in men or a kidney stone, diabetes and other chronic illnesses that may impair the immune system, medications that lower immunity, the prolonged use of tubes (catheters) in the bladder.

Not all the people with UTI develop recognizable signs and symptoms, but most people have one or more, including burning sensation during urination, frequent urination, urgent urination, dysuria, turbid urine occasionally with unpleasant smell, hematuria. When infection reaches the kidneys, fever, vomiting or flank pain will be present.

1. 留意

"留意"的意思和"关心"、"注意"差不多，多用于对某些事物的特别关注。

The meaning of "留意" is similar as "关心" or "注意", it is often used to concern with sth., e.g. 你应该留意你的健康问题。

2. 保证

"保证"和"确保"、"承诺"差不多，多用于确定能做到某事。

It is similar as "确保" or "承诺", often used to make sure to do sth., e.g. 我保证按时完成全部任务。

慢性肾功能不全

夜尿	yèniào	名	nocturia
肿胀	zhǒngzhàng	形	swollen
头昏眼花	tóuhūnyǎnhuā	形	groggy
浮肿	fúzhǒng	名	dropsy; edema
胃液	wèiyè	名	gastric juice
苦胆水	kúdǎnshuǐ	名	bile
灼热感	zhuórègǎn	名	burning sensation
梗阻	géngzǔ	名	obstruction
收集	shōují	动	collect
萎缩	wěisuō	名	atrophy
尿素氮	niàosùdàn	名	blood urea nitrogen（BUN）
肌酐	jīgān	名	creatinine（Cr）
尿蛋白	niàodànbái	名	urine protein
肾小球肾炎	shènxiǎoqiúshènyán	名	glomerulonephritis
肾功能不全	shèngōngnéngbùquán	名	renal failure（dysfunction）
腹膜透析	fùmótòuxī	名	peritoneal dialysis
毒素	dúsù	名	toxic substances
（冲洗）排出	（chōngxǐ）páichū	动	flush out
提醒	tíxǐng	动	remind

地点：肾脏内科门诊
人物：李医生（主任医师）
陈伟（病人，男，50 岁）

李医生　早上好，陈先生，我是李医生。请问您哪里不舒服？

陈　伟　我**夜尿**增多六个月了，而且我四个月前体重开始下降。

李医生　还有别的不舒服吗？您的小便跟以前有什么不同？

陈　伟　有，小便颜色比以前深，是暗红色的。有时候我还怀疑是不是小便里带血了。

李医生　您还有其他不舒服的吗？

陈　伟　有啊，有几回，我早上感到恶心。晚上工作后觉得小腿**肿胀**。而且最近几周来，我总觉得**头昏眼花**，没什么胃口，体重也下降了。

李医生　体重降了多少？呕吐过吗？除了腿**浮肿**以外还有其他部位肿吗？

陈　伟　体重降了大约 6 公斤。前两天呕吐过一次，不过都是**胃液**和苦胆水，没吃东西，吐不出其他东西。有时候感觉眼睛也有点肿。

李医生　这种情况持续多久了？

陈　伟　大概 4 个月吧。

李医生　您以前小便有过异常吗？

陈　伟　有过，两年前我曾在小便的时候感觉尿道有**灼热感**。医生检查后说我有高血压，并给了我一些药片吃，吃了之后就好了。

李医生　您血压最高多少？平时监测血压吗？还在吃降压药吗？

陈　伟　记不太清楚了，收缩压最高大概有 180mmHg，舒张压大概 100mmHg 吧。因为平时没有感觉不舒服，自己也没监测血压。之前吃过药，最近半年没吃了。

李医生　好的，我来给您检查一下。

（10 分钟后，体格检查结束。）

李医生　我想您的问题有可能是长期高血压，由于血压控制不好导致的肾脏并发症。您需要做血液和肾功能检查，以及肾脏超声检查来判断肾脏有没有**梗阻**情况。同时，您还需要**收集** 24 小时小便做尿液检查，具体怎样做护士会告诉您。

陈　伟　好的。

（3 天后，病人检查全部完成）

李医生　请进！陈先生，您好！请坐！

陈　伟　李医生好！我的肾有什么问题吗？

李医生　您的肾脏超声提示两肾**萎缩**，肾功能检查显示**尿素氮** 21.5mmol/L，**肌酐** 480μmol/L，24 小时**尿蛋白** 4.2g。这些结果提示您得了慢性**肾小球肾炎**，并且出现了**肾功能不全**，也就是意味着您的肾功能受到了损害。

陈　伟　那慢性肾小球肾炎严重吗？针对肾功能损害有好的治疗方法吗？

李医生　当然有。您需要住院进行治疗，我们将会一直跟踪您的病情。我们要在您的腹部放个管子，进行**腹膜透析**，通过液体流通达到清洗血液的作用，同时也把血液中的**毒素排出**。

陈　伟　那我大概需要住院多长时间？是不是需要停止工作？

李医生　大概 3 到 4 周。您**提醒**我了，您从事的是什么职业？

陈　伟　我是一名教师。

李医生　那样的话，我建议您休息 2 个月。

陈　伟　谢谢您，医生。

李医生　不用客气。

Chronic Renal Failure

SITE: Nephrology Clinic

CHARACTERS: Doctor Li (Chief physician)

Chen Wei (Patient, Male, 50 years old)

Dr. Li: Good morning, I am Dr. Li. What's the matter with you, Mr. Chen?

Chen Wei: Well, my nocturia has increased for six months and I started losing weight four months ago.

Dr. Li: Any other problems? Have you noticed any changes in your urine?

Chen Wei: Yes, it's darker reddish. I wonder if it could be blood.

Dr. Li: Any other uncomfortable?

Chen Wei: Yes. I've felt sick several times in the morning and I've noticed my legs are swollen after work in the evening. Furthermore, I've felt really groggy and no appetite. My weight lost during the past weeks.

Dr. Li: How much? Have you vomited? Have there been other parts bloated besides your legs?

Chen Wei: About 6kg. I vomited once several days ago and threw out just gastric juice and bile because I ate nothing. Sometimes I felt my eyes a little bloated.

Dr. Li: How long have you had this trouble?

Chen Wei: About 4 months.

Dr. Li: Have you ever had trouble with your urine before?

Chen Wei: Yes. Two years ago I had a burning sensation of my urethra when I passed water. The doctor said that I had high blood pressure as well after examination and it cleared up.

Dr. Li: What about your highest blood pressure? Did you monitor your blood pressure and take antihypertensive drugs?

Chen Wei: I couldn't remember clearly. It seemed that my systolic pressure was about 180mmHg and the diastolic pressure was 100mmHg. I didn't monitor my blood pressure because I didn't feel uncomfortable. I had eaten drugs before but stopped for six months.

Dr. Li: Well, I'd like to do physical examine for you.

(10 minutes later, the physical examination done)

Dr. Li: Well, it looks like that you have some reduced kidney function from prolonged hypertension uncontrolled. You need to take blood and kidney function tests, and an ultrasound examination of the kidneys to make sure there is no obstruction. At the same time, you need to collect your urine for 24 hours to do urine tests. The nurse will tell you exactly what to do.

Chen Wei: Ok.

(3 days later, all of the tests finished)

Dr. Li: Please come in! Hello, Mr. Chen. Take your seat, please.

Chen Wei: Hello! Dr. Li. Can you tell me exactly what is wrong with my kidneys?

Dr. Li: Well, your kidney ultrasonography shows the two kidneys atrophy and kidney function shows that blood urea nitrogen (BUN) is 21.5mmol/L and creatinine (Cr) is 480μmol/L. The urine protein for 24 hours is 4.2g. All the tests indicate that you've got chronic glomerulonephritis with renal disfunction, which has caused damage to your kidneys.

Chen Wei: Is the chronic glomerulonephritis severe? Are there any good treatments to repair the kidney damage?

Dr. Li:　Yes, of course. You'd better stay in the hospital for treatments and observation. We'll have to insert a tube into your abdomen to flush out toxic substances in the blood.

Chen Wei:　How long shall I have to stay in hospital? Shall I have to stop working?

Dr. Li:　For about 3~4 weeks. You have reminded me. What's your job?

Chen Wei:　I'm a teacher.

Dr. Li:　Well, I should advise you to have a 2-month long rest.

Chen Wei:　Thank you, doctor.

Dr. Li:　You are welcome.

疾病介绍

慢性肾病

慢性 肾脏 疾病，也 称 为 慢性 肾病，是 一种 肾功能 在 数月 或 数年 内 逐渐 丧失 的 疾病。在 肾功能 逐渐 恶化 的 过程 中 症状 通常 不 典型，可能 仅仅 感觉不 舒服 或 食欲 不佳、没 胃口。通常 情况 下，慢性 肾脏 疾病的 诊断 是 基于 筛查 患 肾脏 疾病 风险 高 的 人群，如 患有 高血压、糖尿病 以及 其他 与 慢性 肾病 密切 相关 疾病 的 病人。本 病 也可 通过 它 导致 的 并发症 来 加以 辨识，如 心血管疾病、贫血、心包炎 或 肾性 骨病。慢性 肾脏病 是 一个 长期 的 肾脏 疾病 过程，因此，它 与 急性 肾脏 疾病（急性 肾 损伤 ）的 区别 在于 肾功能 下降 必须 在3个月 以上。慢性 肾病 是 一种 国际 公认 的 公共 卫生 问题，世界 上 5%~10% 的 人口 受到 这种 疾病 的 困扰。

Chronic Kidney Disease

Chronic kidney disease (CKD), also known as chronic renal disease, is progressive loss in kidney function over a period of months or years. Its symptoms are not specific during the worsening progress of kidney function, and might only involve slight discomfort and a reduced appetite. Therefore, chronic kidney disease is generally found as a result of screening of people known to be at risk of kidney problems, such as those with high blood pressure, diabetes or disease closely related to CKD. This disease may also be identified by its recognized complications, such as cardiovascular disease, anemia, pericarditis or renal osteodystrophy. CKD is a long-term process of kidney disease, thus it is differentiated from acute kidney disease (acute kidney injury) in that the reduction in kidney function must have been present for at least 3 months. CKD is an internationally recognized public health problem affecting 5%~10%.

语言点

意味着

"意味着"多用于表示某种含义、含有某种意义，连接两个有关联的词语或句子。"A 意味着 B""A means B". Usually use to connect two coordinate words or sentences, e.g. 忘记过去意味着背叛。

练习

> 听力练习

一、听录音,选择你听到的词语

( )1. A. 大便　　　　B. 排便　　　　C. 小便　　　　D. 方便

( )2. A. 血尿　　　　B. 血管　　　　C. 血压　　　　D. 血糖

( )3. A. 尿痛　　　　B. 尿急　　　　C. 尿液　　　　D. 尿频

( )4. A. 感动　　　　B. 感染　　　　C. 感冒　　　　D. 感伤

( )5. A. 酸痛　　　　B. 绞痛　　　　C. 隐痛　　　　D. 疼痛

( )6. A. 恶化　　　　B. 恶变　　　　C. 恶人　　　　D. 恶心

( )7. A. 浮力　　　　B. 浮肿　　　　C. 浮动　　　　D. 浮浅

( )8. A. 肌肉　　　　B. 肌力　　　　C. 肌酐　　　　D. 肌酸

( )9. A. 蛋清　　　　B. 蛋糕　　　　C. 蛋白　　　　D. 蛋壳

( )10. A. 透亮　　　B. 透析　　　　C. 透明　　　　D. 透光

二、请选出与所听录音相符的答案

( )1. A. 尿频　　　　B. 尿急　　　　C. 血尿　　　　D. 尿痛

( )2. A. 患者喝水很多　　　　　　　B. 患者受凉感冒了

　　　C. 患者喝水很少　　　　　　　D. 患者没有感觉很累

( )3. A. 患者有高血压病　　　　　　B. 患者平时不监测血压

　　　C. 患者吃过降压药　　　　　　D. 患者目前在吃降压药

( )4. A. 恶心　　　　B. 腿肿胀　　　C. 体重下降　　D. 腰部酸痛

( )5. A. 血常规　　　B. 肾功能　　　C. 超声　　　　D. X线

三、听录音,完成下面的练习

1. 根据所听到的录音判断对错

1)这个病人不是第一次腰腹部酸痛了。(　　　)

2)这个病人以往治疗过肾结石。(　　　)

3)这个病人平时不喜欢喝水。(　　　)

4)这个病人第一次出现腰腹部绞痛。(　　　)

5)病人不是第一次有发热、尿频、尿急症状。(　　　)

6)病人做血常规检查后发现白细胞增多。(　　　)

7)病人需要注射抗生素抗感染治疗。(　　　)

2. 听录音,选择正确答案回答问题

1)现在,这个病人是第几次住院了? (　　　)

　　A. 第一次　　　　B. 第二次　　　　C. 第三次　　　　D. 第四次

2)病人是什么时候发现血肌酐偏高的? (　　　)

　　A. 今年　　　　　B. 半年前　　　　C. 两年前　　　　D. 十年前

3)这次,病人不是因为什么来医院看病的? (　　　)

　　A. 多尿　　　　　B. 恶心　　　　　C. 头昏　　　　　D. 少尿

4)这次入院检查哪项指标明显下降? (　　　)

　　A. 血肌酐　　　　B. 尿素氮　　　　C. 血压　　　　　D. 血红蛋白

5)下面哪项不是医生考虑的初步诊断? (　　　)

　　A. 2 型糖尿病　　　　　　　　　　B. 糖尿病酮症酸中毒

C. 慢性肾功能不全　　　　　　D. 糖尿病肾病

➤ 词汇和语法练习

一、给下列词语标注拼音

1. 膀胱＿＿＿＿＿＿＿＿＿＿＿＿　　2. 梗阻＿＿＿＿＿＿＿＿＿＿＿＿

3. 萎缩＿＿＿＿＿＿＿＿＿＿＿＿　　4. 泌尿道＿＿＿＿＿＿＿＿＿＿＿

5. 输尿管＿＿＿＿＿＿＿＿＿＿＿　　6. 尿素氮＿＿＿＿＿＿＿＿＿＿＿

7. 腹膜透析＿＿＿＿＿＿＿＿＿＿　　8. 精疲力尽＿＿＿＿＿＿＿＿＿＿

9. 头昏眼花＿＿＿＿＿＿＿＿＿＿　　10. 肾小球肾炎＿＿＿＿＿＿＿＿＿

二、选词填空

混浊　　肌酐　　中段尿培养　　胃口　　过敏　　胃液　　体检　　抗生素

1. 正常情况下,尿液是很清澈的淡黄色,不应该出现＿＿＿＿＿＿＿＿＿的现象。

2. 定期进行＿＿＿＿＿＿＿＿＿有助于发现身体的异常情况,尽早发现疾病。

3. 你需要进行＿＿＿＿＿＿＿＿＿来明确是哪种细菌感染。

4. 我不能吃鸡蛋、牛奶之类的食物,因为我对它们＿＿＿＿＿＿＿＿＿。

5. 我最近特别想吃东西,＿＿＿＿＿＿＿＿＿特别好。

6. 她刚刚呕吐过一次,没有吐出什么东西,基本上都是＿＿＿＿＿＿＿＿＿。

7. 慢性肾病病人的肾功能检查通常会提示＿＿＿＿＿＿＿＿＿偏高。

8. 您现在明确有细菌感染,需要＿＿＿＿＿＿＿＿＿治疗。

三、用指定的词语或结构完成句子或对话。

1. 一旦活动量过大,＿＿＿＿＿＿＿＿＿。(觉得……)

2. 我每天工作都很忙,＿＿＿＿＿＿＿＿＿。(来不及)

3. 希望您做一下泌尿系 B 超检查,＿＿＿＿＿＿＿＿＿。(以便于……)

4. ＿＿＿＿＿＿＿＿＿,还有其他部位肿吗?(除了……)

5. 我们要在您的腹部放个管子,＿＿＿＿＿＿＿＿＿。(达到……的作用)

6. 您目前出现了肾功能不全,＿＿＿＿＿＿＿＿＿。(意味着……)

四、把下列词语排列成句子

1. 小便　我还　很　颜色　发现　混浊

2. 您的　可能　问题　是　感染　泌尿道

3. 膀胱炎　超声　泌尿系　提示　急性

4. 我　有点肿　有时候　觉得　眼睛

5. 需要　您　肾功能　检查　进行

➤ 阅读与应用练习

一、根据课文内容补全对话

病人：医生,您好。您能确切告诉我＿＿1＿＿?

医生：您的肾脏超声提示＿＿2＿＿,肾功能检查显示尿素氮 21.5mmol/L,肌酐 480μmol/L,＿＿3＿＿4.2g,这些检查结果提示您得了＿＿4＿＿,并且出现了＿＿5＿＿,也就是意味着您的＿＿6＿＿。

病人：那慢性肾小球肾炎＿＿7＿＿吗? 有＿＿8＿＿肾功能损害的好的＿＿9＿＿吗?

医生：当然有的。您需要＿＿10＿＿,我们将会一直＿＿11＿＿。我们要在您的＿＿12＿＿放个管子,进行
＿＿13＿＿,通过液体流通达到＿＿14＿＿的作用,同时也把血液中的＿＿15＿＿。

病人：那我大概需要＿＿16＿＿? 是不是需要＿＿17＿＿?

医生：大概 3 到 4 周。＿＿18＿＿了,您是＿＿19＿＿?

病人：我是一名教师。

医生：那样的话我___20___。

二、根据课文内容回答问题

1. 张丽有哪些症状？

2. 张丽的尿常规检查有什么异常？

3. 医生对张丽的诊断是什么？

4. 张丽的病最根本的病因是什么？

5. 医生建议张丽在生活方面注意哪些问题？

6. 陈伟的症状有哪些？

7. 陈伟的肾脏超声检查显示了什么？

8. 陈伟的肾功能检查有什么异常？

9. 医生对陈伟的诊断是什么？

10. 医生对陈伟采用哪种治疗方法？

三、写作练习

请简单描述会话一中病人张丽的主要临床表现。（不少于 30 字）

四、交际练习

参考括号里的词语进行情景对话。

情景：病人的肾功能检查和肾脏 B 超检查报告出来了，医生就检查报告跟病人家属进行解释，并简单向病人家属介绍治疗的方法。

（肾功能，尿素氮，肌酐，萎缩，尿蛋白，慢性肾小球肾炎，慢性肾功能不全，腹膜透析）

血 液 内 科

 缺铁性贫血

缺铁性贫血	quētiěxìngpínxuè	名	iron deficiency anemia
耳鸣	ěrmíng	动	tinnitus
节食	jiéshí	动	on diet
浓茶	nóngchá	名	strong tea
记忆力	jìyìlì	名	memory
月经	yuèjīng	名	menstruation
规律	guīlù	形	regular
卫生巾	wèishēngjīn	名	sanitary pad
痛经	tòngjīng	名	dysmenorrhea
硫酸亚铁	liúsuānyàtiě	名	ferrous sulfate
疗效	liáoxiào	名	curative effect
详细	xiángxì	形	detailed; in detail
血红蛋白	xuèhóngdànbái	名	hemoglobin
血清铁	xuèqīngtiě	名	serum iron
血清铁蛋白	xuèqīngtiědànbái	名	serum ferritin
重度	zhòngdù	形	severe
子宫肌瘤	zǐgōngjīliú	名	hysteromyoma
剂量	jìliàng	名	dose; dosage
胃黏膜	wèiniánmó	名	gastric mucosa
刺激	cìjī	动	stimulate
吩咐	fēnfù	名	instruction; command
营养	yíngyǎng	名	nutrition
偏食	piānshí	名	food preference
瘦肉	shòuròu	名	lean meat
木耳	mùěr	名	black fungus
蘑菇	mógu	名	mushroom

地点:血液内科门诊
人物:刘明(主治医师)
　　　林晓(病人,女,38 岁)

林　晓	刘医生,您好！这是我的挂号单,我是三号。
刘医生	您好,请坐！您哪儿不舒服啊?
林　晓	医生,我最近总是觉得身上没力,做事没劲,很容易疲劳,而且还经常感到头昏。
刘医生	什么时候开始出现头昏、乏力的?
林　晓	大概 5 个月前吧。
刘医生	当时是因为做了什么才感到头昏的呢?
林　晓	也没做什么,突然就觉得头昏、乏力。
刘医生	平时情况怎么样?
林　晓	平时还好,就是感觉身上没力,头有点儿晕,而且一旦走路快了,就觉得喘不过气来,感觉心都要跳出来了。前两天我回家爬楼梯的时候,差点儿晕倒了,休息了好一会儿才好。
刘医生	我知道了。还有什么地方不舒服吗?
林　晓	我有时候还**耳鸣**。
刘医生	胃口好吗?
林　晓	不想吃东西,没什么食欲。
刘医生	您平时**节食**吗?
林　晓	我饭量一直比较小,我喜欢吃蔬菜,肉吃得很少。
刘医生	喜欢喝茶吗?
林　晓	对,我喜欢喝**浓茶**。
刘医生	睡眠好吗?
林　晓	不好,经常做梦,我感觉**记忆力**也下降了。
刘医生	大小便怎么样? 正常吗?
林　晓	正常的。
刘医生	**月经**正常吗?
林　晓	还比较规律。就是月经量有点儿多,有时候有暗红色的血块,每次来月经都得用两包多**卫生巾**,大概要 9 到 10 天才能结束。
刘医生	月经一直都这样吗?
林　晓	大概五年前开始这样的。
刘医生	有**痛经**吗?
林　晓	没有。
刘医生	之前有没有去医院看过医生或做过检查呢?
林　晓	有。两个多月前在我们当地的第三人民医院看过,当时大夫说我是贫血。
刘医生	用过什么药吗?
林　晓	给我开了**硫酸亚铁**。
刘医生	怎么样? 有没有效果?
林　晓	我吃了三天后,觉得恶心、胃不舒服就停掉了。
刘医生	当时这个药是怎么吃的?
林　晓	每天 6 片。
刘医生	哦。还有没有做过别的治疗?
林　晓	后来我又吃了一个月的中药,但是也没有什么**疗效**,一直没有好转。
刘医生	噢！那我现在给您做一下体格检查。

林　晓	好的。
	（10分钟后,体格检查结束。）
刘医生	根据您的病史和体格检查,我初步判断,您得的是贫血。
林　晓	哦。我的贫血是因为什么引起的呢?
刘医生	这样,您先验血,等检查结果出来后,我再**详细**跟您讲。
林　晓	好的。
	（血常规检查结果出来了。）
林　晓	刘医生,这是我的检查报告单!
刘医生	好,我看一下。**血红蛋白**比较低,只有 60g/L;**血清铁** 2.5μmol/L,**血清铁蛋白** 3.84μg/L,这两项也比较低。所以根据您的病史、临床表现和检查结果,我判断您得的是缺铁性贫血,而且贫血的程度已经接近**重度**。
林　晓	我这个病是不是因为我节食造成的啊?
刘医生	节食应该不是主要原因,这个病与您长期月经量多有直接关系。所以,您还要去查一下妇科。
	（妇科检查结果出来了。）
林　晓	刘医生,妇科医生说我有**子宫肌瘤**,我以前都不知道。
刘医生	好的。现在我给您开药,口服铁剂。
林　晓	这个硫酸亚铁我以前吃过,吃了胃里不舒服。
刘医生	那很可能是您上次服用的**剂量**比较大或者是服用时间不当引起的。这次,您在饭后或者饭间服用,这样可以减轻药物对**胃黏膜**的**刺激**,记得不要用茶水吞服。
林　晓	好的,我一定按照您的**吩咐**吃药。
刘医生	另外,您要注意补充**营养**,改掉**偏食**的习惯,多吃一些富含铁质的食物,比如动物肝脏、**瘦肉**、动物血液、**木耳**、**蘑菇**、蔬菜等! 等贫血纠正后,一定要抓紧时间去看妇科,否则您的缺铁性贫血很难根治。
林　晓	好的! 我记住了。谢谢医生。

Iron Deficiency Anemia

SITE:　　　　Hematology Outpatient Department

CHARACTERS:　Liu Ming (Attending physician)

　　　　　　　Lin Xiao (Patient, female, 38 years old)

Lin Xiao:　Hi, Dr. Liu. This is my registration card. I'm number 3.

Dr. Liu:　Hi, have a seat, please! What's wrong with you?

Lin Xiao:　I have been feeling weak recently so that I don't have energy to do anything. I've also got tired easily and felt dizzy.

Dr. Liu:　When did your feelings start?

Lin Xiao:　About 5 months ago.

Dr. Liu:　What made you feel dizzy at that time?

Lin Xiao:　I suddenly felt dizzy and fatigued, even with the slightest activity.

Dr. Liu:　What do you feel usually?

Lin Xiao:　I'm alright except that I feel weak and slightly dizzy. In addition, I'm breathless when I walk fast. The day before yesterday, I almost fainted while climbing the stairs on my way home. But I felt better only after I rested for a while.

Dr. Liu:　I see. Is there any other part of your body you don't feel well?

Lin Xiao:　I have tinnitus sometimes.

Dr. Liu:　How's your appetite?

Lin Xiao:　I don't want to eat anything.

Dr. Liu:　Are you on a diet?

Lin Xiao:　I never eat a big dinner and I like to eat vegetables and not too much meat.

Dr. Liu:　Do you like to drink tea?

Lin Xiao:　Yes, I like to drink strong tea.

Dr. Liu:　How's your sleep at night?

Lin Xiao:　Not good. I'm always troubled with bad dreams and I feel my memory is getting worse.

Dr. Liu:　How about your urine and stool? Are they normal?

Lin Xiao:　Yes, they are.

Dr. Liu:　How's your menstruation? Is it regular?

Lin Xiao:　Yes, it is, but the bleeding is quite heavy, and sometimes it looks dark. I need to use two sanitary pads each time and each menstruation cycle lasts 9~10 days.

Dr. Liu:　Has it always been like this?

Lin Xiao:　Yes, it is. It started about 5 years ago.

Dr. Liu:　Do you suffer from dysmenorrhea?

Lin Xiao:　No, I don't.

Dr. Liu:　Have you been to the hospital taking tests before?

Lin Xiao:　Yes, I went to the Third People's Hospital in my local city and was diagnosed with anemia two months ago.

Dr. Liu:　What medicine did you take?

Lin Xiao:　The doctor prescribed Ferrous Sulfate.

Dr. Liu:　How was it? Did the medicine work or not?

Lin Xiao:　I took it for 3 days and felt nauseated, so I stopped taking it.

Dr. Liu:　How did you take the medicine?

Lin Xiao:　6 tablets a day.

Dr. Liu:　Oh, I see. Did you undergo any other treatment after that?

Lin Xiao:　Yes, I took some Chinese medicines for one month, but I did not get better. There was no curative effect.

Dr. Liu:　Well, I'll examine you.

Lin Xiao:　Sure.

　　　　　(10 minutes later, the physical examination done)

Dr. Liu:　According to your physical examination and case history, I think that you have got anemia.

Lin Xiao:　What caused the anemia?

Dr. Liu:　Now, you'll have a blood test and I'll explain to you in detail based on the test report.

Lin Xiao:　Ok.

　　　　　(The blood test report is out.)

Lin Xiao:　Doctor, this is my blood test report.

Dr. Liu:　Let me have a look. Your hemoglobin is rather low, just 60g/L. Your serum iron 2.5μmol/L and serum ferritin 3.84μg/L are also quite low. According to your case history, clinical evidence and examination results, I think you have Iron Deficient Anemia that is close to the severity of anemia.

Lin Xiao:　Is it because I'm on a diet?

Dr. Liu:　It is not the main reason. It is also due to your heavy bleeding during menstruation. Thus, it is better to go to the Gynecology Department for a checkup.

(The report from gynecology is done.)

Lin Xiao:　Doctor Liu, the doctor of Gynecology Department told me that I have myoma of the uterus. I was not aware of this.

Dr. Liu:　Oh, now I am going to prescribe you oral iron.

Lin Xiao:　I took it before and had stomach discomfort.

Dr. Liu:　It may be that your previous dosage was too much or you used it incorrectly. Take it after or during meals, which can reduce the stimulation for gastric mucosa. And don't take it with tea, either.

Lin Xiao:　Ok, I will follow your instructions.

Dr. Liu:　Another point, you need to pay attention to your nutrition and also change your eating habit, eat more food that contains iron, such as meat, animal blood, fungus, mushroom, vegetables and so on. You have to wait until your anemia has been dealt with. Then go to the Gynecology Department, otherwise it will be hard to treat your iron-deficiency anemia.

Lin Xiao:　Ok, I see. Thank you.

疾病介绍

^{quētiěxìngpínxuè}
缺铁性贫血

缺铁性贫血是指病人的血液里没有足够的铁。铁是非常重要的，它可以帮助血液把氧气输送到细胞中。贫血会使人乏力、易倦、烦躁、面色苍白。医生会建议病人服用铁剂，多吃含铁量丰富的食物。

中度的缺铁性贫血可能不会引起明显的症状。重度贫血的症状表现有：体弱、疲劳、乏力、活动时气短、头痛、注意力不易集中、易怒、头晕、皮肤苍白等。

缺铁性贫血的治疗方法主要是增加体内铁的贮存量。当铁达到正常水平的时候，就可以控制贫血带来的症状。如果贫血是由于某种疾病或某些情况引起的，比如胃出血，医生会采取措施纠正这些问题。如果是由于饮食中铁含量不够或者是身体不能吸收铁引起的，医生会针对病人的情况制订计划增加病人体内的铁含量。

服用铁补充剂或通过饮食获取足够的铁，可以治疗大部分的缺铁性贫血病例。一般每天服用1到3次。维生素C可以促进铁剂的吸收，所以配合维生素C或者橙汁服用铁剂，可以使铁剂的效果最大化。

Iron Deficiency Anemia

Iron deficiency anemia means that there is insufficient iron in the blood. Iron is important in helping blood carry oxygen to the cells. Anemia may cause weakness, tiredness, grumpiness and paleness. Doctors will prescribe iron pills and suggest healthier food rich in iron.

Mild iron deficiency anemia may not cause noticeable symptoms, but severe iron deficiency anemia manifests as weakness, fatigue, or lack of stamina, shortness of breath during exercise, headache, poor concentration, irritability, dizziness and pale skin.

Treatment for iron deficiency anemia focuses on increasing the iron stores up to normal levels to control conditions caused by anemia. If anemia is caused by some diseases or conditions such as gastric hemorrhage, your doctor will take steps to correct the problem. If anemia is caused by insufficient iron in the diet or physical inability to absorb iron, doctors will develop a plan to increase the iron levels in the body.

Increasing iron intake by taking iron supplement pills 1~3 times a day or by diet will correct most cases of iron deficiency anemia. To get the most benefit, iron pills can be taken with vitamin C or orange juice, which helps the body absorb more iron.

1. ……性

词语后缀,表示事物的某种性质或性能,可以构成名词或形容词。如:科学性、严重性、可能性、动物性(蛋白质)、细菌性(食物中毒)、先天性(病变)。

It is a suffix, used after a word to form a noun or an adjective to express the quality or property of something, e.g. 发生这种情况的可能性不大。

2. 一旦……就……

"一旦"用在动词前,作状语,表示新情况的出现或假设。

It is used as adverbial before a verb to indicate or suppose new situation, e.g. 一旦着火,那损失就大啦。

3. 跟……有关系

"跟"是介词,引出对象。"跟……有关系"格式,在句子中可以做谓语、定语,做定语时,需要后面加"的",常用于口语。

"跟"educes an object as a preposition. The structure of "跟……有关系" can be a predicate or an attribute in a sentence. When it is used as an attribute, "的" must be used after it. It is often used in oral communication, e.g. ①你的病跟你的生活习惯有关系;②任何跟这件事有关系的人都不得离开这里。

白 血 病

词汇

白血病	báixuèbìng	名	leukemia
疲劳	píláo	形	fatigue
基本上	jīběnshàng	副	basically; mostly
下肢	xiàzhī	名	lower limb
肩关节	jiānguānjié	名	shoulder joint
肋骨	lèigǔ	名	rib
手臂	shǒubì	名	arm
淤斑	yūbān	名	bruise; ecchymosis

挠	náo	动	scratch
异常	yìcháng	形	abnormal
血小板	xuèxiǎobǎn	名	blood platelet
血红蛋白	xuèhóngdànbái	名	hemoglobin
骨髓象	gúsuǐxiàng	名	myelogram
增生	zēngshēng	名	hyperplasia
原幼淋巴细胞	yuányòulínbāxìbāo	名	lymphoblast and prolymphocyte
遗传	yíchuán	形	hereditary
造血干细胞	zàoxuègānxìbāo	名	hematopoietic stem cell
分化	fēnhuà	动	differentiate
癌变	áibiàn	动	cancerate
节制	jiézhì	动	restraint
侵犯	qīnfàn	动	invade
淋巴结	línbājié	名	lymph node
不治之症	búzhìzhīzhèng	名	incurable disease
化疗	huàliáo	名	chemotherapy
破坏	pòhuài	动	destroy
损伤	sǔnshāng	动	damage
方案	fāngàn	名	schema; plan

地点：血液科门诊
人物：赵伟业（主治医师）
　　　王丹霞（病人，女，30 岁）
　　　李国强（病人丈夫，男，31 岁）

赵医生　您好，请坐。您叫什么名字？多大了？

王丹霞　我叫王丹霞，今年 30 岁。

赵医生　您哪儿不舒服？

王丹霞　我最近总感到**疲劳**，还经常发热。

赵医生　量过体温吗？多少度？

王丹霞　量过了，一般都是 38℃左右，最高 39.1℃。

赵医生　这种发热的情况有多长时间了？

王丹霞　差不多 3 个星期了吧。

赵医生　您一般都是什么时候发热呢？

王丹霞　**基本上**都是下午或者晚上。

赵医生　咳嗽吗？

王丹霞　咳嗽，不过没有痰。

赵医生　刷牙时牙龈出血吗？

王丹霞　有时候会出血。

赵医生　身上有什么地方痛吗？

王丹霞　三个月前我左**下肢**开始痛，后来左边**肩关节**痛，两边**肋骨**也痛。

赵医生　我看您**手臂**上有**淤斑**，这是怎么弄的？

王丹霞 我最近身上很容易出现淤斑,**挠**一挠或者碰到什么就容易有,还容易出血。

赵医生 出血一般要多久才能止住?

王丹霞 至少要十几分钟才能止住。

赵医生 好,我大致了解您的情况了。我给您开化验单,您去做一下血常规检查。等检查结果出来,叫您家人陪您一起过来,好吗?

王丹霞 好的。谢谢医生。

(血常规检查结果出来后)

李国强 赵医生,这是我爱人的检查报告,您看一下。有**异常**吗?

赵医生 情况恐怕不太好。白细胞增多、**血小板**减少、**血红蛋白**下降。这样,我给您爱人开住院单,你们先住下来,我们再给您爱人做全面的检查。

李国强 好的,那我们今天就办理住院手续。

(几天后**骨髓象**检查结果出来了)

李国强 医生,我爱人的骨髓象检查有什么问题吗?

赵医生 我看一下。骨髓象检查结果显示**增生**明显活跃,**原幼淋巴细胞**占90%。根据您爱人的临床表现和检查结果,她得的应该是急性淋巴细胞白血病。

李国强 啊? 这么严重! 她怎么会得白血病的呢? 白血病是什么原因导致的?

赵医生 白血病的确切病因目前还不太清楚。**遗传**因素或者某些特定化学物质的影响可能是其病因。

李国强 总是听人说白血病、白血病,没想到落到自己家人头上了。究竟什么是白血病呢?

赵医生 简单来说,白血病是指**造血干细胞**在**分化**成为白细胞的过程中产生了**癌变**,然后受累的细胞无**节制**地增长,最终占据骨髓,代替正常造血细胞。白血病细胞也有可能**侵犯**其他脏器,比如肝、脾、**淋巴结**、肾脏等。

李国强 得了白血病是不是就没有救了?

赵医生 也不是。白血病并非**不治之症**,**化疗**是白血病目前常用的治疗方法。通过治疗,很多病人的病情可以得到缓解、控制和长期存活,甚至治愈。

李国强 但是我听说化疗特别痛苦,还有很多化疗反应,呕吐啊、掉头发啊什么的,是不是还会抑制骨髓再生?

赵医生 化疗药物在**破坏**癌细胞的同时也会**损伤**正常细胞,因此,我们会根据您爱人的情况选择最有效的**方案**进行治疗。

李国强 好的,谢谢您。

Leukemia

SITE: Hematology Out-patient Department

CHARACTERS: Zhao Weiye (Attending physician)

Wang Danxia (Patient, female, 30 years old)

Li Guoqiang (Patient's husband, male, 31 years old)

Dr. Zhao: Have a seat, please! What is your name? How old are you?

Wang Danxia: My name is Wang Danxia, 30 years old.

Dr. Zhao: What is the trouble with you?

Wang Danxia: I've felt fatigued recently and always have a fever.

Dr. Zhao: Did you take your body temperature? What was it?

Wang Danxia: Yes, I did. It was around 38℃, the highest one 39.1℃.

Dr. Zhao: How long have you had this kind of fever?

Wang Danxia:	It's almost 3 weeks.
Dr. Zhao:	When do you have the fever?
Wang Danxia:	Mostly in the afternoon or at night.
Dr. Zhao:	Do you have a cough?
Wang Danxia:	Yes, but there is no sputum.
Dr. Zhao:	Does your gum bleed when you brush your teeth?
Wang Danxia:	Yes, sometimes.
Dr. Zhao:	Do you feel a pain in any other part of your body?
Wang Danxia:	Yes, I do. It started from my left lower limb to my left shoulder joint and then to both sides of my ribs 3 months ago.
Dr. Zhao:	I have noticed that there are bruises on your arms. What happened?
Wang Danxia:	The bruise appears often recently. I get bruised every time when I scratch myself or bump into something. Also I bleed easily.
Dr. Zhao:	How long does it take for the bleeding to stop?
Wang Danxia:	At least more than 10 minutes.
Dr. Zhao:	Oh, I see. Now I understand your situation and I'll give you a laboratory test form, and then you will have a blood test. After the test results come out, ask your family to accompany you to come to me, ok?
Wang Danxia:	Ok, thank you.
	(Blood test results come out.)
Li Guoqiang:	Here are my wife's test results, Dr. Zhao. Is there anything abnormal?
Dr. Zhao:	The condition is not optimistic, for her white blood cell has increased while her blood platelet and hemoglobin have decreased. I will give you an admission form. Don't worry. We will give your wife a comprehensive examination.
Li Guoqiang:	Ok, we'll go through the admission procedure today.
	(The myelogram test results were taken to Dr. Zhao a few days later.)
Li Guoqiang:	Is there any problem with my wife's myelogram test?
Dr. Zhao:	Let me have a look. It shows that the hyperplasia exists and lymphoblast and prolymphocyte are 90%. I suspect she has acute lymphoblastic leukemia according to your wife's symptoms and the test results.
Li Guoqiang:	How did she get leukemia? What caused the disease?
Dr.Zhao:	It's not clear. Genetic factors or the effects of certain chemicals may be the causes of the disease.
Li Guoqiang:	I have heard of leukemia, but I did not expect someone in my family to have it. What exactly is leukemia?
Dr.Zhao:	In simple terms, leukemia results from the process of maturation from stem cell to white blood cell, which produces a cancerous change. The affected cells multiply without restraint and ultimately occupy the bone marrow, replacing the cells that produce normal blood cells. Leukemic cells may also invade other organs, such as the liver, spleen, lymph nodes, kidneys, and so on.
Li Guoqiang:	Is it incurable ?
Dr.Zhao:	No, it isn't. It is currently treated with chemotherapy that has been proven to be effective. After treatment, there are many patients with the disease that has been alleviated, who have a long-term survival, and even get cured.
Li Guoqiang:	But I heard that chemotherapy is particularly painful and there are a lot of adverse effects, such

as nausea, vomiting and hair loss. Also it may depress bone marrow, right?

Dr. Zhao: The drugs, which can destroy cancer cells, will be harmful to normal cells as well. However, we will choose the most effective treatment according to her situation.

Li Guoqiang: Ok, thank you very much.

急性淋巴细胞白血病

急性淋巴细胞白血病是白血病的一种，它从骨髓中的白细胞开始，由淋巴细胞或淋巴母细胞发展而来。淋巴母细胞是一种未成熟的淋巴细胞。

急性淋巴细胞白血病侵犯血液系统，并且会蔓延至身体的其他器官，如肝、脾和淋巴结等，但是它不会像其他癌症那样会产生肿瘤。它是急性的，病程很快。如果治疗不及时，几个月内就会死亡。

对于大多数人来说，急性淋巴细胞白血病的致病原因是未知的。因此，现在没有办法可以预防，但目前已知导致这种白血病的高风险因素有：高强度的辐射；某些化学物品，如苯；遗传综合征。该病起初症状并不明显，所以一旦需要就医，病情就已经非常严重了。急性淋巴细胞白血病的症状表现不一，包括：全身无力、疲倦、贫血、头晕、经常莫名发烧或感染、体重下降、食欲减退、淤伤增多、骨痛、关节痛、气促、淋巴结、肝、脾大、下肢或腹部水肿、皮肤有出血点。

急性淋巴细胞白血病是一组病的总称，所以对它的治疗需要考虑它的下属类型和其他因素。治疗方法包括：化疗；抗癌药物的联合疗法；靶向治疗针，对特定癌变细胞用药，副作用比化疗小；骨髓移植，造血干细胞移植之后，还需要高剂量的化疗和放疗。

Acute Lymphocytic Leukemia

Acute lymphoblastic leukemia (ALL) is a type of leukemia that starts from white blood cells in the bone marrow and develops from lymphocytes or lymphoblasts, an immature type of lymphocyte.

Acute lymphoblastic leukemia invades the blood system and can spread to other organs such as the liver, spleen, and lymph nodes. Unlike other cancers, however, it won't cause tumor. It is an acute type of leukemia and progresses quickly. Without immediate treatment, it can be fatal within a few months.

Nowadays, it's not clear how to prevent ALL due to the fact that its cause is still unknown. However, a few risk factors such as exposure to high levels of radiation and certain chemicals like benzene as well as an inherited genetic syndrome are known.

Initial symptoms of ALL are not specific, but it has become very serious once medical assistance is sought.

The symptoms of ALL are variable and may include generalized weakness and fatigue, anemia, dizziness, frequent or unexplained fever and infection, weight loss and/or loss of appetite, excessive and unexplained bruising, bone pain, joint pain, polypnea, enlarged lymph nodes, liver and/or spleen, pitting edema (swelling) in the lower limbs and/or abdomen, petechiae, which are tiny red spots or lines on the skin.

ALL is a general term of a group of related diseases, therefore its subtypes and other factors need to be considered during treatment. More than one treatment will be used, including chemotherapy, the use of anticancer drugs in combination; targeted therapy, drugs targeting specific parts of cancer cells with fewer or less severe side effects than chemotherapy; a bone marrow transplant, hematopoietic stem cell transplantation, both followed by high doses of chemotherapy and radiation.

语言点

1. 弄
"弄"的意思和"搞"、"做"差不多,多用于不好的方面。

The meaning of "弄" is similar to "搞" or "做", often used in bad situations, e.g. 妹妹把衣服弄得很脏。

2. 究竟
"究竟"常用于问句,表示进一步追究,有加强语气的作用,常用于书面。

"究 竟" is always used in a question, indicating further investigation with emphasis. It is often used in writing, e.g. 问题究竟出在哪里呢?

➢ 听力练习

一、听录音,选择你听到的词语
( )1.	A. 食品	B. 食堂	C. 食欲	D. 饮食
( )2.	A. 耳鸣	B. 耳朵	C. 外耳	D. 鸣叫
( )3.	A. 经络	B. 痛经	C. 神经	D. 月经
( )4.	A. 效果	B. 疗效	C. 疗法	D. 药效
( )5.	A. 手续	B. 手术	C. 程序	D. 继续
( )6.	A. 牙垢	B. 牙齿	C. 牙科	D. 牙龈
( )7.	A. 胸骨	B. 肋骨	C. 肋间	D. 肋膜
( )8.	A. 恶变	B. 癌症	C. 癌变	D. 恶化
( )9.	A. 黑斑	B. 雀斑	C. 淤斑	D. 祛斑
( )10.	A. 红细胞	B. 白细胞	C. 单细胞	D. 多细胞

二、请选出与所听录音相符的答案
( )1.	A. 腹痛	B. 乏力	C. 没有食欲	D. 身上有淤斑
( )2.	A. 患者食欲大	B. 患者吃素食	C. 患者喜欢吃鱼	D. 患者想减肥
( )3.	A. 患者月经规律	B. 患者月经量多	C. 患者月经天数短	D. 患者月经中会有血块
( )4.	A. 左腿痛	B. 左肩痛	C. 心绞痛	D. 肋骨痛
( )5.	A. 胸透	B. CT	C. B超	D. 血常规

三、听录音,完成下面的练习
1. 根据短文1回答第1~4题

1) 病人有什么生活习惯?

2）病人的症状有哪些？

3）她觉得她的情况跟什么有关系？

4）前天发生了什么突发情况？

2. 根据短文2回答第5~7题

1）病人的主要症状有哪些？

2）病人的家属担心什么？

3）李医生是怎么劝说他们的？

➢ 词汇和语法练习

一、给下列词语标注拼音

1. 牙龈＿＿＿＿＿＿＿＿＿＿＿＿ 2. 化疗＿＿＿＿＿＿＿＿＿＿＿＿＿

3. 血清铁＿＿＿＿＿＿＿＿＿＿＿ 4. 胃黏膜＿＿＿＿＿＿＿＿＿＿＿

5. 骨髓象＿＿＿＿＿＿＿＿＿＿＿ 6. 血小板＿＿＿＿＿＿＿＿＿＿＿

7. 淋巴结＿＿＿＿＿＿＿＿＿＿＿ 8. 不治之症＿＿＿＿＿＿＿＿＿＿

9. 造血干细胞＿＿＿＿＿＿＿＿＿ 10. 原幼淋巴细胞＿＿＿＿＿＿＿＿

二、选词填空

根治　　耳鸣　　血小板　　遗传　　偏食　　子宫肌瘤　　淤斑　　痛经

1. 您得改掉＿＿＿＿＿＿＿＿＿的毛病,蔬菜、肉类、鸡蛋都要吃,营养要均衡。

2. 这种皮肤病很难＿＿＿＿＿＿＿＿,非常容易复发。

3. 妇科医生说我有＿＿＿＿＿＿＿＿,吓死我了,这个病严重吗？

4. 我妻子来月经的时候经常＿＿＿＿＿＿＿＿,有时候甚至疼得无法正常工作。

5. 我爷爷说他有时候会＿＿＿＿＿＿＿＿,耳朵里像打雷一样,影响他睡眠。

6. 他昨天摔了一跤,膝盖上有一块青紫色的＿＿＿＿＿＿＿＿。

7. 血常规检查显示病人＿＿＿＿＿＿＿＿减少。

8. 眼睛近视会不会＿＿＿＿＿＿＿＿给下一代？

三、用指定的词语或结构完成句子或对话。

1. ＿＿＿＿＿＿＿＿,我就觉得头晕、无力。(一旦)

2. 这几天我总是觉得恶心,＿＿＿＿＿＿＿＿。(差点儿)

3. 还算比较规律,＿＿＿＿＿＿＿＿。(就是)

4. 你一定要把烟戒掉,＿＿＿＿＿＿＿＿。(否则)

5. 我以为我爱人只是普通的感冒、咳嗽,＿＿＿＿＿＿＿＿。(没想到)

6. ＿＿＿＿＿＿＿＿,我们会组织专家进行会诊。(等……出来)

7. 现在医疗技术取得了极大的进步,你的病＿＿＿＿＿＿＿＿。(并非)

四、把下列词语排列成句子

1. 我　感觉　都要　了　跳出来　心

2. 已经　重度　程度　贫血的　接近

3. 不是　主要　节食　应该　原因

4. 的　确切　原因　还不太　清楚　白血病

5. 也　白血病　细胞　侵犯　有可能　其他脏器

➢ 阅读与应用练习

一、根据课文内容补全对话。

家属：　医生,这是我爱人的检查结果,您看一下。＿1＿?

医生： 情况恐怕不太好。____2____增多、____3____减少、____4____降低。而且骨髓象检查结果显示____5____。所以,她得的应该是____6____。

家属： 啊？她怎么会得白血病的呢？____7____？

医生： 白血病的确切病因还不太清楚。____8____。

家属： 究竟什么是白血病呢？

医生： 白血病是指____9____在分化成为白细胞的过程中____10____,然后受累的细胞____11____,最终____12____,代替正常造血细胞。白血病细胞也有可能侵犯其他脏器,比如____13____等。

家属： 得了白血病是不是基本上就没有救了？。

医生： 白血病并非____14____,目前____15____,效果还是可以的。

二、根据课文内容回答问题

1. 林晓的血常规检查有什么异常？

2. 医生对林晓的诊断是什么？

3. 林晓的病可能跟什么疾病有关系？

4. 王丹霞的发热症状有什么特点？

5. 王丹霞的骨髓象检查有什么异常？

6. 医生对王丹霞采用哪种治疗方法？

三、写作练习

请简单描述会话一中病人林晓的主要临床表现。(不少于60字)

四、交际练习

参考括号里的词语进行情景对话。

情景:病人的血常规检查和骨髓象检查报告出来了,医生就检查报告跟病人家属进行解释,并简单向病人家属介绍治疗的方法。

(白细胞,血小板,骨髓象,增生,原幼淋巴细胞,急性淋巴细胞白血病,不治之症,化疗,反应)

第八章 普 通 外 科

急性阑尾炎

词汇

阑尾炎	lánwěiyán	名	appendicitis
肚脐	dùqí	名	umbilicus
转移	zhuǎnyí	动	move
隐隐作痛	yǐnyǐnzuòtòng	动	dull pain
辅助	fǔzhù	形	assistant
以便	yǐbiàn	连	in order that
血淀粉酶	xuèdiànfěnméi	名	serum amylase
计数	jìshù	名	count
升高	shēnggāo	动	increase
炎症	yánzhèng	名	inflammation
触诊	chùzhěn	名	palpation
麦氏点	màishìdiǎn	名	McBurney point
压痛	yātòng	名	tenderness
反跳痛	fǎntiàotòng	名	rebound tenderness
肠鸣音	chángmíngyīn	名	bowel sound
减弱	jiǎnruò	动	weaken
腹膜刺激征	fùmócìjīzhēng	名	peritoneal irritation
波及	bōjí	动	spread to
结合	jiéhé	动	combine
体征	tǐzhēng	名	sign
大致	dàzhì	副	generally
切除术	qiēchúshù	名	resection

地点：急诊科外科门诊
人物：张医生（主治医师）
　　　哈斯夫（住院医师）
　　　李刚（病人，男，20 岁）

张医生　您好，请坐。我是您的主治医师，我姓张。您哪儿不舒服？
李　刚　张大夫，我肚子痛得很厉害。
张医生　什么时候开始痛的？
李　刚　昨天晚上睡觉前，大约十点左右。
张医生　这几天吃什么不干净的食物了吗？
李　刚　没有。
张医生　能指一下是哪儿痛吗？
李　刚　这里（指右下腹）。一开始是**肚脐**周围痛，现在又变成这里痛了。
张医生　经过多长时间**转移**到这里的？
李　刚　大约七八个小时吧。
张医生　是一直这么痛还是慢慢痛起来的？
李　刚　一开始是**隐隐作痛**，到后来就痛得很厉害了。
张医生　是一种什么样的痛？
李　刚　感觉是绞痛。
张医生　肚子痛的时候身体其他部位痛吗？比如肩部或背部？
李　刚　没有。不过，我还感觉恶心，刚才在家还呕吐了一次。
张医生　量体温了吗？
李　刚　刚才量了，39℃。
张医生　从您的症状来看，我怀疑您得了急性阑尾炎。请躺到那边床上，让哈斯夫大夫给您检查一下。另外，我们还需要给您做一些**辅助**检查，**以便**进一步明确诊断。
李　刚　好的，谢谢大夫。
　　　　（30 分钟后，医生拿到了病人所有的检查结果。）
哈斯夫　张老师，病人的检查结果出来了。尿常规和**血淀粉酶**水平都正常。血常规显示白细胞**计数升高**，大约 14×10^9/L，**炎症**反应非常明显。
张医生　刚才的体格检查有什么发现？
哈斯夫　我给他做了**触诊**，他的**麦氏点**有明显**压痛**。腹肌非常紧张。不但有压痛，还有**反跳痛**，而且**肠鸣音**也**减弱**了。这是**腹膜刺激征**吧？
张医生　对，这说明病人阑尾的炎症已经**波及**腹膜了。根据检查结果，**结合**病人的症状和**体征**，我们**大致**可以确定他得了急性阑尾炎。为了避免发生更严重的并发症，要尽快让病人住院，并安排阑尾**切除术**。

Acute Appendicitis

SITE:　Emergency Surgery Clinic
CHARACTERS:　Doctor Zhang (Attending physician)

　　　　　　　Hassif (Resident doctor)

　　　　　　　Li Gang (Patient, male, 20 years old)

Dr. Zhang:　Hello! Sit down, please. I am your attending physician, Doctor Zhang. What brings you to the emergency room?

Li Gang: Doctor, I have got severe pain in my belly.

Dr. Zhang: When did it start?

Li Gang: Around 10 o'clock last night before I went to bed.

Dr. Zhang: Did you eat unclean food these days?

Li Gang: No.

Dr. Zhang: Please show me the most harmful site with your fingers.

Li Gang: Right here (Point to the right lower abdominal region). The pain began in the periumbilical region, and later moved and fixed here.

Dr. Zhang: How long did the pain move over here?

Li Gang: About 7 to 8 hours.

Dr. Zhang: Did the pain occur suddenly or did it develop slowly over time?

Li Gang: At the beginning, it was a dull pain, and then it was becoming worse gradually.

Dr. Zhang: What was it like?

Li Gang: It was colic.

Dr. Zhang: Did you feel painful in other parts of the body when it hurt, such as your shoulder or back?

Li Gang: No, I didn't, but I felt nauseous and vomited once at home.

Dr. Zhang: Did you take your temperature?

Li Gang: Yes, I did. It was 39℃.

Dr. Zhang: According to your symptoms, I suspect you have got acute appendicitis. Please lie down on the examination table and Dr. Hassif will give you a physical exam. Besides, you still need some additional tests before we can confirm your diagnosis.

Li Gang: I see. Thank you, Doctor.

(Thirty minutes later, the doctor has got all the examination results.)

Hassif: Dr. Zhang, the patient's test results have come out. The routine urine and serum amylase are normal. However, the routine blood test shows leukocytosis with white blood cell count of 14×10^9/L. Therefore, inflammation is apparent.

Dr. Zhang: What's the result of the physical exam?

Hassif: There was tenderness in the McBurney point that I palpated. The patient has abdominal muscle rigidity and decreased bowel sound. There was not only tenderness but also rebound tenderness. Do these sings indicate peritoneal irritation?

Dr. Zhang: Yes. They show the appendicitis has spread to the peritoneum. According to the examination results and the patient's symptoms and signs, we can roughly determine acute appendicitis. In order to avoid more severe complications, we must admit him and perform appendectomy as quickly as possible.

疾病介绍

jíxìnglánwěiyán
急性阑尾炎

jíxìnglánwěiyán shì lánwěi de jíxìng huànóngxìng yánzhèng　　yěshì wàikē zuìchángjiànde jífùzhèng zhīyī　　qí fābìnglǜ yuēwéi
急性阑尾炎 是 阑尾 的 急性 化脓性　炎症 ，也是 外科 最常见的 急腹症 之一 ，其 发病率 约为

　　　　duō jiàn yú　　　　　　suì deshàonián hé qīngnián　　　　sǐwánglǜ xiǎoyú　　　　　lánwěiqiāngguǎn gěngzǔ shì zuìchángjiàn de
1∶1000, 多 见 于 10~30 岁 的少年 和 青年 。死亡率 小于 0.1% 。　阑尾腔管 梗阻 是 最常见 的

bìngyīn　　cǐwài xìjūn gǎnrǎn hé wèichángdào yánzhèng yěhuì dǎozhì jíxìng lánwěiyán
病因，此外 细菌 感染 和 胃肠道 炎症 也会 导致 急性 阑尾炎 。

zhǔyào línchuáng biǎoxiàn yǒu　　zhuǎnyíxìng yòuxiàfù téngtòng　　wèichángdào zhèngzhuàng　rúyànshí　ěxin　ǒutùděng
主要 临床 表现 有：① 转移性 右下腹 疼痛 ；② 胃肠道　症状 ，如厌食 、恶心 、呕吐等 ；

xìtǒng zhòngdú zhèngzhuàng　rú fálì　fārè　xīndòng guòsù děng　　línchuáng shàng　zǎoqī dānchúnxìng lánwěiyán kěyǐ
③ 系统 中毒　症状 ，如乏力 、发热 、心动 过速 等 。 临床 上 ，早期 单纯性 阑尾炎 可以

xuǎnzé yǒuxiào de kàngshēngsù zhìliáo　ér jíxìnglánwěiyán yǐjīng quèzhěn　yuánzéshàng yīng jǐnzǎo shǒushù zhìliáo
选择 有效 的 抗生素 治疗 ，而 急性阑尾炎 一经 确诊 ，原则上 应 尽早 手术 治疗 。

Acute Appendicitis

Acute appendicitis is an acute suppurative inflammation of appendix. It is the most common one of acute abdomen diseases. The incidence of acute appendicitis is about 1:1000, with the peak incidence occurring between the age of 10 and 30. The mortality risk is less than 0.1%. The obstruction of lumen is the most common cause of acute appendicitis. Bacterial infection and gastrointestinal inflammation are also the causes.

Major clinical manifestations include: ①shifting right lower abdominal pain; ②symptoms of gastrointestinal tract, such as poor appetite, nausea, vomit and so on; ③systemic toxic manifestations, such as fatigue, pyrexia, tachycardia, etc. Effective antibiotic therapy is recommended for early simple appendicitis while surgery is often suggested when the acute appendicitis is confirmed.

语言点

1. 一开始……到后来……

这是一个描述过程的常用格式,表示步骤的先后次序。如果步骤不止两个,也可以在中间插入"接着"、"又",构成"一开始……,接着……,又……,到后来……"等格式。

This is a common pattern used to describe a process, indicating the order. If there are more than two steps, "接着", "又" can be added between the two words to form the pattern of "一开始……,接着……,又……,到后来……", e.g. 一开始是隐隐作痛,到后来就痛得很厉害了。

2. 从……来看

这个结构常单独放在句子开头做状语,强调说话所依据的理由或者看问题的角度、范围等。"从"也可以换成"由"、"就"。

This pattern is often placed at the beginning of a sentence, used as an adverbial alone. It emphasizes the reason or the point of view, with the meaning of "viewed from …". "从" can be replaced by "由" and "就", e.g. 从目前的情况来看,他暂时还不需要手术。

胆　结　石

词汇

胆结石	dǎnjiéshí	名	gallstone, cholelithiasis
割	gē	动	cut or slice (with a knife)
发冷	fālěng	动	be algid; feel chilly
发病	fābìng	动	(a disease) occur; (of a person) fall ill

暴饮暴食	bàoyǐnbàoshí	名	eat and drink too much
油腻	yóunì	形	pinguid; greasy; oily
肩部	jiānbù	名	shoulder
止痛药	zhǐtòngyào	名	pain-killer
露	lù	动	show
蜷	quán	动	curl up
胆囊	dǎnnáng	名	gallbladder; cholecyst
触痛	chùtòng	名	tenderness
墨菲征	mòfēizhēng	名	Murphy's sign
胆囊炎	dǎnnángyán	名	cholecystitis
直径	zhíjìng	名	diameter
厘米	límǐ	名	centimeter
尽早	jǐnzǎo	副	as early as possible
腹腔镜	fùqiāngjìng	名	laparoscope
创伤	chuāngshāng	名	trauma
复发	fùfā	动	relapse
胆管	dánguǎn	名	bile duct
加强	jiāqiáng	动	Promote
胆固醇	dǎngùchún	名	cholesterol
代谢	dàixiè	名	metabolism
鱼籽	yúzǐ	名	fish roe
内脏	nèizàng	名	internal organ; viscus
过度	guòdù	形	excessive; over

地点：急诊科

人物：周医生（主治医师）

陈明（病人，男，43岁）

周医生 来，来，快坐下！是肚子疼吗？

陈 明 是啊，医生，疼得不行了。

周医生 肚子哪个部位疼？上腹还是下腹？

陈 明 上腹，右侧比较疼（指右上腹）。

周医生 什么时候开始疼的？

陈 明 大约一天前。一开始我没太在意，只是一阵阵的隐痛，后来越来越痛，现在变成了持续的绞痛，像刀**割**一样。疼得我坐也不是，躺也不是，疼死了。

周医生 有没有呕吐和拉肚子的症状？

陈 明 只是觉得恶心，但没有呕吐，也没有拉肚子。

周医生 量体温了吗？发没发烧？

陈 明 没量，光想着疼了，也不知道发没发烧，就觉得一阵阵**发冷**。

周医生 您这次是怎么**发病**的？有没有**暴饮暴食**或吃**油腻**的东西？

陈 明 哦，我想起来了。两天前朋友过生日，我们在一起喝了很多啤酒，还吃了不少烤肉，吃完就觉得

　　　　不太舒服。

周医生　您还有其他地方不舒服吗?

陈　明　我的右**肩部**和腰背部也很疼。

周医生　您以前这样疼过吗?

陈　明　有,近两年来发作过几次,但每次都只是隐痛,没有这次严重。一直以为是胃痛,吃点抗生素和**止痛药**就好了,也就没有太在意。

周医生　您回忆一下,每次发作是不是都发生在进食油腻食物之后?

陈　明　好像是这样。有时候太累了也感觉不舒服。

周医生　请到这边躺下,我给您做一下腹部检查。请拉起衣服,**露**出腹部,双腿**蜷**起来,放松。我检查的时候,您要是觉得疼就告诉我,现在慢慢深吸气……

陈　明　嗯。……啊,好痛!

周医生　起来吧。我刚才给您做的是**胆囊**触诊,发现您的胆囊肿大,有**触痛**,**墨菲征**阳性。

陈　明　什么是墨菲征?

周医生　就是把手指放在您腹部胆囊的位置上,当您深吸气时,发炎的胆囊碰到我的手指,您会因疼痛而突然停止吸气,这在医学上叫墨菲征阳性。这是胆囊急性炎症特有的表现。

陈　明　哦,我知道了。那我得的是**胆囊炎**?

周医生　我怀疑您得了胆结石,可能还伴有急性胆囊炎。为了进一步确诊,您还需要做一个腹部 B 超。

陈　明　好的,我这就去做。

　　　　(30 分钟后,病人拿着 B 超检查结果回来)

周医生　B 超显示您的胆囊肿大,里面有多个结石,最大的**直径**有 2~3 **厘米**。结合您的病史和这次发病的症状、体征,我们可以确诊,您得了胆结石,并发急性胆囊炎。

陈　明　那该怎么治疗呢?

周医生　应该**尽早**进行胆囊切除术。

陈　明　不能保守治疗吗?

周医生　由于您的症状非常明显,结石也比较大,最好还是做手术。

陈　明　做手术是不是要住很长时间的院?

周医生　不用,现在胆囊手术可以使用**腹腔镜**,**创伤**小,恢复很快。您只需要住院一个星期左右就可以了。

陈　明　好吧,那我就做腹腔镜手术吧。做完手术后,胆结石还会**复发**吗?

周医生　一般来说,手术后胆囊结石就不会复发了,但是**胆管**里可能会再次出现结石。所以手术后您要按时服用**加强胆固醇代谢**的药物。

陈　明　手术后是不是也不能吃油腻的东西?

周医生　是的,平时要少吃鸡蛋黄、**鱼籽**和动物**内脏**等胆固醇含量高的食物。要多喝水,减少盐、糖的摄入,多吃富含维生素的水果和蔬菜。此外,还要保持精神愉快,养成良好的生活习惯,避免暴饮暴食和**过度**劳累。这样才能有效地预防胆管结石的发生。

Cholelithiasis

　　　　 SITE:　 Emergency Department

CHARACTERS:　 Doctor Zhou (Attending physician)

　　　　　　　　 ChengMing (Patient, male, 40 years old)

　Dr. Zhou:　 Come here! Sit down, please. You have a stomachache, don't you?

Chen Ming:　 Yes, I do. I can't endure any more.

Dr. Zhou: Where is the pain? Is it in the upper or lower part?

Chen Ming: Here, in the upper right side. (Point to right upper abdomen.)

Dr. Zhou: How long has it been like this?

Chen Ming: About one day. At first, I didn't pay too much attention and there were waves of dull pain, later it became worse and worse, and turned into persistent colicky pain, like being cut by a knife. It's all the same whether I am sitting up or lying down. Oh, it's killing me.

Dr. Zhou: Do you have any symptoms of vomiting and diarrhea?

Chen Ming: I just felt sick without vomiting or diarrhea.

Dr. Zhou: Have you taken your temperature? Do you have a fever?

Chen Ming: I only felt painful and didn't take the temperature to check for a fever. I just felt chilly.

Dr. Zhou: What do you think really made you ill? Have you eaten or drunk too much or had any greasy foods before the onset of illness?

Chen Ming: About two days ago, I ate a lot of roast meat and drank much beer with my friends. I felt uncomfortable after eating.

Dr. Zhou: Do you have other trouble?

Chen Ming: I have aches in my right shoulder, back and waist, too.

Dr. Zhou: Have you had that abdominal pain previously?

Chen Ming: Yes, I have attached by such aches several times during the past two years, which were only a dull pain and not like this time. I thought it was stomachache and would be alleviated by taking some antibiotics and pain-killer. So I didn't pay much more attention on it.

Dr. Zhou: Please try to recall that whether you were attacked each time after eating too much greasy stuff?

Chen Ming: Mostly it is. It sometimes also happens as a result of tiredness after working too hard.

Dr.Zhou: Let me examine you. Please lie down and unbutton your clothes. Show me your abdomen and curl your legs. Take it easy. Tell me where the pain is when I push on your abdomen.

Chen Ming: Ok···Ah! It hurts a lot.

Dr. Zhou: Ok, you can get up now. I gave you a cholecystic palpation now. You have an enlarged gallbladder and Murphy's sign is positive.

Chen Ming: What is "Murphy's sign"?

Dr. Zhou: Just now, I placed my finger at the approximate location of your gallbladder. When you inhaled, the gallbladder came in contact with my finger. If you stopped breathing due to pain, it means Murphy's sign is positive. It often occurs in acute cholecystitis.

Chen Ming: Oh, I see. Do I have cholecystitis?

Dr. Zhou: I suspect you suffer from gallstone with cholecystitis and you need have a B ultrasound to confirm the diagnosis.

Chen Ming: Ok, I will go and have the test right away.

            (After thirty minutes, the patient came back with the result of ultrasound.)

Dr. Zhou: The result of B ultrasound shows that you have a swollen gallbladder and there are several stones in it. The biggest one is about 2~3cm in diameter. Combined with the history and your symptoms and signs, our initial diagnosis can be confirmed.

Chen Ming: How should be that treated?

Dr. Zhou: You should accept the cholecystectomy operation as early as possible.

Chen Ming: Does non-surgical treatment work?

Dr. Zhou: Because your symptoms are very apparent and the stone is rather big, operative treatment is the best approach.

Chen Ming:　Do I need a long stay in hospital if I choose the operation?

Dr. Zhou:　Don't worry. We have a new method that enables us to use laparoscopy to do the operation. It has less trauma and good effect. You just need to be hospitalized for about a week.

Chen Ming:　Ok, I prefer the surgery. Will there be a recurrence after the operation?

Dr. Zhou:　Generally, you won't get recurrence after gall bladder calculi surgery, but it may recur in bile duct. After the operation, you should take the drugs in time to improve cholesterol metabolism.

Chen Ming:　Should I not eat anything oily after the operation?

Dr. Zhou:　Of course. You should eat little food with high fat and cholesterol, such as egg yolk, fish roe and viscera as possible as you can, drink more water, eat more green vegetables and fruit high in vitamins. You should keep a happy mood and form good living habits. Don't eat or drink too much and overwork. You can effectively prevent bile duct stones relapse when you live this way.

疾病介绍

dǎnjiéshí
胆结石

胆结石 是 最常见 的 胆道 疾病，包括 胆囊 结石 和 胆管 结石，其中 胆囊 结石 占 全部 结石 的 50% 左右。绝大多数人（80%）没有 任何 症状，20% 的 胆囊 结石 会 并发 急性 或 慢性 胆囊炎。胆囊 结石 的 发生 受 多种 因素 的 影响，包括 种族、性别 和 遗传学。胆囊 结石 主要 见 于 成人，女性 多于 男性。40 岁 以后，胆囊 结石 的 发生率 随 年龄 增长 而 增高。胆汁 淤积 是 各种 胆石 形成 的 首要 条件，治疗 方法 首选 腹腔镜 胆囊 切除术。

Cholelithiasis

Cholelithiasis is the most common biliary tract disease. It includes gallbladder stone and bile duct stone, and gallbladder stone takes up about 50% of total calculosis. The vast majority (80%) do not have any symptoms while 20% may develop into acute or chronic cholecystitis. The prevalence of cholelithiasis is affected by many factors, including ethnicity, gender and genetics. It is mainly found in adult and more in women than men. After the age of 40, the risk of developing gallstones increases with aging. Cholestasis is the primary condition of the gallstone formation. The preferred therapy is laparoscopic cholecystectomy.

语言点

1. 疼死了。(adj.+ 死)

"死" 在这里表示程度达到极点，跟 "adj. + 极了" 意思差不多。句子的主语也可放在 "死" 的后面。

"死" refers to the highest degree. The subject of the sentence can also be placed after the word "死"，e.g. ①难受死了！②困死我了！

2. 伴有……

"伴有" 表示一种伴随状态，通常指两种或两种以上疾病并存。

It is an attending circumstance, means two or more diseases coexisting, e.g. 我怀疑您得了胆结石，可能还

伴有胆囊炎。

3. ……的话

"……的话"多用于口语,表示假设语气。一般用在前一个分句的末尾,表示假设。后面分句表示假设的结果,常跟"就"或"也"配合使用,"就"或"也"放在动词或能愿动词前边。

"……的话" is commonly used in spoken language, including the hypothetical tone. It is often used at the end of a preceding clause for assumption, and the following clause expresses the results of assumption. It is often used together with "就" or "也", "就" or "也" can be put before the verb or auxiliary verb, e.g. 手术顺利的话,你明天就可以出院了。

4. 一般来说

"一般来说"也作"一般说来",常用在句子的开头,有停顿,有时也可以放在主语的后面,表示从一般的情况说,根据通常的情况来看。

It is also used as "一般说来", often used at the beginning of the sentence with a pause. Sometimes it can also be used after the subject, indicating according to the usual conditions, e.g. ①一般来说,没有复发的可能;②手术一般来说不会超过 6 个小时。

➢ **听力练习**

一、听录音,选择你听到的词语

( ) 1. A. 妒忌	B. 肚脐	C. 神奇	D. 东西
( ) 2. A. 专业	B. 专一	C. 转椅	D. 转移
( ) 3. A. 几束	B. 奇数	C. 寄书	D. 计数
( ) 4. A. 叩诊	B. 口罩	C. 寇准	D. 扣子
( ) 5. A. 牙痛	B. 丫头	C. 压痛	D. 岩洞
( ) 6. A. 绞痛	B. 交通	C. 搅动	D. 交工
( ) 7. A. 细腻	B. 油腻	C. 油泥	D. 有你
( ) 8. A. 使命感	B. 死刑案	C. 失心肝	D. 实性感
( ) 9. A. 直径	B. 止境	C. 死心	D. 实现
( ) 10. A. 内向	B. 内脏	C. 弄脏	D. 内战

二、请选出与所听录音相符的答案

( ) 1. A. 患者没在家吃饭　　　　　B. 患者吃饭不规律
　　　 C. 患者吃了不干净的食物　　D. 患者没吃不干净的食物

( ) 2. A. 患者左下腹痛　　　　　　B. 患者右下腹痛
　　　 C. 患者一直是肚脐周围痛　　D. 患者的疼痛从右下腹转移到肚脐

( ) 3. A. 尿常规　　　B. B 超　　　C. 血淀粉酶　　　D. 血常规

( ) 4. A. 患者一直是持续的绞痛　　B. 患者躺着就不疼了
　　　 C. 患者一开始是隐痛　　　　D. 患者已经死了

( ) 5. A. 患者吃了许多油腻的东西　B. 患者没有恶心的感觉
　　　 C. 患者回家就吐了　　　　　D. 患者回家后就感觉不舒服

三、听录音,完成下面的练习

1. 根据所听到的录音判断对错

1) 今天科里来了一位腹泻的患者。(　　)

2) 这个患者有恶心呕吐的症状。(　　)

3) 这个患者的麦氏点有压痛。（　　　）

4) 这个患者的白细胞计数不高。（　　　）

5) 医生建议患者立即接受手术。（　　　）

2. 听录音,选择正确答案回答问题

1) 病人右上腹疼痛有多长时间了?（　　　）

　　A. 八年　　　　　B. 五年　　　　　C. 三年　　　　　D. 六年

2) 病人的症状和体征中**没有**下面哪项?（　　　）

　　A. 转移性腹痛　　B. 放射痛　　　　C. 墨菲氏征阳性　　D. 胆囊肿大

3) 病人还需要做什么检查才能确诊?（　　　）

　　A. 尿常规　　　　B. 血常规　　　　C. 脑电图　　　　　D. B 超

➤ 词汇和语法练习

一、给下列词语标注拼音

1. 阑尾炎＿＿＿＿＿＿＿＿＿＿　　2. 胆囊炎＿＿＿＿＿＿＿＿＿＿

3. 腹膜＿＿＿＿＿＿＿＿＿＿＿　　4. 炎症＿＿＿＿＿＿＿＿＿＿＿

5. 腹腔镜＿＿＿＿＿＿＿＿＿＿　　6. 麦氏点＿＿＿＿＿＿＿＿＿＿

7. 肠鸣音＿＿＿＿＿＿＿＿＿＿　　8. 预防＿＿＿＿＿＿＿＿＿＿＿

9. 切除术＿＿＿＿＿＿＿＿＿＿　　10. 墨菲征＿＿＿＿＿＿＿＿＿＿

二、选词填空

阑尾炎	直径	触诊	绞痛	减弱	麦氏点	尽快	含量	转移	加强

1. 一开始是隐痛,后来越来越重,变成了＿＿＿＿＿＿＿＿。

2. 我初步判断这个病人得了急性＿＿＿＿＿＿＿。

3. 我给他做了腹部＿＿＿＿＿＿＿,他的＿＿＿＿＿＿＿有压痛。

4. 最大的结石＿＿＿＿＿＿＿有 3 厘米。

5. 病人的疼痛从肚脐＿＿＿＿＿＿＿到右下腹了。

6. 动物内脏和煎蛋的胆固醇＿＿＿＿＿＿＿很高。

7. 她听诊时发现病人的肠鸣音＿＿＿＿＿＿＿了。

8. 由于他的症状比较典型,应该＿＿＿＿＿＿＿安排阑尾切除手术。

9. 您可以服用一些＿＿＿＿＿＿＿胆固醇代谢的药物。

三、用指定的词语或结构完成句子或对话。

1. 一开始只有肚子痛,＿＿＿＿＿＿＿＿。(到后来)

2. 你要少吃油腻的东西,＿＿＿＿＿＿＿＿。(复发)

3. 我给病人做了腹部检查,＿＿＿＿＿＿＿＿。(不但……还……)

4. ＿＿＿＿＿＿＿＿,你就会被社会淘汰。(不……的话)

5. ＿＿＿＿＿＿＿＿,我怀疑您得了胆囊结石。(从……来看)

四、把下列词语排列成句子

1. 还需要　辅助检查　你　进一步　做一些　以便　确诊

2. 我怀疑　胆囊炎　还伴有　您得了　可能　胆结石

3. 压痛　不但　他的　还有　反跳痛　有　腹部

4. 右肩部　也　我的　腰背部　疼　很　和

5. 治疗　不好　不做　的话　效果　手术

➢ 阅读与应用练习

一、根据课文内容补全对话

主治医师： 病人哪儿不舒服？

住院医师： 他有典型的__1__腹痛,还有__2__和胃肠道症状。

主治医师： 你的初步诊断是什么？

住院医师： 我怀疑他是__3__。

主治医师： 还有其他的体征吗？

住院医师： 我给他做了__4__,他的__5__有压痛,还有__6__。

主治医师： 血常规结果如何？

住院医师： __7__计数升高,__8__反应很明显。

主治医师： 现在可以__9__了,要尽快给他做__10__。

二、根据课文内容回答问题。

1. 李刚的腹痛多长时间从肚脐转移到右下腹？

2. 李刚做了哪些辅助检查？

3. 陈明有几年的腹痛病史？

4. 胆囊切除术后会不会复发？

5. 胆囊切除术后的病人饮食上要注意什么？

三、写作练习

请简单描述会话二中病人陈明的主要临床表现。(不少于30字)

四、交际练习

学生两人一组,扮演下列角色并进行对话练习。

A:住院医师,今天有一位病人刚住院,你去问过了他的病情,并检查了他的身体。回到医生办公室向主治医师汇报情况。

B:主治医师,让住院医师找新病人询问病史并做体格检查,做完后问他检查的结果。根据住院医师说的情况,指导他进行诊断。

第九章　　　心 胸 外 科

 会话一　　　**先天性心脏病**

词汇

先天性	xiāntiānxìng	名	congenital
青紫	qīngzǐ	名	cyanose
下蹲	xiàdūn	动	to squat
痰	tán	名	phlegm
怀孕	huáiyùn	名	pregnancy
紧张	jǐnzhāng	名	nervous
法洛四联症	fǎluòsìliánzhèng	名	tetralogy of Fallot
胎儿	tāier	名	fetus
发育	fāyù	动	growth
早期	zǎoqī	动	early stage

地点:心外科门诊
人物:唐医生(主治医师)
　　　邹维(患儿,男,15个月,母亲陪同)

唐医生　请进! 你们好! 我是唐医生。请坐! (患儿在哭闹)小朋友怎么了? 哪儿不舒服啊?

母　亲　大夫,最近我发现儿子哭闹后,嘴唇会慢慢变紫。还有,他在学走路的时候,每走几分钟就会蹲下,而且有点喘,嘴唇的颜色也会加深。是不是有什么问题?

唐医生　他出现嘴唇**青紫**这种情况多长时间了?

母　亲　刚出生的时候没发现,大概 6 个月前发现他在哭闹后嘴唇会变紫。最近这两个月,哭闹后嘴唇青紫得越来越厉害了。

唐医生　什么时候发现他走路后出现**下蹲**?

母　亲　他是两个月前开始学走路的。刚开始学走路的时候,就出现下蹲和哭闹的情况了。

唐医生　他经常咳嗽吗?

母　亲　经常咳嗽。

唐医生　有**痰**吗? 痰是什么颜色的?

母　亲　有痰,是白色的。

唐医生　他是您的第一个孩子吗? 您**怀孕**的时候做过什么检查?

母　亲　他是我的第一个孩子。我家在农村,离县城医院比较远,怀孕的时候没有做过什么检查。

唐医生　您夫妻双方亲戚的身体都怎么样?

母　亲　我哥哥很小的时候就不在了,具体死亡原因,我也不太清楚。另外,我有一个叔叔也去世了,过世的时候挺年轻的,才 27 岁,听说是因为心脏病的原因。

唐医生　哦! 孩子以前还得过什么病吗?

母　亲　他经常感冒和发烧。我常带他去村里的小诊所看病,每次医生都是给他开点退烧药,有时候吃药没效果就给他打抗生素。

唐医生　您在怀孕期间生过什么病吗?

母　亲　没有。

唐医生　好的。现在我要给他做一下体格检查。请把他抱到检查床上。

母　亲　好的。

　　　　(10 分钟后,体格检查结束。)

唐医生　根据病史和体格检查,我考虑他可能是先天性心脏病,但是请您不要**紧张**。我们还需要给他做心脏超声检查以及心电图和胸部 X 线片检查,才能确诊。

母　亲　好的。

唐医生　这是检查申请单,等检查完,拿到结果后您再来找我。还有其他问题吗?

母　亲　没有了。谢谢医生!

唐医生　不用谢!

　　　　(三天后,病人检查都已经完成。)

母　亲　唐医生好! 请您看看我儿子的检查结果怎么样?

唐医生　根据您儿子的症状、体征和所有的检查结果来看,您儿子得的是一种先天性心脏病——**法洛四联症**。

母　亲　什么是先天性心脏病和法洛四联症? 严重吗?

唐医生　先天性心脏病是指**胎儿**还在母亲肚子里的时候,由于心脏和大的血管没有**发育**成正常的形状,从而导致胎儿的心脏和血管功能异常的一类疾病。这种疾病的严重程度取决于胎儿非正常发育的程度,法洛四联症是这类疾病中比较严重、也比较常见的一种。

母　亲　那该怎么治疗啊?

唐医生　我建议您马上让孩子住院,准备手术治疗。

母　亲　一定要手术吗? 吃药可以吗?

唐医生　这是一种先天性疾病,吃药只能缓解他的部分症状,不能根治,如果不在**早期**进行手术治疗,可能会危及他的生命。

母　亲　医生,那什么时候可以手术呢?

唐医生　您先别急,我先给您开住院通知单,等入院后再决定手术的时间。

母　亲　好的。谢谢唐医生!

唐医生　不用谢! 希望孩子早日康复!

Congenital Heart Disease

SITE:　Cardiac Surgery Clinic

CHARACTERS:　Doctor Tang (Attending physician)

　　　　　　Zou Wei (Patient, male, 15 months old, accompanied by his mother)

Dr. Tang:　Come in, please. I am Dr. Tang. Sit down, please. (The baby is crying.) What's the matter with your little baby?

Mother:　Hello, Dr. Tang. I found that my son's lip became purple as soon as he cried. Moreover, he always squats and breaths rapidly, while the color of his lips deepen after walking for a few minutes. What's the matter with him?

Dr. Tang: How long has your son have cyanotic lips?

Mother: It didn't occur at birth and began to become purple after crying 6 months ago. It has been serious in recent 2 months.

Dr. Tang: When did you find his squat after walking?

Mother: 2 months ago, when he started learning to walk, he usually began squatting and crying after a few minutes of walking.

Dr. Tang: Does the child cough often?

Mother: Yes, he dose.

Dr. Tang: Does he have phlegm? What color is it?

Mother: Yes, he coughs often with white phlegm.

Dr. Tang: Is he your first child? During the pregnancy, did you undergo any checks for the baby as well as you?

Mother: My son is our first child. I didn't have any checks before his birth because I live at the countryside where is far away from the hospital in the town.

Dr. Tang: Did you have any relatives who have any special medical history?

Mother: My brother died of an unknown sickness when he was very young. And my uncle, in his 27 years old, died of heart disease.

Dr. Tang: Oh! Have your son ever seen the doctor before ?

Mother: We have seen doctor several times in the small village clinic because he often has a cold or fever, the doctor gave him some antipyretics, but sometimes he gave antibiotics if the medicines had no effect.

Dr. Tang: Did you have any illness during pregnancy?

Mother: No.

Dr. Tang: Well, now I'll examine him. Please take him on the bed.

Mother: Ok.

(10 minutes later, the physical examination is over.)

Dr. Tang: Based on the medical history and physical examination, he may be suffering a congenital heart disease. Don't worry. Heart ultrasound, electrocardiogram and chest X-ray examination are needed to make the final diagnosis.

Mother: I see.

Dr. Tang: These are some examination forms. Wait till you get the results and then come back to see me. Do you have any other questions?

Mother: No, thank you, doctor.

Dr. Tang: You're welcome.

(Three days later, all the examinations were completed.)

Mother: Hello, Dr. Tang. These are my son's test results.

Dr. Tang: According to all the symptoms, signs and examination results, your son is suffering from a congenital heart disease—tetralogy of Fallot.

Mother: I'm sorry, doctor. I have no idea about the congenital heart disease and tetralogy of Fallot. Is it severe?

Dr. Tang: Basically, the congenital heart disease means a problem in the structure of the heart or large vessel of the fetus during the development in mother's abdomen, the signs and symptoms of which depend on the state of abnormal growth, while the tetralogy of Fallot is a common and severe one among this kind of disease.

Mother: What can we do now?

Dr. Tang: I suggest that you should immediately let the child stay in hospital and prepare for surgery!

Mother:　　It must be surgical treatment? Could it be treated with medicines?

Dr. Tang:　　This is a congenital disease. Medication can only alleviate symptoms and may endanger his life if not in the early surgical treatment.

Mother:　　When will he be operated?

Dr. Tang:　　Don't worry. I'll admit him first and the surgery time will be determined after he is in hospital.

Mother:　　Thank you!

Dr. Tang:　　You are welcome and I hope your son will recover soon.

疾病介绍

先天性心脏病

先天性心脏病 是 由于 在 胎儿期 心脏血管 发育 异常 而致的 心脏 血管 畸形，是 小儿 时期 最常见 的 心脏病。遗传 是 主要 的 内因，在 胎儿期 任何 影响 心脏 胚胎 发育 的 因素 均 可能 造成 心脏 畸形。常见 的 先天性心脏病 分为 非青紫型 和 青紫型 两类。

一般 先天性心脏病 中 仅有 少数 类型 的 可以 自然 恢复，有 的 则 随着 年龄 的 增大，并发症 会 增多，病情 也 逐渐 加重。简单 而 轻微 的 畸形 对 血流动力学 无 明显 影响，可以 终身 不 需 任何 治疗。严重 的 先天性心脏病 在 出生 后 必须 立即 手术，否则 患儿 将 无法 生存。

先天性心脏病 的 外科 手术 方法 主要 根据 心脏 畸形 的 种类 和 病理 生理 改变 的 程度 等 综合 因素 来 确定，手术 方法 可 分为：根治 手术、姑息 手术 和 心脏移植 三类。根治 手术 可以 使 病人 的 心脏 解剖 回到 正常人 的 结构。姑息 手术 仅 能 起到 改善 症状 的 作用 而 不能 起到 根治 效果，主要 用于 目前 尚无 根治 方法 的 复杂 先天性心脏病，或者 作为 一种 预备 手术，为 根治 手术 创造 条件。心脏移植 主要 用于 终末性心脏病 及 无法 用 目前 的 手术 方法 治疗 的 复杂 先天性心脏病。

Congenital Heart Disease

Congenital heart disease (CHD) refers to abnormal heart disease caused by cardiovascular development abnormalities during maternal pregnancy, which is the most common type of pediatric cardiovascular disease. Any factor influencing the development of embryonic heart during prenatal period may contribute to cardiac malformation, but genetics is the main internal cause. Congenital heart disease is divided into two main groups: non-cyanotic heart diseases and cyanotic heart diseases.

Generally only few CHD cases improve gradually without treatment. Some cases may suffer more complications with age and their conditions will worsen gradually. Simple and slight malformations don't have obvious influence on the patient's hemodynamics, thus no treatment is needed during his/her whole life. Severe congenital heart disease must be operated immediately after birth, otherwise the patient will not be able to survive.

The surgical procedure of congenital heart disease is mainly based on the types of cardiac malformations and the degree of pathological changes, and surgical methods can be divided into: radical surgery, palliative surgery and heart transplantation. Radical surgery can make a patient's heart anatomy back to his normal structure. Palliative operation only serves to improve symptoms and fails to have a curative effect. Heart transplantation is mainly used for end-stage heart disease and those complicated ones which can't be operated by the current surgical methods.

…仅…

"仅"在这里是副词,意思是只,仅仅。

It is an adverb here, it means only or merely, e.g. 这些也仅是工作的一小部。

肺 癌

肺癌	fèiái	名	lung cancer
部位	bùwèi	名	site
剧烈	jùliè	名	severe
刺	cì	动	prick
血丝	xuèsī	名	blood-streaked
乏力	fálì	形	fatigue
青霉素	qīngméisù	名	penicillin
病史	bìngshǐ	名	medical history
包块	bāokuài	名	mass
性质	xìngzhì	名	nature
纤维支气管镜	xiānwéizhīqìguǎnjìng	名	fiber bronchoscopy
经验	jīngyàn	名	experience
组织学	zǔzhīxué	名	histology
根治性	gēnzhìxìng	形	radical
化学治疗	huàxuézhìliáo	名	chemotherapy
放射治疗	fàngshèzhìliáo	名	radiotherapy
免疫治疗	miǎnyìzhìliáo	名	immunotherapy
胸腔	xiōngqiāng	名	pleural
积液	jīyè	名	effusion
保守治疗	báoshǒuzhìliáo	名	conservative treatment
治愈率	zhìyùlù	名	cure rate
分期	fēnqī	动	stage

地点：胸外科门诊
人物：李医生（主治医师）
张翰（病人，男，58岁）
刘霞（病人妻子）

李医生　请坐，张先生。您好，我是李医生，请问有什么不舒服？

张　翰　大夫，您好！我这几天胸口疼得厉害，一直咳嗽！

李医生　胸口哪个**部位**痛？痛了多长时间了？是什么样的痛？

张　翰　我从两个月前开始感觉到右侧胸口闷闷地痛。开始的时候不太**剧烈**，但咳嗽时疼痛就会加重，感觉像针刺一样。

李医生　咳嗽时有痰吗？痰是什么颜色的？

张　翰　是干咳，痰很少，但从上周开始咳嗽比以前厉害了，最严重的是，有几次痰里有鲜红色的**血丝**，所以才来医院就诊。

李医生　发烧吗？

张　翰　开始没烧，最近感觉有点低烧。

李医生　以前有类似的情况发生吗？

张　翰　没有。

李医生　近期有没有感冒或受凉？

张　翰　没有。

李医生　睡觉醒来后有没有出现全身大汗、感觉**乏力**的情况？

张　翰　没有。

李医生　您抽烟喝酒吗？

张　翰　抽烟，从上中学就开始抽了。开始的时候，每天抽一包，工作以后，每天抽两包左右。

李医生　您是做什么工作的？

张　翰　我是做房地产销售的。每天接待客户，烟抽得比较多，但是我不怎么喝酒，偶尔喝点啤酒。

李医生　您以前检查或治疗过吗？用过什么药？效果如何？

张　翰　因为工作忙，没有看过医生。每次咳嗽的时候，我就自己买点儿抗生素吃。

李医生　您吃过什么抗生素？

张　翰　吃过**青霉素**类和头孢类抗生素。

李医生　您有其他什么特殊疾病吗？比如高血压、糖尿病等。

张　翰　没有。

李医生　您家人身体状况怎么样？您的父母和兄弟姐妹有没有得过什么病？

张　翰　没有。

李医生　请您躺到床上，我需要给您做一下体格检查。
　　　　（10分钟后，体格检查结束。）

李医生　张先生，根据您的**病史**和体格检查，您需要做进一步的检查，包括胸部 X 线片、CT 和血液检查等。等您拿到所有结果后，我们才能决定下一步的诊断治疗。

张　翰　好的。
　　　　（三天后，病人检查都已经完成。）

李医生　请进！请坐！

刘　霞　李医生好！请您看看我丈夫的检查结果怎么样？

李医生　您看，胸部 X 线片和 CT 都显示他的肺部有一个**包块**。他的咳嗽可能是这个肺部包块引起的。

刘　霞　那这个包块是什么？严重吗？

李医生　包块的具体**性质**目前还不能确定。他最好住院做进一步检查，如**纤维支气管镜**检查。

刘　霞　根据您的**经验**判断,他可能会是什么病?

李医生　从他的病史和检查结果来看,包块可能是恶性的,也就是癌。当然,包块的最终性质必须要做组织学检查才能确定。

刘　霞　医生,我丈夫得了肺癌了吗?

李医生　只是有这个可能性。

刘　霞　那他还有救吗?

李医生　您先别着急。目前还不能确定,还需要进一步的**组织学**检查才能确诊。就算是肺癌,也不是完全没有办法治疗。目前,肺癌的**根治性**治疗方式主要是手术治疗。当然,根据病人的情况,我们也可以采用**化学治疗**、**放射治疗**以及**免疫治疗**等。

刘　霞　如果做手术,会不会发生手术意外呢?

李医生　只要是手术就有可能出现并发症,比如说出血、**胸腔积液**和肺功能不全等!

刘　霞　如果出现并发症,那该怎么办呢?

李医生　这些都要根据具体情况而定,有的可以**保守治疗**,有的可能需要再次手术治疗。

刘　霞　如果我丈夫真的是肺癌,手术后他就没事了吗?

李医生　这还不好说,如果是早期的话,手术的**治愈率**相对较高。

刘　霞　根据您的经验判断,他这种情况属于早期吗?

李医生　现在,我还没法儿回答您的这个问题。判断肺癌的**分期**还需要很多方面的资料,比如 CT 或 MRI 的结果。一方面,我们需要知道癌细胞有没有转移到周围淋巴结或是转移到身体其他器官;另一方面,还要看每个人的身体状况。因此,我建议他尽快住院检查,这样我们才能最终确诊,抓紧时间治疗。

刘　霞　好的,谢谢医生。

Lung cancer

SITE:　Thoracic Surgery Clinic

CHARACTERS:　Doctor Li (Attending physician)

Zhang Han (Patient, male, 58 years old)

Liu Xia (The patient's wife)

Dr. Li:　Sit down, please. I am Doctor Li. What's the matter with you?

Zhang Han:　Hello, doctor. I get chest pain and cough these days.

Dr. Li:　How long have you had chest pain? Show me your chest pain site and tell me what pain you have as well as much as you can about your symptoms.

Zhang Han:　I felt a bit of pain located in the right chest before 2 months. At the beginning it was not so violent, while it became too severe to suffer when I coughed, which made me feel painful like pinprick. It always locates in the right chest.

Dr. Li:　Do you have cough with any sputum? What color is it if you do?

Zhang Han:　Basically, I got dry cough, sputum rarely. However, since last week, I've coughed more and more. Particularly, several times I found there were some bright red blood streaks in the sputum, which made me go and see the doctor.

Dr. Li:　With some fever?

Zhang Han:　No, I didn't at the beginning. I've recently got a little.

Dr. Li:　Did it happen before?

Zhang Han:　No.

Dr. Li:	Did you have a cold recently?
Zhang Han:	No.
Dr. Li:	Are you getting sweating when you get up? Is there any sense of fatigue ?
Zhang Han:	No.
Dr. Li:	Do you smoke and drink?
Zhang Han:	Yes, I do. I've smoked since high school, almost one pack per day, while it increases to 2 per day because of my job.
Dr. Li:	What's your job?
Zhang Han:	I'm a salesman, engaged in real estate sales. Because I contact with many customers every day, I smoke more, but I do not drink, and occasionally drink a little beer.
Dr. Li:	Have you been to any treatment before you came here? Any checks were undergone? Did you take any medicine? How did it work?
Zhang Han:	As you know, I've got plenty of work to do, therefore I had no time to see the doctor and just took some antibiotics.
Dr. Li:	What antibiotics did you take?
Zhang Han:	Somehow like penicillin or cephalosporin.
Dr. Li:	Do you have any other diseases, such as high blood pressure, diabetes, etc.?
Zhang Han:	No.
Dr. Li:	How are your family members such as your mother, brothers and sisters?
Zhang Han:	They are healthy.
Dr. Li:	I see. I'll give you a physical examination. Please lie down on the bed.
	(10 minutes later, the physical examination is over.)
Dr. Li:	Mr. Zhang, based on your medical history as well as your physical examination, some checks including CT scanner and chest X-ray are necessary. Moreover, the blood examination also is needed, and you must come back when you get all the results. And then we'll decide the treatment.
Zhang Han:	Ok.
	(Three days later, all the examinations have been completed.)
Dr. Li:	Come in. Take a seat, please!
Liu Xia:	Hi, doctor Li. Could you take a look for my husband's examination results?
Dr. Li:	Chest X-ray and CT show a mass in his lungs. I think his current symptoms are caused by it.
Liu Xia:	What kind of the mass is? Is it serious?
Dr. Li:	Well, actually, I can't tell you at the moment what kind of mass he has before performing further examination such as fiber bronchoscopy.
Liu Xia:	What kind of disease does he probably have based on your experience?
Dr. Li:	Personally, based on his medical history and examination results, the nature of the mass probably is malignant, which is the cancer people often call. Of course, the definite nature of the mass will be confirmed by histological examination.
Liu Xia:	You mean my husband has got lung cancer!
Dr. Li:	It might be.
Liu Xia:	Is he savable?
Dr. Li:	Don't worry. It is not clear that further histological examination is needed to confirm the diagnosis. If it is lung cancer, we still have some options. The radical treatment is surgery currently. Of course, we have other options such as chemotherapy, radiotherapy, and immunotherapy and so on.
Liu Xia:	Does the surgery have any accidents?

Dr. Li: What you said, the medically unexpected situations, is called complications. It is possible to have some complications, such as bleeding, pleural effusion and pulmonary insufficiency, etc. as long as we do surgery.

Liu Xia: What should we deal with them if complications take place?

Dr. Li: It depends. We shall give conservative treatment for some cases, while sometimes it may require surgical procedure again.

Liu Xia: Will my husband be all right after the operation if he has been diagnosed lung cancer?

Dr. Li: Cure rate varies from person to person. If it is in early stage, the cure rate is relatively high.

Liu Xia: What about his situation according to your experience?

Dr. Li: Judgment of lung cancer staging requires a lot of data, such as CT or MRI results to investigate whether there is metastasis of lymph nodes or of other organs of the body, plus the evaluation of the physical condition of each person, therefore I can't answer your question until I get all the test results. I advise him to be hospitalized as soon as possible.

Liu Xia: Thank you, doctor.

肺癌

肺癌 发生 于 支气管 黏膜 上皮 ，近 50 年 来 发病率 显著 增高 。在 欧美 工业 发达 国家 和 我国 的 一些 工业 大城市 中 ，肺癌 发病率 在 男性 恶性肿瘤 中 居 首位 ，女性 发病率 也 迅速 增高 ，占 女性 常见 恶性肿瘤 的 第 2 位 或 第 3 位 ，成为 危害 生命 健康 的 一种 主要 疾病 。肺癌 早期 多 无 症状 ，几乎 2/3 的肺癌 病人 在 就诊 时 已 是 晚期 ，原发瘤、转移瘤、全身 症状 或 肿瘤 伴随 症状 均 可以 是 病人 的 首诊 症状 。肺癌 的 治疗 有 外科 治疗、放射 治疗、化学 疗法 和 免疫 疗法 。外科 治疗 已 被 公认 为 治疗 肺癌 的 首选 方法 ，要 依据 肺癌 临床 分期 选择 治疗 方案 。根治性 切除 到 目前 为止 是 唯一 有 可能 使 肺癌 病人 获得 治愈 从而 恢复 正常 生活 的 治疗 手段 。

Lung Cancer

Lung cancer occurs in the bronchial epithelium, the incidence of which has significantly increased in the last 50 years. It has got the first place in the malignant tumors found in man in the developed countries of Europe and America as well as the industrial cities in China; In women, the incidence of the disease also has increased rapidly to be the second or third of the common malignant tumors. Lung cancer has become one of the main diseases endangering life and health. In the early stage, the patients with lung cancer have no symptoms but almost 2/3 patients are in advanced stage when diagnosed. The primary tumor, metastatic tumor, systemic symptoms or tumor-associated symptoms usually are the first symptoms of the patient. At present, the treatment of lung cancer includes surgical treatment, radiotherapy chemotherapy and immunotherapy. Surgical treatment has been recognized as the first choice. Treatment options should be based on the clinical stage of lung cancer.

Radical resection is the only treatment possible to help patients with lung cancer restore their normal life and recover.

语言点

1. 在……中

"在"是介词,表示位于其中。

"在" is a preposition, it means "among", e.g. 在全班同学中,他最高。

2. 只要……就……

"只要……就……"在这里是连词,表示条件非唯一,有之必然。

"只要……就……" is a conjunction here, which means the condition is not unique and it is inevitable, e.g. 只要做手术就会有风险。

练习

> **听力练习**

一、听录音,选择你听到的词语

( )1.	A. 心脏	B. 心情	C. 心肌	D. 心悸
( )2.	A. 导管	B. 导尿	C. 导游	D. 倒灌
( )3.	A. 分手	B. 分流	C. 疯牛	D. 回流
( )4.	A. 搜狐	B. 守护	C. 手术	D. 售后
( )5.	A. 花瓣	B. 瓣膜	C. 观摩	D. 航模
( )6.	A. 吸烟	B. 喜宴	C. 炊烟	D. 溪水
( )7.	A. 专一	B. 专业	C. 专员	D. 转移
( )8.	A. 链霉素	B. 青霉素	C. 氯霉素	D. 青面兽
( )9.	A. 根治性	B. 观众席	C. 公正性	D. 工作鞋
( )10.	A. 临床表现	B. 理财保险	C. 令出必行	D. 临床工作

二、请选出与所听录音相符的答案

( )1.	A. 父母陪同	B. 同事陪同	C. 病人自己	D. 医生陪同
( )2.	A. 嘴唇青紫	B. 皮肤红润	C. 巩膜黄染	D. 眼睛青紫
( )3.	A. 说话后大声喘气	B. 行走后眼冒金星	C. 行走后蹲踞	D. 吃饭后喜欢蹲踞
( )4.	A. 每年吸 20 支烟	B. 每天吸 40 包烟	C. 每天喝 20 公斤酒	D. 每天吸 20 支烟
( )5.	A. 化学疗法是根治性治疗		B. 放射疗法是根治性治疗	
	C. 免疫疗法是根治性治疗		D. 手术是根治性治疗	

三、听录音,完成下面的练习

1. 根据所听到的录音判断对错

1)严重先天性心脏病病人在婴幼儿时期没有症状。(   )

2)可通过腹部 B 超诊断是否患有先天性心脏病。(   )

3)根据先天性心脏畸形的范围和程度确定治疗方案。(   )

4)先天性心脏病病人都需要行手术治疗。(   )

5)新生儿患严重先天性心脏病,待成年后方可手术治疗。(   )

2. 听录音,选择正确答案回答问题

1)下列哪一项是肺癌的首发症状? (   )

A. 咯血   B. 胃炎   C. 嘴唇青紫   D. 夜尿增多

2) 肺癌病人可能**没有**以下哪一项表现？（　　　　）

A. 食欲增加   B. 咳嗽   C. 胸痛   D. 咯血

3) 肺癌的治疗方式**不包含**以下哪一项？（　　　　）

A. 手术   B. 化学疗法   C. 抗结核治疗   D. 放射疗法

➢ 词汇和语法练习

一、给下列词语标注拼音

1. 先天性＿＿＿＿＿＿＿＿＿＿   2. 蹲踞＿＿＿＿＿＿＿＿＿＿

3. 心电图＿＿＿＿＿＿＿＿＿＿   4. 手术＿＿＿＿＿＿＿＿＿＿

5. 胸痛＿＿＿＿＿＿＿＿＿＿   6. 转移＿＿＿＿＿＿＿＿＿＿

7. 根治性手术＿＿＿＿＿＿＿＿   8. 青霉素＿＿＿＿＿＿＿＿＿＿

9. 临床表现＿＿＿＿＿＿＿＿   10. 移植＿＿＿＿＿＿＿＿＿＿

二、选词填空

非青紫型   分钟   心脏移植   痰   也就是   法洛四联症

1. 先天性心脏病可分为青紫型及＿＿＿＿＿＿＿＿。

2. 病人在行走几＿＿＿＿＿＿＿＿后喜欢蹲踞。

3. 对于目前无法行相关治疗方式治疗的终末期心脏病，可以行＿＿＿＿＿＿＿＿。

4. 肺癌病人常常表现为干咳，＿＿＿＿＿＿＿＿中可见鲜红色血丝。

5. 独生子女，＿＿＿＿＿＿＿＿说每个家庭只有一个孩子。

6. ＿＿＿＿＿＿＿＿是最常见的先天性心脏病。

三、用指定的词语或结构完成句子或对话

1. 对于原发性肺癌，＿＿＿＿＿＿＿＿。（唯一）

2. 对于症状严重的先天性心脏病，＿＿＿＿＿＿＿＿。（仅）

3. ＿＿＿＿＿＿＿＿，都可能有咳嗽的临床表现。（几乎）

4. ＿＿＿＿＿＿＿＿，肺癌是发病率第一的肿瘤。（在……中）

四、把下列词语排列成句子

1. 就 出生前 心脏病 先天性心脏病 是 已有的

2. 心脏解剖 正常 病人 手术使 结构 回到

3. 是 遗传 内因 的 主要

4. 迅速 发病率 也 女性 增高

5. 生命健康 主要疾病 危害 的 肺癌成为

➢ 阅读与应用练习

一、根据课文内容补全对话

病人：大夫，我最近这几天＿＿1＿＿得很厉害。

医生：能说一下具体＿＿2＿＿和性质吗？

病人：开始的时候不＿＿3＿＿，但当我＿＿4＿＿时候加重。

医生：有多长＿＿5＿＿了？

病人：从开始＿＿6＿＿的时候到现在两个月。

医生：做过什么＿＿7＿＿或是接受过治疗吗？

病人：只是自己吃了点＿＿8＿＿，但是没有明显的效果。

二、根据课文内容回答问题

1. 先天性心脏病分为哪几种类型？

2. 青紫型先天性心脏病的患儿常见的临床表现是什么？

3. 先天性心脏病的治疗方式包括什么？

4. 肺癌的主要临床表现是什么？

三、写作练习

请简单描述会话二中病人肺癌的主要相关因素。（不少于50字）

四、交际练习

参考括号里的词语进行情景对话。

情景：肺癌病人的所有检查结果出来了准备手术，医生和病人进行对话。

（肺癌，手术，转移，并发症，治疗效果）

 骨 折

CHAPTER 10

词汇

骨折	gǔzhé	名	bone fracture
摔倒	shuāidǎo	动	fall down
手腕	shǒuwàn	名	wrist
伸	shēn	动	stretch out
撑	chēng	动	prop up
喷	pēn	动	spray
敷	fū	动	apply (medicine)
减轻	jiǎnqīng	动	alleviate
可能性	kěnéngxìng	名	possibility
X 线片	Xxiànpiàn	名	X ray
扭伤	niǔshāng	名	sprain
腕关节	wànguānjié	名	wrist joint
桡骨	ráogǔ	名	radius
远端	yuǎnduān	名	distal end
采取	cǎiqǔ	动	adopt
复位	fùwèi	动	reduce
石膏	shígāo	名	plaster
绷带	bēngdài	名	bandage
固定	gùdìng	动	fix
移位	yíwèi	名	displacement
拆	chāi	动	take apart; take off
愈合	yùhé	动	heal; unite
康复	kāngfù	名	rehabilitation; recovery
指关节	zhǐguānjié	名	finger joint; knuckle
防止	fángzhǐ	动	prevent
发麻	fāmá	动	numb

地点：骨科门诊

人物：王医生（主治医师）

李强（病人，男，21 岁）

王医生　您好，请坐。您这是怎么了？

李 强 您好,大夫!我上午上体育课的时候,打篮球**摔倒**了,右**手腕**一直疼得厉害,我担心是不是骨折了。

王医生 来,我看一下。

李 强 (**伸**出右手)大夫,您看,从上午到现在,这儿一直肿着。

王医生 现在,右手能动吗?

李 强 没法儿动,一动就疼得特别厉害。

王医生 您摔倒的时候,手腕是怎么受伤的?

李 强 我记得摔倒的时候,右手好像在地上**撑**了一下。站起来以后,手腕就疼得没法儿动了。

王医生 摔伤以后,您用了什么药吗?

李 强 我**喷**了点儿云南白药,还用冰**敷**了几个小时,但是疼痛一直没有**减轻**。

王医生 您这手腕确实肿得挺厉害的,目前,还不能排除骨折的**可能性**,您还是先去拍个 X **线片**吧。

李 强 好,那就麻烦您给我开检查单吧。

(X 线片结果出来后)

李 强 王大夫,这是我的 X 线片,请您看看。

王医生 来,我看看。您这还真不是**扭伤**,是骨折了。您看,您的**腕关节**在这儿,这是**桡骨**。您的桡骨**远端**骨折了。

李 强 啊?!大夫,那怎么办啊?

王医生 一般手腕骨折有两种治疗方法。一种是保守治疗,另一种是手术治疗。从您的 X 线片上看,骨折不是特别严重,我建议先**采取**保守治疗。

李 强 保守治疗是怎么治疗的?

王医生 保守治疗就是先把骨折的地方**复位**,然后打上**石膏**,再用**绷带固定**。

李 强 打石膏要打多长时间啊?

王医生 至少得三个月。

李 强 这么长时间啊!

王医生 俗话说"伤筋动骨一百天",可不是得三个月嘛。

李 强 哎,这三个月我都不能打篮球了!

王医生 不但不能打篮球,您还要注意右手不能用力。如果骨折的地方再发生**移位**,就得做手术了。

李 强 哦,那**拆**了石膏,我就可以打篮球了吧?

王医生 拆了石膏,您也别急着去打球。如果**愈合**得好,手腕活动不会受到太大的影响,但也要做一些**康复**练习,才能慢慢恢复腕关节的功能。拆石膏以后可不能马上做剧烈运动。

李 强 这样啊,我明白了。我还是听您的,先打石膏吧。

王医生 好,我给您开单子。您拿着单子和您的 X 线片去治疗室就可以了。

李 强 好的。打石膏以后,我还要注意什么吗?

王医生 每个月您要定期来医院复查。我们得根据您骨骼愈合的情况,才能确定什么时候可以拆石膏。另外,您要经常活动活动**指关节**,**防止**肌肉萎缩。如果出现手指**发麻**、发黑的情况,一定要马上到医院来复诊。

李 强 好的,我明白了。谢谢,大夫!

Bone fracture

SITE: Orthopedic Clinic

CHARACTERS: Doctor Wang (Attending orthopedist);

Li Qiang (Patient, male, 21 years old)

Dr. Wang: Please sit down. What's wrong with you?

Li Qiang: Hi, Doctor. I fell when I was playing basketball in the PE class this morning. My right wrist has been very painful since then. I'm worrying if my wrist is broken.

Dr. Wang: Oh, let me see.

Li Qiang: (Stretch out his right hand) Doctor, look, until now, here is still swollen.

Dr. Wang: Can you move your right hand now?

Li Qiang: No, it is really painful if I move it a little bit.

Dr. Wang: Do you remember how your wrist was hurt when you fell?

Li Qiang: My right hand propped up on the ground when I fell. Then, I found that my wrist could not move after I stood up.

Dr. Wang: Did you use any medicine after that?

Li Qiang: I sprayed Yunnan Baiyao Aerosol, and iced my wrist for a couple of hours, but the pain didn't be alleviated.

Dr. Wang: Your wrist did swell badly. It cannot be ruled out that it has possibilities of bone fracture. You'd better take an X-ray examination.

Li Qiang: Ok, please prescribe the examination sheet for me.
            (After the X-ray)

Li Qiang: Dr. Wang, this is my X-ray film. Please look at it.

Dr. Wang: You did have bone fracture instead of sprain. Please look at here. This is your wrist joint, and this one is your radius. The distal end of your radius is broken.

Li Qiang: Oh, my God! What shall I do?

Dr. Wang: Generally speaking, there are two kinds of treatment for wrist bone fracture, conservative treatment and surgical treatment. Your fracture, showed on the X-ray film, is not that severe, therefore I suggest conservative treatment first.

Li Qiang: What is conservative treatment?

Dr. Wang: I'll reduce your broken bones first, and then fix them with plaster cast.

Li Qiang: How long shall I have it?

Dr. Wang: At least three months.

Li Qiang: It needs such a long time!

Dr. Wang: As the saying goes: "It takes 100 days to recover for the injuries in the sinews or bones". Doesn't it need three months?

Li Qiang: Well, I cannot play basketball at all during these three months!

Dr. Wang: Of course not. Besides, you cannot use your right hand after fixation. If the broken bones displace again, you have to have surgery.

Li Qiang: So, I can play basketball after taking off the plaster cast, right?

Dr. Wang: No, you can't indeed. You cannot rush to play basketball. The function of your wrist won't be influenced too much if the broken bone unites well. However, you also need to take rehabilitation practice to regain joint function. You cannot take intensive exercises right after taking off the plaster cast.

Li Qiang: Well, I see. I will take your advice to have fixation first.

Dr. Wang: Ok, I will prescribe treatment sheet for you. You need to go to the treatment room with this sheet and your X-ray film.

Li Qiang: Ok, what shall I pay attention to after fixation?

Dr. Wang: You'll come to hospital to take reexamination each month. When the plaster cast can be taken off depends on how your bones unite. Besides, you need to move your finger joints time to time to prevent muscle atrophy. If your fingers become numb or darken, you must come to hospital immediately.

Li Qiang: Ok, I understand. Thank you, doctor.

骨折

骨折指骨结构的完全或部分断裂。常见的骨折类型包括青枝骨折、移位性骨折、粉碎性骨折、嵌入骨折和开放性（复合性）骨折。病理性骨折是指病骨发生的骨折。疲劳性或应力性骨折是指骨骼由于长距离步行或跑步等运动出现重复性创伤而造成的骨折。

骨的愈合是指骨骼断裂处的重新连接生长。骨骼的复位有助于促进骨骼的愈合。复位就是将骨折中出现错位的骨骼恢复到其解剖学位置。复位后，需要通过固定来避免骨折处产生过度运动而导致再次错位。骨折的固定可分为外部固定和内部固定两种。外部固定主要通过夹板或石膏固定，内部固定则通过钢钉或钢板与螺丝进行固定。移位性骨折如复位不佳可能导致畸形愈合，即不完全愈合或错位愈合。

Bone Fracture

A fracture is a complete or partial break in a bone. Some of the common types of fracture include greenstick fracture, displaced fracture, comminuted fracture, impacted fracture and open (compound) fracture. A pathological fracture is fracture in a diseased bone. A fatigue or stress fracture is due to repeated minor trauma caused by sports like long-distance marching or running.

When the fragments of a broken bone heal and join together, they unite. Union may be promoted, or helped, by reducing the fracture-replacing the fragments in their anatomical position if they are displaced. After reduction, excessive movement of the broken bone is prevented by fixation-either external, for example a splint or plaster of Paris cast, or internal, for example a pin or a plate and screws. A displaced fracture which is not reduced may result in malunion-incomplete or incorrect union.

语言点

1. 排除……的可能(性)

"可能"这里是一个名词，也可以说"可能性"。"排除……的可能(性)"常用于鉴别诊断。

"可能" is a noun here, the same as "可能性". This structure means "rule out the possibility of …" and is often used in the context of differential diagnosis, e.g. 到目前为止，我们还不能排除胃出血的可能。

2. 受(到)……影响

"受"表示被动语态，后面接宾语。

"受" indicates passive voice and an object is used after it. The structure means "be influenced", e.g. 你手腕的功能不会受到太大影响。

 **会话二**

腰椎间盘突出

 词汇

腰椎间盘突出	yāozhuījiānpántūchū	名	lumbar disc herniation
磁共振	cígòngzhèn	名	magnetic resonance imaging (MRI)
图像	túxiàng	名	image
清晰	qīngxī	形	clear
费用	fèiyong	名	fees
报告	bàogào	名	report
结论	jiélùn	名	conclusion
四周	sìzhōu	名	surrounding
膨出	péngchū	动	bulge out
硬膜囊	yìngmónáng	名	dural sac
压迫	yāpò	动	press
有效	yǒuxiào	形	effective
推拿	tuīná	名	massage
针灸	zhēnjiǔ	名	acupuncture
存在	cúnzài	动	exist
风险	fēngxiǎn	名	risk
适当	shìdāng	副	properly
增强	zēngqiáng	动	strengthen
尽量	jǐnliàng	动	try one's best to
久坐	jiǔzuò	动	be sedentary

地点:骨科门诊
人物:李医生(主治医师)
　　　王春梅(病人,女,65岁)
　　　刘明(病人儿子)

刘　明　大夫,您好。这是我母亲。她最近总是说左腿发麻,走路使不上劲儿。麻烦您看看,我妈是怎么了。

李医生　好的。王阿姨,您一般什么时候觉得腿麻?

王春梅　如果走得时间长了,就觉得有点儿麻。另外,晚上睡觉,也觉得腿麻。

李医生　都是左腿麻吗?

王春梅　是的,都是左腿。右腿没什么不舒服的。

李医生 除了左腿麻,还有别的地方不舒服吗?

刘 明 最近,我妈还总说腰疼。

王春梅 对。一干活儿,腰就疼得厉害。

李医生 一般干什么活儿会觉得腰疼呢?

王春梅 我也就是在家干点儿家务活儿,像洗碗、洗衣服什么的。干活的时候,腰一直弯着。如果弯得久了,腰就开始疼了。还有长时间坐着的话,腰也疼得不行。

李医生 是什么样的痛?是一阵阵地痛吗?

王春梅 不是,是持续地疼,像针刺一样,有时候会突然疼得特别厉害。

李医生 出现这种情况大概多长时间了?

王春梅 差不多半年多吧。以前,我也腰疼,我觉得可能就是人老了,腰不好了。可是最近一两个月,疼得特别厉害,有时候疼得连腰都弯不了。

李医生 是什么时候开始觉得腿麻的呢?

王春梅 也是最近一两个月。刚开始,就是睡觉的时候觉得有点麻,我也没在意。后来,觉得越来越麻,走路也有点困难了。我觉得不太对劲儿,就赶紧让儿子带我来医院了。

李医生 根据您说的症状,我们考虑您可能是患了腰椎间盘突出,但是还需要做 CT 或者 MRI 检查,才能最后确诊。

王春梅 大夫,CT 我知道,可您说的 MRI 是什么?

李医生 MRI 也叫**磁共振**,跟 CT 差不多,但是 MRI 的**图像**要比 CT **清晰**,不过,MRI 的**费用**比较高。你们商量商量是做 CT 还是磁共振。

刘 明 大夫,不用商量了,就给我妈做磁共振吧。贵点儿没关系,只要能把我妈的病看好就行。
 (磁共振检查结果出来后)

刘 明 大夫,您好!这是我妈的磁共振**报告**,上面写的**结论**是腰椎间盘突出。

李医生 没错。您看,片子显示您母亲的 $L_{1\sim2}$ 和 $L_{2\sim3}$ 椎间盘向后突出,$L_5\sim S_1$ 椎间盘向**四周膨出**,硬膜囊受压,所以她总是出现腰疼的症状。

刘 明 哦,那她又为什么会腿疼呢?

李医生 腰椎间盘突出后**压迫**了神经,就会引起腿部麻痛。

刘 明 原来是这样。那她现在的情况严重吗?要怎么治疗?

李医生 目前,腰椎间盘突出还没有特别**有效**的治疗方法。从磁共振看,现在您母亲的情况还不是特别严重,我建议先进行物理治疗,比如**推拿**、**针灸**什么的。

王春梅 大夫,我听说腰椎间盘突出不是得做手术吗?

李医生 并不是所有的腰椎间盘突出病人都需要手术治疗。手术治疗是**存在**一定**风险**的。只有病情较重,影响正常行走了,我们才考虑手术。您目前的情况还不需要手术,我建议还是先采取保守治疗。

王春梅 哦,那我需要吃什么药吗?

李医生 不需要。不过,您平时要注意休息;不要剧烈运动,可以**适当**做一些**增强**腰背部肌肉的运动;不要干重体力活儿;少用腰,像弯腰拖地、洗衣服这些家务活儿,要少做;还有**尽量**不要**久坐**,晚上最好睡硬板床。

王春梅 好的,我一定注意。谢谢李大夫!

Lumbar Disc Herniation

SITE: Orthopedic Clinic

CHARACTERS: Doctor Li (Attending orthopedist);

Wang Chunmei (Patient, female, 65 years old)

Liu Ming (Patient's son)

Liu Ming: Hello, doctor. This is my mother. Recently, she has kept complaining about numbness and muscle weakness in her left leg. Could you tell us what is going on?

Dr. Li: When do you feel numb, Mrs. Wang?

Wang Chunmei: It takes place not only when I walk for a long time but also at night.

Dr. Li: Does it all happen to your left leg?

Wang Chunmei: Yes, it does. There is nothing wrong with my right leg.

Dr. Li: Do you have any more troubles besides numbness in your left leg?

Liu Ming: My mum also complained a lot about waist pain as well.

Wang Chunmei: Yes, I have. Recently, my waist is painful whenever I work.

Dr. Li: What kind of work makes your lumbago?

Wang Chunmei: They are household chores, like washing dishes, washing clothes and so on. Usually, I have to bend when doing those things. If I bent for a long time, I will have severe waist pain. Besides, I also have waist pain if I am seated for a long time.

Dr. Li: What kind of pain it is? Is it intermittent?

Wang Chunmei: No, it's constant and tingles. Sometime, the pain becomes sharp suddenly.

Dr. Li: How long does this kind of condition last?

Wang Chunmei: About half a year. I had waist pain before and I just thought it was due to my old age. However, it became severer one or two months ago. Sometimes, it was so painful that I could not bend my back.

Dr. Li: I see. When did you start to feel numb in your left leg?

Wang Chunmei: It also started one or two months ago. In the beginning, I didn't care because I just felt a little numb during sleep, but I've felt difficult when walking since the numbness became severer and severer. I think something is going wrong, so I asked my son to take me to hospital.

Dr. Li: According to the symptom you told me, we consider that you've got lumber disc herniation that will be diagnosed only after CT or MRI examination.

Wang Chunmei: Dr. Li, I know CT exam. What is MRI?

Dr. Li: It is also called magnetic resonance imaging, similar to CT. Its image is clearer than CT, but expense is relatively higher. Do you need to discuss which you want to take, CT or MRI?

Liu Ming: No, we don't, Dr. Li. We choose MRI. It's ok for the expense, only if it detects the cause of my mum's sickness.

(After MRI result came out)

Liu Ming: Hi, doctor. This is my mum's MRI report. Its conclusion is "lumber disc herniation".

Dr. Li: That's right. Look, your mother's MRI film shows that her L_{1-2} and L_{2-3} discs herniated backwards and her $L_5 \sim S_1$ disc bulged out, so her dural sacs suffered pressure. That's why she always has waist pain.

Liu Ming: Well, why did she also have leg pain?

Dr. Li: If herniated lumber discs press nerve, the numbness in leg takes place.

Liu Ming: Oh, I see. Is her condition severe? How to treat it?

Dr. Li: No, it isn't. Your mother's condition is not that severe based on her MRI. There is no really effective treatment for lumber disc herniation. My suggestion is to take physical therapy first, such as massage and acupuncture.

Wang Chunmei: I hear that lumber disc herniation needs surgery, right?

Dr. Li: No, not all the patients with lumber disc herniation need surgery. There is a risk in surgical treatment. We would consider surgery only if patient's herniation is really severe and affects walking. Considering your condition, you don't need surgery now. I suggest taking conservative treatment at first.

Wang Chunmei: Ok. What medicine shall I take now?

Dr. Li: Actually, no need for medication. You need to take a good rest. Avoid strenuous exercise. You can try some exercises to strengthen your back or waist muscles. Don't work too hard and use strength of your waist less. You cannot do the chores, like mopping floor and washing clothes. In addition, you cannot be seated for long time either, and you'd better sleep on hard mattress.

Wang Chunmei: Ok. I'll pay attention. Thank you, Dr. Li!

疾病介绍

腰椎间盘突出

随着 年龄 的 增长，椎间盘 可能 出现 失水 干瘪 而 发生 变形，导致 外部 较为 坚硬 的 环状 结构 发生 退行性 改变，使得 内部 的 核区 或 环状 组织 向外 膨出，出现 椎间盘 膨隆。如果 椎间盘 退行性 改变 或 脊椎 劳损 情况 未 得到 改善，可能 导致 纤维环 破裂，髓核 从 纤维环 破裂处 突出，也就是 椎间盘突出。突出 的 髓核 组织 可能 压迫 椎间盘 后方 的 神经根，从而 引起 疼痛 、无力 、麻木 等 症状。椎间盘 突出 多 发于 腰椎，特别 是 腰 4~5 以及 腰 5~ 骶 1 。

腰椎间盘突出 的 症状 因 椎间盘突出 发生 的 位置 及其 所压迫 神经根 的 不同 而 不同 。 最常见 的 腰椎间盘突出 症状 主要 有 以下 几类：间断性 或 连续性 腰部 疼痛，疼痛 因 运动 或 久坐 等 加重；坐骨神经痛，也就是 疼痛 由 背部 或 臀部 向 下肢大腿 、小腿 、足部 游走；下肢 肌无力；下肢 麻木；膝关节 或 踝关节 灵活性 下降；泌尿 功能 或 胃肠 功能 变化 。

Lumber Disc Herniation

As we age, the intervertebral disk may lose fluid and become dried out. As it happens, the disk compresses, which may lead to the deterioration of the tough outer ring allowing the nucleus, or the inside of the ring, to bulge out. This is considered a bulging disk. As the disk continues to degenerate, or with continued stress on the spine, the inner nucleus pulposus may actually rupture out from the annulus. This is considered a ruptured, or herniated disk. The fragments of disk material can then press the nerve roots that are located just behind the disk space, which can cause pain, weakness, or numbness. Disk herniation commonly happens at the lower lumbar spine, especially at the L_{4-5} and $L_5 \sim S_1$ levels.

The symptoms of lumbar disk disease vary depending on the position where the disk has herniated and which nerve root it compresses. The following are the most common symptoms of lumbar disk disease: intermittent or continuous back pain, which may be made worse by movement, or sitting for long periods of time; sciatica, that is, a pain that starts near the back or buttock and travels down the leg to the calf or into the foot;

muscle weakness in the legs; numbness in the leg or foot; decreased reflexes at the knee or ankle and changes in bladder or bowel function.

语言点

1. 在……情况下

指所处的环境。

It means "under the condition of …", e.g. 在大多数情况下,病人还是愿意接受药物治疗。

2. 存在……风险

"存在……风险"的意思是"It exists the risk of …",常用于医生向病人解释治疗风险时。如:

"存在……风险" means "It exists the risk of …", usually is used when doctors explain treatment risk to patients, e.g.:①这个手术存在很大的风险;②他目前的情况存在瘫痪风险。

练习

➤ **听力练习**

一、听录音,选择你听到的词语

( )1. A. 骨骼　　　　　B. 骨折　　　　　C. 骨裂　　　　　D. 骨穿

( )2. A. 受伤　　　　　B. 摔伤　　　　　C. 扭伤　　　　　D. 撞伤

( )3. A. 指骨　　　　　B. 掌骨　　　　　C. 桡骨　　　　　D. 尺骨

( )4. A. 减轻　　　　　B. 减慢　　　　　C. 减少　　　　　D. 减弱

( )5. A. 前端　　　　　B. 近端　　　　　C. 远端　　　　　D. 末端

( )6. A. 用劲儿　　　　B. 得劲儿　　　　C. 对劲儿　　　　D. 使劲儿

( )7. A. 采取　　　　　B. 提取　　　　　C. 支取　　　　　D. 领取

( )8. A. 牙膏　　　　　B. 石膏　　　　　C. 软膏　　　　　D. 药膏

( )9. A. 胆囊炎　　　　B. 硬膜囊　　　　C. 网膜囊　　　　D. 滑膜囊

( )10. A. 膨胀　　　　 B. 胀气　　　　　C. 膨出　　　　　D. 突出

二、请根据录音判断正误,对的写"T",错的写"F"

( )1. 病人的脚腕骨折了。

( )2. 医生已经决定给病人拆石膏了。

( )3. 打石膏以后,一定会出现手指发黑、发麻的情况。

( )4. 病人的疼痛像针刺一样。

( )5. 病人的 $L_{1\sim2}$ 和 $L_5\sim S_1$ 椎间盘都向后突出。

三、听录音,完成下面的练习

1. 根据所听到的录音判断对错

1) 患者因为运动左手腕骨折了。( )

2) 患者受伤后,用冰敷了以后,好点儿了。( )

3) 患者手腕疼痛持续四小时以上。( )

4) 患者来看病的时候,手腕又痛又肿。( )

5) 医生说一个月以后可以拆石膏。( )

2. 听录音,选择正确答案回答问题

1) 病人觉得什么地方发麻? ( )

A. 腹部　　　　　B. 背部　　　　　C. 腿部　　　　　D. 腰部

2) 病人做了什么检查？（　　　）

    A. X 线片　　　　　　B. B 超　　　　　　C. CT 检查　　　　　D. 磁共振

3) 病人最后确诊是什么问题？（　　　）

    A. 颈椎病　　　　　B. 腰椎间盘突出　　C. 腰椎劳损　　　　D. 腰椎错位

4) 医生建议做什么治疗？（　　　）

    A. 物理治疗　　　　B. 化疗　　　　　　C. 手术　　　　　　D. 放疗

➤ 词汇和语法练习

一、给下列词语标注拼音

1. 桡骨＿＿＿＿＿＿＿＿＿＿＿＿　　2. 远端＿＿＿＿＿＿＿＿＿＿＿＿

3. 压迫＿＿＿＿＿＿＿＿＿＿＿＿　　4. 愈合＿＿＿＿＿＿＿＿＿＿＿＿

5. 萎缩＿＿＿＿＿＿＿＿＿＿＿＿　　6. 摔倒＿＿＿＿＿＿＿＿＿＿＿＿

7. 磁共振＿＿＿＿＿＿＿＿＿＿＿　　8. 硬膜囊＿＿＿＿＿＿＿＿＿＿＿

9. 椎间盘＿＿＿＿＿＿＿＿＿＿＿　　10. 腕关节＿＿＿＿＿＿＿＿＿＿＿

二、选词填空

防止　　采取　　固定　　喷　　可能性　　不对劲儿　　风险　　尽量　　压迫　　增强

1. 吃完这个药，我觉得有点儿＿＿＿＿＿＿＿＿＿，我就不敢再吃了。

2. 为了＿＿＿＿＿＿＿＿＿出现错误，请大家再认真检查检查。

3. 这个手术的＿＿＿＿＿＿＿＿很大，你们要有一定的心理准备。

4. 他之所以看不见，是因为他的视神经受到了＿＿＿＿＿＿＿＿。

5. 从目前的情况看，他盆骨骨折的＿＿＿＿＿＿＿＿很大。

6. 我先给您开点儿外用药，每天＿＿＿＿＿＿＿＿三次。

7. 这个病人一直动，没法治疗，麻烦你们帮忙把他的手＿＿＿＿＿＿＿＿一下。

8. 你怎么总是感冒？你得多锻炼锻炼身体，＿＿＿＿＿＿＿＿免疫力。

9. 手术以后，您要＿＿＿＿＿＿＿＿多走动走动，别一直躺在床上。

10. 病人出现了这种情况，我们应该先＿＿＿＿＿＿＿＿什么治疗？

三、用指定的词语或结构完成句子或对话

1. 根据病人的病史和体格检查结果，＿＿＿＿＿＿＿＿＿＿。（考虑）

2. 从他目前的情况来看，＿＿＿＿＿＿＿＿＿＿。（存在）

3. 他还需要做一些检查，＿＿＿＿＿＿＿＿＿＿。（排除……的可能性）

4. ＿＿＿＿＿＿＿＿＿＿，我们不得不采取这种特殊的治疗方法。（在……情况下）

5. 他恢复得很好，以后下肢的功能＿＿＿＿＿＿＿＿＿＿。（受到……影响）

四、把下列词语排列成句子

1. 更　CT 的　比　MRI 的　清晰　图像

2. 麻痛　腰椎间盘　是　引起　腿部　的　突出

3. 可能性　不能　骨折的　我们　排除　还

4. 萎缩　指关节　防止　经常　肌肉　要　活动

5. 手腕的　影响　活动　太大　受到　病人　没有

➤ 阅读与应用练习

一、根据课文内容补全对话

主治医师：阿里，你带这个病人去打一下石膏？

实习医生：好的。（对病人说）来，跟我走。

实习医生：请坐,刚才王医生说您是__1__骨折。现在,我要先给您__2__,然后再__3__石膏。

患　　者：好的。大夫,打石膏会不会很疼?

实习医生：复位的时候,可能会__4__。您忍一忍。石膏打好了,就不疼了。

　　　　　(打石膏以后)

实习医生：好了,我再给您用__5__固定一下。

患　　者：大夫,我什么时候可以__6__?

实习医生：至少__7__。您要注意右手__8__,如果骨折的地方__9__,就得做手术了。

患　　者：好的。那我多久以后要来医院__10__?

实习医生：您每个月都要__11__来医院复查。我们要根据__12__,才能确定__13__。

患　　者：好的,我明白了。

二、根据课文内容回答问题

1. 病人什么时候开始觉得腰痛? 是什么样的痛?

2. 病人一般什么时候觉得腿麻?

3. 医生建议病人做什么检查? 为什么?

4. 病人的检查结果怎么样? 结论是什么?

5. 目前,医生建议病人采取什么治疗? 为什么?

三、写作练习

请简单描述会话一中骨折病人的主要治疗方法。(不少于60字)

四、交际练习

学生两人一组,扮演下列角色并进行对话练习。

A:实习医生 A,今天在骨科门诊实习,带教医生接诊了一位腕关节骨折的病人,并进行了相应的治疗。

B:实习医生 B,今天在骨科门诊实习,带教医生接诊了一位腰椎间盘突出的病人,并给出了相应的治疗建议。

两位实习医生下班后,互相交流今天所遇到的病例以及带教医生所做出的治疗。

 会话一　　　　　　　脑　外　伤

词汇

脑外伤	nǎowàishāng	名	traumatic brain injury
抢救室	qiǎngjiùshì	名	first-aid room
车祸	chēhuò	名	car accident
稳定	wěndìng	形	steady
烦躁	fánzào	形	agitated
撞	zhuàng	动	hit
意识	yìshí	名	consciousness
右颞部	yòunièbù	名	right tempus
多发	duōfā	形	multiple
散在	sànzài	形	diffuse
脑挫伤	nǎocuòshāng	名	cerebral contusion
出血量	chūxuèliàng	名	bleeding amount
观察	guānchá	动	observe
脱离	tuōlí	动	be out of
密切	mìqiè	副	closely
尽力	jìnlì	动	try one's best
呈	chéng	动	appear
喷射状	pēnshèzhuàng	名	spurting pattern
面积	miànjī	名	area
神志不清	shénzhìbùqīng	动	be unconscious
危重	wēizhòng	形	critical
开颅手术	kāilúshǒushù	名	craniotomy
签字	qiānzì	动	sign

地点：抢救室
人物：谢医生（神经外科主任医师）
　　　陈医生（急诊科住院医师）
　　　付静（病人，女，30 岁）
　　　王成（病人丈夫）

陈医生　　谢主任，您来了。您看一下，这是刚送进来的**车祸**病人。

谢医生　病人生命体征怎么样?

陈医生　心率、呼吸、血压都比较**稳定**,但是病人很**烦躁**。

谢医生　家属在哪儿?

王　成　在这儿。我是她丈夫。

谢医生　她是怎么受伤的?

王　成　我也不太清楚。晚上,我骑电动车带她回家。在路上,骑着骑着,突然被车**撞**了。我们俩都从车上摔了下来。我爬起来一看,她躺在地上,满头都是血。

谢医生　付静,你现在身上哪里痛吗?

付　静　头痛!啊……头痛!

陈医生　刚才我们问了。她**意识**不太清楚,情绪也不太稳定。

谢医生　赶紧先去拍个头部 CT 吧。

　　　　(CT 结果出来后)

谢医生　家属,她的 CT 检查显示是**右颞部多发散在**的**脑挫伤**,伴有脑出血。从目前她的颅内**出血量**来看,我们考虑暂时不手术,继续**观察**。

王　成　那她现在是不是没有危险了?

谢医生　不,她现在还没**脱离**危险。因为她发生脑外伤的时间还比较短,颅内出血量**随时**可能增加。我们要**密切**观察她的病情,如果颅内出血量继续增加,也可能还需要手术。

王　成　好,好。大夫,您一定要救救我妻子啊!

谢医生　我们一定会**尽力**治疗,您放心!

　　　　(半个小时以后)

陈医生　谢主任,病人刚才出现了呕吐,**呈喷射状**,呕吐量比较大。

谢医生　马上去复查头颅 CT!

　　　　(第二次 CT 结果出来了)

谢医生　从第二次 CT 结果来看,病人颅内出血的**面积**变大了。现在病人已经**神志不清**了,病情比较**危重**,我们建议马上做**开颅手术**。

王　成　她现在就需要手术吗?

谢医生　现在这样的情况,必须要做手术。如果不做,会有生命危险!您考虑下吧,如果您同意手术,我们马上做手术准备。

王　成　那还是手术吧。请你们赶紧安排吧。

谢医生　好,那您来**签**一下**字**吧。

王　成　好的。

Traumatic Brain Injury

SITE:　　　First-aid Room

CHARACTERS:　Doctor Xie (Chief neuron surgeon);

　　　　　　Doctor Chen (Resident in ER);

　　　　　　Fu Jing (Patient, female, 30 years old);

　　　　　　Wang Cheng (Patient's husband)

Dr. Chen:　Dr. Xie, here you are! Please check out this patient injured in a car accident.

Dr. Xie:　How are patient's vital signs?

Dr. Chen:　Her heart rate, respiration and BP (blood pressure) are relatively steady, but she is agitated.

Dr. Xie:　Where is her family?

Wang Cheng:	Here am I.
Dr. Xie:	How did she get hurt?
Wang Cheng:	I don't know clearly. I took her back home by e-bike this evening. We were suddenly hit by a car when riding on the road. Both of us fell from the bike. When I stood up, I found that she was lying on the ground with blood all over her head.
Dr. Xie:	Where is painful, Fu Jing?
Fu Jing:	Headache! Ah··· headache!
Dr. Chen:	We already asked her, but she is not quite conscious, and her emotion is not stable.
Dr. Xie:	Well, take her to have a head CT immediately.
	(The CT result is taken to Dr. Xie.)
Dr. Xie:	Mr. Wang, Fu Jing's CT report shows she has multiple diffuse cerebral contusions on her right tempus, with intracranial hemorrhage. Based on her present cerebral hemorrhage amount, we'll observe her instead of operation now.
Wang Cheng:	So, she has been out of danger, hasn't she ?
Dr. Xie:	No, she hasn't got out of danger now. Her intracranial hemorrhage may increase at any time since she suffered from traumatic brain injury in a short time. We will monitor her closely. She needs surgery if her wound keeps bleeding.
Wang Cheng:	Ok, ok, doctor. Please save my wife!
Dr. Xie:	Don't worry. We'll try our best to save her.
	(Half an hour later)
Dr.Chen:	Dr. Xie, the patient just has spurting vomiting, and vomits badly.
Dr. Xie:	Take her to have a head CT again right away!
	(After the second CT)
Dr. Xie:	Observing from the second CT scan, the intracranial hemorrhage area of your wife has become larger. Now, she turned into unconscious in a critical condition. She needs surgery immediately.
Wang Cheng:	She has to take surgery now?
Dr. Xie:	Yes, she has. Craniotomy is definitely necessary based on her present condition. Her life would be in danger if she hasn't got operation. You can consider it for a while. If you agree to take the surgery, we'll prepare for it immediately.
Wang Cheng:	I choose to have the surgery. Please arrange it soon.
Dr. Xie:	Ok, then please go to sign your name.
Wang Cheng:	Ok.

疾病介绍

脑外伤

脑外伤 一般 指 由 突发性 外力 造成 的 脑部 损伤 ，是 最为 常见 的 成人 致残 和 致死 原因 之一 。其 脑部 损伤 可 分 为 局灶性损伤（ 损伤 只 发生 在 脑部 某一 特定 区域 ）和 弥散性损伤（ 损伤 发生 在 脑部 多处 组织 ）两类 。不同 程度 的 脑损伤 可 引起 不同 的 症状 ，轻则 引起 轻度 脑震荡 ，重则 导致 昏迷 甚至 死亡 。

脑外伤 又 可 分 为 闭合性脑外伤 和 穿透性脑外伤 。 闭合性脑外伤 是 指 未 出现 颅骨 骨折 的 无 穿透性脑部损伤 。 大脑 快速 前后 运动 或 晃动 ，与 头骨 发生 碰撞 引起 脑组织 和 脑血管 的 挫伤 或 撕裂，均 可 造成 闭合性脑外伤 。 闭合性脑外伤 多发 于 车祸 、 坠落 ，也 越来越多 出现 在 运动 损伤 中 。 猛烈 摇晃 婴儿 也 会 导致 闭合性脑外伤 ，又 称为 摇晃婴儿综合征 。 穿透性 或 开放性脑外伤 是 指 出现 颅骨 骨折 的 脑部 损伤 ，比如 脑部 穿透性枪伤 。

Traumatic Brain Injury

Traumatic brain injury (TBI) happens when a sudden, external, physical assault damages the brain. It is one of the most common causes of disability and death in adults. The damage can be focal (confined to one area of the brain) or diffuse (happens in more than one area of the brain). The severity of a brain injury can range from a mild concussion to a severe injury that results in coma or even death.

Brain injury may be divided into two types: closed brain injury and penetrating brain injury. The former takes place when there is a nonpenetrating injury to the brain with no break in the skull. The latter is caused by a rapid forward or backward movement and shaking of the brain inside the bony skull that results in bruising and tearing of brain tissue and blood vessels. Closed brain injuries are usually caused by car accidents, falls, and increasingly occur in sports. Shaking a baby can also result in this type of injury (called shaken baby syndrome). Penetrating, or open head injuries happen when there is a break in the skull, such as the wound penetrating the brain with a bullet.

语言点

1. 呈

"呈"常用于表示物体出现或呈现的形状、颜色和性质等，多用于正式文体。

"呈" is often used formally to indicate shape, color or property in something, means "appear", e.g. 病人的呕吐呈喷射状。

2. ……状

"状"可用作词缀，用于表示物体的形状。

"状" is used as a suffix, with the meaning of "shape", e.g. 喷射状、片状、粉状、柱状、球状。

颅 内 血 肿

颅内血肿	lúnèixuèzhǒng	名	intracranial hematoma
转（科）	zhuǎn（kē）	动	transfer department
额叶	éyè	名	frontal lobe

骨板	gǔbǎn	名	bone lamella
清除	qīngchú	动	clean away
畸形	jīxíng	名	malformation
破裂	pòliè	动	burst
动脉瘤	dòngmàiliú	名	aneurysm
自发性	zìfāxìng	形	spontaneous
占位性病变	zhànwèixìngbìngbiàn	名	space-occupying lesion
脑室	nǎoshì	名	encephalocoele
中线	zhōngxiàn	名	midline
肿瘤	zhǒngliú	名	tumor
判断	pànduàn	动	judge
先兆	xiānzhào	名	sign;forerunner;premonition
昏倒	hūndǎo	动	faint
模糊	móhu	形	vague; dim
瞳孔	tóngkǒng	名	pupil
反射	fǎnshè	名	reflex
偏	piān	动	deviate
抽动	chōudòng	动	twitch
配合	pèihé	动	cooperate
偏瘫	piāntān	名	hemiplegia
昏迷	hūnmí	名	coma
保命	bǎomìng	动	keep alive
恢复	huīfù	动	recover; restore
修复	xiūfù	动	repair

地点：实习生宿舍
人物：王大伟（神经外科实习生）
　　　苏达明（急诊科实习生）

苏达明　大伟，你可回来了！下午从我们急诊**转**到你们**科**的那个病人王阳，怎么样了？

王大伟　王主任给他做了手术，手术挺成功的，我刚把他送进 ICU 观察。

苏达明　那就好，希望他没事。他那么年轻，才 22 岁，怎么会颅内大出血？是不是还有血肿？

王大伟　是啊！他右侧**额**叶有一个很大的血肿。手术的时候，他颅骨的部分**骨板**都被拿掉了。王主任把血肿**清除**了以后，发现他有血管**畸形**，他的颅内出血就是畸形的血管**破裂**造成的。

苏达明　原来真的是这样啊！下午 CT 结果出来之前，王主任就已经初步诊断，他可能有脑**动脉瘤**或血管畸形引起的**自发性**脑出血了。

王大伟　王主任的经验还真丰富啊！下午我也看了他的 CT 片子，CT 显示有颅内**占位性病变**，颅内出血的面积很大，血液都已经进入**脑室**，连**中线**都发生移位了。

苏达明　你刚说的"颅内占位性病变"是什么啊？

王大伟　王主任说"颅内占位性病变"一般就是出现了颅内血肿或者**肿瘤**。像他这种情况，应该可以**判断**是颅内血肿。不过，他发病这么急，好像一点儿**先兆**都没有，是不是？

苏达明　是的。他妈妈说他今天早上起床以后,就一直说头痛得厉害,面色苍白,全身冒冷汗,他想给老板打个电话请假,可电话还没打,人就**昏倒**了。他妈妈马上打 120,把他送到急诊了。

王大伟　他到你们急诊的时候,情况怎么样?

苏达明　他来的时候,意识就有些**模糊**了,心跳也比较快。我给他做了**瞳孔反射**检查,瞳孔反应比较差,还有点儿**偏**大。另外,他还特别烦躁,身体一直无意识地**抽动**,根本控制不住。

王大伟　对,本来术前王主任要安排他去做 CTA 检查,看看他脑部血管的情况。但是因为他的头一直动,根本没法**配合**检查。最后,没做 CTA,王主任只能直接开颅手术了。

苏达明　你刚说的 CTA 是什么啊?

王大伟　CTA 就是 CT 血管造影啊。

苏达明　哦,那不做 CTA,开颅的风险是不是比较大?

王大伟　当然了。王主任让家属签手术同意书的时候,我听王主任跟他妈妈说术后可能存在**偏瘫**、长期**昏迷**的风险。

苏达明　但是即使有风险,他还是得先做手术**保命**吧。

王大伟　是啊,不做手术,连命都保不住了。

苏达明　现在就看他术后恢复得怎么样了。

王大伟　是的。王主任说如果他明天能**恢复**意识,应该就算脱离危险了,不过以后他还得做颅骨**修复**手术。

苏达明　希望他明天能清醒!

Intracranial Hematoma

SITE:　Interns' dorm
CHARACTERS:　Wang Dawei (Intern in Neuron surgery department)
　　　　　　　Su Daming (Intern in Emergency department)

Su Daming:　Dawei, you came back finally! How is Wang Yang, the patient transferred from ER to your department this afternoon?

Wang Dawei:　He was just out of surgery, and the surgery is successful. I sent him into ICU for observation.

Su Daming:　Well, I hope he'll be fine. He is so young, only 22 years old. How could he have such a server intracranial hemorrhage? Did he have intracranial hematoma as well?

Wang Dawei:　Yes, he did. In his surgery, Dr. Wang had to take out his bone lamella since he had got a large hematoma in his right frontal lobe. And a malformed blood vessel was found after Dr. Wang eliminated the hematoma. It is the burst of the malformed blood vessel that caused his intracranial hemorrhage.

Su Daming:　Wow! That is the reason, indeed. Dr. Wang already made a primary diagnosis that he got spontaneous intracranial hemorrhage caused by either a cerebral aneurysm or a malformed blood vessel before his CT results came out this afternoon.

Wang Dawei:　Dr. Wang really is an experienced neuron surgeon. I also saw his CT film this afternoon. His CT indicates that he has got intracranial space-occupying lesion and massive hemorrhage, and blood had already penetrated into his encephalocoele, which even caused his brain midline shifted.

Su Daming:　What is "intracranial space-occupying lesion" you just said?

Wang Dawei:　Dr. Wang said intracranial space-occupying lesion usually indicates intracranial hematoma or tumor. Based on his condition, we can estimate that it is hematoma. It seemed that his hemorrhage developed rapidly without any signs, didn't it?

Su Daming: Yes, it did. His mother told us that he looked pale and complained of a headache with cold sweats all over his body after getting up this morning. He would call in sick; however, he fainted even before he made the call. Then his mother called 120 and sent him to ER right away.

Wang Dawei: How was he when sent to ER?

Su Daming: He was confused and his heart beat was rapid at that time. I took pupillary reflex examination for him and found his pupillary response was worse and his pupil was relatively dilated. Besides, he was agitated and unconsciously twitching all the time. His body was totally out of control.

Wang Dawei: That was true. In order to get a clearer image of his cerebral blood vessels, Dr. Wang scheduled CTA for him to get a view of his brain vessels before the operation, however, he was moving his head all the time and was unable to cooperate with the examination. Dr. Wang had to perform craniotomy on him directly without CTA at last.

Su Daming: What is CTA you just mentioned?

Wang Dawei: CTA is CT angiography.

Su Daming: Oh, I see. Is it at a high risk to perform craniotomy without CTA?

Wang Dawei: Yes, of course. When Dr. Wang asked the patient's family to sign the surgery agreement, I heard Dr. Wang told the patient's mother that it might have the risk of hemiplegia and long-term coma after surgery.

Su Daming: Even so, he still had to take this surgery to keep alive first, right?

Wang Dawei: That's right. There was no other option. His mother had to agree to the surgery.

Su Daming: Now, let's see how his recovery is after the surgery.

Wang Dawei: Right. Dr. Wang said that he would be out of danger if he could regain conscience the next day, but he still needed skull prosthesis later.

Su Daming: I hope he'll come round tomorrow!

疾病介绍

颅内血肿
lúnèixuèzhǒng

颅内血肿是指血液集聚于脑内或者脑与颅骨之间所形成的血肿。

颅内血肿可能出现的症状包括持续性头痛、嗜睡、意识模糊、记忆变化、偏瘫、语言障碍等。根据血肿的来源和部位,颅内血肿包括硬膜外血肿,即血肿形成于颅骨和硬脑膜之间;硬膜下血肿,即血肿形成于硬脑膜与蛛网膜之间;脑内血肿,即血肿形成于大脑内。

绝大部分的硬膜外和脑内血肿以及部分硬膜下血肿发病迅速,几分钟内即可出现症状。较大的颅内血肿压迫大脑可能导致大脑肿胀或脑疝。脑疝可能导致意识丧失、昏迷、全瘫或偏瘫、呼吸困难、心跳放缓,甚至死亡。而有些血肿,尤其是硬膜下血肿,发病缓慢,可能导致病人,特别是老年病人,逐渐出现意识混乱和记忆丧失。

颅内血肿的诊断主要是基于CT或MRI检查的结果,其治疗方案取决于颅内血肿的类型、

<ruby>血肿<rt>xuèzhǒng</rt></ruby> 的 大小 以及 血肿 所 造成 的 颅压 的 大小 。

（拼音标注：xuèzhǒng de dàxiǎo yǐjí xuèzhǒng suǒ zàochéng de lúyā de dàxiǎo）

Intracranial Hematomas

Intracranial hematomas are accumulations of blood within the brain or between the brain and the skull.

Symptoms may include a persistent headache, drowsiness, confusion, memory changes, paralysis on the opposite side of the body, speech or language impairment. According to the position where the hematoma comes or forms, intracranial hematomas include epidural hematomas, which form between the skull and dura mater; subdural hematomas, which form between the dura mater and arachnoid mater; intracerebral hematomas, which form within the brain.

Most epidural and intracerebral hematomas and many subdural hematomas develop rapidly and cause symptoms within minutes. Large hematomas press the brain and may cause swelling and herniation of the brain. Herniation may cause loss of consciousness, coma, paralysis on one or both sides of the body, breathing difficulties, slowing heartbeat and even death. Some hematomas, particularly subdural hematomas, may develop slowly and cause gradual confusion and memory loss, especially in older people.

Diagnosis is usually based on results of computed tomography (CT) or magnetic resonance imaging (MRI). Treatment depends on the type and size of the hematoma and how much pressure has built up in the brain.

语言点

1. A（就）是 B 造成的

"A 就是 B 造成的"用于强调导致某一结果的原因，其中，"A"表示结果，而"B"表示原因。

"A 就是 B 造成的" is used to emphasize the cause that leads to some consequence. "A" indicates the consequence, while "B" indicates its cause, e.g. ①他的颅内压升高是颅内肿瘤造成的；②病人双下肢麻木是腰椎间盘突出压迫神经根造成的。

2. V.+ 住

用在动词后，作补语，表示动作的停止、稳固、牢固等。该结构可插入"得"或"不"。

"住" used after a verb in this structure as a complement, means cessation or fastness of action. "得" or "不" can be used in the middle of the structure, e.g. ①用药以后，病人的病情基本控制住了；②大夫，实在太疼了，我忍不住了；③王护士，来帮我按住这个病人的手臂。

➢ 听力练习

一、听录音，选择你听到的词语

(　)1. A. 脑外伤　　　　B. 脑重伤　　　　C. 脑挫伤　　　　D. 脑损伤

(　)2. A. 颞叶　　　　　B. 额叶　　　　　C. 枕叶　　　　　D. 顶叶

(　)3. A. 变形　　　　　B. 整形　　　　　C. 奇形　　　　　D. 畸形

(　)4. A. 瞳孔　　　　　B. 鼻孔　　　　　C. 椎孔　　　　　D. 毛孔

(　)5. A. 瘫痪　　　　　B. 面瘫　　　　　C. 偏瘫　　　　　D. 截瘫

(　)6. A. 骨裂　　　　　B. 破裂　　　　　C. 龟裂　　　　　D. 开裂

(　)7. A. 急躁　　　　　B. 焦躁　　　　　C. 暴躁　　　　　D. 烦躁

（　　）8. A. 脱离　　　　　　B. 逃离　　　　　　C. 远离　　　　　　D. 游离

（　　）9. A. 预兆　　　　　　B. 前兆　　　　　　C. 凶兆　　　　　　D. 先兆

（　　）10. A. 昏死　　　　　B. 昏厥　　　　　　C. 昏倒　　　　　　D. 昏迷

二、请根据录音判断正误，对的写"T"，错的写"F"

（　　）1. 病人的生命体征和情绪都比较稳定。

（　　）2. 病人现在还没脱离危险。

（　　）3. 病人被送进来时，神志不清、心率过慢。

（　　）4. 颅内占位性病变包括颅内血肿和颅内肿瘤。

（　　）5. 病人的脑中线移位引起了颅内出血。

三、听录音，完成下面的练习

1. 根据所听到的录音判断对错

1）患者骑电动车被撞了。（　　　　）

2）患者刚到抢救室时，意识模糊。（　　　　）

3）患者刚到抢救室时，出现了呕吐。（　　　　）

4）一开始，患者的脑出血并不严重。（　　　　）

5）半小时后，患者出现了脑挫伤。（　　　　）

2. 听录音，选择正确答案回答问题

1）王阳为什么被送到了医院？（　　　　）

　　A. 头痛　　　　　B. 昏倒　　　　　　C. 车祸　　　　　　D. 冒冷汗

2）下面哪个**不**是王阳刚到医院时出现的症状？（　　　　）

　　A. 神志不清　　　B. 身体无意识抽动　　C. 瞳孔反应差　　　D. 呕血

3）CT 显示王阳的颅内血肿的位置是哪儿？（　　　　）

　　A. 右侧额叶　　　B. 左侧额叶　　　　　C. 颞叶　　　　　　D. 不清楚

4）手术中，医生发现什么？（　　　　）

　　A. 血肿　　　　　B. 血管畸形　　　　　C. 脑出血　　　　　D. 肿瘤

➤ 词汇和语法练习

一、给下列词语标注拼音

1. 额叶＿＿＿＿＿＿＿＿＿＿＿＿＿　　2. 观察＿＿＿＿＿＿＿＿＿＿＿＿＿

3. 车祸＿＿＿＿＿＿＿＿＿＿＿＿＿　　4. 意识＿＿＿＿＿＿＿＿＿＿＿＿＿

5. 颅内＿＿＿＿＿＿＿＿＿＿＿＿＿　　6. 血肿＿＿＿＿＿＿＿＿＿＿＿＿＿

7. 放射科＿＿＿＿＿＿＿＿＿＿＿＿　　8. 抢救室＿＿＿＿＿＿＿＿＿＿＿＿

9. 动脉瘤＿＿＿＿＿＿＿＿＿＿＿＿　　10. 神志不清＿＿＿＿＿＿＿＿＿＿＿

二、选词填空

呈　　伴　　偏　　撞　　配合　　清除　　控制　　尽力　　脱离　　密切

1. 病人的出血一直＿＿＿＿＿＿＿＿＿＿不住，非常危险。

2. 一般，新生儿的肺＿＿＿＿＿＿＿＿＿鲜红色。

3. 你一定要好好＿＿＿＿＿＿＿＿＿＿治疗，这样才能尽早康复。

4. 做人工呼吸以前，要先＿＿＿＿＿＿＿＿＿病人口鼻中的血、痰等污物。

5. 目前，这个病人还没有＿＿＿＿＿＿＿＿危险。你们要＿＿＿＿＿＿＿＿＿观察病情。

6. 医生的诊断结果是胆结石，＿＿＿＿＿＿＿＿＿有胆囊炎。

7. 我们一定会＿＿＿＿＿＿＿＿＿抢救病人的生命，您放心！

8. 他被车＿＿＿＿＿＿＿＿＿得很厉害，下肢粉碎性骨折。

9. 血常规检查发现病人血红蛋白＿＿＿＿＿＿＿＿＿低。

三、用指定的词语或结构完成句子或对话

1. 不好意思,能让我先做 B 超吗?我憋了一个小时的尿,已经＿＿＿＿＿＿＿＿。(V.+ 住)

2. 病人的乙肝检查结果＿＿＿＿＿＿＿＿。(呈)

3. 医生说,他的脑出血＿＿＿＿＿＿＿＿。(是……造成的)

4. 他的颅内出血量很大,＿＿＿＿＿＿＿＿。(连……都……)

5. 虽然病人的手术比较成功,但是＿＿＿＿＿＿＿＿。(存在……的风险)

四、把下列词语排列成句子

1. 伴有 右颞 有 脑挫伤 脑出血 病人 还

2. 血管 引起 畸形 脑出血 自发性 会 破裂

3. 颅内 随时 病人 的 增加 出血量 可能

4. 造成 脑卒中 他的 偏瘫 的 是

5. 呕吐 出现 病人 了 喷射状

➤ 阅读与应用练习

一、根据会话二补全对话

主治医师: 病人家属,我现在给您讲一下病人的情况。

家　　属: 好的。大夫,我儿子他到底怎么了?

主治医师: 他被送来的时候,意识 1 , 2 明显, 3 差。我们考虑他可能是 4 引起的 5 。现在,从 CT 检查结果来看,确实是这样。CT 显示出血已经进入 6 了,连 7 都 8 。

家　　属: 那他现在可以做手术了吗?

主治医师: 可以,但是这个手术的 9 很大,术后存在 10 的风险。你们考虑一下,同意不同意手术?

家　　属: 如果 11 ,会怎么样?

主治医师: 不手术,很可能就会死亡。

家　　属: 我们同意,请你们赶紧给他做手术吧!

主治医师: 好,请你们签一下 12 。

二、根据会话一内容回答问题。

1. 病人刚被送进抢救室的时候,情况怎么样?

2. 病人第一次 CT 检查的结果怎么样?

3. 做完第一次 CT 后,医生的建议是什么?

4. 病人为什么又做了第二次 CT 检查?

5. 第二次 CT 检查的结果怎么样?医生建议做什么?

三、写作练习

请简单描述会话二中病人出现颅内血肿的原因。(不少于 60 字)

四、交际练习

学生两人一组,根据会话二内容,扮演下列角色并进行对话练习。

A:神经外科主任医生

B:急诊科医生

病人因突然昏倒送入抢救室,急诊科医生请神经外科医生来会诊,医生 A 与 B 讨论病人的病情及治疗方案。

 会话一

尿路结石

 词汇

尿路结石	niàolùjiéshí	名	urinary stone
搀扶	chānfú	动	support sb. with one's hand
弓着腰	gōngzheyāo	动	stoop
叩诊	kòuzhěn	名	percussion
肾盂积水	shènyújīshuǐ	名	hydronephrosis
阿托品	ātuōpǐn	名	atropine
肾衰竭	shènshuāijié	名	kidney failure
止痛剂	zhǐtòngjì	名	analgetic (pain reliever)
止血剂	zhǐxuèjì	名	hemostatic

 地点：急诊外科
人物：周医生（主治医师）
　　　田华（病人，男，36岁）

田　华　哎哟，大夫，救救我，我快疼死了！（在家属**搀扶**下，病人**弓着腰**来到急诊外科）

周医生　快扶他坐下。请问哪里疼？是一种什么样的疼痛？

田　华　医生，我腰疼，就像刀割一样，有时候还一阵阵地绞痛，疼得我实在是受不了啦！

周医生　哪边腰疼？右边还是左边？还是两边都疼？

田　华　右边。

周医生　疼痛从什么时候开始的？

田　华　大概两小时前，当时我正在睡觉，突然一阵剧烈的疼痛把我疼醒了。开始还想忍忍等天亮再来医院，结果实在是疼得太厉害了，刚才还呕吐了一次，于是我就来医院了。

周医生　疼痛前有没有其他不舒服的感觉？

田　华　有的。今天白天上班时，总觉得腰部这里酸酸的，当时没有在意，以为是上班累着了，没想到半夜突然疼得厉害。

周医生　小便时感觉疼痛吗？

田　华　哦，没有，但是刚才小便时我发现尿液颜色有点深，好像有点儿红，不知道是不是尿血？

周医生　有可能，一会儿我给您做个尿液检查。您有没有总想上厕所、憋不住尿的感觉？

田　华　没有。这是第一次疼得这么厉害。大夫，我得的什么病？严重吗？会不会疼死？

周医生　别担心，您先躺到检查床上，我来给您检查一下。（周医生给病人做两侧肾区**叩诊**检查）这样疼吗？

田　华　哎呀,疼,右边疼,左边不疼。

周医生　腹部按压疼吗?

田　华　不疼。

周医生　好的,我给您开了化验单。让家属扶您去化验小便,再去做个泌尿系统的 B 超,结果出来后立刻到急诊室。

（15 分钟后,检查结果出来,病人回到急诊室。）

田　华　医生,检查结果出来了。我到底得了什么病?

周医生　我看看。尿液常规显示有肉眼血尿和镜下血尿,B 超检查结果提示轻度**肾盂积水**并有结石。您只有右侧腰痛、伴有恶心和呕吐的症状,而没有尿频、尿急和尿痛。同时,您的右侧背部肾区有叩击痛。根据这些结果,可以确诊您得的是肾结石。

田　华　结石为什么会这么疼?

周医生　疼痛厉害的原因是因为小的结石通过输尿管排出体外的时候,卡在了输尿管狭窄的地方,引起了梗阻性疼痛。只要结石排出去,消除了梗阻,疼痛自然就消失了。别急,我马上给您用**阿托品**止痛。

田　华　哦! 那结石梗阻很严重吗? 会导致**肾衰竭**吗?

周医生　别担心,肾结石如果没有引起严重的肾盂积水,只要治疗及时,一般不会导致肾衰竭的。

田　华　好的。这下我放心啦!

周医生　我给您开了**止痛剂**和**止血剂**。请家属先去缴费拿药,然后带病人去观察室输液,疼痛很快会缓解的。另外,我还给您开了口服的排石冲剂,是中药,一次一包,一天三次。疼痛缓解后,要大量饮水,适当运动。跳绳是最好的运动方式,有利于排石。

田　华　好的。今后有什么要注意的吗?

周医生　饮食上要注意少吃高钙食物,平时多运动,多喝水,预防结石的形成。

田　华　好的! 谢谢医生。

Urinary Stone

SITE:　Emergency Surgery

CHARACTERS:　Doctor Zhou (Attending physician)

　　　　　　TianHua (Patient, male, 36 years old)

Tian Hua:　Oh, Doctor, save me! Please save me! I am dying of the bad pain! (The patient went into the emergency surgery room, stooping double, supported by his family)

Dr. Zhou:　Please help him sit down quickly. What's the matter with you? Where is the pain? Can you tell me?

Tian Hua:　Oh, I can, Doctor. I have a sharp pain in my low back as if it was being cut with a knife, with a colic pain sometimes. It is so unbearable.

Dr. Zhou:　Which side is the pain on? Right ?　Left or both sides?

Tian Hua:　Right.

Dr. Zhou:　When did the pain start?

Tian Hua:　Two hours ago, I was wakened by a suddenly sharp pain at night. At first, I thought I could bear it till dawn, but it was so severe that I vomited. So I came to the hospital now.

Dr. Zhou:　Did you feel uncomfortable in other parts before it took place?

Tian Hua:　Yes, my lower back was sore when I was working at daytime, but I didn't care. I thought it was due to my fatigue. I didn't expect a suddenly severe pain would attack me at night.

Dr. Zhou:　Does it hurt when you urinate?

Tian Hua: No, it doesn't. However, I found the color of the urine was red when I passed water just now. I'm not sure whether there is blood in the urine or not.

Dr. Zhou: There might be. I'll make a urine routine examination for you. Did you have urinary urgency that was unable to control?

Tian Hua: No, I didn't. This is the first time for me to have such a sharp pain. What's wrong with me, Doctor? Is it serious? Shall I die of it?

Dr. Zhou: Don't worry about it. Please lie on the examining table. I'll make a physical examination for you. (Dr. Zhou made the percussion inspection for the patient on both sides of the kidney area) Is it painful when I tap here?

Tian Hua: Oh! It's the pain on the right, but not on the left.

Dr. Zhou: Is it painful when I palpate the abdomen?

Tian Hua: No.

Dr. Zhou: I see. They are the medical checklists. Let your family send you to take the urine routine examination and B ultrasound to check the urinary system as soon as possible. Go back to the emergency room when the results come out.

(15 minutes later, the results come out and the patient come back to the emergency room)

Tian Hua: Doctor, here are the results. What is my disease?

Dr. Zhou: Well, let me see. The urine routine examination results show that you have microscopic hematuria and gross hematuria. The results of B ultrasound demonstrate that you have urinary stone with mild hydronephrosis. Based on the symptoms, the right low back colic pain, nausea and vomit, you haven't frequent micturition, urgent urination and micturition pain. I am sure you have got the kidney stone with the sign of percussion pain in the right kidney

Tian Hua: Why is it so painful, Doctor?

Dr. Zhou: The cause of the pain is that the stricture of pyeloureteric junction is blocked by stone. If the stone is passed out of the body, the blockage would relieve and the pain would disappear. Don't worry about it. I'll give you the atropine to relieve it.

Tian Hua: Oh! Is the blockage serious? Does it cause the kidney failure?

Dr. Zhou: Take it easy. If the kidney stone does not cause serious hydronephrosis, it'll not lead to the kidney failure as long as it is treated in time.

Tian Hua: Oh, I see! I set my heart at rest now.

Dr. Zhou: I'll give you analgetic and hemostatic. The family pays the fee and gets the drug, then take the patient to the transfusion room and put him on a drip. The pain will ease soon. In addition, I prescribe you removing stone granules, a kind of Chinese medicine, once a pack, three times a day. After the pain eases, you have to drink a plenty of water and exercise properly. The best one is rope skipping. That is beneficial to remove the stone.

Tian Hua: Thank you, doctor! Are there any other matters I'll pay attention to?

Dr. Zhou: Pay more attention to eating less food rich in calcium, doing more exercise and drinking much water to prevent the formation of stones.

Tian Hua: I see! Thank you, doctor!

尿路结石

尿路结石 是 最 常见 的 泌尿 外科 疾病 之 一 ，可 分 为 上尿路结石 和 下尿路结石 。上尿路结石 包括 肾结石 和 输尿管结石 ，下尿路结石 包括 膀胱结石 和 尿道结石 。尿路结石 好 发于 男性 ，男女 之比 约 3：1~4：1 。

上尿路结石 的 主要 症状 是 腰痛 ，可 放射 至 腹部 或 腹股沟 ，有时 伴有 血尿 ，其 结石 多 为 草酸钙结石 ；下尿路结石 的 主要 症状 是 尿频 、尿急 、尿痛 等 尿路 刺激征 ，其 结石 多 为 磷酸镁铵结石 。结石 形成 的 原因 可能 和 饮食 习惯 、代谢 异常 、感染 因素 和 药物 因素 等 有关 。

尿路结石 的 诊断 可 根据 典型 的 临床 症状 ，并 结合 尿常规 、B 超 、X 线片 或 膀胱镜 检查 等 确诊 。治疗 方法 包括 解痉 止痛 ，排石 冲剂 和 适当 运动 排出 结石 ，大 的 结石 可 采用 超声波 碎石 或 手术 取石 。预防 结石 的 关键 在 于 养成 良好 的 饮食 习惯 ，少 食 用 含钙 高 的 食物 ，多 喝水 ，适当 运动 ，避免 感染 。

Urinary Tract Stone

Urinary tract stone is one of the most common urological diseases. It can be divided into upper urinary tract calculi and lower urinary tract calculi. The upper urinary tract calculi include kidney stones and ureteral stones. The lower urinary tract calculi include bladder stones and urethral stones. Urinary calculi are most common in the male. The ratio of the disease in the male to female is about 3：1 to 4：1.

The main symptoms of upper urinary tract stones are low back pain which can spread to the abdomen or groin. Most of the upper urinary tract stones are calcium oxalate stones. The main symptoms of lower urinary tract stones are frequent urination, urgent urination, dysuria and other urinary tract irritation, and most of the stones are magnesium ammonium phosphate. Possible reasons for stone formation may be associated with the eating habits, metabolism, infection factors and drug factors.

Diagnosis of urinary tract stones is based on typical clinical symptoms, combined with the urinalysis, B ultrasound, X-rays and cystoscopy. Treatments include the drugs for relieving spasm and pain, removing stone granules and physical exercise to remove the calculus. Extracorporeal shock wave lithotripsy can be used for large stones. Some of them may need surgery. The key to the prevention of stone formation is to develop a good eating habit with less food rich in calcium, drink plenty of water, exercise properly and avoid infection.

1. 把

"把"字句型，是汉语中的一种主动式动词谓语句。"把"在此处为介词。常见句型：主语 + "把" +

宾语＋动作。

　　"把", a preposition, conducts an active verb predicate sentence. The common sentence pattern: subject+ "把" + object + verb, e.g. 疼痛把我弄醒了。

　　2. 到底……？

　　"到底……？"意思是"究竟……？"常用于疑问句,表示进一步追究,加强语气。

　　"到底" means "on earth", usually used in general questions to emphasize the expression, e.g. 我到底得了什么病?

　　3. 有利于……

　　有利于……,常用句型:A 有利于 B。

　　To benefit…, generally used as: A benefits B, e.g. 多喝水有利于排出结石。

前 列 腺 炎

前列腺炎	qiánlièxiànyán	名	prostatitis
难以启齿	nányǐqíchǐ	形	be too shy to speak out
生殖器	shēngzhíqì	名	genitals
肛门	gāngmén	名	anus
坠胀感	zhuìzhànggǎn	名	tenesmus
尿不尽	niàobújìn	形	incomplete emptying
臀部	túnbù	名	buttocks
膝胸卧位	xīxiōngwòwèi	名	kneechest position
直肠指检	zhíchángzhǐjiǎn	名	digital rectal exam
细菌培养	xìjūnpéiyǎng	名	bacterial culture
药物敏感性试验	yàowùmǐngǎnxìngshìyàn	名	drug susceptibility test
挤压	jǐyā	动	extrude
卵磷脂小体	luǎnlínzhīxiǎotǐ	名	lecithin body
革兰阴性	gélányīnxìng	名	Gram-negative
大肠埃希菌	dàchángāixījūn	名	*Escherichia coli*
大环内酯类	dàhuánnèizhǐlèi	名	macrolide
性病	xìngbìng	名	venereal disease
病原体	bìngyuántǐ	名	pathogen
手淫	shǒuyín	名	masturbation
酗酒	xùjiǔ	名	intemperance
疑难杂症	yínánzázhèng	名	incurable diseases
医嘱	yīzhǔ	名	doctor's order
红霉素	hóngméisù	名	erythromycin
坐浴	zuòyù	动	sit bath

地点:泌尿外科门诊

人物:李医生

　　　石鹏(病人,男,41岁)

李医生　下午好! 我是李医生。

石　鹏　下午好,李医生,我叫石鹏。

李医生　您怎么了? 看起来怎么愁眉苦脸的?

石　鹏　唉! 说来话长,我这病真是**难以启齿**啊,拖了好久了,我都不好意思来医院。

李医生　怎么回事呢?

石　鹏　最近我肚子总是隐隐作痛,有时候**生殖器**及周边部位也疼,**肛门**有**坠胀感**,很不舒服。

李医生　像这样有多长时间了?

石　鹏　差不多半年。

李医生　您去医院看过吗?

石　鹏　没有。

李医生　排尿有异常吗?

石　鹏　总想上厕所,有时候晚上还起来两三次,严重影响我的睡眠,偶尔还有**尿不尽**的感觉。

李医生　以前得过尿路结石吗?

石　鹏　没有。

李医生　请问您是什么职业?

石　鹏　我是卡车司机。

李医生　那经常跑长途吗?

石　鹏　是的。

李医生　请把裤子脱下,趴在检查床上,抬高**臀部**,**膝胸卧位**,我要给您做**直肠指检**,检查前列腺,并取
　　　　点儿前列腺液。您需要做前列腺液的常规检查、**细菌培养**和**药物敏感性试验**。

石　鹏　好的。这样对吗?

李医生　对,很好,请放松。我开始挤压了,有点不舒服,疼吗? (医生做直肠指检,**挤压按摩前列腺**)

石　鹏　有点疼。

李医生　好了,您可以起来了,请把前列腺液标本送到检验科。您还需要做尿常规和泌尿系统B超检查,
　　　　这是检查单。一会儿您去检验科取一个尿杯,接一点中段尿送到检验科;最后去做 B 超检查。

石　鹏　好的,谢谢医生。

李医生　不客气。

　　　　(五天后,病人来到医生办公室)

石　鹏　医生,我的检查结果都出来了。这个药敏试验结果等了五天才拿到,真慢。等得我好着急啊!

李医生　是的,这个试验 3~5 天才能出结果,需要耐心等待,但是这个检查必须做。这样我们才能有针
　　　　对性地选择敏感性药物。

石　鹏　我到底得的是什么病?

李医生　您的尿液常规检查结果都正常,B 超检查没有发现结石,但前列腺轻度增大。

石　鹏　大夫,您看看这两张化验单,好像很多项都不太正常。

李医生　是的。您的前列腺液常规检查结果显示白细胞 +++、脓细胞 +、红细胞 1~3、**卵磷脂小体**少。前
　　　　列腺液细菌培养结果阳性,我们在前列腺液中发现了**革兰阴性**的**大肠埃希菌**。药物敏感性试
　　　　验显示该大肠埃希菌对**大环内酯类药物**敏感。根据您的检查结果和临床症状,您得的是慢性
　　　　细菌性前列腺炎。

石　鹏　前列腺炎是**性病**吗? 我怎么会得这个病呢?

李医生　别紧张,前列腺炎不是性病,是男性生殖系统的一种常见病。其原因可能是**病原体**感染、长期

久坐、运动少、性生活不规律,经常**手淫**、**酗酒**以及心理等因素也可能导致前列腺炎。

石 鹏 前列腺炎好治吗? 广告里常提到的男科**疑难杂症**是不是也包括前列腺炎呢?

李医生 有些心理因素引起的非细菌性前列腺炎治疗起来的确有难度,但是您的前列腺炎属于细菌性前列腺炎,按照**医嘱**正规治疗,很快就会好的。

石 鹏 那要怎么治疗?

李医生 根据您的药物敏感性试验结果,我给您开了**红霉素**,先输液治疗三天,然后改为口服治疗,连续口服 4~6 周。此外,我还给您开了中药,可以缓解您的症状。

石 鹏 平时还有什么需要注意的吗?

李医生 平时多喝水,不憋尿,不要久坐,适当运动。每天可以热水**坐浴** 1~2 次,节制性生活,保持愉快的心情,注意卫生。记得一个月后来复诊。

石 鹏 好的,谢谢医生。

Prostatitis

SITE: Urologic Surgery Clinic

CHARACTERS: Doctor Li (Attending physician)

Shi Peng (Patient, male, 41 years old)

Dr. Li: Good afternoon! I am Dr. Li.

Shi Peng: Good afternoon, Dr. Li. I am Shi Peng.

Dr. Li: What's the matter with you? Why are you in a bad mood?

Shi Peng: Oh, It's a long story. I can't speak out and see a doctor for shame. I am suffering the disease for a long time.

Dr. Li: What's wrong with you?

Shi Peng: Recently, I always have abdominal pain. Sometimes I have the genitals and anus pain. The feelings of rectal tenesmus and anal discomfort are hard for me to bear.

Dr. Li: How long have you been like this?

Shi Peng: About half a year.

Dr. Li: Did you go to see a doctor?

Shi Peng: No.

Dr. Li: Did you have trouble with urination?

Shi Peng: Yes, I urinate frequently, 2~3 times per night. Sometimes, I have a sensation of incomplete emptying. It seriously affects my sleep.

Dr. Li: Did you have urinary stones?

Shi Peng: No.

Dr. Li: What's your job?

Shi Peng: I am a truck driver.

Dr. Li: Do you often drive long-distance?

Shi Peng: Yes.

Dr. Li: Please take off your pants and lie on the examining table in a knee-chest position. I'll check your prostate with a rectal examination and take a little prostatic fluid to take the routine laboratory examination, bacterial culture and the drug susceptibility test.

Shi Peng: Ok. Like this?

Dr. Li: Yes. It's very good. Try to relax, please. I start to palpate so that you will feel uncomfortable. Is that painful? (The doctor made a digital rectal examination and massaged the prostate.)

Shi Peng: A little bit pain.

Dr. Li: Ok. Please take on your pants and send the prostatic fluid to the clinical laboratory. In addition, here is the checklist for urine routine and B ultrasound of urinary system. First, you take a urine cup from the clinical laboratory. Then, you go to the bathroom to get a little midstream urine and send it to the clinical laboratory. At last, you go to the B ultrasound room to do the B ultrasound with the checklist.

Shi Peng: Ok. Thank you very much. Doctor Li.

Dr. Li: You are welcome.

(Five days later, the patient comes to the doctor's office)

Shi Peng: Dr. Li, these are my results. It's very slow for the drug susceptibility test. I was anxious for it for five days.

Dr. Li: Yes, it's slow. This test takes 3~5days. I need the result to select the sensitive drugs for you. So, you have to do this examination and wait for the results patiently.

Shi Peng: What illness have I got?

Dr. Li: The urine routine is normal. There is no urinary stone with B ultrasound results. But the prostate gland is a little enlarged.

Shi Peng: Look at these two laboratory reports, Dr. Li. There are so many abnormal items.

Dr. Li: Yes. Prostate fluid routine shows that WBC: +++, pus: +, RBC: 1~3, lecithin body: less. Bacterial culture of the prostate fluid is positive. We find the gram-negative *Escherichia coli* in the prostatic fluid. Susceptibility test tells us that the bacteria are sensitive to the macrolides antibiotics. You have got the chronic bacterial prostatitis according to your test results and your symptoms.

Shi Peng: Is prostatitis a venereal disease? How did I get this disease?

Dr. Li: Take it easy. Prostatitis is not a sexually transmitted disease. It's a common disease for the man. Researches show that the causes for the prostatitis maybe associate with the pathogen infection, long-term sedentary, lack of exercise, irregular sexual life, masturbation, intemperance, psychological factors and so on.

Shi Peng: Is it easy to cure? The advertisement often mentions the male difficult incurable diseases. Is prostatitis one of them?

Dr. Li: Nonbacterial prostatitis caused by some psychological factors is indeed difficult to treat, but what you have got is the bacterial prostatitis. You'll be well soon if you take the regular treatment according to my advice.

Shi Peng: How to treat?

Dr. Li: According to your drug sensitivity test results, I choose the erythromycin. You need transfusion treatment for three days, then change to oral medication for 4~6 weeks. In addition, I'll give you some traditional Chinese medicine. They can relieve your symptoms.

Shi Peng: What else should I pay attention to?

Dr. Li: You should drink plenty of water, exercise properly, not hold back the urine, not sit for a long time, take a hot water sitting bath once or twice a day, and avoid sexual activity, be happy and pay attention to hygiene. You should return visit a month later.

Shi Peng: I see. Thank you, Doctor Li.

前列腺炎
qiánlièxiànyán

前列腺炎 是 泌尿 外科 的　常见病 ，50 岁 以下 男性 病人 居首位。 1995 年 NIH 将 前列腺炎

分 为 四型： I 型 为 急性 细菌性 前列腺炎 ， II 型 为 慢性 细菌性前列腺炎 ， III 型 为 慢性

前列腺炎 / 慢性　盆腔疼痛综合征 ， IV 型 为　无症状性前列腺炎 。 其中 非细菌性前列腺炎

远 较 细菌性前列腺炎 多见 。

前列腺炎 的 常见　症状 包括 盆骶疼痛（ 可 放射 至 会 阴部 、腹部 、尿道 等 ）、排尿

异常（ 尿频 、尿急 、尿痛 、排尿 不畅 、夜尿 增多 等 ）和 性功能　障碍（ 性欲 减退 、早泄 、

阳痿 等 ）等 前列腺炎 综合征 。 I 型 常 发病 突然 ， 表现 为 寒战 、发热 、疲乏 无力 等

全身　症状 。 IV 型 无 临床　症状 。

病原体 感染 、排尿 功能 障碍 、精神 心理 因素 、神经 内分泌因素 、免疫 反应 异常 、氧化

应激 和 下尿路 上皮 功能 障碍 等 均 可 引起 前列腺炎 的 发生 。 前列腺 的 治疗 方法 可 针对

不同 的 型别 采用 抗菌 药物 、消炎 止痛 药物 、物理 疗法 、M- 受体 拮抗剂 、α- 受体 拮抗剂 、中医

中药 等 方法 行 个体化 治疗 。

Prostatitis

Prostatitis is a common disease of urology. It is the number-one reason for the male patients under age 50 who visit a urologist. According to the National Institutes of Health in 1995, prostatitis was divided into four types: acute prostatitis (type I), chronic bacterial prostatitis (type II), chronic prostatitis/chronic pelvic pain syndrome (type III), asymptomatic prostate inflammation (type IV). Chronic nonbacterial prostatitis was far more common than bacterial prostatitis.

The symptoms of prostatitis include syndromes of the basin of sacral pain (It may radiate to the perineum, abdomen, urinary tract, etc.), abnormal urination (frequent urination, urgent urination, pain during urination, difficult urination, urine increased during night, etc.), sexual dysfunction (decreased libido, premature ejaculation, impotence, etc.) and so on. Type I is often sudden onset, manifested as chills, fever, fatigue, weakness and other symptoms. Type IV has no clinical symptoms.

The cause of prostatitis may be related to the following factors, such as pathogen infection, voiding dysfunction, psychological factors, neuroendocrine factors, abnormal immune response, oxidative stress theory, lower urinary tract epithelial dysfunction and so on. Personalized treatment is used for prostatitis according to the type the patient has, which includes antibiotics, pain relievers, physical therapy, muscle relaxants (M-receptor antagonists, α -receptor antagonist), traditional Chinese medicine and other methods.

语言点

1. 先……,然后……,再……

"先……,然后……,再……"是一组表示动作先后顺序的句型。

The pattern "First……, then……, at last……" indicates the action order, e.g. 你先去检验科检验尿液,然后去 B 超室做 B 超,等所有结果出来后,再到医生办公室找我。

2. 有……感

少数名词、形容词或动词短语后面加后缀"感",可以构成一个新名词,表示有某种感觉,如灼热感、责任感、安全感、亲切感、好感等。

The suffix "感" can be used after noun and adjective and verbal phrase to form new nouns, indicating to have some kind of feeling, e.g. 下蹲后起身太快会有眩晕感。

➤ 听力练习

一、听录音,选择你听到的词语

( )1. A. 尿频　　　　B. 尿急　　　　C. 尿痛　　　　D. 尿血

( )2. A. 疼痛　　　　B. 隐痛　　　　C. 钝痛　　　　D. 绞痛

( )3. A. 结石　　　　B. 结核　　　　C. 结实　　　　D. 结合

( )4. A. 梗阻　　　　B. 更足　　　　C. 梗塞　　　　D. 梗死

( )5. A. 彷徨　　　　B. 膀胱　　　　C. 旁观　　　　D. 旁顾

( )6. A. 衰败　　　　B. 衰竭　　　　C. 衰减　　　　D. 衰落

( )7. A. 刺杀　　　　B. 次级　　　　C. 此举　　　　D. 刺激

( )8. A. 甲状腺　　　B. 前列腺　　　C. 肾上腺　　　D. 消化腺

( )9. A. 红霉素　　　B. 青霉素　　　C. 氯霉素　　　D. 链霉素

( )10. A. 病原体　　　B. 松果体　　　C. 支原体　　　D. 衣原体

二、请选出与所听录音相符的答案

( )1. A. 在病人的家里　　B. 在医院 B 超室内　　C. 在医生家里　　D. 在医院门诊部

( )2. A. 性传播疾病　　　B. 感染性疾病　　　C. 血液疾病　　　D. 恶性肿瘤

( )3. A. 结石梗阻很容易导致肾功能衰竭

　　　B. 结石梗阻不会导致肾功能衰竭

　　　C. 结石梗阻不会导致肾积水

　　　D. 结石梗阻导致严重的肾积水有可能导致肾功能衰竭

( )4. A. 多喝水可以预防结石的形成　　　　B. 多运动可以预防结石的形成

　　　C. 少食用含钙高的食物可预防结石的形成　　D. 低盐饮食可以预防结石的形成

三、听录音,完成下面的练习

1. 根据所听到的录音判断对错

1) 这个患者是一位肾结石病人。(　　　)

2) 这个患者的主要症状是腹痛。(　　　)

3) 医生给患者开了止痛药。(　　　)

4) 医生给患者做了肾脏检查。(　　　)

5) 医生建议患者多喝水、多运动帮助排石。(　　　)

2. 听录音,选择正确答案回答问题

1) 患者有什么病史? (　　　)
　　A. 肾结石　　　　　B. 慢性前列腺炎　C. 急性前列腺炎　D. 前列腺增生

2) 患者经过前期治疗后还有下面哪种症状? (　　　)
　　A. 尿频　　　　　　B. 夜尿　　　　　C. 尿不尽　　　　D. 腰骶痛

3) 医生建议患者做以下哪一种继续治疗? (　　　)
　　A. 放射线治疗　　　B. 口服抗生素　　C. 输液治疗　　　D. 理疗

> **词汇和语法练习**

一、给下列词语标注拼音

1. 狭窄＿＿＿＿＿＿＿＿＿＿＿＿＿　　2. 叩诊＿＿＿＿＿＿＿＿＿＿＿＿＿

3. 梗阻＿＿＿＿＿＿＿＿＿＿＿＿＿　　4. 血尿＿＿＿＿＿＿＿＿＿＿＿＿＿

5. 性病＿＿＿＿＿＿＿＿＿＿＿＿＿　　6. 医嘱＿＿＿＿＿＿＿＿＿＿＿＿＿

7. 绞痛＿＿＿＿＿＿＿＿＿＿＿＿＿　　8. 肾盂积水＿＿＿＿＿＿＿＿＿＿＿

9. 前列腺＿＿＿＿＿＿＿＿＿＿＿＿　　10. 肾衰竭＿＿＿＿＿＿＿＿＿＿＿

11. 生殖器＿＿＿＿＿＿＿＿＿＿＿＿　　12. 直肠指检＿＿＿＿＿＿＿＿＿＿

13. 药敏试验＿＿＿＿＿＿＿＿＿＿＿　　14. 细菌培养＿＿＿＿＿＿＿＿＿＿

15. 病原体＿＿＿＿＿＿＿＿＿＿＿＿

二、选词填空

| 直肠指检　　尿频　　中段尿　　医嘱　　药物敏感性试验 |
| 狭窄　　排石冲剂　　尿不尽　　绞痛　　叩诊 |

1. 您得的是前列腺炎,按照＿＿＿＿＿＿＿＿＿＿正规治疗,很快就会好的。

2. 尿路刺激征的主要症状包括＿＿＿＿＿＿＿＿＿、尿急和尿痛等。

3. 您有夜尿和尿不尽的症状,可能前列腺有问题,我要给您做＿＿＿＿＿＿＿。

4. 您用尿杯到厕所留取一点＿＿＿＿＿＿＿＿＿送到检验科做尿常规检查。

5. 医生,我夜尿次数增多,有时候还有＿＿＿＿＿＿＿＿＿感觉。

6. 结石卡在了输尿管＿＿＿＿＿＿＿＿＿的地方引起了梗阻性疼痛。

7. 我给您开了口服的中药＿＿＿＿＿＿＿＿＿,服用方法:一次一包,一天三次。

8. 请您把前列腺液送到检验科做细菌培养和＿＿＿＿＿＿＿＿＿的检查。

9. 医生,我的腰一阵阵地＿＿＿＿＿＿＿＿＿,疼得我实在受不了啦!

10. 医生正在给病人做两侧肾区的＿＿＿＿＿＿＿＿＿检查。

三、用指定的词语或结构完成句子或对话

1. ＿＿＿＿＿＿＿＿＿＿,我确定您患有肾结石。(根据)

2. 您应该少食用含钙高的食物,＿＿＿＿＿＿＿＿＿。(预防)

3. 结石卡在输尿管狭窄的地方＿＿＿＿＿＿＿＿。(引起)

4. ＿＿＿＿＿＿＿＿＿＿,肾结石一般不会导致肾衰竭。(只要)

5. 药物敏感试验结果显示,＿＿＿＿＿＿＿＿＿＿。(对……敏感)

四、把下列词语排列成句子

1. 肾衰竭　肾盂积水　严重　的　导致　会

2. 有　请问　您　的　憋不住尿　感觉　吗

3. 确诊　您　可以　患有　肾结石

4. 耐心　您　等待　要　结果　药物敏感性　试验

5. 心理因素　前列腺炎　引起　会　可能

➢ **阅读与应用练习**

一、根据课文内容补全对话

病人：大夫,我最近总觉得肚子__1__,有时候生殖器及周边部位也疼,肛门向下有__2__,很不舒服。

医生：多长时间了?

病人：__3__半年了。

医生：排尿有__4__吗?

病人：总想上厕所,有时候晚上起来上 2~3 次厕所,严重__5__我的睡眠,有时还有__6__的感觉。

医生：您以前__7__结石吗?

病人：没有。

医生：请把裤子脱下,趴在检查床上,我要给您做__8__,检查前列腺,并取一点前列腺液。您需要做前列腺液的__9__、__10__和药物敏感性试验。

病人：好的。

二、根据课文内容回答问题

1. 田华除了有肾绞痛的症状之外,还有哪些症状?

2. 田华为什么会出现绞痛?

3. 医生给田华的诊断是什么? 如何治疗?

4. 石鹏的前列腺炎为什么拖延了半年才来医院?

5. 石鹏的前列腺炎诊断依据是什么?

三、写作练习

根据课文内容简单描述前列腺炎有哪些临床表现。(不少于 60 字)

四、交际练习

参考括号里的词语进行情景对话。

情景:病人的检查报告出来了,医生和病人进行对话。

(肛门指检,慢性细菌性前列腺炎,前列腺液检查,细菌培养,药敏试验,尿常规检查)

第十三章　烧伤与整形外科

烧　伤

词汇

烧伤	shāoshāng	名	burn
瘢痕	bānhén	名	scar
水疱	shuǐpào	名	blister
创面	chuāngmiàn	名	wound
深度	shēndù	形	deep
浅Ⅱ度	qiǎn Ⅱ dù	形	superficial Ⅱ degree
冷疗	lěngliáo	名	cold therapy
包扎	bāozā	动	bandaging
破伤风	pòshāngfēng	名	tetanus
忌	jì	动	avoid

地点：烧伤科门诊
人物：冯医生（主治医师）
　　　李晓亮（病人，男，38 岁）

冯医生　您好，请坐！我是冯医生，您右前臂是怎么受伤的？

李晓亮　您好！冯医生，是被热水烫的。

冯医生　多长时间了？现在疼痛能忍受吗？

李晓亮　20 多分钟，还能忍。

冯医生　好的，赶紧过来用冷水冲，这样能减轻疼痛，也有利于创面愈合。热水是刚烧开的吗？

李晓亮　热水烧开后，放置了大概 20 分钟。

冯医生　那还好，要是刚烧开的水烫伤，就很严重了。

李晓亮　医生，我目前这种情况严重吗？会留下**瘢痕**吗？

冯医生　是否会留下瘢痕，主要看创面的深度。您这种情况属于轻度烧伤，起了几个大**水疱**，**创面深度**为**浅Ⅱ度**，一般需要 2 周左右愈合，如果没感染，不会留下瘢痕。

李晓亮　那我就放心了。我需要输液治疗吗？

冯医生　就您目前的情况来看，暂时没有必要输液，先**冷疗** 20 分钟吧。

　　　　（20 分钟后）

冯医生　我先给您处理一下创面，然后再给您**包扎**。

李晓亮　医生，现在天气这么热，是包扎好，还是不包扎好？

冯医生　还是包扎治疗的效果好。包扎有利于创面的愈合，同时也有利于您从事一些简单的活动。

李晓亮   您看我这手臂烫伤了这么一大片,不需要住院治疗吗?

冯医生   一般浅度烫伤面积达到 5 个巴掌大小,也就是身体皮肤总面积的 5%,我们才考虑住院治疗。您手臂烫伤的创面面积只有两个巴掌大,只占体表总面积(TBSA)的 2%,不需要住院治疗。

李晓亮   那我什么时候来换药?

冯医生   您明天就需要来门诊换药。过一会儿,您还需要到急诊科打一针**破伤风**抗毒素才能回家。

李晓亮   好的,谢谢大夫! 还有其他需要注意的吗?

冯医生   在家不要饮酒,**忌辛辣**食物。

李晓亮   好的,谢谢!

冯医生   不客气! 祝您早日康复!

Burn

SITE: Burn and Plastic Clinic

CHARACTERS: Doctor Feng (Attending physician)

Li Xiaoliang (Patient, male, 38 years old)

Dr. Feng: Sit down, please! I'm doctor Feng. How did you hurt your right forearm?

Li Xiaoliang: Hi, Dr Feng. My right forearm was burned by hot water.

Dr. Feng: How long has it been? Can you stand the pain now?

Li Xiaoliang: It happened about twenty minutes ago. I can endure it.

Dr. Feng: Well, please flush it with clean cold water quickly, which helps ease your pain, and it would be conducive to the wound healing. Is the hot water just boiling?

Li Xiaoliang: The water has been placed for 20 minutes after boiling.

Dr. Feng: The injury would be very serious if it was boiling.

Li Xiaoliang: Is the present condition serious? Will it leave scar?

Dr. Feng: Whether to leave a scar mainly depends on the depth of the wound. The injury is minor burns, covered by several large blisters, belonging to a superficial II degree due to the depth of wound. It generally takes two weeks to heal. If the wound isn't infected, it will not leave scar.

Li Xiaoliang: I see. I can set my mind at rest. Do I need infusion treatment?

Dr. Feng: Depending on your situation, there is no need for infusion treatment. Then take cold therapy for 20 minutes.

(After 20 minutes)

Dr. Feng: Let me check your wound. I'll deal with the wound and bandage it.

Li Xiaoliang: Doctor, since the weather is so hot, is bandage treatment better?

Dr. Feng: It is better to bandage the wound, and it is conducive to the wound healing. At the same time, you can do some simple activities.

Li Xiaoliang: Since my right forearm was burned so large, don't I need hospital treatment?

Dr. Feng: Generally, the patient with the wound area reached five percent of the total body, that is, the same as the size of five palms, will be admitted. You'll not because your burn area is the size of two palms, only accounting for 2% of your total body surface area (TBSA).

Li Xiaoliang: When shall I come to change the dressing if in outpatient treatment?

Dr. Feng: You can do it tomorrow. Then you'll go to the emergency surgery to inject tetanus antitoxin before you go home.

Li Xiaoliang: Ok, good bye. What should I pay attention to?

Dr. Feng: Do not drink and avoid spicy food at home.

Li Xiaoliang:　Ok, thank you!

Dr. Feng:　Well, you're welcome! Get better soon.

shāoshāng
烧伤

烧伤 一般 系 指 火焰、热液、高温 气体、激光、炽热 金属液体 或 固体 等 因素 引起 的 组织 损害。

烧伤 病情 严重 程度 一般 按 烧伤 面积 及 创面 深度 判断。病人 五指 并拢 的 手掌 面积 为 体表 面积 的 1%。Ⅰ 度 烧伤，皮肤 有 红斑、烧灼感，3~5 天 脱皮屑 后 愈合，不留 瘢痕。浅 Ⅱ 度 烧伤，出现 大小 不一 水疱，去除 疱皮，基底 红，疼痛 剧烈，渗出 多，一般 需要 2 周 左右 愈合，愈合 后 可 有 色素 沉着，不留 瘢痕。深 Ⅱ 度 烧伤，一般 见 小水疱，创面 肿胀；通常 需要 3~4 周 左右 愈合，愈合 后 会 出现 瘢痕 或者 色素 沉着。Ⅲ 度 烧伤，焦痂 形成，基底 蜡白 或 见 栓塞 的 血管网，干燥，基本 不 渗出，创面 发凉，一般 需要 手术 植皮 治疗，愈合 后 多 留有 瘢痕。一般 四肢 小 面积 的 浅度 烧伤 采用 包扎 疗法，头 面 颈、臀部 及 会阴部 烧伤，外涂 磺胺嘧啶银 或 其他 药物 后，采用 暴露 疗法。

Burn

Burns generally refer to tissue damaged by the flame, hydrothermal, high temperature gas, laser, and hot metal liquid or solid.

The severity of the disease is usually judged according to the area of burn and the depth of the wound. The hand area with five fingers together is about 1% of the body surface area. The first degree burn reveals erythematous skin with burning sensation, healing after the exfoliation of scurf three or five days later, no scar left. The superficial second degree burn bears blisters of all sizes. After the skin of the blisters is removed, the base appears red, severely painful with much exudation. It generally takes two weeks to heal and there will be some pigmentation left after healing, no scar left. The second degree burn generally bears small blisters and swelling wound surface. It generally takes three to four weeks to heal with scars or pigmentation left after healing. The third degree burn has eschar formed, pale base and vasoganglion with embolization. The wound surface appears dry with scarce exudation and low skin temperature. It needs surgery to graft skin and scars will be left after healing. The superficial burn of a small area of limbs can be treated by bandaging therapy, and the burn of head, face, neck, buttock and perineum is often coated with sulfadiazine or other drugs and exposed to the air afterwards.

1. 属于

"属于"表示为某方所有。

"属于" means "belong to", e.g. 这种药物属于麻醉药品。

2. 好，还是……好

"好，还是……好" 常用在疑问句中。

It means "which one is better", e.g. ①病人疼痛难忍，口服药物好，还是肌注药物好？②发热时，用物理降温好，还是用药物降温好？

3. 如果……，可以

"如果……，可以" 表示前提条件。

It means "if…", e.g. 如果明天天气好，我们可以去郊游。

 **蹼 状 瘢 痕**

整形	zhěngxíng	名	plastic
胳膊	gēbo	名	arm
药膏	yàogāo	名	ointment
涂抹	túmǒ	动	smear
腋窝	yèwō	名	armpit
疤瘌	bāla	名	scar
麻醉	mázuì	名	anesthesia
禁忌证	jìnjìzhèng	名	contraindication
植皮	zhípí	动	skin-grafting
蹼状	pǔzhuàng	形	webbed
传统	chuántǒng	形	tradition
皮瓣	píbàn	名	flap
拆线	chāixiàn	动	take out stitches

 地点：整形科门诊

人物：王医生（主治医师）
　　　刘利军（病人，男，40岁）

王医生　您好，请坐！我是王医生，有什么需要帮助的吗？

刘利军　您好，大夫，我**胳膊**活动不灵活。

王医生　多长时间了？您能把上衣脱下来吗？

刘利军　有两年了，当时左肩部被热水烫伤过。

王医生　两年前被热水烫伤时，去医院了吗？烫伤创面多长时间愈合的？

刘利军　没有去医院。烫伤后，我自己在药店买了**药膏**，**涂抹**治疗了一个半月，才长好。

王医生　创面愈合后，用过抑制瘢痕药物吗？给予压迫治疗没有？

刘利军　没有，我左侧**胳膊**活动时感觉肩膀处很紧，不能上举，是不是因为我**腋窝**处的这个伤疤？

王医生　是的。您这个疤，俗称"**疤瘌**"。主要就是它影响了您胳膊的活动。

刘利军　为什么我腋窝处会留下这么大的一个疤呢？

王医生　您腋窝处形成的瘢痕与皮肤烫伤的深度、部位有关。腋窝处不易包扎、不易制动，容易留下瘢痕。另外，根据您创面愈合的时间来看，当时的烫伤创面可能是Ⅲ度，Ⅲ度创面愈合后也会留下瘢痕。

刘利军　那怎样才能恢复我手臂的活动能力呢？

王医生　您需要住院手术治疗。

刘利军　要住院啊？这个手术门诊可以做吗？

王医生　不行。门诊一般只能做局部麻醉的小手术，这个手术需要在全身**麻醉**下才能进行。

刘利军　好的。那我什么时候可以入院安排手术？

王医生　今天就可以办理入院手续。如果您今天入院，明天就可以进行术前相关检查，没有手术**禁忌证**的话，后天就可以进行手术了。

刘利军　好的，谢谢！手术是怎么做的？需要**植皮**吗？

王医生　您左腋窝处的瘢痕呈**蹼状**，一般采用**传统**的 Z 字成形手术治疗，不需要植皮。

刘利军　那我多长时间才能出院？

王医生　手术后要根据伤口愈合的情况才能决定出院的日期。如果手术部位没有感染，**皮瓣**血液运行良好，术后一周，就可以考虑出院了。出院后，您还需要到门诊换药、**拆线**。

刘利军　手术后我胳膊的活动能恢复到什么程度呢？

王医生　如果手术恢复顺利的话，经过一段时间的康复，您左胳膊的功能基本都能恢复。

刘利军　好的，谢谢王医生。

王医生　不客气。您今天办理住院吗？

刘利军　是的。麻烦您给我开住院通知单，我这就去办入院手续。

Webbed Scar

SITE:　　　　Burn and Plastic Clinic

CHARACTERS:　Doctor Wang (Attending physician)

　　　　　　　Liu Lijun (Patient, male, 40 years old)

Dr. Wang:　Hello! Sit down, please. I'm doctor Wang. Can I help you?

Liu Lijun:　Good morning, Doctor. My arm is not flexible.

Dr. Wang:　How long has it lasted? Can you take off your coat and show me?

Liu Lijun:　Yes, of course. The left shoulder was burned by hot water two years ago.

Dr. Wang:　Did you go to hospital at that time? When did the wound heal?

Liu Lijun:　I didn't go to hospital. I bought some ointment in a drugstore and smeared to my wound for one and half months.

Dr. Wang:　I see. Did you use inhibition scar drugs for external application or pressure therapy after wound healing?

Liu Lijun:　No, I didn't. The left arm is difficult to move upward. Is it due to the scar in my armpit?

Dr. Wang:　Yes, it is. Popularly said "scar". The scar is the main cause for your arm's activities.

Liu Lijun:　Why is there a scar left in my armpit?

Dr. Wang:　Its formation is associated with the depth of the wound and position of the wound. It is difficult to bandage in the armpit. According to the healing time, the wound may be Ⅲ degree at that time. The Ⅲ degree burn would leave scar.

Liu Lijun:　How to restore my arm's activities?

Dr. Wang: You need surgery treatment in hospital.

Liu Lijun: Do I need surgery treatment in hospital? Can I have the operation in outpatient service?

Dr. Wang: No, you can't. Because only simple surgery can be performed under local anesthesia in clinic, but your operation needs to be carried out under general anesthesia.

Liu Lijun: Oh, I see. When shall I be hospitalized? And what time to perform the surgery?

Dr. Wang: You can go into ward today and finish the preoperative examination tomorrow. If there is no contraindication, you would be performed surgery the day after tomorrow.

Liu Lijun: Ok, thank you! How to implement the operation? Do I need skin grafting surgery?

Dr. Wang: The scar in your left armpit looks like the duck webbed. Generally Z-plastic surgery will be performed. There is no need to perform skin grafts.

Liu Lijun: How long shall I stay in the hospital?

Dr. Wang: The date of discharge can be determined according to the condition of healing. If operative site is not infected and each flap blood supply is well, you can go home within one week after operation. Go to the outpatient clinic dressing and take out the stitches.

Liu Lijun: And to what extent can my arm function recover?

Dr. Wang: If recovery goes well, your left arm can restore the basic function after a period of rehabilitation.

Liu Lijun: Ok, thanks!

Dr. Wang: You're welcome! Are you hospitalized today?

Liu Lijun: Yes, I'll go through the formalities of hospitalization now.

疾病介绍

蹼状瘢痕

蹼状瘢痕呈皱襞状，形似鸭蹼状，故称蹼状瘢痕。好发于关节的屈侧，多由垂直跨越关节屈侧的长条形创面愈合后所形成的瘢痕自两端向中央逐渐收缩而形成。随着瘢痕的短缩，出现关节的屈曲变形。烧伤是导致蹼状瘢痕形成的常见原因。

蹼状瘢痕一般采取手术治疗，最宜采用Z成形术，以挛缩蹼的游离缘为轴，按单一或连续Z成形术作切口，将蹼状皱襞均匀剖分为等厚的两层，并形成一对或几对互相对应的三角形皮瓣，将互相对应的三角形皮瓣交错缝合修复创面。采用多个Z成形术后切口呈锯齿状，可防止直线的瘢痕挛缩，从而获得较好的疗效。

Webbed Scar

The fold scar shaped like a duck web is always called the webbed scar, appearing mostly at the flexure of joint. It is because the long strip wound surface is perpendicular to the flexure of joint, its both ends contracting to the central after healing. Along with the scar contraction appears the deformation of the joint. Burn is a common cause of webbed scar.

Webbed scar is generally treated with surgery and the most appropriate one is flap Z-plastic pivoted on the free edge of contracture web. Incised with a single or continuous flap Z-plastic, webbed plica can be evenly divided into two layers of the same thickness, consequently forming a pair or several pairs of triangular skin flaps corresponding to each other. Then interlacing suture is used on the skin flaps to repair the wound surface. After adopting several flaps Z-plastic, the incision is serrated, which can prevent scar from contracting of straight line and achieve satisfactory therapeutic effects.

语言点

1. 当时

"当时"指过去发生某件事情的时候。

It means "at that time", e.g. 当时看到他晕倒在地,我都不知所措了。

 练习

➢ 听力练习

一、听录音,选择你听到的词语

( ) 1. A. 烧伤　　　　B. 冻伤　　　　C. 烫伤　　　　D. 刀伤

( ) 2. A. 深度　　　　B. 浅度　　　　C. 纬度　　　　D. 温度

( ) 3. A. 包扎　　　　B. 暴露　　　　C. 包装　　　　D. 报销

( ) 4. A. 蹼状　　　　B. 瀑布　　　　C. 形状　　　　D. 普通

( ) 5. A. 二度　　　　B. 三度　　　　C. 一度　　　　D. 四度

( ) 6. A. 上肢　　　　B. 前臂　　　　C. 下肢　　　　D. 躯干

( ) 7. A. 创面　　　　B. 创伤　　　　C. 伤面　　　　D. 伤口

( ) 8. A. 色素　　　　B. 毒素　　　　C. 激素　　　　D. 肝素

( ) 9. A. 口服　　　　B. 肌注　　　　C. 静注　　　　D. 静滴

( ) 10. A. 水疱　　　　B. 水饺　　　　C. 冷疗　　　　D. 冷冻

二、请选出与所听录音相符的答案

( ) 1. A. 在病人单位　　B. 在银行里　　　C. 在医院里　　　D. 在社区诊所

( ) 2. A. 有点恶心　　　B. 不想吃东西　　C. 有点心慌　　　D. 头痛

( ) 3. A. 先给予冷水冲洗　　　　　　B. 先给予冰块冷敷

　　　C. 先外涂牙膏　　　　　　　　D. 先给予干净毛巾包扎

( ) 4. A. 患者没必要服药　　　　　　B. 患者需要服药

　　　C. 患者三天内需要服药　　　　D. 患者三天内不需要服药

( ) 5. A. 患者现在需要住院　　　　　B. 患者以前没住院

　　　C. 患者刚出院不久　　　　　　D. 患者不想住院

三、听录音,完成下面的练习

1. 根据所听到的录音判断对错

1) 这个患者是热水烫伤。( )

2) 这个患者平常不喝酒,也不吸烟。( )

3) 患者对青霉素过敏。( )

4) 患者因皮肤裂伤住院治疗过。( )

5) 患者需要注射破伤风抗毒素。( )

6) 从严重程度看,患者属于重度烧伤。(　　　)

2. 听录音,选择正确答案回答问题

1) 现在,这个患者来就诊,主要因为哪个部位留下瘢痕了? (　　　)

　　A. 左手　　　　　　B. 左腋窝　　　　　C. 左肘部　　　　　D. 右腋窝

2) 患者左腋窝的瘢痕是什么形状? (　　　)

　　A. 条索状　　　　　B. 蹼状　　　　　　C. 疙瘩状　　　　　D. 菜花状

3) 蹼状瘢痕需要什么样的手术治疗? (　　　)

　　A. 切除缝合　　　　B. Z 成形术　　　　C. V 成形术　　　　D. 切除植皮

➢ **词汇和语法练习**

一、给下列词语标注拼音

1. 烧伤_____　　　　　2. 面积_____

3. 深度_____　　　　　4. 手术_____

5. 重度_____　　　　　6. 水疱_____

7. 蹼状瘢痕_____　　　8. 疼痛_____

9. 包扎治疗_____　　　10. 瘢痕_____

二、选词填空

> 烧伤　　冷疗　　包扎　　浅Ⅱ度　　特重度烧伤
> 蹼状瘢痕　　瘢痕增生　　Z 成形术　　皮瓣

1. 一般把热水、热油、火焰导致的皮肤损害统称_____。

2. 被热水烫伤后,需要立即给予_____。

3. 烧伤病人的肢体浅度创面一般需要_____治疗。

4. 烧伤部位散在大水疱,基底红,疼痛剧烈,创面深度属于_____。

5. 一般烧伤面积如超过 50% TBSA,属于_____。

6. 蹼状瘢痕一般采取_____手术治疗。

7. 瘢痕呈皱襞状,形似鸭蹼状,故称_____。

8. Z 成形术中,将蹼状皱襞均匀剖分为等厚的两层,并形成一对或几对互相对应的三角形_____
_____。

9. 手术切口瘢痕如出现充血、增宽、变硬,高于皮肤,并伴有痛和痒的症状,称之为_____。

三、用指定的词语或结构完成句子或对话

1. _____,现在您不会留下瘢痕。(当时)

2. 如烫伤后立即冷疗,_____。(就……)

3. 烧伤后留下瘢痕,主要_____。(与……有关)

4. 腋窝处的蹼状瘢痕不仅影响功能,_____。(而且也)

5. 热水烫伤后,不要自行外涂药物,_____。(还是……好)

四、把下列词语排列成句子

1. 烧伤　影响　深度　创面　愈合

2. 烧伤　水疱　创面　可见　Ⅱ度

3. 蹼状　常需　手术　Z 成形术　治疗　瘢痕

4. 一般　2 周　可以　出院　住院

5. 在　局部麻醉　门诊　下　可行　小手术　治疗

➢ **阅读与应用练习**

一、根据课文内容补全对话

病人： 这种情况需要___1___治疗吗？如需手术，门诊可以做吗？

医生： 需要住院治疗，这种手术需要在全身___2___下进行。门诊一般只能开展局部麻醉下的小手术。

病人： 好的，那我什么时候入院手术？

医生： 今天就可以办理入院手续，明日进行术前相关检查，没有手术___3___的话，后天就可以手术治疗。

病人： 好的，谢谢！手术是怎么做的，需要___4___吗？

医生： 您左腋窝处的瘢痕呈___5___，一般采用传统的 Z 字成形手术治疗，不需要植皮。

病人： 多长时间能出院？我胳膊的活动度能恢复到什么程度？

医生： 手术后要根据伤口愈合的情况才能决定出院的日期，如术区无感染，各个___6___血液运行良好，手术后一周，就可以考虑出院，出院后可以到门诊换药，拆线。手术伤口恢复顺利的话，经过一段时间的___7___，您左胳膊的功能基本都能恢复。

病人： 好的，谢谢医生。

二、根据课文内容回答问题

1. 李晓亮烫伤后都有哪些症状？

2. 医生给李晓亮的诊断属于什么程度的烧伤？

3. 腋窝处的瘢痕怎么称呼？如何治疗？

4. 烫伤后需要紧急的处理措施是什么？

5. 刘利军左肩部烫伤的深度是几度？形成的蹼状瘢痕常规切除缝合行吗？

三、写作练习

请简单描述会话一中病人李晓亮的主要临床表现。(不少于 50 字)

四、交际练习

参考括号里的词语进行情景对话。

情景:病人的诊断明确,腋窝处蹼状瘢痕,医生和病人进行对话。

(手术,Z 成形术,全身麻醉,住院等)

第四篇 妇产科学

第十四章 妇科（1）

会话一 外阴阴道炎

词汇

外阴阴道炎	wàiyīnyīndàoyán	名	vulvovaginitis
阴道	yīndào	名	vagina
瘙痒	sàoyǎng	形	pruritic
更换	gēnghuàn	动	replace；change
白带	báidài	名	leucorrhea；vaginal discharge
红肿	hóngzhǒng	形	red and swollen
稠厚	chóuhòu	形	thick
豆渣	dòuzhā	名	bean dregs
臭味	chòuwèi	名	foul smell
类似的	lèisìde	形	similar
妇科	fùkē	名	gynaecology
进一步	jìnyībù	副	more；further
黏膜	niánmó	名	mucosa
霉菌	méijūn	名	fungus；fungi
菌丝	jūnsī	名	hyphae
孢子	bāozǐ	名	spore
外阴阴道假丝酵母菌病	wàiyīnyīndàojiǎsījiàomǔjūnbìng	名	vulvovaginal candidiasis；
氟康唑	fúkāngzuò	名	fluconazole
仅	jǐn	副	only；merely
克霉唑	kèméizuò	名	clotrimazole
阴道栓	yīndàoshuān	名	vaginal suppository
塞	sāi	动	stuff，fill in
传播	chuánbō	动	spread；transmit

地点：妇科门诊
人物：王刚（主治医师）
　　　张洁（病人，女，31岁，已婚）

王医生　张女士，您好，我是您的主治医师王刚。

张　洁　王医生，您好！

王医生　请问您哪儿不舒服？

张　洁　我觉得"下面"很痒。

王医生　您的意思是**阴道瘙痒**，对吗？

张　洁　是的。阴道里面很痒。

王医生　请问您这样不舒服有多长时间了？

张　洁　两天前开始的，这两天越来越厉害了！

王医生　您觉得这次不舒服的原因是什么？比如最近有没有**更换**过卫生巾品牌？有没有性生活？

张　洁　哦，两天前和老公"在一起"后才这样的。

王医生　除了阴道瘙痒外，还有其他不舒服的吗？比如**白带**异常、外阴疼痛、**红肿**、尿频、尿痛等。

张　洁　白带也不太正常。

王医生　怎么不正常？

张　洁　白带量很多，白色的，**稠厚**，像**豆渣**，没有**臭味**。

王医生　您以前有过**类似的情况**吗？

张　洁　以前身体不好的时候或劳累后、月经后，甚至旅游以后，也会出现阴道瘙痒，但这次痒得比较厉害。

王医生　以前看过医生吗？做过什么治疗没有？

张　洁　看过。医生诊断是阴道炎，哪一种类型的阴道炎我记不清了，用过阴道内用药物，后来好起来了，就没有去医院复查。

王医生　您这次去其他医院检查或治疗过吗？

张　洁　没有。

王医生　张女士，请您跟我到检查室做**妇科**检查和白带常规检验，等检查结果出来再进行**进一步**的治疗。

张　洁　好的。

　　　（检查完成后）

王医生　您好，张女士。妇科检查发现您的阴道**黏膜**充血比较明显，阴道内有大量的白色豆渣样白带。阴道瘙痒伴随白带异常，是阴道炎症的临床表现。现在我们会进行白带常规的检查，根据检查结果进一步明确诊断，再进行治疗。

张　洁　好的。谢谢您，王医生。

　　　（白带检查结果见到大量**霉菌菌丝**及**孢子**生长）

王医生　张女士，您的白带检查结果出来了。您得的是**外阴阴道假丝酵母菌病**，是阴道炎的一种。

张　洁　请问我应该怎么治疗？

王医生　我给您开两种药物。一种是**氟康唑**片，口服，每天两次，每次两片，**仅**服用一天；另一种是**克霉唑阴道栓**，每天塞阴道一粒，连用7天。

张　洁　谢谢医生，还有什么要注意的吗？

王医生　请您用药两周后到医院复查。另外，阴道炎可能通过性生活**传播**，所以建议您的丈夫也到泌尿外科检查检查。

张　洁　好的，我明白了。谢谢王医生，再见。

王医生　再见。

Vulvovaginitis

SITE: Gynecology Clinic Consulting Room

CHARACTERS: Wang Gang (Attending physician)

Zhang Jie (Patient, female, 31 years old, married)

Dr. Wang: Good morning, Ms. Zhang. I am Dr. Wang Gang.

Zhang Jie: Good morning, Dr. Wang!

Dr. Wang: Are you feeling unwell?

Zhang Jie: I have itchiness "down there".

Dr. Wang: Do you mean vaginal pruritus?

Zhang Jie: Oh, it is. My vagina is quite itchy.

Dr. Wang: Could you tell me how long have you had the symptom like this?

Zhang Jie: It started two days ago. The itchiness worsened in the past two days!

Dr. Wang: What do you think of the possible causes? Have you changed the brand of sanitary pads recently? Have you been sexually active?

Zhang Jie: Oh, it started after I had been together with my husband two days ago.

Dr. Wang: Do you have any other discomfort, such as abnormal vaginal discharge, vulvar pain, redness and swelling, frequent or painful urination, etc. in addition to vaginal itching?

Zhang Jie: I have abnormal vaginal discharge.

Dr. Wang: Could you tell me about your vaginal discharge in detail?

Zhang Jie: There's an increasing amount of thick, white and no foul smell vaginal discharge, like bean dregs.

Dr. Wang: Did you ever have any similar conditions?

Zhang Jie: I had vaginal itching before when I was ill, tired, after menstruation, even after travel. But this time it's more severe than before.

Dr. Wang: What was your diagnosis in the past? Did you receive any treatment?

Zhang Jie: The doctor's diagnosis was vaginitis and I cannot recall which type of vaginitis it is. I only remember having taken vaginal medication before I got better. I didn't go to the hospital for follow-up.

Dr. Wang: Did you go to other hospitals for examination or treatment?

Zhang Jie: No, I didn't.

Dr. Wang: Ms. Zhang, please follow us to the inspection chamber for gynecologic evaluation, and then we'll take a routine vaginal discharge test. Wait for the results before further diagnoses and treatment.

Zhang Jie: Okay.

(After physical examination)

Dr. Wang: Hello, Mrs. Zhang. The physical examination shows significant mucosal congestion, and indeed generous amount of white cottage cheese-like vaginal discharge. Vaginal pruritus and discharge are consistent with the clinical manifestations of vaginitis. Now we will proceed to take routine vaginal discharge test. A definitive diagnosis and treatment plan will be made according to the test results.

Zhang Jie: Okay. Thank you, Dr. Wang.

(Discharge test shows abundant fungal hyphae and spores.)

Dr. Wang: Ms. Zhang, I've got your lab test results. According to your clinical manifestations and routine discharge test results, the primary diagnosis is vulvovaginal candidiasis, a type of vaginitis.

Zhang Jie: What's the treatment for me?

Dr. Wang: I will prescribe two medications for you. One is fluconazole, two tablets each time, twice orally a day only for one day. Another is clotrimazole vaginal suppository, one of which is put into your vagina every day for 7 days.

Zhang Jie: Thank you, doctor. Is there anything else I should pay attention to?

Dr. Wang: Come to the hospital after 2 weeks for follow-up. Also, vaginitis can be sexually transmitted, so I advise your husband to have a checkup in the Urology Department.

Zhang Jie: I see. Thank you, Dr. Wang. Goodbye.

Dr. Wang: Goodbye.

外阴阴道炎
wàiyīnyīndàoyán

外阴 及 阴道 炎症 是 妇科 最 常见 疾病，各 年龄组 均可 发病。外阴、阴道 与 尿道 和 肛门 邻近，局部 潮湿，易受 污染；生育 年龄 妇女 性 生活 频繁，且 外阴阴道 是 分娩、宫腔 操作 的 必经 之 路，容易 受到 损伤 及 外界 病原体 的 感染；绝经 后 妇女 及 婴幼儿 雌激素 水平 低，局部 抵抗力 下降，也 容易 发生 感染。外阴 及 阴道 炎症 可 单独 存在，也 可 两者 同时 存在。

Vulvovaginitis

Vulvovaginitis is the most common gynecologic disease, which can manifest in any age groups. Vulva and vagina are near the urethra and anus, partially damp, and susceptible to contamination; women of reproductive age are sexually active, and vulva and vagina are the route of delivery and uterine cavity operation, which are vulnerable to damage and infection with external pathogens; postmenopausal women and children have low estrogen levels and are prone to infection due to the weakened local defenses. Vulvar and vaginal inflammation can occur individually, or simultaneously.

1. 下面

中国人往往比较含蓄地用"下面"这个词来表达女性外生殖器。

Chinese people often use the phrase "下面" to implicitly refer to the female genitals, e.g. 我"下面"很痒。

2. ……得很

"adj.+ 得很"表示程度高。

It expresses a high degree of sth., e.g. 疼得很。

3. 越来越……

常用在形容词前，也可以用在某些动词前，表示程度随时间的推移而增加。

It means "the more …the more…", usually used before an adjective, and also before some verbs to show waxing degree as the time goes on, e.g. 治疗效果越来越好。

4. 在一起

中国人往往比较含蓄地用"在一起"来表达性交。

Chinese people often use the phrase "在一起" to implicitly refer to sexual intercourse, e.g. 我和他很久没有"在一起"了。

 **先 兆 流 产**

先兆流产	xiānzhàoliúchǎn	名	threatened abortion
停经	tíngjīng	动	menopause, suppressed menstruation, amenorrhea
一阵一阵	yízhènyízhèn	副	intermittently
化验	huàyàn	动	test
黄体酮	huángtǐtóng	名	progesterone
保胎	bǎotāi	名	tocolysis
初产妇	chūchǎnfù	名	primipara
趋势	qūshì	名	tendency
区别	qūbié	动	differ, distinguish
流产	liúchǎn	名	abortion
异位妊娠	yìwèirènshēn	名	ectopic pregnancy
鉴别	jiànbié	动	differentiate, identify

地点:妇产科病房
人物:王刚(主治医师)
　　　赵敏(实习医生)
　　　李萍(病人,女,31 岁,已婚)

赵医生　您好,我是实习医生赵敏。我需要详细了解一下您的病史。

李　萍　您好。我是昨天突然感到肚子痛,还有阴道流血,到急诊室看病,被诊断为**先兆流产**,所以住院的。

赵医生　请问您最后一次月经是什么时候?

李　萍　2016 年 4 月 20 日。

赵医生　嗯,那么您现在应该是**停经** 65 天。能详细讲下肚子痛的情况吗?

李　萍　好的,我前天上班后有点累,昨天开始觉得肚子有点疼,但不是很厉害,隐隐地痛,**一阵一阵**地。到医院时,肚子痛没有加重,但也没有好起来。

赵医生　阴道流血的情况呢?

李　萍　肚子痛以后,就出现了阴道流血,量不多,鲜红色,到医院时,流血就停止了。

赵医生　除了阴道流血和腹痛外,还有其他不舒服吗? 比如发烧,拉肚子等。

李　萍　没有。

赵医生　请问您以前怀孕过吗?

李　萍　没有,这是我第一次怀孕。

赵医生　您到医院后,都做了哪些检查?

李　萍　在急诊室做了妇科检查、血液检查,还做了超声检查。

赵医生　住院后,您用过什么药吗?

李　萍　住院后医生让我卧床休息,还给我打了**黄体酮针保胎**。

赵医生　您现在感觉怎么样?

李　萍　哦,现在好多了。肚子也不痛了,也不流血了。

赵医生　好的,祝您早日康复。

李　萍　谢谢!

（医生办公室）

赵医生　王老师,这个病人是**初产妇**,末次月经 2016 年 4 月 20 日,目前停经 65 天,昨天在劳累后出现下腹痛伴有阴道流血。下腹痛为阵发性,不剧烈,没有加重**趋势**。阴道流血量少,鲜红色。到急诊室就诊,经过妇科检查、血液**化验**和超声检查后,初步诊断为先兆流产,并收住院。入院后,经过卧床休息、肌注黄体酮后,腹痛消失、阴道出血停止,目前病情稳定。

王医生　很好。流产的主要临床表现为停经后腹痛和阴道流血。通过病史、临床表现、体格检查,再结合辅助检查来**区别流产**的类型,进行初步诊断。同时,需要**与异位妊娠**等疾病进行**鉴别诊断**。

Threatened Abortion

SITE:　Maternity Ward

CHARACTERS:　Wang Gang (Attending physician)

Zhao Min (Intern student)

Li Ping (Patient, female, 31 years old, married)

Dr. Zhao:　Good morning, I am an intern, Dr. Zhao Min. Dr. Wang sent me to ask for a complete medical history.

Li Ping:　Good morning. Yesterday I felt a sudden pain in my belly and had vaginal bleeding. I went to the emergency room and was diagnosed as threatened abortion, so I was hospitalized.

Dr. Zhao:　When was your last menstrual period?

Li Ping:　April 20th, 2016

Dr. Zhao:　Oh, so you've had amenorrhea for 65 days. Could you tell me in detail?

Li Ping:　Well, I was a bit tired after work the day before yesterday and I have been feeling a pain in my lower abdomen since yesterday, but it was not severe, and it was a dull pain that occurred intermittently. When I arrived at the hospital, neither did it worsen nor alleviate.

Dr. Zhao:　What about the vaginal bleeding?

Li Ping:　After the abdominal pain, vaginal bleeding followed in small quantity, which looked bright red. The bleeding stopped after my arriving at the hospital.

Dr. Zhao:　Do you have any complaints other than vaginal bleeding and abdominal pain such as fever, diarrhea, etc.?

Li Ping:　No, I have nothing else.

Dr. Zhao:　Were you pregnant before?

Li Ping:　No, this is my first pregnancy.

Dr. Zhao:　What examinations did you take after you came to the hospital?

Li Ping:　I had gynecologic examination in the E.R, blood test, and also ultrasound.

Dr. Zhao:　Did you take any medications after being hospitalized?

Li Ping:　Yes, I did. In the wards the doctor told me to stay in bed and injected me with progesterone for tocolysis.

Dr. Zhao: So how are you feeling now?

Li Ping: Oh, much better now. The abdominal pain is gone, and there isn't vaginal bleeding any more.

Dr. Zhao: Alright, get well soon.

Li Ping: Thanks.

(Director's Office)

Dr. Zhao: Teacher Wang, this is a primipara, LMP on April 20th, 2016, amenorrhea for 65 days, presented with a lower abdominal pain accompanied by vaginal bleeding yesterday. The lower abdominal pain was intermittent, not intense, with no aggravation. The vaginal bleeding was in a small amount and looked bright red. After gynecologic examination, blood tests and ultrasound at the ER, primary diagnosis was threatened abortion, and she was admitted immediately. With bed rest and treatment with progesterone, she is currently stable, without lower abdominal pain and the vaginal bleeding have not recurred.

Dr. Wang: That's good. The main clinical manifestations of miscarriage are post-amenorrheal abdominal pain and vaginal bleeding. The type of abortion can be distinguished and the primary diagnosis can be made based on the medical history, clinical manifestations, physical examination, along with supplementary examinations. It also needs to be differentiated from other diseases, like ectopic pregnancy.

疾病介绍

先兆流产

妊娠 不足 28 周、胎儿 体重 不足 1000 克而 终止 妊娠 称为流产，妊娠 12 周末 前 终止 称为 早期 流产，妊娠 13 周 至 不足 28 周 终止 称为 晚期 流产。妊娠 20 周 至 不足 28 周间 流产、体重 在 500 克 至 1000 克 之间、有 存活 可能 的 胎儿，称为 有生机儿。因此，美国 把 孕 20 周 前 终止 妊娠 定义 为 流产。先兆流产 表现 为 停经 后 出现 少量 阴道 流血，常 为 暗红色 或 血性 白带，流血 后 数小时 至 数日 可 出现 轻微 下腹痛 或 腰骶部 胀痛；宫颈口 未开，无 妊娠物 排出；子宫 大小 与 停经 时间 相 符合。经 休息 及 治疗，症状 消失，可 继续 妊娠。如 症状 加重，难免 流产。

Threatened Abortion

Abortion is the termination of pregnancy before 28 weeks of gestation or the fetal weight is less than 1000g. Early abortion refers to termination of pregnancy before 12 weeks of gestation and late abortion refers to termination of pregnancy between 13 and 28 weeks of gestation. Fetuses are viable when the abortion occurs between 20 and 28 weeks of gestation, weighting between 500g and 1000g, and have chance of survival. Therefore, the United States defines abortion as termination of pregnancy before 20 weeks of gestation. Threatened abortion manifests as scant vaginal bleeding after amenorrhea, usually dark red or bloody discharge. There may be slight lower abdominal or lumbosacral pain hours or days after the bleeding; the cervix is not dilated and there is no passage of products of conception; uterus size is consistent with duration of amenorrhea. The symptoms disappear after rest and treatment, and the pregnancy may continue. Aggravation of symptoms may lead to inevitable abortion.

语言点

1. 末次月经

"末次月经"指最后一次月经来潮的第一天时间。一般妊娠妇女的预产期和孕龄都是根据末次月经来计算的。

It refers to the first day of the last menstrual period. The expected date of confinement for pregnant women and the gestational age are calculated based on the last menstrual period, e.g. 请问您末次月经是什么时候？

2. 好多了（adj.+ 多了）

"多了"用在形容词后,表示程度高。

It is used after an adjective to express a higher degree, e.g. 我觉得肚子痛好多了。

➤ 听力练习

一、听录音,选择你听到的词语

( )1. A. 阴道　　　　B. 阴暗　　　　C. 阴雨　　　　D. 阴唇
( )2. A. 里面　　　　B. 下面　　　　C. 面条　　　　D. 上面
( )3. A. 白色　　　　B. 白带　　　　C. 白云　　　　D. 白斑
( )4. A. 性病　　　　B. 性别　　　　C. 性格　　　　D. 性交
( )5. A. 超人　　　　B. 超声　　　　C. 超车　　　　D. 超级
( )6. A. 流星　　　　B. 流行　　　　C. 流产　　　　D. 流血
( )7. A. 停下　　　　B. 停止　　　　C. 停经　　　　D. 停车
( )8. A. 前途　　　　B. 前面　　　　C. 前进　　　　D. 前天
( )9. A. 妇科检查　　B. 产科检查　　C. 阴道检查　　D. 腹部检查
( )10. A. 异位妊娠　　B. 宫颈妊娠　　C. 早期妊娠　　D. 初次妊娠

二、请选出与所听录音相符的答案

( )1. A. 在病人家里　　B. 在医生家里　　C. 在医院住院部　　D. 在医院门诊部
( )2. A. 双脚　　　　　B. 双腿　　　　　C. 腹部　　　　　　D. 阴道
( )3. A. 白带　　　　　B. 出血　　　　　C. 大便　　　　　　D. 小便
( )4. A. 做相关的检查　　　　　　　　　B. 直接进行治疗
　　　 C. 把病人转诊给其他医院　　　　　D. 参考其他医院的检查结果
( )5. A. 妇科检查—白带检验—诊断治疗　　B. 诊断治疗—白带检验—妇科检查
　　　 C. 白带检验—诊断治疗—妇科检查　　D. 诊断治疗—妇科检查—白带检验

三、听录音,完成下面的练习

1. 根据所听到的录音判断对错

1) 这个病人发生阴道炎是第一次。(　　)
2) 这个病人这次发生阴道炎的症状比上次要厉害。(　　)
3) 这个病人这次发病原因是和老公性交过。(　　)
4) 这个病人这次发病不想做检查。(　　)

5) 这个病人上次发病治疗方法是口服药。（　　）
2. 听录音,选择正确答案回答问题
1) 病人主要因为什么来看病？（　　）
　　A. 阴道瘙痒　　　　B. 白带增多　　　C. 尿频尿痛　　　D. 外阴疼痛
2) 病人什么时候开始出现不舒服的？（　　）
　　A. 一天前　　　　B. 两天前　　　C. 三天前　　　D. 一周前
3) 病人出现阴道瘙痒的原因是什么？（　　）
　　A. 游泳　　　　B. 更换卫生巾　　　C. 性交　　　D. 做过妇科手术
4) 对病人妇科检查可能发现的体征,**除了**（　　）
　　A. 阴道大量出血　　　　　　　B. 阴道黏膜充血
　　C. 外阴皮肤抓痕　　　　　　　D. 阴道内分泌物增多
5) 对这个病人的初步诊断,首先考虑的是（　　）
　　A. 阴道炎　　　B. 子宫肌瘤　　　C. 盆腔炎　　　D. 先兆流产

➢ 词汇和语法练习
一、给下列词语标注拼音
1. 白带常规＿＿＿＿＿＿＿＿　　　2. 瘙痒＿＿＿＿＿＿＿＿
3. 卫生巾＿＿＿＿＿＿＿＿　　　4. 阴道炎症＿＿＿＿＿＿＿＿
5. 外阴阴道假丝酵母菌病＿＿＿＿＿　　6. 停经＿＿＿＿＿＿＿＿
7. 怀孕＿＿＿＿＿＿＿＿　　　8. 黄体酮＿＿＿＿＿＿＿＿
9. 初产妇＿＿＿＿＿＿＿＿　　　10. 异位妊娠＿＿＿＿＿＿＿＿
二、选词填空

| 尿频尿痛　性生活　阴道炎　豆渣　妇科检查 |
| 急诊室　先兆流产　隐隐地　黄体酮　早日康复 |

1. 前天我出现阴道瘙痒症状,到医院检查,结果诊断是＿＿＿＿＿＿＿。
2. 医生告诉我在治疗阴道炎期间,不能＿＿＿＿＿＿＿。
3. 医生说如果阴道炎合并有＿＿＿＿＿＿＿症状,要排除泌尿系统感染。
4. 这两天白带很不好,虽然没有臭味,但量很多,像＿＿＿＿＿＿＿。
5. 如果发生妇科疾病,＿＿＿＿＿＿＿是必要的检查方法之一。
6. 现在我怀孕60天,昨天开始阴道流血,经过检查,医生诊断我是＿＿＿＿＿＿＿。
7. 我现在在住院治疗,医生给我用的药是＿＿＿＿＿＿＿。
8. 医生,我肚子痛得不是很厉害,是那种＿＿＿＿＿＿＿痛。
9. 请按照医生的话按时服药,祝您＿＿＿＿＿＿＿。
10. 昨晚我发高烧了,到＿＿＿＿＿＿＿去看病。
三、用指定的词语或结构完成句子或对话
1. 昨天她开始出现阴道瘙痒不舒服,＿＿＿＿＿＿＿。（越来越……）
2. ＿＿＿＿＿＿＿,医生,能不能赶快给我开点止痛药。（……得很）
3. 这里有阳光、大海、沙滩、绿树,像一幅画一样,＿＿＿＿＿＿＿。（……极了）
4. ＿＿＿＿＿＿＿,但他仍然不愿意到医院看病。（根据……初步诊断为……）
5. 我给您开了这种药物,＿＿＿＿＿＿＿,请按时服药。（每天……,每次……）
6. 医生,经过您的治疗,＿＿＿＿＿＿＿。（……多了）
7. 医生,我现在很不舒服,＿＿＿＿＿＿＿。（除了……,还……）
8. 这个病人的临床表现,除了要考虑先兆流产,＿＿＿＿＿＿＿。（鉴别）

9. _____,肯定是怀孕了！（停经）

10. 经过治疗,她目前病情很稳定,_____。（没有……,也没有……）

四、选择句子完成对话

A. 到医院检查过吗

B. 以前有过类似的情况吗

C. 当时并不严重

D. 还有什么其他症状

E. 然后再做一些化验

医生：您觉得阴道瘙痒是什么时候开始的?

病人：一周前和老公同房后开始的,___1___。

医生：___2___?

病人：以前身体劳累的时候,也有过几次。

医生：___3___?

病人：这次没有去过医院。

医生：除了阴道瘙痒外,___4___?

病人：嗯,还有白带增多。

医生：那我先给您做个妇科检查,___5___,再进一步治疗,好吗?

病人：好的,谢谢!

五、排列下列句子的顺序

(   )A. 主要表现为白色稠厚的白带增多,像豆渣,没有臭味。

(   )B. 未到其他医院检查和治疗。

(   )C. 不伴有外阴疼痛和红肿,也没有尿频、尿痛的表现。

(   )D. 病人2天前性交后出现阴道瘙痒的症状,

(   )E. 伴随有白带异常,

六、把下列词语排列成句子

1. 阴道 瘙痒得 越来越 病人 厉害

2. 检查结果 根据 诊断为 阴道炎 初步

3. 出现过 以前 类似的 情况 病人

4. 最近 有没有 卫生巾 更换 过

5. 阴道 黏膜 病人 充血 很明显

6. 末次月经 您 的 是 什么时候

7. 做了 检查 哪些 您 都

8. 给 医生 保胎 黄体酮 用 我

9. 辅助检查 通过 异位妊娠 鉴别 来

10. 劳累后 伴随 下腹痛 阴道流血 出现

➤ **阅读与应用练习**

一、根据课文内容补全对话

(一) 病人： 医生,我这几天___1___瘙痒很厉害。

　　　医生： 那您觉得是什么原因哪?

　　　病人： 两天前和老公___2___后开始的。

　　　医生： 除了阴道瘙痒,有没有___3___异常。

　　　病人： 量多,稠厚,像___4___,还有异味。

　　　医生： 那您有没有到医院___5___过。

病人： 没有。

医生： 根据刚刚检查的结果,初步诊断为__6__。

(二)病人： 我昨晚因为肚子痛,还有__7__到急诊室看病。

医生： 当时急诊的诊断是什么?

病人： 当时诊断我是__8__。

医生： 那你看好急诊后,一定是__9__治疗了。

病人： 对的,医生给我做了妇科检查,化验了血,还做了__10__检查,然后住院的。

医生： 住院后用了哪些药物?

病人： 我打了__11__保胎。

医生： 那祝您__12__!

二、根据课文内容回答问题

1. 张洁患阴道炎的主要临床表现是什么? 发病原因是什么?

2. 张洁患阴道炎后白带的性状是怎样的?

3. 根据课文,请问外阴阴道假丝酵母菌病的治疗方案是什么?

4. 请问在阴道炎治疗方面的注意事项有哪些?

5. 请问先兆流产的症状有哪些?

6. 根据课文,诊断先兆流产前,医生一般需要做哪些检查?

7. 根据课文,先兆流产的治疗方案有哪些?

8. 先兆流产主要与哪种疾病相鉴别?

三、写作练习

根据第一篇会话内容,写出一篇字数不少于 60 个字的概述,简单介绍病人临床表现和诊断治疗情况。

四、交际练习

根据括号里的词语进行场景对话。

(腹痛,阴道流血,停经,超声,先兆流产,住院,药物治疗,病情稳定)

子宫肌瘤

词汇

子宫肌瘤	zǐgōngjīliú	名	uterine myoma
经量增多	jīngliàngzēngduō	名	excessive menstruation
周期	zhōuqī	名	cycle
分娩	fēnmiǎn	名	delivery
剖宫产	pōugōngchǎn	名	caesarean section
肿块	zhǒngkuài	名	mass；lump
肌壁间肌瘤	jībìjiānjīliú	名	intramural myoma
生育年龄	shēngyùniánlíng	名	reproductive age
雌激素	cíjīsù	名	estrogen
绝经	juéjīng	名	menopause
消退	xiāotuì	动	regress
微创手术	wēichuàngshǒushù	名	minimally invasive surgery
二胎	èrtāi	名	second child
琥珀酸亚铁	hǔpòsuānyàtiě	名	ferrous succinate
诊断性刮宫	zhěnduànxìngguāgōng	名	diagnostic curettage
宫颈刮片	gōngjǐngguāpiàn	名	cervical smear
细胞学检查	xìbāoxuéjiǎnchá	名	cytological examination

地点：妇科门诊
人物：刘医生（主任医师）
　　　王婷（病人，女，33 岁）

王　婷　大夫，我最近几个月的月经不规律，**经量增多**，经期很长。
刘医生　您经期大概多长时间？
王　婷　10 天左右。
刘医生　月经**周期**多少天？
王　婷　大概 22 天。
刘医生　您这属于月经周期缩短。还有其他症状吗？
王　婷　我还经常感觉头晕、乏力。

刘医生	我看您的脸色有些苍白,好像贫血。这些症状有多长时间了?
王 婷	大概也有半年了。
刘医生	您结婚了吗? 有几个孩子?
王 婷	结婚了。有一个男孩,5 岁。
刘医生	您是阴道**分娩**还是**剖宫产**?
王 婷	阴道分娩。
刘医生	您做过手术吗?
王 婷	没有。
刘医生	抽烟、喝酒吗?
王 婷	我不抽烟,也不喝酒。
刘医生	嗯,以前去医院检查过吗?
王 婷	没有。
刘医生	为了进一步明确诊断,您先去做个妇科 B 超和血常规检查。
	(1 小时后,病人拿着检查结果回来。)
王 婷	刘医生,这是我的检查结果。
刘医生	让我看看,B 超显示您有子宫**肿块**。根据临床表现及超声检查结果,首先考虑为子宫肌瘤。只有一个肌瘤,大小为 6.6cm × 6.2cm,而且超声显示肌瘤位置不好,是**肌壁间肌瘤**。血常规显示您的血红蛋白为 82g/L,属于中度贫血。
王 婷	啊! 我怎么会长子宫肌瘤呢?
刘医生	子宫肌瘤常见于**生育年龄**妇女,可能与女性的**雌激素**水平有关系,**绝经**后可以萎缩或**消退**。
王 婷	我这病应该怎么治疗呢?
刘医生	我建议您尽快做肌瘤切除术。
王 婷	刘医生,我害怕做手术。可以吃药保守治疗吗?
刘医生	您的肌瘤这么大,症状又这么明显,吃药意义不大,手术是最好的办法。您可以选择剖腹手术,也可以选择腹腔镜下肌瘤切除术。
王 婷	腹腔镜下肌瘤切除属于**微创手术**吗?
刘医生	是的。
王 婷	刘医生,我打算生**二胎**,肌瘤切除后会影响生育吗?
刘医生	恢复良好的话对生育影响不大。
王 婷	那我什么时候可以要孩子呢?
刘医生	这要根据术中情况才能确定。手术后再给您最佳妊娠时间的建议。
王 婷	好的。顺便问一下,如果做肌瘤切除术,我需要做什么准备吗?
刘医生	手术前,您可以先口服一些补血药物纠正贫血,如硫酸亚铁,**琥珀酸亚铁**等。
王 婷	需要服多久?
刘医生	术前治疗 1~2 个月就可以了。
王 婷	好的,手术前我还用做其他检查吗?
刘医生	是的,您还需要做**诊断性刮宫**和**宫颈刮片细胞学检查**,排除子宫的恶性病变。
王 婷	大夫,手术后,我的子宫肌瘤还会复发吗?
刘医生	这个不好说,子宫肌瘤有一定的复发几率。
王 婷	好的,我明白了。谢谢刘医生。

Uterine Myoma

SITE:　Gynecology Clinic

CHARACTERS: Doctor Liu (Chief physician)

                 Wang Ting (Patient, female, 33 years old)

Wang Ting: Doctor, I have been experiencing irregular menses with excessive menstruation and prolonged periods in recent months.

Dr. Liu: How long is your period?

Wang Ting: About 10 days.

Dr. Liu: How long is your menstrual cycle?

Wang Ting: About 22 days.

Dr. Liu: Your menstrual cycle is shortened. Do you have other symptoms?

Wang Ting: I usually feel dizzy and fatigued.

Dr. Liu: You look pale and anemic. How long have you had these symptoms?

Wang Ting: About half a year.

Dr. Liu: Did you get married? How many children do you have?

Wang Ting: Yes, I did and have one child, 5-year-old boy.

Dr. Liu: Did you have a vaginal delivery or a caesarean section?

Wang Ting: I had the former.

Dr. Liu: Did you have the history of surgery?

Wang Ting: No, I didn't.

Dr. Liu: Do you smoke or drink alcohol?

Wang Ting: No, I do neither of them.

Dr. Liu: Oh, did you go to hospital for a check-up?

Wang Ting: No, I didn't.

Dr. Liu: First, you need have gynecologic ultrasonography and then take the blood routine test for diagnosis. (An hour later, the patient comes back with all the examination results)

Wang Ting: Doctor Liu, here are my examination results.

Dr. Liu: Let me see. The gynecologic ultrasonography shows that you have a uterine mass. Uterine myoma is first considered based on your clinical manifestation and the results of ultrasonography. You have only one myoma, with the size of 6.6cm × 6.2cm. It is an intramural myoma, the location of which is not good. Your blood routine test shows your Hb is 82g/L and you suffer from moderate anemia.

Wang Ting: Ah! What causes uterine myoma?

Dr. Liu: It often occurs in woman of reproductive age. It may be related to the levels of estrogen, usually shrinking or regressing after menopause.

Wang Ting: How to treat it?

Dr. Liu: I suggest you should accept myomectomy as soon as possible.

Wang Ting: Doctor Liu, I am afraid of operation. Can I have conservative therapy by taking some medicine?

Dr. Liu: At present, your myoma is very big with apparent symptoms, so medication doesn't work. Surgery is optimal. You can choose laparotomy or laparoscopic myomectomy.

Wang Ting: Does laparoscopic myomectomy belong to minimally invasive surgery?

Dr. Liu: Yes.

Wang Ting: Doctor Liu, I plan to have a second child. Will this myomectomy affect reproduction?

Dr. Liu: This will have little influence on reproduction if you get fully recovered.

Wang Ting: When can I be pregnant?

Dr. Liu: I will give you suggestions about the best time for pregnancy based on the surgery.

Wang Ting: Ok. By the way, what can I prepare if I accept myomectomy?

Dr. Liu: You can take oral antianemia drugs such as ferrous sulfate or ferrous succinate to correct anemia.

Wang Ting: How long should I take the medicine?

Dr. Liu: One to two months before the surgery.

Wang Ting: Ok. Do I need other examination besides the drugs?

Dr. Liu: Yes, you need do diagnostic curettage, cervical smear and cytological examination to exclude malignant diseases of uterus.

Wang Ting: Doctor, is there any possibility that the uterine myoma will recur after myomectomy?

Dr. Liu: It's hard to say and there is some possibility.

Wang Ting: Ok. I see. Thank you, Doctor Liu.

疾病介绍

子宫肌瘤
zǐgōngjīliú

子宫肌瘤是女性最常见的良性肿瘤，主要包括肌壁间肌瘤、浆膜下肌瘤和黏膜下肌瘤。子宫肌瘤可以是一个，也可以是多个。子宫肌瘤的确切病因尚不明确，但由于肌瘤主要常见于生育年龄，尤其是30岁以上的妇女，绝经后会萎缩或消退。因此其发生可能与女性雌激素水平有关。有些研究显示，子宫肌瘤也与遗传因素有关。子宫肌瘤多无明显症状，通常在体检时偶然发现，但有些肌瘤会出现明显症状，如经量增多、经期延长、下腹包块、白带增多、尿频、便秘、腹痛等，有些会导致贫血或不育。子宫肌瘤可以根据病史和体征进行诊断，也可以通过B超、MRI、宫腔镜、腹腔镜等协助诊断。治疗应根据病人症状、年龄、生育要求进行。无症状或症状轻的，一般不需要治疗，随访观察即可；症状明显的，可根据肌瘤大小、数量、位置等具体情况，采用肌瘤切除术或子宫切除术。

Uterine Myoma

Uterine myoma is the most common benign tumor in women mainly including intramural myoma, subserous myoma and submucous myoma. There can either be one myoma or many small ones. There is no definite known cause of uterine myoma, but the levels of estrogen may contribute to its development because uterine myoma often occurs in women of reproductive age, more common in women over the age of 30 and shrinks or regresses after menopause. What's more, some studies show that genetic factors can also lead to uterine myoma. In most cases, uterine myoma does not produce any obvious symptoms, often being detected incidentally during a routine physical examination. But some myomas can produce obvious symptoms, such as excessive menstruation, prolonged periods, abdominal lump, leukorrhagia, frequency of urination, constipation and abdominal pain. Some can lead to anemia or infertility. Diagnosis can be made by medical history and physical signs. B-ultrasound, MRI, hysteroscope, laparoscope can also be applied to help make diagnosis. The treatments can depend on the patient's symptoms, age, childbearing plans. If there is no symptom or few symptoms, the patients need follow-up observation with no treatments. If the symptoms are obvious, the myomectomy or hysterectomy can be considered based on the size, number and location of the myoma.

1. 是……还是

用于询问, 表示选择。

It is used to make a choice, e.g. 您是阴道分娩还是剖宫产?

2. 最好

"最好" 用在动词前, 表示建议。

It is used in front of verbs, implying a suggestion or advice, e.g.

最好做肌瘤切除术。

3. 动词重叠

动词重叠表示动作经历的时间短促或轻松、随便, 有时也表示尝试。

Some verbs can be reduplicated to show short duration or ease and casualness of an act, and sometimes they mean to have a try. The reduplication form of a monosyllabic verb is "AA" and that of a disyllabic verb "ABAB", e.g. ①我想听听音乐; ②大家一起来讨论讨论这个病例。

盆 腔 炎

盆腔炎	pénqiāngyán	名	pelvic inflammatory disease
无痛人流	wútòngrénliú	名	painless abortion
间歇性的	jiànxiēxìngde	形	intermittent
抬举	táiju	动	lift
按	àn	动	press
双附件	shuāngfùjiàn	名	bilateral adnexal
增厚	zēnghòu	动	thicken
分泌物	fēnmìwù	名	secretion
宫腔内	gōngqiāngnèi	名	intrauterine
残留	cánliú	名	residue
检测	jiǎncè	动	detect
淋病奈瑟菌	lìnbìngnàisèjūn	名	gonococcus
沙眼衣原体	shāyǎnyīyuántǐ	名	*Chlamydia trachomatis*
后遗症	hòuyízhèng	名	sequela
不孕	búyùn	名	infertility
反复	fǎnfù	形	repeating
体位引流	tǐwèiyǐnliú	名	postural drainage

地点：妇科门诊
人物：刘医生（主任医师）
　　　李玟（病人，女，28 岁）

李　玟　　大夫，我 10 天前做了**无痛人流**，最近两天开始下腹痛，还发烧。

刘医生　　用消炎药了吗？发烧多少度？

李　玟　　没用过。38.5℃左右。

刘医生　　下腹痛是**间歇性的**疼痛还是持续性的疼痛？

李　玟　　持续性疼痛。

刘医生　　手术后有过性生活吗？

李　玟　　有过一次。

刘医生　　您还有别的症状吗？

李　玟　　没有了。

刘医生　　您以前做过手术吗？

李　玟　　没有。

刘医生　　您有药物过敏史吗？

李　玟　　也没有。

刘医生　　我先给您检查一下。您现在体温 38.8℃，血压 100/60mmHg，心率 101 次 / 分。请躺下！把下腹露出来，我这样逐渐深压下腹，您感觉痛吗？

李　玟　　哎呀，好痛！

刘医生　　我这样突然抬手，您觉得更疼了？

李　玟　　是的。

刘医生　　我现在给您做妇科检查，请把内裤脱下来。这样（**抬举**宫颈），痛吗？

李　玟　　痛。

刘医生　　您的子宫正常大小。这样（**按子宫**），痛吗？

李　玟　　痛。

刘医生　　**双附件稍增厚**。我按压的时候痛吗？

李　玟　　痛。

刘医生　　您有粉红色的阴道**分泌物**。好了，检查完了，请穿上衣服吧。

李　玟　　哦，我这是得了什么病？

刘医生　　我怀疑您是急性盆腔炎。您先去做一下血常规、妇科 B 超、阴道分泌物和宫颈管分泌物检查，以便进一步明确病因。

　　　　　（1 个小时后，病人带来了所有的检查结果）

刘医生　　把您的检查结果给我。血常规检查白细胞总数 15×10^9/L，中性粒细胞比例 83%。妇科 B 超显示**宫腔内未见残留**。阴道分泌物检查没有**检测出淋病奈瑟菌**，宫颈管分泌物检查没有检测**出沙眼衣原体**。

李　玟　　刘医生，我的病很严重吗？需要住院吗？

刘医生　　您别着急，不是特别严重，用不着住院。

李　玟　　太好了！那应该怎么治疗呢？

刘医生　　我给您开一些口服抗生素，回家按时服用就可以了。

李　玟　　好的。对了，刘医生，盆腔炎能彻底治愈吗？会影响我以后要宝宝吗？

刘医生　　大多数病人如果能及时、恰当地使用抗生素治疗就能彻底治愈，对以后生育影响不大。如果治疗不及时的话，就会引发后遗症。盆腔炎的**后遗症有不孕**、异位妊娠、慢性盆腔痛、盆腔炎**反复**发作等。

李 玟   这么严重呀！我一定积极配合医生治疗。还有其他的预防措施吗？

刘医生   您应该加强营养，保持**体位引流**，防止炎症波及上腹部，预防再次感染。

李 玟   知道了，谢谢刘医生。

Pelvic Inflammatory Disease（PID）

SITE: Gynecology Clinic

CHARACTERS: Doctor Liu (Chief physician)

Li Wen (Patient, female, 28 years old)

Li Wen: Dr. Liu, I had painless abortion 10 days ago, and I have a lower abdominal pain with a fever for two days.

Dr. Liu: Did you take any antibiotics after the abortion? What is your temperature?

Li Wen: No, I didn't. It's about 38.5℃.

Dr. Liu: Is your pain intermittent or durative?

Li Wen: It is durative.

Dr. Liu: Did you have sexual life after abortion?

Li Wen: Yes, I had once.

Dr. Liu: Do you have other symptoms?

Li Wen: No, I don't.

Dr. Liu: Did you undergo any surgery?

Li Wen: No, I didn't.

Dr. Liu: Did you have drug allergy history?

Li Wen: No, I didn't, either.

Dr. Liu: Now I'll give you physical examination. Your temperature is 38.8℃, your blood pressure is 100/60mmHg and your heart rate is 101bmp. Please lie down and unbutton your clothes. Do you feel painful when I gradually press deeply here (lower abdomen)?

Li Wen: Ow! I feel very painful.

Dr. Liu: Do you feel more painful when I raise my hand suddenly?

Li Wen: Yes, I do.

Dr. Liu: I'll carry out a gynecological examination for you. Please take off your underwear. Do you feel painful this way (when I lift your cervix)?

Li Wen: Yes, I do.

Dr. Liu: The size of your uterus is normal. Do you feel painful this way (when I press your uterus)?

Li Wen: Yes, I do.

Dr. Liu: Your bilateral adnexa are slightly thickened. Do you feel painful when I press them?

Li Wen: Yes, I do.

Dr. Liu: You have pink vaginal discharge. It is all right. I have finished checking, please put on your clothes.

Li Wen: What disease do I have?

Dr. Liu: I suspect you have got acute pelvic inflammatory disease(PID). You need to take blood routine test, gynecologic ultrasonography and the examinations of the cervix secretion and vaginal discharge to confirm the diagnosis.

(1 hour later, the patient brings all the examination results)

Dr. Lu: Give me your results, please. Your blood routine test shows that your WBC is 15×10^9/L, NEUTP 83%

and gynecologic ultrasonography shows that there is no intrauterine residue. Gonococcus is not detected in samples from vaginal discharge and CT DNA is not detected in samples from the cervix secretion, either.

Li Wen: Am I seriously ill, Doctor Liu? Need I be hospitalized?

Dr. Liu: Don't worry. It is not very serious. You needn't be hospitalized.

Li Wen: Great! And what treatment should I have?

Dr. Liu: I will prescribe some oral antibiotics for you, and you can take them at home on time.

Li Wen: Ok. By the way, doctor Liu. Can it be cured completely? Will it influence my having a baby?

Dr. Liu: Most patients can be cured by using antibiotics immediately and appropriately. It has little influence on your pregnancy, but it will lead to sequelae if not treated in time. PID sequelae contain infertility, ectopic pregnancy, chronic pelvic pain and recurrent bouts of PID.

Li Wen: It's so serious that I must positively cooperate with the doctor in the treatment. What other precautions should I take?

Dr. Liu: You are supposed to improve nutrition, keep postural drainage to prevent inflammation spreading to the upper abdomen and prevent reinfection.

Li Wen: I got it. Thank you, doctor Liu.

疾病介绍

盆腔炎

盆腔炎 是 女性 上 生殖道（子宫、输卵管、卵巢）的 感染，可能 引发 子宫内膜炎、输卵管炎、腹膜炎 等。盆腔炎 的 发病 原因 包括 妇科 手术、剖宫产、流产、宫内 避孕器 的 放置 及 经期 不卫生。急性 盆腔炎 一般 症状 为 下腹部 疼痛、白带 增多、脓性 白带，部分 病人 会 出现 高热、月经 不规律。查体 时，发现 宫体 及 附件区 有 压痛，有时 能 触及 压痛 包块，血常规 结果 显示 白细胞 计数 升高。根据 病史、症状、体征、妇科 检查，可 做出 初步 诊断。尽快 进行 治疗 可 降低 出现 盆腔炎 后遗症 的 可能性，如 不孕、异位妊娠、慢性 盆腔痛。病情 较轻 时 可 口服 抗生素，较重 时 可 采用 静脉 给药、脓肿 穿刺 引流、腹腔镜 下 手术 引流、切除 附件 或 子宫 等 个性化 处理。

Pelvic Inflammatory Disease

Pelvic inflammatory disease (PID) is an infection of the upper genital tract: uterus, fallopian tubes and ovaries, which can cause endometritis, salpingitis, peritonitis, etc. The factors leading to PID include gynecologic surgery, C-section, abortion, IUD insertion and unhygienic practices during menses. The common symptoms of acute PID are lower abdominal pain, leukorrhagia, purulent leucorrhea, and some patients with high fever and irregular menses. Bimanual examination demonstrates uterine tenderness, adnexal tenderness and occasional lump. Blood routine test shows that WBC is increased. Preliminary diagnosis can be made based on medical history, symptoms, physical signs and pelvic examination. Timely treatment can reduce the incidence of its sequelae (infertility, ectopic pregnancy, chronic pelvic pain). When the illness is slight, oral antibiotics can be taken. When the illness is serious, personalized treatments can be applied, such as intravenous antibiotics, puncture drainage for abscess, laparoscopic drainage, adnexectomy or hysterectomy.

语言点

1. 如果……，就……

"如果……"表示假设，"就"表示假设的结果。

The former is used to indicate an assumption in the first clause, and the latter is in the second clause indicating the result produced by the assumption, e.g. 如果盆腔炎治疗不及时的话，就会引发后遗症。

2. ……后遗症有……

"……后遗症有……"用来列举说明某种疾病、治疗或外伤带来的后遗症。如：

It is used to list sequelae resulting from a disease, therapy or trauma, e.g. 盆腔炎后遗症有不孕、异位妊娠、慢性盆腔痛等。

 练习

➤ **听力练习**

一、听录音，选择你听到的词语

( ) 1. A. 经历	B. 经量	C. 精良	D. 净量
( ) 2. A. 头晕	B. 头疼	C. 头沉	D. 头昏
( ) 3. A. 声音	B. 剩余	C. 生育	D. 培育
( ) 4. A. 复发	B. 继发	C. 开发	D. 诱发
( ) 5. A. 流动	B. 流产	C. 顺产	D. 人流
( ) 6. A. 综合征	B. 三联症	C. 后遗症	D. 腹痛症
( ) 7. A. 下腹痛	B. 上腹痛	C. 下部痛	D. 肚子痛
( ) 8. A. 顺产史	B. 助产士	C. 自然产	D. 剖宫产
( ) 9. A. 轻度贫血	B. 中度贫血	C. 重度贫血	D. 微度贫血
( ) 10. A. 子宫肌瘤	B. 子宫肿瘤	C. 平滑肌瘤	D. 子宫内膜

二、请选出与所听录音相符的答案

( ) 1. A. 月经不规律　　B. 经期较长　　C. 经常腹痛　　D. 经量增多

( ) 2. A. 吃药治疗　　B. 保守治疗　　C. 子宫切除术　　D. 肌瘤切除术

( ) 3. A. 肌瘤切除术后不会复发　　　　B. 肌瘤切除术后可能复发
　　　C. 肌瘤切除术后有后遗症　　　　D. 可以进行肌瘤切除术

( ) 4. A. 两天前做的人流手术　　　　B. 两周前做的人流手术
　　　C. 发烧两天　　　　D. 腹痛两天

( ) 5. A. 病人需要静脉输液抗生素　　　　B. 病人需要口服抗生素
　　　C. 病人需要住院治疗　　　　D. 病人得了慢性盆腔炎

三、听录音，完成下面的练习

1. 根据所听到的录音判断对错

1) 这个患者有过分娩史。(　　　)

2) 这个患者最近一年月经不规律。(　　　)

3) 这个患者患有多发子宫肌瘤。(　　　)

4) 医生建议子宫切除术。（　　　）

5) 术前可以口服铁剂纠正贫血,控制症状。（　　　）

2. 听录音,选择正确答案回答问题。

1) 这个讲话者是谁? （　　　）

    A. 医生　　　　　　B. 护士　　　　　　C. 学生　　　　　　D. 病人

2) 对于该病人的描述**不**包括哪一项? （　　　）

    A. 压痛　　　　　　B. 宫颈举痛　　　　C. 发烧　　　　　　D. 月经不规律

3) 该病人得了什么病? （　　　）

    A. 急性盆腔炎　　　B. 慢性盆腔炎　　　C. 子宫肌瘤　　　　D. 阑尾炎

> ➤ 词汇和语法练习

一、给下列词语标注拼音

1. 月经＿＿＿＿＿＿＿＿＿＿＿＿＿＿＿＿　　2. 萎缩＿＿＿＿＿＿＿＿＿＿＿＿＿＿＿＿

3. 宫颈＿＿＿＿＿＿＿＿＿＿＿＿＿＿＿＿　　4. 下腹痛＿＿＿＿＿＿＿＿＿＿＿＿＿＿

5. 盆腔炎＿＿＿＿＿＿＿＿＿＿＿＿＿＿　　6. 双附件＿＿＿＿＿＿＿＿＿＿＿＿＿＿

7. 反复发作＿＿＿＿＿＿＿＿＿＿＿＿＿　　8. 阴道分泌物＿＿＿＿＿＿＿＿＿＿＿＿

9. 宫腔内残留＿＿＿＿＿＿＿＿＿＿＿＿　　10. 微创手术＿＿＿＿＿＿＿＿＿＿＿＿

二、选词填空

| 残留　　　缩短　　　肌瘤切除术　　　乏力　　　持续性的　　　妇科 B 超 |
| 抗生素　　　后遗症　　　月经　　　妇科检查 |

1. 大夫,我最近几个月总是＿＿＿＿＿＿＿＿＿不规律,经量增多,经期较长。

2. 我患有贫血,经常感觉头晕,＿＿＿＿＿＿＿＿。

3. 妇科 B 超显示宫腔内未见＿＿＿＿＿＿＿＿。

4. 现在你的肌瘤这么大,最好的办法是＿＿＿＿＿＿＿＿＿。

5. ＿＿＿＿＿＿＿＿＿显示您患有子宫肿块。

6. 盆腔炎的＿＿＿＿＿＿＿＿＿包括不孕、异位妊娠、慢性盆腔痛等。

7. 我现在给您做个＿＿＿＿＿＿＿＿,请把内裤脱下来。

8. 您的月经周期是 22 天,您是周期＿＿＿＿＿＿＿＿。

9. 大多数盆腔炎病人及时、恰当地使用＿＿＿＿＿＿＿＿治疗能彻底治愈。

10. 你下腹痛是间歇性的疼痛还是＿＿＿＿＿＿＿＿疼痛?

三、用指定的词语或结构完成句子或对话。

1. 你现在发烧、腹痛,＿＿＿＿＿＿＿＿。(最好)

2. 她得了盆腔炎,＿＿＿＿＿＿＿＿。(后遗症有……)

3. 这个病人下腹痛＿＿＿＿＿＿＿＿? (是……还是……)

4. 医生建议她做肌瘤切除术,术前＿＿＿＿＿＿＿＿。(除了……以外)

5. 对于大多数盆腔炎病人,＿＿＿＿＿＿＿＿。(如果……就……)

四、把下列词语排列成句子

1. 做　我　保守治疗　肌瘤切除术　可以　吗　害怕

2. 可能性　有　子宫肌瘤　复发的

3. 可以　一些　你　纠正　口服　铁剂　贫血

4. 能　吗　彻底　盆腔炎　治愈

5. 这个　最近　下腹　持续性　病人　两天　疼痛

➤ 阅读与应用练习

一、根据课文内容补全对话

病人： 大夫,我最近几个月总是___1___,经量增多,经期较长。

医生： 您___2___大概多长时间?

病人： 大概 10 天左右。

医生： 您___3___多长时间?

病人： 大概 22 天。

医生： 我看您脸色有些苍白,您___4___吗?

病人： 不知道呀。

医生： 这些___5___大概有多长时间了?

病人： 大概也得半年了。

医生： 为了进一步明确诊断,您去做个___6___,再做个血常规。

病人： 好的。

医生： 现在 B 超显示子宫肿块。根据临床表现及超声检查结果,首先考虑诊断为___7___。

病人： 子宫肌瘤是什么引发的呢?

医生： 可能与女性的___8___有关系。

二、根据课文内容回答问题

1. 王婷有哪些症状?

2. 医生让王婷做什么检查来进一步明确诊断?

3. 医生给王婷的初步诊断是什么? 如何治疗?

4. 李玟为何患了急性盆腔炎?

5. 盆腔炎的后遗症有哪些?

三、写作练习

根据第二个会话中李玟的主要临床表现及诊断治疗情况,写出一篇短文,要求字数不少于 60 个字。

四、交际练习

参考括号里的词语进行情景对话。

情景:病人的检查报告出来了,医生和病人进行对话。

(妇科 B 超,血常规,子宫肌瘤,药物治疗,肌瘤切除术)

会话一 产前检查

词汇

产前检查	chǎnqiánjiǎnchá	名	prenatal care
妊娠	rènshēn	名	gestation
脚踝	jiǎohuái	名	ankle
下腔静脉	xiàqiāngjìngmài	名	inferior vena cava
阻碍	zǔài	动	block
左侧卧位	zuǒcèwòwèi	名	left lateral position
姿势	zīshì	名	position
便秘	biànmì	动	constipation
粗粮	cūliáng	名	roughage
胎动	tāidòng	名	fetal movement
胎心率	tāixīnlǜ	名	fetal heart rate（FHR）
入盆	rùpén	名	engagement
胎心监护	tāixīnjiānhù	名	fetal heart monitoring
海带	hǎidài	名	kelp
羊水	yángshuǐ	名	amniotic fluid
待产	dàichǎn	动&形	awaiting delivery；predelivery
假临产	jiǎlínchǎn	动	false labor
见红	jiànhóng	动	bloody show
破水	pòshuǐ	动	amniotic fluid escaped
胎头下降感	tāitóuxiàjiànggǎn	名	lightening

 地点：产科门诊
人物：杨医生（产科医生）
　　　李小妍（病人，女，30岁）

杨医生　您好，我是杨医生，请坐。怀孕多长时间了？
李小妍　医生，您好。我怀孕9个多月了。
杨医生　末次月经是哪天？
李小妍　5月26日。

杨医生	您以前月经周期规律吗？多长时间一次？一次持续多长时间？月经量怎么样？
李小妍	还行吧，25 天的周期，挺规律的。一次持续 4~5 天，月经量也正常。
杨医生	好的，我帮您算一下，您已经是**妊娠** 38 周了。感觉怎么样？
李小妍	最近这几周**脚踝**和小腿都肿了，晚上睡觉特别不舒服。
杨医生	休息后，水肿能减轻吗？
李小妍	能好点儿。
杨医生	水肿是由于增大的子宫压迫**下腔静脉**，阻碍血液回流导致的。您睡觉的时候可以采取**左侧卧位**的睡姿，将枕头夹在两腿间或放于腹部下面，单腿或双腿保持弯曲，看看哪一种**姿势**更舒服吧。除了水肿之外，还有其他不舒服的地方吗？比如说眩晕或者头疼？
李小妍	没有，就是最近有点**便秘**。
杨医生	便秘不要紧，怀孕期间比较常见。您平时多喝点水，多吃一些纤维含量高的食物，吃点**粗粮**，这样会好些。
李小妍	哦，那就好。
杨医生	这几天**胎动**怎么样？
李小妍	感觉挺正常的，白天动得少，晚上动得多一些。
杨医生	好的，以前有高血压或糖尿病的病史或家族史吗？
李小妍	没有。
杨医生	做过口服葡萄糖耐量试验了吗？
李小妍	做过了，都正常。
杨医生	好，我现在给您量一下血压。
李小妍	好的。
杨医生	血压 117/68mmHg，很正常。请躺下，我给您检查一下。
李小妍	好的。
杨医生	**胎心率**正常，每分钟 156 次，胎头半**入盆**了。您现在 38 周了，需要做彩色超声来看一下胎儿的发育情况。另外，还要做**胎心监护**及血常规、尿常规检查。
	（1 小时后，病人将所有的检查报告拿给医生。）
杨医生	尿常规正常，没有蛋白尿。胎心也正常。血常规显示血红蛋白含量是 95g/L，正常应该至少有 110g/L，说明您有轻度的贫血。
李小妍	医生，要紧吗？会不会影响孩子？
杨医生	您别紧张，只是轻度的缺铁性贫血，暂时不会影响到胎儿，平时注意食补就行了，回家要多吃含铁比较高的食物，比如动物肝脏、瘦肉、木耳、**海带**等。
李小妍	好的。彩超结果怎么样？
杨医生	彩超挺正常，胎儿的大小与孕周相符，**羊水**和胎心都在正常范围以内。
李小妍	哦，那我就放心了。
杨医生	挺好的，您和孩子都很健康，可以继续在家**待产**。
李小妍	对了，医生，最近我还经常觉得肚子一阵阵发硬发紧。
杨医生	疼不疼？有规律吗？
李小妍	不疼，也没什么规律。
杨医生	这是**假临产**的表现，是子宫肌肉通过收缩来为即将到来的分娩做准备。
李小妍	这是不是说明我马上就要生了？
杨医生	不是的，真正临产子宫收缩会疼，而且有规律。您回去安心待产吧。适当饮水，避免过度劳累，不要憋尿，仔细监测胎动。如果出现有规律的腹痛、**见红**、**破水**和胎头下降感就马上来医院。
李小妍	好的，谢谢医生。

Prenatal care

SITE: Obstetrics Clinic

CHARACTERS: Doctor Yang (Obstetrician)

Li Xiaoyan (Patient, female, 30years old)

Dr. Yang: Hello, I am Doctor Yang. Sit down, please. How long have you been pregnant?

Li Xiaoyan: Hello, doctor. About 9 months pregnant.

Dr. Yang: When was your last menstrual period?

Li Xiaoyan: May 26th.

Dr. Yang: Is your menstrual cycle regular? How often is it? How long does it last each time ? How about the menstrual blood volume?

Li Xiaoyan: Well, I think it is regular with a cycle of every 25 days. It lasts 4~5 days each time with normal volume.

Dr. Yang: Ok. Let me see. Now you have reached 38 weeks gestation. How are you feeling ?

Li Xiaoyan: My ankles and legs are swollen in recent weeks and it is very uncomfortable at night.

Dr. Yang: Can the swelling be relieved when you take a rest for one night?

Li Xiaoyan: Yes, it can.

Dr. Yang: The cause of edema is that the enlarged uterus compresses inferior vena cave, which blocks blood back flow. You may sleep in the left lateral position. Place a pillow between your legs or under your abdomen and bend one or both legs, whichever is more comfortable. Do you have any other discomfort, such as dizziness or headache?

Li Xiaoyan: No, I don't feel unwell except mild constipation.

Dr. Yang: Don't worry about it. Constipation is quite common during pregnancy. You can drink plenty of water, take food rich in fiber and eat more roughage. That will help.

Li Xiaoyan: Oh! I see.

Dr. Yang: How about the fetal movement?

Li Xiaoyan: I think it's normal. The fetal movement is more frequent in the daytime than at night.

Dr. Yang: Ok. Have you and your family ever had a history of hypertension or diabetes?

Li Xiaoyan: No, we haven't.

Dr. Yang: Did you have the oral glucose tolerance test?

Li Xiaoyan: Yes, I did and the result is normal.

Dr. Yang: Good. Let me check your blood pressure.

Li Xiaoyan: Ok.

Dr. Yang: The blood pressure is 117/68mmHg, which is normal. Please lie on your back. I will give you a check, Ok?

Li Xiaoyan: All right.

Dr. Yang: The fetal heart rate (FHR) is normal with 156 bmp. The state of the fetal head is half engagement. Now, you are in 38 weeks of pregnancy. You need a color ultrasonography to estimate the development of your fetal. In addition, you also need a fetal monitoring and both blood and urine routine test.

(One hour later, the patient gave the report to the doctor.)

Dr. Yang: Your urine is normal without protein in it and the fetal heart rate is very good. Blood routine shows that the content of hemoglobin is 95g/L, while the normal level should be at least 110g/L, which means that you have got mild anemia.

Li Xiaoyan: Does it matter, doctor? Will it affect the fetus?

Dr. Yang: Don't worry. It is just mild iron-deficiency anemia and will not affect the fetus. It only needs diet therapy. You'd better take food rich in iron, such as liver, lean meat, agaric and kelp, etc.

Li Xiaoyan: Oh, I see. How about the result of color ultrasonography?

Dr. Yang: It is normal. The fetal size is consistent with gestational week and the amniotic fluid and the fetal heart are all within the normal range.

Li Xiaoyan: I'm happy to hear that.

Dr. Yang: You and your baby are all right. You can stay at home before giving birth.

Li Xiaoyan: But I often feel my abdomen contracts recently.

Dr. Yang: Is it painful regularly?

Li Xiaoyan: No, it isn't.

Dr. Yang: This is called false labor, in which uterine muscles prepare for the upcoming labor through contractions.

Li Xiaoyan: Does it indicate that I am going to give birth?

Dr. Yang: No, not yet. You will feel painful because of regular contractions in labor. You may go home and wait for it. You'd better drink proper water, avoid over exertion and monitor fetal movement carefully without holding back make water. Be sure you have to come to the hospital right away when you have the definite signs such as the regular contractions of your uterus, bloody show, amniotic fluid escaped and lightening.

Li Xiaoyan: I see. Thank you!

chǎnqiánjiǎnchá
产前检查

产前 检查，也 称 为 产前 保健，是 为 妊娠期 妇女 提供 的 一系列 预防性 医疗 和 护理 建议 或 措施，其 目的 是 通过 定期 检查，医生 或 助产士 在 整个 怀孕 过程 中，为 产妇 提供 正确 的 治疗 建议 并 预防 潜在 的 健康 问题，同时 建立 有利 于 母亲 和 孩子 的 健康 生活 方式。产前 诊断 或 产前 筛查，可以 在 胎儿 或 胚胎 出生 之前 监测 疾病 或 异常 状况 。 产科 医生 和 助产士 通过 一系列 常规 检查，能够 监测 母亲 怀孕 期间 的 健康 和 胎儿 的 发育 状况 。

Prenatal Care

Prenatal care, also known as antenatal care, is a type of preventive healthcare with the goal of providing regular check-ups that allow doctors or midwives to treat and prevent potential health problems throughout the course of the pregnancy as well as promoting healthy lifestyles that benefit both mother and child. Prenatal diagnosis or prenatal screening is to test diseases or abnormal conditions in a fetus or embryo before it is born.

Obstetricians and midwives have the ability to monitor mother's health and prenatal development during pregnancy through series of regular check-ups.

1. ……是由……导致的

"是"前面是结果。"由"是介词,引出原因。

It means "results from", e.g. 肺炎常常是由细菌或病毒导致的。

2. 只要……就行了

口语中表示条件和结果关系的常用句型,强调做了"只要"后面所说的事情,自然可以达到目的。

It is a pattern to express the relation between condition and result. If the requirements after "只要" are satisfied, the aim can be achieved certainly, e.g. 这种病只要按时服药就行了。

3. ……和……相符

表示两个事物(在数量、质量、形式、性质等方面)彼此一致。

It indicates two things that are equivalent in number, quality, shape, or property, e.g. 她的子宫大小和孕周相符。

会话二　　临　产

词汇

预产期	yùchǎnqī	名	due date of delivery
宫高	gōnggāo	名	fundal height
腹围	fùwéi	名	abdominal perimeter
头位	tóuwèi	名	head position
宫缩	gōngsuō	名	uterine contraction
胎方位	tāifāngwèi	名	fetal position
枕后位	zhěnhòuwèi	名	occipitosacral position
羊膜囊	yángmónáng	名	amniotic membrane
人工破膜	réngōngpòmó	名	artificial rupture of membranes
催产素	cuīchǎnsù	名	oxytocin
产力	chǎnlì	名	puerperal force
先露	xiānlù	名	presentation
胎位不正	tāiwèibúzhèng	名	malposition
枕后位	zhěnhòuwèi	名	occiput posterior
手转胎头术	shǒuzhuǎntāitóushù	名	manual rotation of fetal head
胎盘	tāipán	名	placenta
会阴	huìyīn	名	perineum

撕裂	sīliè	名	lacerations
缝合	fénghé	动	suture；stitch
母乳喂养	mǔrǔwèiyǎng	名	breast feeding
乳汁	rǔzhī	名	milk
房事	fángshì	名	sexual activity
盆浴	pényù	名	tub

地点：产科急诊室；分娩室
人物：孙医生（产科医生）
　　　助产士
　　　张欣（病人，女，28岁）

（在产科急诊室）

孙医生　您好，女士。您怎么了？

张　欣　大夫，我从凌晨四点开始，肚子就一阵一阵地疼，去卫生间发现有水流出来。

孙医生　水流得多吗？

张　欣　不多，就一点。

孙医生　肚子多长时间疼一次？有没有规律？

张　欣　一开始半小时一次，一阵比一阵疼得厉害，现在大约十分钟一次。我是不是快生了？

孙医生　每次疼多长时间？

张　欣　大约一分钟左右吧。

孙医生　见红了吗？

张　欣　没有。

孙医生　您**预产期**是哪天？

张　欣　还有四天才到。

孙医生　您这是第几胎？以前做过流产手术吗？

张　欣　没有做过流产，第一胎。

孙医生　您身高有多少？

张　欣　165cm。

孙医生　请您躺下，我给您检查一下。

张　欣　好的。

孙医生　**宫高**35cm，腹围100cm，胎儿头位，已经入盆了。估计胎儿大小能有3500g左右。胎心每分钟150次，**宫缩**目前2~3分钟一次。接下来我要为您做一下阴道内诊检查。

张　欣　好的。

孙医生　羊水流出少量，宫颈口扩张3cm，**胎方位为枕后位**。您现在**羊膜囊**还没有完全破，我要给您进行**人工破膜**，您同意吗？

张　欣　同意。

孙医生　羊水比较清澈，您现在进入第一产程，我送您去分娩室待产。

　　　　（在分娩室）

张　欣　护士，我肚子越来越疼了，实在受不了了！什么时候能生啊？

助产士　要等宫颈口扩张得足够大，就可以生了。现在给您监测胎心和宫缩。

张　欣　好的。

助产士	胎心正常,您的宫缩有点不好,需要给您打一些**催产素**来增加**产力**,有了想要拉大便的感觉就告诉我。
	(3个小时后,宫颈口开全,**先露** +2)
张 欣	大夫,我有想要拉大便的感觉了。
助产士	这是要生了。来,我扶您上产床。
张 欣	好的,谢谢。
助产士	张女士,您的**胎位不正**,是持续性**枕后位**。
张 欣	那是不是要剖宫产啊?
助产士	不用,但需要实施**手转胎头术**。您的丈夫已经在同意书上签字了。
张 欣	好的。
	(经过手转胎头处理后)
助产士	现在宫口已经开全,可以用力了! 在肚子痛的时候深吸一口气,然后屏气,像拉大便一样用力!
张 欣	好。
助产士	没有宫缩的时候,您可以休息一下,深呼吸。
张 欣	又有宫缩了!
助产士	好,继续,用力! 再来,屏住呼吸,用力!
	(30分钟后)
助产士	恭喜您生了个女儿,体重 3200 克。
张 欣	太好了!
助产士	现在我帮您娩出**胎盘**,另外您的**会阴**部有轻度的**撕裂**,我给您**缝合**一下。
张 欣	谢谢您。
助产士	好了,您还需要在分娩室继续观察两个小时。
张 欣	好。
	(两个小时以后)
助产士	产后出血不多,一切正常,您可以回病房休息了。
张 欣	我需要注意什么吗?
助产士	回去注意休息,加强营养。建议您用**母乳喂养**,让孩子尽早吸吮乳头,每天 8~12 次,这样不但能促进**乳汁**分泌,还有利于子宫收缩,帮助您身体恢复。产后 42 天内禁**房事**、**免盆浴**,保持外阴清洁。如果有腹痛、异常阴道流血及发热等情况让家属随时找我。
张 欣	好的,谢谢您。

Labor

SITE: Obstetrical Emergency Room and Delivery Room

CHARACTERS: Doctor Sun (Obstetrician)

Doctor Liu (Midwife)

Zhang Xin (Patient, female, 28 years old)

（In obstetrical Emergency Room）

Dr. Sun: Hello, Ms Zhang. What happened?

Zhang Xin: Doctor, I've been feeling painful since 4 am before dawn and I noticed a little water flowing out in the toilet.

Dr. Sun: Is the water much?

Zhang Xin: No, not much and just a little.

Dr. Sun: How often is the pain? Do you feel it regularly?

Zhang Xin: Every half an hour at the beginning and the pain gradually increased. Now, every ten minutes. Am I going to labor?

Dr. Sun: How long does it last?

Zhang Xin: About 1 minute.

Dr. Sun: Is there any blood?

Zhang Xin: No, not yet.

Dr. Sun: When is the due date of delivery?

Zhang Xin: Four days left.

Dr. Sun: How many children do you have? Did you ever have a surgical abortion before?

Zhang Xin: No, I haven't. This is my first baby.

Dr. Sun: How tall are you?

Zhang Xin: 165cm.

Dr. Sun: Please lie on your back. You need a check.

Zhang Xin: Ok.

Dr. Sun: The fundal height is 35cm and the abdominal perimeter is 100cm. The fetal head has entered the basin. The weight of your baby is estimated 3500g. FHR is 150bpm, and the contraction occurs every 2~3 minutes. You need a further vaginal examination.

Zhang Xin: All right.

Dr. Sun: A small amount of amniotic fluid outflows and the cervix has dilated 3cm, the fetus being in the occipitosacral position. Your amniotic membranes are not completely broken and you need artificial rupture of membranes. Do you agree?

Zhang Xin: Yes, I do.

Dr. Sun: The amniotic fluid is clear. You are at the first stage of labor. I'll send you to the delivery room now.

(In the delivery room)

Zhang Xin: Doctor, I'm feeling more and more painful intensively. I can't bear it anymore! When shall I give birth?

Dr. Liu: When the cervix opens enough to allow the baby to come out, you'll be ready to give birth with an effort while we'll monitor the fetal heart rate and the uterine contraction.

Zhang Xin: Ok. FHR is normal, but you have no adequate uterine contractile forces and you need some oxytocin to increase the puerperal force. Please tell me if you have the feeling of bowel movement.

(The cervix fully dilated with fetal presentation +2cm 3 hours later.)

Zhang Xin: Doctor, I have the feeling of shit.

Dr. Liu: You'll give birth right now. Come on. Let me hand you up on the obstetric table.

Zhang Xin: Thank you.

Dr. Liu: Your baby is in malposition that is persistent occiput posterior, Ms. Zhang

Zhang Xin: Do I need a cesarean section?

Dr. Liu: No, you don't but your fetal head has to be rotated with hand. Your husband has signed on the informed consent.

Zhang Xin: Ok.

(After the manual rotation)

Dr. Liu: Your cervix has full dilation and you can push. At the time of abdominal pain, take a deep breath, hold it and make an effort as you are having a bowl movement.

Zhang Xin: I see.

Dr. Liu: You can have a rest during the break of contractions. Take a breath.

Zhang Xin: The contractions come again!

Dr. Liu: Good, go on, push! Again, hold breath! Push!

         (30 minutes later.)

Dr. Liu: Congratulations! It is a girl, 3200g!

Zhang Xin: Great!

Dr. Liu: Now, I will help you labor the placenta. What's more, your perineum has slight lacerations which need suture.

Zhang Xin: Thank you!

Dr. Liu: Ok. You need to be observed in the delivery room for two hours.

         (2 hours later.)

Dr. Liu: The postpartum bleeding is little and everything is ok! You can go back to the ward and have a good rest.

Zhang Xin: What else do I need to do?

Dr. Liu: Have a good rest and more nutritious foods. Breastfeeding is preferred. Let the baby suck the nipple as soon as possible, 8~12 times per day, which can not only enhance lactation, but also help the uterine contractions contributing to your quick recovery. The sexual activity is banned and genitals vulvae should be kept clean within the 42 days after the childbirth. Please come up to me when you have the symptoms of abdominal pain, abnormal vaginal bleeding and fever.

Zhang Xin: I see! Thanks!

疾病介绍

临产的诊断与产程
（línchǎndezhěnduànyǔchǎnchéng）

一、临产的诊断
（yī línchǎn de zhěnduàn）

临产开始的标志为有规律且逐渐增强的子宫收缩，持续30秒或以上，间歇5~6分钟，同时伴随进行性宫颈管消失、宫口扩张和胎先露部下降，用镇静药物不能抑制临产。

二、总产程及产程分期
（èr zǒng chǎnchéng jí chǎnchéng fēnqī）

总产程即分娩全过程，是指从开始出现规律宫缩直到胎儿胎盘娩出。分为3个产程：

第一产程，又称宫颈扩张期。从子宫肌层出现规律的、具有足够频率(5~6分钟一次)、强度和持续时间的收缩，导致宫颈管逐渐消失、扩张直至宫口完全扩张即开全为止。初产妇的宫颈较紧，宫口扩张较慢，需11~12小时；经产妇的宫颈较松，宫口扩张较快，需6~8小时。

<ruby>第二<rt>dìèr</rt></ruby> <ruby>产程<rt>chǎnchéng</rt></ruby>，<ruby>又<rt>yòu</rt></ruby> <ruby>称<rt>chēng</rt></ruby> <ruby>胎儿<rt>tāier</rt></ruby> <ruby>娩出期<rt>miǎnchūqī</rt></ruby>。<ruby>从<rt>cóng</rt></ruby> <ruby>宫口<rt>gōngkǒu</rt></ruby> <ruby>完全<rt>wánquán</rt></ruby> <ruby>扩张<rt>kuòzhāng</rt></ruby>（<ruby>开全<rt>kāiquán</rt></ruby>）<ruby>到<rt>dào</rt></ruby> <ruby>胎儿<rt>tāier</rt></ruby> <ruby>娩出<rt>miǎnchū</rt></ruby> <ruby>结束<rt>jiéshù</rt></ruby>，<ruby>是<rt>shì</rt></ruby> <ruby>娩出<rt>miǎnchū</rt></ruby> <ruby>胎儿<rt>tāier</rt></ruby> <ruby>的<rt>de</rt></ruby> <ruby>全<rt>quán</rt></ruby> <ruby>过程<rt>guòchéng</rt></ruby>。<ruby>初产妇<rt>chūchǎnfù</rt></ruby> <ruby>一般<rt>yìbān</rt></ruby> <ruby>需<rt>xū</rt></ruby> 1~2 <ruby>小时<rt>xiǎoshí</rt></ruby>；<ruby>经产妇<rt>jīngchǎnfù</rt></ruby> <ruby>通常<rt>tōngcháng</rt></ruby> <ruby>数分钟<rt>shùfēnzhōng</rt></ruby> <ruby>即可<rt>jíkě</rt></ruby> <ruby>完成<rt>wánchéng</rt></ruby>，<ruby>但<rt>dàn</rt></ruby> <ruby>也有<rt>yěyǒu</rt></ruby> <ruby>长达<rt>chángdá</rt></ruby> 1~2 <ruby>小时者<rt>xiǎoshízhě</rt></ruby>。

<ruby>第三<rt>dìsān</rt></ruby> <ruby>产程<rt>chǎnchéng</rt></ruby>，<ruby>又<rt>yòu</rt></ruby> <ruby>称<rt>chēng</rt></ruby> <ruby>胎盘<rt>tāipán</rt></ruby> <ruby>娩出期<rt>miǎnchūqī</rt></ruby>。<ruby>从<rt>cóng</rt></ruby> <ruby>胎儿<rt>tāier</rt></ruby> <ruby>娩出<rt>miǎnchū</rt></ruby> <ruby>开始<rt>kāishǐ</rt></ruby> <ruby>到<rt>dào</rt></ruby> <ruby>胎盘<rt>tāipán</rt></ruby> <ruby>胎膜<rt>tāimó</rt></ruby> <ruby>娩出<rt>miǎnchū</rt></ruby> <ruby>即<rt>jí</rt></ruby> <ruby>胎盘<rt>tāipán</rt></ruby> <ruby>剥离<rt>bōlí</rt></ruby> <ruby>和<rt>hé</rt></ruby> <ruby>娩出<rt>miǎnchū</rt></ruby> <ruby>的<rt>de</rt></ruby> <ruby>过程<rt>guòchéng</rt></ruby>。<ruby>需<rt>xū</rt></ruby> 5~15 <ruby>分钟<rt>fēnzhōng</rt></ruby>，<ruby>不应<rt>bùyìng</rt></ruby> <ruby>超过<rt>chāoguò</rt></ruby> 30 <ruby>分钟<rt>fēnzhōng</rt></ruby>。

The Diagnosis about Labor and Its Phase

I. The diagnosis about labor

The sign of labor is regular and growing uterine contraction which lasts over 30 seconds with 4~5 minutes pauses, accompanied by progressive effacement and dilation of cervix, fetal presentation and descending. Sedative drugs can't restrain labor.

II. Total stage of labor and its phase

The entire process of birth is from the beginning of regular contraction till delivery of the placenta and the fetus, which is called "the total stage of labor". Clinical stages of labor are divided into three phases:

The first stage of labor: it is also called the stage of dilatation of cervix. It is from regular uterine muscular contraction with enough frequency (5~6 minutes each time), intensity and duration till the time when cervix dilation is big enough to deliver the fetus and placenta. The cervix of primipara is tight and dilatation of uterus cervix is slow, so it needs about 11~12 hours. On the contrary, the multipara needs about 6~8 hours.

The second stage of labor: it is also called fetal delivery period. It is from cervical dilation to fetus delivery. The primipara needs 1~2 hours. The multipara needs from several minutes to 1~2 hour.

The third stage of labor: it is also called placental delivery period. It is from the delivery of fetus to the delivery of placenta and embryolemma which is the process of placental separation and delivery. It will take 5~15 minutes, less than 30 minutes.

语言点

1. 对……来说

用在句子开头，表示从某人或某事的角度看待事物。

It's a phrase, placed at the beginning of a sentence, meaning "from one's perspective or for something", e.g. 对于您的身高来说,孩子不算大。

2. 受不了

不能忍受或接受某种不好的事情,如疾病、痛苦、不好的生活习惯、坏脾气等,前面常用"真"、"真是"、"实在"、"简直"等词语。

It means "can not endure or accept…" and "真", "真是", "实在", "简直" are often used before it for emphasis, e.g. 我肚子越来越疼,实在受不了!

3. 在……上

介词短语"在……上"用在动词前,表示处所。

It means "on, above or beyond", e.g. 麻烦您在手术同意书上签字。

练习

➤ 听力练习

一、听录音,选择你听到的词语

(　)1. A. 怀疑　　　　B. 回忆　　　　C. 怀孕　　　　D. 管用
(　)2. A. 分娩　　　　B. 危险　　　　C. 非典　　　　D. 肤浅
(　)3. A. 绚丽　　　　B. 怀孕　　　　C. 眩晕　　　　D. 前进
(　)4. A. 必要　　　　B. 憋尿　　　　C. 偏向　　　　D. 泌尿
(　)5. A. 临产　　　　B. 遗产　　　　C. 理财　　　　D. 理睬
(　)6. A. 肥牛　　　　B. 维修　　　　C. 垂柳　　　　D. 回流
(　)7. A. 临床　　　　B. 星辰　　　　C. 凌晨　　　　D. 黎明
(　)8. A. 心脏　　　　B. 扩张　　　　C. 快枪　　　　D. 哭腔
(　)9. A. 取舍　　　　B. 凄惨　　　　C. 轻松　　　　D. 清澈
(　)10. A. 撕裂　　　　B. 世界　　　　C. 输液　　　　D. 思念

二、请选出与所听录音相符的答案

(　)1. A. 病人月经周期不规律　　　　　B. 病人月经周期30天一次
　　　　　C. 病人的月经周期比较规律　　　D. 病人没有月经
(　)2. A. 病人的水肿减轻了　　　　　　B. 病人的水肿加重了
　　　　　C. 病人的水肿没有改善　　　　D. 病人没回答医生的问题
(　)3. A. 病人的胎儿大　　　　　　　　B. 病人的羊水不正常
　　　　　C. 病人的彩超结果都正常　　　D. 病人的胎心不正常
(　)4. A. 病人肚子疼没有规律　　　　　B. 病人的肚子一直在疼
　　　　　C. 病人肚子疼得不厉害　　　　D. 病人肚子疼一直在加重
(　)5. A. 病人有拉大便的感觉　　　　　B. 病人需要打催产素
　　　　　C. 病人宫缩正常　　　　　　　D. 病人胎心不正常

三、听录音,完成下面的练习

1. 根据所听到的录音判断对错

1) 这个病人是第一次怀孕。(　　)

2) 这个病人妊娠反应不太重。 (　　)

3) 这个病人的症状有头晕,恶心和呕吐。(　　)

4) 这个病人尿常规和血常规结果都正常。(　　)

5) 医生不建议病人吃药。 (　　)

2. 听录音,选择正确答案回答问题

1) 病人主要因为什么来就诊? (　　)
　　A. 见红　　　　B. 腹痛　　　　C. 破水　　　　D. 出血

2) 病人什么时候开始出现有规律宫缩的? (　　)
　　A. 凌晨　　　　B. 傍晚　　　　C. 中午　　　　D. 一天前

3) 医生为病人做了什么检查? (　　)
　　A. 血常规　　　　B. 尿常规　　　　C. B超　　　　D. 阴道检查

4) 病人的宫颈口扩张到(　　)
　　A. 4厘米　　　　B. 3厘米　　　　C. 10厘米　　　　D. 5厘米

5) 病人的胎方位是:(　　)

A. 枕后位   B. 左枕前   C. 右枕后   D. 枕前位

➤ 词汇和语法练习

一、给下列词语标注拼音

1. 阻碍_____   2. 临产_____

3. 水肿_____   4. 破水_____

5. 羊水_____   6. 分娩_____

7. 宫缩_____   8. 预产期_____

9. 撕裂_____   10. 人工破膜_____

二、选词填空

待产	扩张	水肿	隐隐约约	破水	枕后位
左侧卧位	妊娠	预产期	食补	撕裂	

1. 您已经_____38 周了。

2. 休息一晚,_____能减轻些吗?

3. 医生建议孕妇睡觉的时候尽量采取_____的睡姿。

4. 您不需要吃药,可以进行_____,多吃些含铁高的食物。

5. 您和孩子都很健康,可以继续在家_____。

6. 这个孕妇还有四天才到_____,今天提前_____了。

7. 该孕妇宫颈口_____3 厘米,胎头的位置为_____。

8. 您的会阴部有轻度的_____,我给您缝合一下。

三、用指定的词语或结构完成句子或对话

1. 我感冒了,医生说是_____。(由……导致)

2. 高血压一般不需要住院,_____。(只要……就行了)

3. 老师仔细检查了他的证件,照片_____。(相符)

4. _____,这次考试太简单了。(对……来说)

5. 他收到了公司的通知,让他_____面试。(在……上)

四、把下列词语排列成句子

1. 肿了 这一周 我的 最近 脚踝

2. 您 做 胎心监护 一个 还需要

3. 可以 扩张 完全 就 宫颈口 生了

4. 把她 分娩室 医生 送进 了

5. 丈夫 了 同意书上 在 签字 已经 您的

➤ 阅读与应用练习

一、根据课文内容补全对话

病人:大夫,我最近这几天脚踝肿得很厉害。

医生:休息一晚,__1__能减轻些吗?

病人:是的,好一点。

医生:还有其他不舒服的地方吗?

病人:还有点__2__。

医生:别担心,这在孕期比较常见。您可以多吃一些__3__含量高的食物,多喝水,多吃__4__。

病人:我最近还经常感觉肚子一阵阵发硬发紧,不觉得疼,也没有什么__5__。

医生:哦。这是__6__的表现,是子宫肌肉通过收缩来为即将到来的分娩准备。

病人：我明白了,还需要注意些什么?

医生：您回去安心待产吧。如果出现规律的肚子疼,___7___、___8___和___9___马上来医院。

二、根据课文内容回答问题

1. 李小妍在医院做了哪些检查?

2. 李小妍出现什么情况需要马上去医院?

3. 张欣因什么原因到医院就诊的?

4. 张欣在生产过程中遇到了什么问题?

5. 张欣生完孩子后需要注意些什么?

三、写作练习

请简单描述会话二中病人张欣的生产过程。(不少于 50 字)

四、交际练习

参考括号里的词语进行场景对话。

情景:病人临产了,到产科就诊,医生和病人进行对话。

(肚子疼,便秘,水肿;头晕;假临产;尿频,见红,破水,胎位,待产)

CHAPTER 17

会话一　　　　　　　　　　　　　**产后出血**

词汇

产后出血	chǎnhòuchūxuè	名	postpartum hemorrhage
顺产	shùnchǎn	名	natural birth
产妇纸	chǎnfùzhǐ	名	maternal paper
宫底	gōngdǐ	名	uterine fundus
轮廓	lúnkuò	名	contour
胎膜	tāimó	名	fetal membrane
软产道裂伤	ruǎnchǎndàolièshāng	名	soft birth canal laceration
凝血功能障碍	níngxuègōngnéngzhàngài	名	coagulation defects
指标	zhǐbiāo	名	index
缩宫素	suōgōngsù	名	oxytocin
贫血貌	pínxuèmào	名	anemic appearance
恶化	èhuà	动	deteriorate
蔗糖铁	zhètángtiě	名	iron sucrose

　　地点：妇产科病房
　　　　人物：周洋（主治医师）
　　　　　　　张芳（病人，28 岁，初产妇）
　　　　　　　徐芳（助产士）

张　芳　医生，我全身没劲，头晕心慌。

周医生　请问您结束分娩多长时间了？

张　芳　大约两个小时，是**顺产**。

周医生　好的，别紧张，我来给您检查一下。脉搏每分钟 95 次，呼吸 30 次，血压 90/60mmHg，您阴道出血多吗？

张　芳　我感觉有好多液体流出来，您看看是不是流了好多血？

周医生　好的，我看看，阴道有出血，颜色暗红、有凝血块。

张　芳　医生，我到底怎么了？严重吗？

周医生　别紧张，我先帮您取出垫在会阴部位的**产妇纸**，称重后计算一下出血量。

张　芳　好的。

周医生　（称重后）您的出血量有 800ml。请您平躺放松，我来摸摸您的子宫怎么样。嗯，**宫底**脐上一指，子宫软,**轮廓**不清。

周医生　(转向助产士)2 床病人分娩时胎盘胎膜娩出是否完整?

徐护士　周医生,2 床病人分娩时我仔细检查过胎盘胎膜,是完整的。

周医生　好。徐护士,请您帮我把她扶到产检床上,我来给她做软产道检查,看看有没有**软产道裂伤**。

　　　　(几分钟后)

周医生　(对病人)请放心,您的宫颈和阴道都正常,会阴也没有裂伤。

张　芳　那我怎么会头晕、浑身没劲呢?

周医生　您这种情况很可能是宫缩乏力造成的产后出血,还需要进一步抽血化验,排除**凝血功能障碍**。

张　芳　好的。

周医生　检查结果出来之前护士会先给您按摩子宫,增强宫缩。

张　芳　好的,谢谢医生。

　　　　(周医生拿着检查结果走进病房)

周医生　这是您的血常规和凝血功能检查结果,所有**指标**都很正常。综合您的各项检查结果分析,您的出血可以排除胎盘因素、软产道裂伤和凝血功能异常,可以确定是由产后宫缩乏力引起的。

张　芳　那怎么办? 总是这么流血会不会很危险?

周医生　请放心! 子宫按摩可以促进宫缩,有助于控制出血。我马上给您静脉滴注**缩宫素**,也可以帮助子宫收缩,逐步减少出血。

　　　　(几分钟后)

周医生　现在感觉怎么样? 好多了吧?

张　芳　出血好像减少了。

周医生　是的,子宫收缩恢复正常后,阴道流血就会明显减少,您会慢慢恢复的。另外,我看您面色苍白,是典型的**贫血貌**,您以前有没有检查过?

张　芳　查过的,我怀孕之前就有点儿贫血,当时也没在意,断断续续地吃过一些补血的药,不过没有坚持。

周医生　产后出血会让您的贫血症状**恶化**,您的乏力、心慌等症状就是明显的反应。

张　芳　那应该怎么治疗呢?

周医生　我先给您静脉滴注几天**蔗糖铁**,补充铁剂,症状好转后再改为口服琥珀酸亚铁片,一天三次,一次一片。坚持用药一段时间,您贫血的情况会明显改善的。

张　芳　谢谢医生,我一定按照您的吩咐,坚持吃药。

Postpartum Hemorrhage

SITE:　　　　　Obstetric Ward

CHARACTERS:　Zhou Yang (Attending physician)

　　　　　　　　Zhang Fang (Patient, 28y, primipara)

　　　　　　　　Xu Fang (Midwife)

Zhang Fang:　I feel weak, flustered and dizzy, Doctor.

　Dr. Zhou:　Could you please tell me how long it is after your delivery?

Zhang Fang:　About two hours and it was a natural birth.

　Dr. Zhou:　Ok, relax yourself. I will examine you. P 95/min, R30/min and BP 90/60mmHg. What about the bleeding in vaginal? Was it too much?

Zhang Fang:　I feel much fluid is flowing from my vagina. Can you have a look whether it is bleeding?

　Dr. Zhou:　Yes, it is with coagulation clots in deep red.

Zhang Fang:	What's wrong with me, doctor? Is it serious?
Dr. Zhou:	Don't worry. Let me take out the maternal paper padded under your perineum and weigh it to see the volume of the bleeding.
Zhang Fang:	Ok.
Dr. Zhou:	(After weighing)800ml. Please supine and relax. I need to palpate your uterus. Yeah, the uterine fundus is 1 finger above the umbilicus. The uterus is soft and its outline is unclear.
Dr. Zhou:	(Turn to Xu)Are the placenta and fetal membrane completely extracted during her delivery?
Nurse Xu:	Dr. Zhou, I've checked them carefully during her delivery and I am sure of their completeness.
Dr. Zhou:	Ok. Please help her get on the examining table. I'll make a soft birth canal examination to find whether there is any laceration.
	(Several minutes later)
Dr. Zhou:	(Turn to the patient)Nothing is serious. Your cervix and vagina are normal, so is your perineum.
Zhang Fang:	But why do I feel so dizzy and weak?
Dr. Zhou:	It may be postpartum hemorrhage caused by uterine atony, but a blood routine test is still needed to exclude the factor of coagulation defects.
Zhang Fang:	Ok.
Dr. Zhou:	We'll start kneading your uterus when waiting for the results.
Zhang Fang:	Thank you.
	(Doctor entered the ward with the results)
Dr. Zhou:	Your test results show that all the indexes are normal. According to the analysis of all the test results, we've excluded the factors of placenta, soft birth canal laceration and blood coagulation defects and confirmed the diagnosis of the cause of uterine atony.
Zhang Fang:	What shall I do? Isn't it dangerous for me with continuous bleeding?
Dr. Zhou:	Take it easy. The kneading of uterine can promote its contraction to reduce the bleeding and the intravenous injection with oxytocin can also help uterine contract. Thus the bleeding will be reduced.
	(Several minutes later)
Dr. Zhou:	What are you feeling now? Better?
Zhang Fang:	It seems that it bleeds less than before.
Dr. Zhou:	Yes, when the uterine returns to normal, the virginal bleeding will be apparently less and you will gradually recover. What's more, you look anemic with a pale face. Did you have a check before?
Zhang Fang:	Yes, I did. I was a little bit anemic before pregnancy. However, I didn't take it serious and just took some medication intermittently.
Dr. Zhou:	Postpartum hemorrhage will deteriorate your anemic symptoms and your dizziness and fluster is the obvious response.
Zhang Fang:	How should that be treated?
Dr. Zhou:	I'll prescribe intravenous infusion of iron sucrose for you, followed by ferrous succinate pills, one pill each time and three times a day, to supplement iron. Keep taking them for a period of time, you will improve anemia status.
Zhang Fang:	Thank you, doctor. I will follow your instruction.

疾病介绍

产后出血
chǎnhòuchūxuè

顺产 后 的 阴道 流血量 超过 500ml ， 剖宫产 后 流血量 超过 1000ml 称 为 产后 出血 。
产后 出血是分娩期 严重 的 并发症 ，也是 产妇 死亡的 重要 原因 之一 。 产后 出血 的 原因
包括 宫缩 乏力 ， 软产道 损伤 ，胎盘 胎膜 残留 和凝血 功能 障碍 4 类 。
治疗 措施 主要 如下 ：① 徒手 按摩 子宫 ；② 采血 做 血型定型 及 交叉 配血 试验 ；③ 观察
血块 ，排除 凝血 异常 ；④ 输液 或者 输血 ；⑤ 仔细 检查 子宫腔 、宫颈 和 阴道 ；⑥ 建立 第二个
静脉通道 。

Postpartum Hemorrhage

Postpartum hemorrhage is defined as blood loss exceeding 500ml in a vaginal delivery and greater than 1000ml in a cesarean section. Postpartum hemorrhage is both a serious complication in delivery and one of the leading causes of maternal mortality. Causes of postpartum hemorrhage include uterine atony, cervical lacerations, placental tissue residues and coagulation defects.

The main treatments are as follows：①manually compressing the uterus；②obtaining blood for typing and cross-matching；③observing blood for clotting to rule out coagulopathy；④beginning fluid or blood replacement；⑤carefully inspecting the uterine cavity, cervix and vagina；⑥inserting a second intravenous catheter for administration of blood or fluids.

语言点

1. ……一下

用于动词后,表示略微之意。

The phase "一下" used after a verb forms verb-complement phrase, meaning a little or slightly, e.g. 称一称重量,了解一下出血量。

2. ……有助于……

对某人或某事有利,能起到帮助与促进的作用。

It means "be beneficial to", e.g. 晚上喝牛奶有助于睡眠。

3. ……下来

"动词 + 下来"表示动作或者某种状态从过去开始一直持续到现在。

"Verb+ 下来" indicates an act or state lasting from the past to the present, e.g. 我刚来中国时学了一年的汉语,因为太忙,没有学下来。

妊娠期高血压疾病

妊娠期高血压疾病	rènshēnqīgāoxuèyājíbìng	名	hypertensive disorders in pregnancy
硝苯地平	xiāoběndìpíng	名	nifedipine
失眠	shīmián	名	insomnia
丙氨酸氨基转移酶	bǐngānsuānānjīzhuǎnyíméi	名	alanine transaminase，ALT
天冬氨酸氨基转移酶	tiāndōngānsuānānjīzhuǎnyíméi	名	aspartate transaminase，AST
低蛋白血症	dīdànbáixuèzhèng	名	hypoproteinemia
左心室	zuǒxīnshì	名	left ventricle
动静脉比	dòngjìngmàibǐ	名	ratio of vein and artery
子痫前期	zixiánqiánqī	名	preeclampsia
宫内窘迫	gōngnèijiǒngpò	名	fetal intrauterine distress
尼卡地平	níkǎdìpíng	名	nicardipine
人体白蛋白	réntǐbáidànbái	名	human albumin
硫酸镁	liúsuānměi	名	magnesium sulfate

地点：妇产科病房
人物：周洋(主治医师)
　　　护士
　　　实习生
　　　吴菲菲(病人，女，32岁，孕36周，初产妇)

周医生　您好，请问您有什么不舒服？

吴菲菲　我头晕，双腿浮肿，每天胃里胀胀的，没有食欲。糟糕的是，眼睛最近看东西也不清楚了，不知道是怎么回事。

周医生　您的产前检查一直在做吗？

吴菲菲　是的，都是在我们县城医院做的。

周医生　有没有什么不正常的？

吴菲菲　怀孕26周的时候检查血压有点高140/90mmHg，但是我没什么不舒服的感觉，就没吃药。后来我妈妈生病了，家里事情多，我就没有再去医院检查血压了。上个星期开始，我头晕得不得了，腿也肿得厉害，躺了好几天也没好转。前几天检查血压160/120mmHg，尿蛋白有三个加号。县医院的医生给我开了**硝苯地平**吃，症状也没有缓解。昨天开始，眼睛看东西也模糊了，肚子也不舒服，医生就让我到你们医院来了。

周医生　请问您怀孕之前有没有高血压？

吴菲菲　没有。

周医生　您家里有人有高血压吗？

吴菲菲　我妈妈有高血压很多年了。

周医生　您最近睡眠怎么样？

吴菲菲　不太好，经常**失眠**。

周医生　别紧张，我先给您检查检查。（给病人做触诊检查）嗯，血压 170/120mmHg，心率每分钟 90 次，**体温 36.8℃**，呼吸每分钟 20 次。（按腹部）没有摸到宫缩，浮肿 +++。我来听听小宝宝怎么样……嗯，胎心正常，小家伙好得很呢。您不用担心。

吴菲菲　谢谢医生。

周医生　您还需要做系统的全身检查，我来给您开检查单，让您的家人扶着您去，注意安全。

吴菲菲　好的，我们会注意的。（翻看化验单）请问医生，为什么还要去眼科呀？

周医生　眼底检查可以反映您全身小动脉的痉挛程度，有助于医生对病情的估计和处理。

吴菲菲　知道了，我这就去。

（几个小时后化验单结果出来了）

周医生　吴小姐，您好，您的检验结果出来了。血常规、心电图、电解质检查结果和肝胆 B 超都正常；尿常规显示您的尿蛋白 +++；肝肾功能检查显示您的肾功能正常，但是**丙氨酸氨基转移酶**和**天冬酰胺氨基转移酶**轻度升高，还有**低蛋白血症**；心脏彩超显示**左心室**略大；眼底检查的**动静脉比**是 1：2。根据您的症状体征和这些检查结果综合判断，您得的是**子痫前期**。

吴菲菲　子痫前期？厉害吗？会不会影响胎儿？

周医生　别担心，但是您一定要配合医生积极治疗，否则会影响胎儿的发育，甚至造成胎儿**宫内窘迫**，危及胎儿生命。

吴菲菲　放心吧，医生，我一定会积极治疗的。

周医生　好好休息，我给您开点儿镇静药。（转向护士）护士，请给她测一下 24 小时的尿量，血压每四小时测一次。

护　士　好的，我记住了，医生。

周医生　从今天开始静脉滴注**尼卡地平**控制您的血压，输入体白蛋白，注意利尿，使用解痉药**硫酸镁**，实习生请注意一下她的毒性反应，随时检查。

实习生　好的。

吴菲菲　医生，孩子出生后我还会有这些症状吗？

周医生　您别紧张，好好治疗，生产后这些症状会逐渐减轻。一般来说，大多数人都能恢复健康的。

吴菲菲　那就好，谢谢医生。

Hypertensive Disorders in Pregnancy

SITE:　Obstetric Ward

CHARACTERS:　Zhou Yang (Attending physician);

Nurse; Interns

Wu Feifei (Patient, female, 32 years old, 36 gestational weeks, primipara)

Dr. Zhou:　Hello! What's wrong with you?

Wu Feifei:　I feel dizzy and have swollen legs as well as poor appetite. The worst thing is that I can't see **things** clearly recently.

Dr. Zhou:　Do you keep taking regular antenatal examinations?

Wu Feifei:　Yes, all have been done in my county hospital.

Dr. Zhou:　Anything abnormal?

Wu Feifei:　Everything went right until the 26th gestational week when my blood pressure rose to 140/90mmHg. My doctor didn't prescribe any medication, for I didn't feel unwell. Then my mother got seriously sick and I was so fully occupied afterwards that I failed to go to hospital later. Last week I felt very dizzy and my legs became more swollen. It didn't get better even after several days' rest in bed. Then I went to the county hospital, where my blood pressure 160/120mmHg and my proteinuria +++ were detected. I didn't feel much better even after taking nifedipine. Yesterday I found I couldn't see things clearly and my upper belly was uncomfortable, so my doctor quickly transferred me to your hospital.

Dr. Zhou: Do you have the symptom of hypertension before pregnancy?

Wu Feifei: No, never.

Dr. Zhou: What about your family members?

Wu Feifei: Oh, my mother has suffered from hypertension for many years.

Dr. Zhou: How about your recent sleep?

Wu Feifei: I often suffer insomnia.

Dr. Zhou: Don't be nervous. Let me examine you by palpation. (Palpate her abdomen) Bp 170/120mmHg, HR 90/min, temperature is 36.8℃ and R 20/min. No uterine contraction touched and edema +++. Then let's check the fetus. The fetal heart is normal, so you needn't worry about it.

Wu Feifei: Thank you, doctor.

Dr. Zhou: My pleasure. I'm afraid that you need a systematic examination. I will write out the checklists for you. Ask your relatives help you and take care.

Wu Feifei: I see. I'll be careful. (Flip through the lab slips) By the way, why do we need to go to the ophthalmology department?

Dr. Zhou: Because the result of your fundus oculi could reflect the degree of the spasm of your overall arteriolae, which helps the doctor estimate your condition and treat you properly.

Wu Feifei: I see. We will go immediately.

(Several hours later, the results have come out)

Dr. Zhou: Hi! Here are your tests results. The blood routine test, electrolyte test and liver B ultrasonic examination appear normal. The urine routine test shows+++ protein on dipstick, and the liver and renal examination indicates a moderate increase in ALT and AST and hypoproteinemia. The ECG is normal but the UCG shows your left ventricle is slightly bigger. The ratio of vein to artery in your fundus oculi test is 1:2. Based on your physical signs and these test results, I think you've got preeclampsia.

Wu Feifei: Preeclampsia? Is it serious? Would it influence my baby?

Dr. Zhou: Don't worry. You'd better cooperate with the doctors actively or it will influence the development of the fetus and even result in fetal intrauterine distress, thus endangering the fetus' life.

Wu Feifei: Rest assured that I will actively follow your treatment.

Dr. Zhou: Have a good rest and I will prescribe some sedatives for you. (Turn to the nurse) Nurse, please test her urine volume for 24 hours and her blood pressure every four hours.

Nurse: Yes. I've got it.

Dr. Zhou: Give her intravenous infusion with nicardipine from today and human albumin and administrate magnesium sulfate. Please monitor her toxic reaction, interns.

Interns: We understand.

Wu Feifei: Doctor, shall I still suffer these after delivery?

Dr. Zhou: Relax, please. The treatment will contribute to the symptoms' reduction gradually after your delivery. Generally speaking, most people will recover.

Wu Feifei: Good news! Thank you, doctor.

疾病介绍

rènshēnqīgāoxuèyājíbìng
妊娠期高血压疾病

妊娠 期间 的 高血压病 分 为 慢性 高血压 和 妊娠 引发 的高血压 。 慢性 高血压 是 指 孕前 、孕20 周 之前 或者 产后 六周 依然 持续 的 高血压 病状 ，妊娠 引发 的 高血压 包括 子痫 前期 、子痫 和妊娠期 高血压 。 患有 子痫 前期 的 少数 患者 会 出现 肝损伤 ，而 肝损伤 与 两种 高患病率 、高 死亡率 的 疾病 关系 密切：HELLP 综合征 和 妊娠期 急性 脂肪肝 。 它们 引发 的常见 并发症 一直 是 发展中 国家 和 发达 国家 孕产妇 死亡 的 最 主要 原因 。

Gestational Hypertension

The categories of hypertension in pregnancy are stratified between chronic hypertension and hypertension specific to pregnancy. Chronic hypertension is defined as hypertension that is present before conception, before 20 weeks gestation or that persists for more than 6 weeks postpartum. Hypertension caused by pregnancy includes preeclampsia, eclampsia and gestational hypertension. Liver injury is seen in a small percentage of patients with preeclampsia and is associated with two diseases in pregnancy with high morbidity and mortality: HELLP syndrome and acute fatty liver of pregnancy (AFLP). Complications from these disorders are consistently among the leading causes of maternal death in both developed and developing countries.

语言点

1. ……得不得了

该结构中的第一个"得"是助词,放在形容词或者动词的后面,"不得了"是程度补语,强调程度很高。

The first "得" in the structure is the auxiliary word used after adjectives or verbs eliciting the complement of degree, and "不得了" serves as the complement of degree, meaning very or extremely, e.g. 这个手术做得很成功,医护人员都高兴得不得了。

2. 这就……

"这就 + 动词"是常用口语。"这"现在的意思,"就"是副词,动作在短时间里就要发生。"这就去"就是"现在立刻去"的意思。

"这就 +v" is a commonly-used oral expression. "这" means now and "就" is an adverb indicating that the action is about to happen within a short time, e.g. 我这就来。

练习

➢ 听力练习

一、听录音,选择你听到的词语

( )1. A. 胎盘　　　　B. 胎膜　　　　C. 胎动　　　　D. 胎位

(）2. A. 心慌   B. 心悸   C. 心律   D. 心衰

(）3. A. 凝血   B. 出血   C. 咯血   D. 输血

(）4. A. 顺产   B. 流产   C. 难产   D. 引产

(）5. A. 阴道   B. 产道   C. 产妇   D. 产检

(）6. A. 缩宫素   B. 青霉素   C. 催产素   D. 抗生素

(）7. A. 白蛋白   B. 尿蛋白   C. 低蛋白   D. 高蛋白

(）8. A. 宫缩   B. 宫底   C. 宫颈   D. 子宫

(）9. A. 血常规   B. 妇科常规   C. 尿常规   D. 大便常规

(）10. A. 功能性   B. 病理性   C. 持续性   D. 生理性

二、请选出与所听录音相符的答案

(）1. A. 病人有贫血的病史   B. 病人没有积极治疗贫血

       C. 病人一直坚持吃药   D. 病人觉得贫血不要紧

(）2. A. 胃疼   B. 视物模糊   C. 头晕   D. 浮肿

(）3. A. 子痫前期会影响胎儿   B. 子痫前期会造成胎儿发育迟缓

       C. 子痫前期可能引起宫内窘迫   D. 子痫前期危及产妇的生命

(）4. A. 凝血异常   B. 软产道裂伤   C. 宫缩乏力   D. 胎盘娩出完整

(）5. A. 病人已经确诊为重度子痫   B. 病人是转科过来的

       C. 病人的病情还需要进一步检查   D. 病人住进了县医院

三、听录音,完成下面的练习

1. 根据所听到的录音判断对错

1）10 床病人是顺产的。(   )

2）病人有阴道出血,颜色暗红,没有凝血块。(   )

3）医生给病人做了触诊、妇检,还开了血常规和 B 超的单子。(   )

4）宫缩乏力引起的产后出血需要子宫按摩和滴注缩宫素。(   )

5）经过及时的治疗,病人的产后出血状况很快好转。(   )

2. 听录音,选择正确的答案回答问题

1）下面关于病人情况的描述哪句话是错误的? (   )

     A. 病人的家属中有高血压病人   B. 病人一直按时孕期检查

     C. 病人的睡眠不太好   D. 病人的血压一直在升高

2）病人是什么时候发现血压高的? (   )

     A. 孕 20 周   B. 孕 26 周   C. 孕 34 周   D. 孕 36 周

3）病人为什么转院治疗? (   )

     A. 病人的眼睛视物不清   B. 病人全身浮肿

     C. 病人头晕头疼   D. 病人尿蛋白 +++

4）使用硫酸镁治疗的时候,要注意什么? (   )

     A. 注意利尿   B. 注意多休息   C. 注意中毒反应   D. 注意保护眼睛

➤ 词汇和语法练习

一、给下列词语标注拼音

1. 胎膜 _____   2. 宫底 _____

3. 失眠 _____   4. 子痫 _____

5. 妊娠 _____   6. 转氨酶 _____

7. 贫血貌 _____   8. 宫内窘迫 _____

9. 宫缩乏力 _____   10. 凝血功能障碍 _____

二、选词填空

排除　　缓解　　指标　　裂伤　　产妇纸　　动静脉比　　断断续续　　按摩子宫

1. 我吃了一个星期的硝苯地平,血压高的情况没有_____。
2. 让我帮您取出垫在会阴部位的_____,称出血量。
3. _____可以控制阴道出血,帮子宫收缩,逐步减少出血。
4. 您的眼底检查显示您的_____是1∶2。
5. 您的血常规和凝血功能的结果出来了,所有_____都很正常。
6. 我要给她做个软产道检查,看看有没有软产道_____。
7. 病人还需要做进一步抽血化验,_____凝血功能障碍。
8. 我曾经吃过一些补血的药,不过_____的,没有坚持下来。

三、用指定的词语或结构完成句子或对话

1. 这两周感觉头_____。(……不得了)
2. 我们看了您的各项检查结果,_____,可以确诊出血的原因是宫缩乏力。(排除……)
3. 因宫缩乏力引起的产后出血,要立刻给病人按摩子宫,_____。(有助于……)
4. _____,我诊断您得了子痫前期。(根据……)
5. 一定要按时吃药,_____。(否则……)

四、把下列词语排列成句子

1. 中毒　注意　病人的　实习生　一下　反应
2. 会　生产后　减轻　症状　逐渐
3. 更加　产后出血　会让　您的贫血症状　恶化
4. 产检床上　帮我　请　扶到　把她
5. 口服　症状　琥珀酸亚铁片　再　好转一些后

➢ 阅读与应用练习

一、根据课文内容补全对话

医生：您好,请问___1___?

病人：我头晕,浮肿,胃里也胀胀的,没有___2___。眼睛___3___。医生,我到底怎么了?

医生：请问___4___?有没有异常情况?

病人：做了。孕周26周的时候血压有点儿高,140/90mmHg,因为没什么感觉,医生没让我吃药。后来家里有事就没有去医院检查了。这两周感觉___5___,___6___,血压升高到160/120 mmHg,___7___,县医院医生给我开了硝苯地平,症状也没有___8___。

医生：血压是挺高的,请问您怀孕前有没有高血压?

病人：没有。

医生：___9___?

病人：哦,我妈妈患高血压已经很多年了。

医生：最近睡眠怎么样?

病人：不太好,夜里老是___10___。

医生：好的,我来给您仔细检查检查。

二、根据课文内容回答问题

1. 10床产妇产后的症状主要有哪些?
2. 产后出血的原因主要有哪些?
3. 由宫缩乏力引起的产后出血主要的治疗措施是什么?
4. 周医生为什么让2床去做眼底检查?

5. 妊娠期高血压对胎儿有什么影响?

三、写作练习

请简单描述会话二里病人吴菲菲的主要临床表现和医生的治疗方案。(不少于 50 字)

四、交际练习

参考括号里的词语进行医患的情景对话。

情景:妇产科病房,病人张芳分娩 2 小时后阴道出血增多。

(产妇纸、触诊、胎盘胎膜完整、软产道裂伤、宫缩乏力、凝血功能障碍、产后出血、按摩、缩宫素)

第十八章	儿科（1）

小 儿 肺 炎

词汇

热性惊厥	rèxìngjīngjué	名	febrile seizures
注意	zhùyì	动	take notice of
埋怨	mányuàn	动	complain; blame
呼吸困难	hūxīkùnnan	形	short of breath
鼻翼扇动	bíyìshāndòng	名	nasal flaring
结核病	jiéhébìng	名	tuberculosis
C反应蛋白	C fǎnyìngdànbái	名	C reactive protein
头孢呋辛	tóubāofūxīn	名	Cefuroxime
化痰	huàtán	动	reduce sputum
止咳	zhǐké	动	relieve coughing
沐舒坦糖浆	mùshūtǎntángjiāng	名	mucosolvin syrup
富露施	fùlùshī	名	fluimucil
雾化	wùhuà	名	nebulization
治疗室	zhìliáoshì	名	treatment room

地点：儿科门诊
人物：吴医生（儿科医生）
乐乐（患儿，女，3岁，由母亲带来就诊）

吴医生　请坐！我是吴大夫，有什么需要帮助的吗？

母　亲　吴大夫，我女儿几天前开始流鼻涕、咳嗽，今天又发起烧来了，我很担心，就带她来医院了。

吴医生　咳嗽几天了？有痰吗？

母　亲　三天了。听着有痰，但是她不会咳出来。

吴医生　宝宝发烧多少度？吃退烧药了吗？

母　亲　最高有39℃了，我怕影响她看病，没有让她吃退烧药。

吴医生　服用退烧药不会影响看病。如果孩子发烧超过38.5℃，最好尽快给她口服退烧药，因为高热可

　　　　　能会导致孩子出现**热性惊厥**,比较危险。

母　亲　是这样啊,我真不懂,下次我一定**注意**!

吴医生　孩子生病后,您有没有带她看过医生?

母　亲　没有!宝宝刚开始就是有点流鼻涕、咳嗽,也不严重,我就没当回事儿,自己喂了点感冒药给她吃,结果也没见好,还发起烧来了。这不,孩子他爸直**埋怨**我。

吴医生　您给她吃的什么感冒药,有抗生素吗?

母　亲　没有,我就给她吃了点中药。

吴医生　孩子还有什么其他不舒服吗?比如呕吐、腹泻、老想睡觉等?

母　亲　这倒是没有,但是孩子有点儿没精神、不爱吃饭。

吴医生　孩子有喘息或**呼吸困难**的症状吗?

母　亲　没看到她喘。怎么判断她是不是呼吸困难?

吴医生　就是孩子是不是呼吸很快,呼吸时**鼻翼扇动**?

母　亲　呼吸好像有点快,鼻翼扇动倒是没有。

吴医生　孩子平时身体怎么样?有没有按时打预防针?

母　亲　乐乐以前身体很好,基本上不怎么生病,但是上幼儿园以后,就老爱生病了。预防针都是按时打的。

吴医生　您家里有人患**结核病**吗?

母　亲　没有。

吴医生　好!现在我来给孩子做一下体格检查,请把孩子抱到检查床上!
　　　　　(面对患儿乐乐)阿姨用这个听诊器和你做个游戏,好不好?一点都不疼,乐乐最乖了!
　　　　　(5分钟后,体格检查结束。)

吴医生　孩子肺里有广泛的湿啰音,根据孩子的病史和体格检查,初步考虑孩子患了肺炎。您先带孩子抽血检查血常规和 C 反应蛋白,看看是什么病原体感染;然后再去拍胸部 X 线片。等结果出来后,您再来找我!

母　亲　好的!
　　　　　(1 小时后,检查结果出来了)

母　亲　吴大夫,宝宝的检查结果已经都出来了,请您看一下!

吴医生　好的!胸片双肺可见点片状阴影,孩子确实是患了肺炎。血常规化验提示白细胞增高,C 反应蛋白增高,考虑细菌感染的可能性大。

母　亲　肺炎是不是很严重?宝宝需要住院治疗吗?

吴医生　孩子目前属于轻症肺炎,可以在门诊治疗。

母　亲　那是吃药还是打针啊?

吴医生　孩子现在是肺炎急性期,有高热、精神差的症状,而且血常规化验白细胞明显增高,在门诊输液治疗吧。

母　亲　用什么药?

吴医生　孩子化验结果支持细菌感染,建议输**头孢呋辛**,对球菌杆菌都有效。

母　亲　那还需要吃药吗?

吴医生　需要,我给您开了**止咳化痰**药物**沐舒坦糖浆**,一天三次,一次 2.5ml。

母　亲　好的。

吴医生　孩子痰多,建议用**富露施雾化**促进排痰,不知道孩子配不配合,您愿意试一下吗?

母　亲　雾化会让孩子很难受吗?

吴医生　雾化没有什么痛苦,但是面罩扣在口鼻处,有的孩子会比较恐惧,不愿接受。

母　亲　做吧,我家宝宝很乖,没有问题!

吴医生　这是您的处方,交费取药后到儿科**治疗室**找护士输液并做雾化。回家后**请按**时服药,三天后到门诊复诊!

母　亲　好的,谢谢您,大夫。

吴医生　不用谢! 好好照顾孩子,尽快康复吧!

Childhood Pneumonia

SITE:　Paediatric Clinic

CHARACTERS:　Doctor Wu (Pediatrician)

Lele (Patient, female, 3 years old, is taken by her mother to the hospital.)

Dr.Wu:　Take your seat, please. I am Dr. Wu. What can I do for you?

Mother:　Dr. Wu, my daughter has running nose and coughed for a few days. Today she started to have a fever. I am so worried about her that I take her here.

Dr.Wu:　How long has she coughed? Is there any phlegm?

Mother:　Three days. It sounds chesty, but she could not cough it up.

Dr.Wu:　Have you taken the temperature when she had a fever? Has she had any antipyretic?

Mother:　It was up to 39℃. I did not give her any medication for the fever, as I'm afraid it may make her symptoms less obvious, which affects the determination of her disease.

Dr.Wu:　Well, if the temperature is higher than 38.5℃, you'd better give her antipyretic to control the fever promptly. It will not have any effect on diagnosis. Sometimes, children could have febrile seizures with high fever, which is dangerous.

Mother:　Oh, I knew nothing about it. I'll take notice of it.

Dr.Wu:　Have you taken her to see a doctor after she was ill?

Mother:　No, I didn't. She only had mild running nose and a cough at first. I didn't take it seriously and gave her some cold & flu medications. She is not getting better and today she has a fever. My husband has been complaining about it.

Dr.Wu:　What kinds of cold & flu tablets did you give to her? Were there any antibiotics?

Mother:　I have no idea about antibiotics. I just gave her Chinese medicine.

Dr.Wu:　Does she have any other problems, like vomit, diarrhea, or somnolence?

Mother:　No, she doesn't. But she looks a bit tired with a poor appetite.

Dr.Wu:　Does she have any wheeze or feel short of breath?

Mother:　No, it doesn't seem that she wheezes. What do you mean by short of breath? How could we tell whether she feels short of breath?

Dr.Wu:　It means that the kid breathes fast or has nasal flaring while breathing.

Mother:　She is breathing a bit fast without nasal flaring.

Dr.Wu:　How about her general health? Has she been vaccinated on schedule?

Mother:　She is always healthy without problems, but he has got sick quite often since she went to kindergarten. She had immunization on time.

Dr.Wu:　Any contact with tuberculosis?

Mother:　No.

Dr.Wu:　Now, I'll examine her. Please put her on the bed.

(Turn to Lele) Shall we play a game with my stethoscope? It won't hurt you at all. You are a quite good girl, aren't you?

(5 minutes later, the physical examination was completed)

Dr.Wu:　There are widespread moist rales over the lung bases. According to the history and examination, it looks as if she has got pneumonia. Let's do some blood tests to judge the pathogen, including FBC(full blood count)and CRP(C reactive protein). The chest X-ray is also needed for the diagnosis. Please come back to me when the results are available.

Mother: Oh, I see.

(The results are available within 1 hour)

Mother: Dr Wu, here are the results. Please have a look.

Dr.Wu: Ok. There were bilateral patchy infiltrations on the chest X-ray, which confirms pneumonia. FBC shows elevated WBC(white blood cell)and the CRP is high, which suggests bacterial infection.

Mother: Is it serious? Does she need to be admitted to the hospital?

Dr.Wu: No, it is mild pneumonia. She'll be treated as outpatient.

Mother: Does she need oral, or IV(intravenous)medications?

Dr.Wu: Yes, she needs the latter. Now that it is in the acute phase with high fever, lethargy, and elevated WBC. She'd better have IV treatment in the outpatient clinic.

Mother: What medications will she have?

Dr.Wu: The blood tests are suggestive of bacterial infection. I'll recommend cefuroxime to her, which is effective to cure both cocci and bacilli infection.

Mother: Does she need any oral medication apart from what you mentioned above?

Dr.Wu: Yes, I'll prescribe mucosolvin syrup to relieve coughing and reduce phlegm. Take 2.5 ml, three times a day.

Mother: Ok.

Dr.Wu: As there is lots of phlegm, I suggest fluimucil nebulization to help clear it up. I am not sure whether Lele will cooperate. Would you like to have a try?

Mother: Is the nebulization painful?

Dr.Wu: No, it's not painful. But some children may feel scary and do not accept it as the mask has to be put over the nose and mouth.

Mother: No problem. She is a really good girl.

Dr.Wu: This is the prescription. Please go to pay for the medicines and then bring them to the nurse in the Pediatric Treatment Room for IV and nebulization. Don't forget to take medicines on time at home. Please bring her back for review after 3 days.

Mother: I see. Thank you, Dr. Wu.

Dr.Wu: Don't mention it. Take care of her so that she'll recover soon.

疾病介绍

xiǎoérfèiyán
小儿肺炎

肺炎 是 肺实质 的 炎症 。大部分 肺炎 是 由 微生物 感染 所致 ，不同 年龄段 感染 的 微生物 不同 。 临床 表现 有发热 、咳嗽 和 呼吸 困难 ， 通常 前期 有上呼吸道 感染史 。 呼吸 增快 是 肺炎 的 重要 体征 ，同时 肺部 听诊 可以 听到 广泛 的 湿啰音 和 喘鸣音 。 胸部 X 线 检查 可以 帮助 确诊 肺炎 。 全血细胞 计数 、C 反应蛋白 和 鼻咽 分泌物 检查 有 助 于 判断 病原体 。 如果 是 细菌性肺炎 ，需要 给予 抗生素 治疗：青霉素 对于 多数 患儿 是 一线 用药 ，

tóubāojūnsù yòngyú yánzhòng de huàn'ér　　rúguǒ bìngyuántǐ shì zhīyuántǐ　zé xūyào jǐyǔ　āqíméisù zhìliáo
头孢菌素 用于 严重 的 患儿 。 如果 病原体 是 支原体 ， 则 需要 给予 阿奇霉素 治疗 。

Childhood Pneumonia

Pneumonia is an inflammation of the parenchyma of the lungs. Most cases of pneumonia are caused by microorganisms and different organisms affect different age groups. The clinical manifestations include fever, cough and breathlessness, usually accompanied by an upper respiratory tract infection in the early stage. Tachypnea is a key sign and chest auscultation may reveal widespread rales and wheezing. A chest X-ray can help confirm the diagnosis. A full blood count, C-reactive protein, and nasopharyngeal aspirate should be carried out in patients for the judgment of the pathogen. Antibiotics are usually given if a diagnosis of bacterial pneumonia is made: penicillin is the first choice to most children and cefuroxime is indicated in severe cases. If mycoplasma is suspected, azithromycin should be given.

1. 当回事儿
认为某人或某事是非常重要的。
It means "take seriously", e.g. 不舒服就马上看病，别不当回事儿。

2. ……见好
表示有所好转；出现好的情况。
It means "get better", e.g. 经过治疗，病人的病情见好。

3. 倒是……
表示跟一般情理相反，出乎意料。
It indicates "contrast to" or "unexpected", e.g. 这样的怪事我倒是第一次听说。

婴 儿 腹 泻

黏液	niányè	名	mucus
脓血	nóngxuè	名	pus and blood
体温计	tǐwēnjì	名	thermometer
配方奶	pèifāngnǎi	名	formula
接种	jiēzhòng	动	vaccinate
轮状病毒	lúnzhuàngbìngdú	名	rotavirus
疫苗	yìmiáo	名	vaccine
前囟凹陷	qiánxìnāoxiàn	名	sunken fontanel（le）
脱水	tuōshuǐ	名	dehydration
酸中毒	suānzhòngdú	名	acidosis

静脉补液	jìngmàibǔyè	名	intravenous rehydration
累计损失	lěijìsǔnshī	名	accumulated deficit
继续丢失	jìxùdiūshī	名	ongoing losses
生理需要	shēnglǐxūyào	名	physiological requirement
口服补液	kǒufúbǔyè	名	oral rehydration
休克	xiūkè	名	shock
心力衰竭	xīnlìshuāijié	名	heart failure
保护剂	bǎohùjì	名	protective agent
蒙脱石散	méngtuōshísàn	名	smecta
益生菌	yìshēngjūn	名	probiotics

地点：儿科门诊
人物：陆医生（儿科医生）
　　　壮壮（患儿，男，10个月，由母亲带来就诊）

陆医生　您好！孩子有什么不舒服吗？

母　亲　陆大夫，宝宝又吐又拉，我很担心他。

陆医生　很严重吗？病了几天了？

母　亲　他两天前开始呕吐，精神还好。这两天，我只喂他吃了些容易消化的食物，也没见好，**昨天又开始拉稀。**

陆医生　孩子一天拉几次？大便什么样？

母　亲　一天快十次了，大便像稀水一样，黄绿色的。

陆医生　大便里面有没有**黏液脓血**？

母　亲　没有。

陆医生　尿少不少？

母　亲　他大小便都在尿布里，看不太清，但感觉尿有点儿少。

陆医生　发不发热？

母　亲　感觉有点儿热，但家里没有**体温计**，没给他量过体温。刚才护士测了体温，告诉我是**38℃**。

陆医生　嗯，孩子除了这些不适，有没有哭闹、腹胀、嗜睡甚至惊厥的情况？

母　亲　没有。他精神还挺好的，就是奶吃得少了。

陆医生　孩子是母乳喂养还是吃**配方奶**？

母　亲　母乳。以前也没生过什么病，这次不知道怎么回事。

陆医生　这次呕吐之前有没有吃什么不干净的东西？

母　亲　没有。我们一直挺注意卫生的。

陆医生　疫苗都按时接种了吗？**接种过轮状病毒**口服**疫苗**吗？

母　亲　预防针都按时打了，没吃过您说的这个疫苗。

陆医生　这两天有没有看过病？化验过大便吗？

母　亲　没有，孩子小，我轻易不愿意带他去医院，怕传染疾病。今天拉得太厉害了，我担心有什么问题，才赶紧把他带来了。

陆医生　请把孩子抱到检查床上平躺，我给他做一下体格检查。

　　　　（5分钟后，体格检查结束）

陆医生 孩子略有口唇干燥、**前囟凹陷**,腹部无压痛,肠鸣音活跃,可以确诊他患了婴儿腹泻、**轻度脱水**。从孩子发病季节和症状看,有可能是轮状病毒肠炎。不过,确诊还需要给孩子做血常规、便常规以及大便轮状病毒抗原化验。另外,再化验一下电解质,了解有无电解质紊乱和**酸中毒**。

母 亲 好的。那是不是做完检查,我们就可以回去了?等化验结果出来后再来找您吗?

陆医生 你们现在可不能回家。孩子目前出现了轻度脱水,又有呕吐、进食差的症状,需要在门诊留观,尽快给予**静脉补液**治疗。等化验结果出来后,我们再决定是否加用抗生素。

母 亲 输液要多长时间?

陆医生 输液分为三个阶段:补充**累计损失**、补充继续丢失和补充**生理需要**,大概需要 24 小时。等孩子不呕吐了,就可以改为**口服补液**治疗了。

母 亲 啊! 那孩子多遭罪啊!

陆医生 因为水分占儿童体重的比例较大,儿童脏器功能发育尚未成熟,体液平衡调节能力差,容易发生脱水。如果不重视,会从轻度转为重度,甚至会出现**休克**,危及生命,但是补液又不能过快,否则容易出现**心力衰竭**。

母 亲 好吧,我懂了。还要开点儿药吃吗?

陆医生 我给他开了肠黏膜保护剂**蒙脱石散**和肠道**益生菌**妈咪爱口服,具体服用方法药师会写在药品包装上。

母 亲 饮食有什么需要注意的吗?

陆医生 目前认为腹泻时继续进食十分重要。待宝宝呕吐好转后可以喂食,辅食要暂停,只母乳喂养就可以了。腹泻好转后可以逐步添加辅食,由少到多,由稀到稠,逐渐恢复正常饮食。

母 亲 明白了。

陆医生 这是处方和化验单,交费取药后到儿科治疗室找护士输液就可以了。化验结果出来后记得再来找我。

(3 小时后,化验结果全部出来)

母 亲 陆大夫,这是孩子的化验结果,请您看看。

陆医生 血常规、便常规大致正常。大便轮状病毒抗原阳性,可以确诊为轮状病毒肠炎。电解质化验提示轻度酸中毒,这个不用特殊治疗,补液后会好转!

母 亲 那我就放心了。

陆医生 您还有什么问题吗?

母 亲 我们输完液后还要做什么?

陆医生 这个您不用担心,壮壮是留观病人,会有值班医生根据孩子的病情决定下一步诊疗计划!

母 亲 太好了,谢谢医生!

Infantile Diarrhea

SITE:　Pediatric Clinic

CHARACTERS:　Doctor Lu (Pediatrician)

　　　　　　Zhuangzhuang (Patient, male, 10 months old, is taken by his mother to the hospital.)

Dr. Lu:　**Hello**, what **brought** you here today?

Mother:　**Dr. Lu**, my baby vomited and had diarrhea. I am really concerned about him.

Dr.Lu:　Oh, when did it start?

Mother:　**The vomiting** started two days ago, and his mental state was not bad at that time. I only gave him some **easily digestible** food to eat, but he didn't get better, and then he had loose bowels yesterday.

Dr.Lu:　How many times a day did he have diarrhea? What did the stool look like?

Mother:　About 10 times a day. The stool was watery, in yellow-greenish colour.

Dr.Lu:　Have you noticed any mucus, pus or blood in it?

Mother:　No.

Dr.Lu:　Did he pass less urine than usual?

Mother:　He was wearing nappies. It was hard to tell. But he did have less wet nappies.

Dr.Lu:　Did he have any fever?

Mother:　I felt he was hot, but I did not check the temperature as I did not have thermometer at home. The nurse just checked it and told me the temperature was 38℃.

Dr.Lu:　Oh, have you noticed that he had irritability, bloating, lethargy, or even seizures besides the symptoms you mentioned?

Mother:　No, he still looks well except for his decreased appetite. He has drunk less milk recently.

Dr.Lu:　Is he breast-fed or formula-fed?

Mother:　Breast-fed. He was really healthy before. I don't know where he got it.

Dr.Lu:　Did he have any unclean food before he got sick?

Mother:　Nothing specific. We are really careful about hygiene.

Dr.Lu:　Has he had vaccination up to date? Has he vaccinated the oral vaccine for rotavirus?

Mother:　Yes, he has all the planned immunization but I don't know the vaccine you mentioned.

Dr.Lu:　Have you brought him to see a doctor recently, and have you tested the stool?

Mother:　No, I haven't. He is so little that I dare not bring him to hospital in case he might get infection from the hospital. But his diarrhea is getting worse, so I am really worried about him and brought him here hastily.

Dr.Lu:　Please take him on his back on the bed. Let me examine him.

　　　　(5 minutes later, the physical examination was completed.)

Dr.Lu:　It showed that there were mild dry mouth and sunken fontanelle and there was no tenderness on his abdomen with active bowel sounds, therefore I'll diagnose infantile diarrhea with mild dehydration. Based on the onset season and his symptoms, rotavirus gastroenteritis is suspected. Let's have some tests to confirm the diagnoses, including FBC(full blood count), faecal MCS(faecal microscopy), and faecal rotavirus antigen. We'll also check electrolytes to make sure whether there is electrolyte disturbance and metabolic acidosis.

Mother:　Ok. Shall we go home after the tests and come back to you when the results are available?

Dr.Lu:　I'm afraid you can't go. I think he has to be kept in the outpatient department for observation at present, and IV(intravenous)rehydration should be given as quickly as possible, for your baby has dehydration and can't tolerate oral fluids due to his poor feeding and ongoing vomiting. We'll wait for the results of chemical examination to see whether we have to give him some antibiotics.

Mother:　How long will it take for IV rehydration?

Dr.Lu:　Gradual IV rehydration over 24 hours is recommended, to replace accumulated deficits, ongoing losses, and physiologic requirements. When the vomiting settles down, we could choose oral rehydration solution.

Mother:　Oh, what a torture for such a little boy!.

Dr.Lu:　Infants are prone to have dehydration due to their high proportion of body water, immature organ function, and poor ability to maintain fluid and electrolyte balance. If not taken seriously, the dehydration could deteriorate quickly, from mild to severe, even lead to shock, which is life-threatening. We have to provide him with intravenous fluid slowly; otherwise congestive heart failure will happen.

Mother:　Oh, I see. Does he need to take any oral medications?

Dr.Lu:　I'll prescribe mucosal protective agent, smecta, and probiotics Medilac-Vita. The pharmacists will write down the instruction details on the package of medications.

Mother:　Is there anything else we have to pay attention to foods?

Dr.Lu:　Currently it is very important to continue feeding while having diarrhea. Once the vomiting settles down, breast feeding could restart but complementary food. When the diarrhea improves, he can be given complementary food gradually, from small to large amount, from fluids to semi solid, and then solid foods.

Mother:　I see.

Dr. Lu:　Here are the prescriptions and laboratory test request forms. After payment, please take the medications to the Paediatric Treatment Room to have IV therapy there. Come back to me when the results are available.

　　　　(The results of laboratory test are available within 3 hours)

Mother:　Dr. Lu, these are the laboratory test reports. Would you like to tell me what they are?

Dr. Lu:　Ok. FBC and faecal MCS are mostly normal. The faecal rotavirus antigen is positive, so acute rotavirus gastroenteritis is confirmed. There is mild metabolic acidosis that'll be resolved by IV fluid therapy, and other treatment is not required.

Mother:　That's good.

Dr.Lu:　Do you have any more questions?

Mother:　What else shall we do after the IV fluid therapy?

Dr.Lu:　Don't worry. Zhuangzhuang will be kept in the hospital for observation, and the doctor on duty who looks after him will check him up and let you know what to do next.

Mother:　That's great. Thank you very much.

疾病介绍

婴儿腹泻

婴儿腹泻是一组由多因素引起的以大便次数增加和大便性状改变为特点的消化道综合征。婴儿容易患腹泻病，病因分为感染性和非感染性。胃肠炎是胃肠道的感染，多由病毒引起，主要表现为腹泻和呕吐。轮状病毒是最常见的病原，特别是在秋冬季发病最多。体格检查中，最重要的体征是有无脱水以及脱水的严重程度。实验室检查包括大便镜检、大便培养和病毒抗原检测。腹泻治疗的关键是补液，维持水电解质平衡。抗生素很少使用，除非是细菌感染。

Infantile Diarrhea

Infantile diarrhea is a gastrointestinal syndrome caused by multiple factors and characterized by the increase of the stool frequency and the change of the stool consistency. Diarrhea is more common in children and can be due to the infectious and noninfectious causes. Gastroenteritis is an infection of the gastrointestinal tract, usually caused by viral, which presents with a combination of diarrhea and vomiting. Rotavirus is the most common pathogen, especially in the fall and winter. The most important physical signs in examination are the presence and severity of dehydration. Laboratory investigations should include stool microscopy, stool culture and stool viral antigen detection. The key to infantile diarrhea is rehydration in order to keep the balance of fluid and electrolyte. Antibiotics are rarely used except for specific bacterial infections.

语言点

1. 又……又……

并列两个动词或形容词,表示"两者都有"或"不仅…而且…"。

Verbs or adjectives are used in the structure, which means "both…and…" or "not only…but also…", e.g. 这里的东西又便宜又好。

2. 轻易……

表示简单容易;随随便便。

It means "easily or lightly", e.g. 胜利不是轻易得到的。

3. ……受罪

指受到折磨,也泛指遇到不顺利或不愉快的事情。

It means "endure hardships, tortures, rough conditions, etc", e.g. 孩子因为生病而受罪了。

 练习

➤ 听力练习

一、听录音,选择你听到的词语

( ) 1. A. 干咳   B. 咳嗽   C. 咳痰   D. 咳喘

( ) 2. A. 喘气   B. 喘憋   C. 喘息   D. 喘鸣

( ) 3. A. 良药   B. 西药   C. 苦药   D. 中药

( ) 4. A. 发呆   B. 发热   C. 发烧   D. 发病

( ) 5. A. 肺炎   B. 鼻炎   C. 咽炎   D. 唇炎

( ) 6. A. 赶快   B. 赶路   C. 赶紧   D. 赶集

( ) 7. A. 留守   B. 留住   C. 留念   D. 留观

( ) 8. A. 平躺   B. 侧躺   C. 斜躺   D. 横躺

( ) 9. A. 肾衰   B. 心衰   C. 肝衰   D. 呼衰

( ) 10. A. 黏液   B. 体液   C. 汁液   D. 唾液

二、请选出与所听录音相符的答案

( ) 1. A. 患儿自己吃了退烧药   B. 患儿自己不吃退烧药

       C. 母亲让患儿吃了退烧药   D. 母亲没有让患儿吃退烧药

( ) 2. A. 患儿没看病也没吃药   B. 患儿没看病吃了药

       C. 患儿看了病吃了药   D. 患儿看了病没吃药

( ) 3. A. 患儿妈妈听说过轮状病毒疫苗   B. 患儿疫苗按时接种了

       C. 患儿没接种过轮状病毒疫苗   D. 患儿妈妈没听说过轮状病毒疫苗

( ) 4. A. 医生要跟患儿做游戏   B. 医生要跟患儿打电话

       C. 医生哄患儿配合检查   D. 医生在询问孩子病情

（　　）5. A. 腹泻患儿继续母乳喂养　　　　　　B. 腹泻患儿继续辅食添加

　　　　　 C. 腹泻患儿可以正常饮食　　　　　　D. 腹泻患儿不能进食

三、听录音，完成下面的练习

1. 根据所听到的录音判断对错

1）医生查体后怀疑妞妞患了支气管炎。（　　　）

2）医生最后确诊妞妞是细菌感染所致的支气管肺炎。（　　　）

3）妞妞住院输了头孢菌素治疗。（　　　）

4）妞妞只输了头孢菌素，病情就有所好转。（　　　）

5）医生建议每日给妞妞静脉输抗生素，直至退热。（　　　）

6）医生说每天除了静脉点滴，还要门诊复诊。（　　　）

2. 听录音，选择正确答案回答问题

1）下面哪一项不是壮壮的症状？（　　　）

　　A. 呕吐　　　　　 B. 腹泻　　　　　 C. 发热　　　　　 D. 尿少

2）下面哪一项不是医生查体发现的体征？（　　　）

　　A. 口唇干燥　　　 B. 眼窝凹陷　　　 C. 前囟凹陷　　　 D. 皮肤苍白

3）医生给出的治疗方案是什么？（　　　）

　　A. 静脉补液　　　 B. 口服补液　　　 C. 抗生素治疗　　　 D. 口服退烧药

➤ **词汇和语法练习**

一、给下列词语标注拼音

1. 喘息＿＿＿＿＿＿＿＿＿＿＿＿　　　　2. 休克＿＿＿＿＿＿＿＿＿＿＿＿

3. 热性惊厥＿＿＿＿＿＿＿＿＿＿　　　　4. 鼻翼扇动＿＿＿＿＿＿＿＿＿＿

5. 听诊器＿＿＿＿＿＿＿＿＿＿＿　　　　6. 止咳化痰＿＿＿＿＿＿＿＿＿＿

7. 静脉补液＿＿＿＿＿＿＿＿＿＿　　　　8. 母乳喂养＿＿＿＿＿＿＿＿＿＿

9. 轮状病毒＿＿＿＿＿＿＿＿＿＿　　　　10. 前囟凹陷＿＿＿＿＿＿＿＿＿＿

二、选词填空

| 治疗室　　脱水　　发烧　　酸中毒　　及时　　便常规 |
| 退烧药　　诊疗计划　　雾化　　不舒服 |

1. 您好，请坐！我是吴大夫，孩子有什么＿＿＿＿＿＿＿＿＿＿吗？

2. 宝宝昨晚开始＿＿＿＿＿＿＿＿＿＿，我很着急，就带她来医院了。

3. 如果孩子发烧大于 38.5℃，最好尽快给孩子口服＿＿＿＿＿＿＿＿＿＿。

4. 孩子有腹泻，我帮您开一下＿＿＿＿＿＿＿＿＿＿化验，协助判断病因。

5. 孩子痰多，建议应用富露施＿＿＿＿＿＿＿＿＿＿促进排痰。

6. 孩子口唇干燥，前囟凹陷，尿量减少，考虑有＿＿＿＿＿＿＿＿＿＿。

7. 这是您的药物处方，交费取药后到＿＿＿＿＿＿＿＿＿＿找护士输液就可以了。

8. 值班医生根据患儿的病情决定下一步的＿＿＿＿＿＿＿＿＿＿。

9. 幸亏患儿的妈妈＿＿＿＿＿＿＿＿＿＿带他来医院，才避免了病情加重。

10. 腹泻合并脱水的患儿容易出现电解质紊乱和＿＿＿＿＿＿＿＿＿＿。

三、用指定的词语或结构完成句子或对话

1. 宝宝腹泻合并脱水，＿＿＿＿＿＿＿＿＿＿呢？（是……还是……）

2. 宝宝刚开始有点咳嗽，＿＿＿＿＿＿＿＿＿＿，后来越来越严重了。（当回事儿）

3. 孩子吃了口服药，＿＿＿＿＿＿＿＿＿＿。（见好）

4. 医生，宝宝＿＿＿＿＿＿＿＿＿＿，您给好好看一下。（又……又……）

5. 我担心医院交叉感染，_____。(轻易)

6. 我_____，不想给宝宝输液治疗。(受罪)

四、把下列词语排列成句子

1. 输液　后　交费取药　到治疗室　找护士

2. 补液　的　孩子　治疗　尽快　脱水　需要

3. 检查　医生　患儿　做　给　体格

4. 不知道　能不能　配合　妈妈　孩子　治疗

5. 化验　找　看　医生　结果　一下

➤ **阅读与应用练习**

一、根据课文内容补全对话

医生：孩子咳嗽几天了？有痰吗？

母亲：咳嗽 3 天了，听着有痰，但他不会吐出来。

医生：孩子生病后，有没有带他看过医生？

母亲：没有！宝宝刚开始就是有点__1__、咳嗽，也不__2__，我就没__3__，自己找了点感冒药给他吃，结果也没__4__，还发起烧来了，最高 39℃。这不，孩子他爸直__5__我。

医生：孩子除了发烧和咳嗽，还有哪儿不舒服吗？

母亲：这倒是没有，但是孩子有点儿没精神，不爱吃饭。

医生：有没有觉得孩子喘息、__6__？

母亲：呼吸好像有点快，没有其他的。

　　　(体格检查发现患儿呼吸稍急促，双肺可闻及细湿啰音)

医生：根据孩子的病史和体格检查，我初步考虑孩子患了__7__，我给你开一下__8__和__9__化验，看看是什么病原感染，另外还需要做一下__10__检查，协助诊断。

二、根据课文内容回答问题

1. 乐乐生病的主要症状有哪些？

2. 医生给乐乐做体格检查时发现的重要体征是什么？

3. 医生给乐乐的确定诊断是什么？建议如何治疗？

4. 壮壮大便性状是什么样子的？排便次数是多少？

5. 针对壮壮的腹泻，医生建议饮食需要注意些什么？

三、写作练习

根据会话二，总结壮壮的主要症状和体征(不少于 40 字)。

四、交际练习

参考括号里的词语进行情景对话。

情景：患儿妞妞，女，3 岁，因"发热伴咳嗽 3 天"，由母亲王女士带来医院儿科门诊就诊。医生和患儿母亲进行情景对话。

(喘息、呼吸困难、鼻翼扇动、退烧药、感冒药、双肺细湿啰音、血常规、C 反应蛋白、胸片、抗生素)

新生儿黄疸

词汇

黄疸	huángdǎn	名	jaundice
皮肤	pífū	名	skin
脸	liǎn	名	face
耽误	dānwu	动	delay
传染病	chuánrǎnbìng	名	infectious disease
消毒	xiāodú	动	disinfect
胆红素	dǎnhóngsù	名	bilirubin
生理	shēnglǐ	名	physiology
数值	shùzhí	名	numerical value
平均值	píngjūnzhí	名	mean
伤害	shānghài	动	harm
照射	zhàoshè	动	shine

地点：儿科门诊

人物：王医生（儿科医生）

贝贝（患儿，男，出生 21 天，由母亲带来就诊）

母　亲　大夫，宝宝的**皮肤**黄得厉害，急死我了！

王医生　别担心。宝宝皮肤黄有几天了？

母　亲　宝宝刚出生挺正常的，从第三天开始，**脸**和身上的皮肤都变黄了，而且越来越黄。刚开始我上网查了相关信息，得知可能是新生儿生理性黄疸，不用治，过些日子会自然消退，我就没有带宝宝来医院。现在已经是出生第二十一天了，黄疸还没退。我有点儿着急，怕**耽误**宝宝的病，赶紧来医院了。

王医生　孩子是母乳喂养还是人工喂养？

母　亲　人工喂养。

王医生　除了皮肤发黄，孩子还有其他症状吗？

母　亲　吃奶不好，有时候呕吐，小便颜色也特别黄，但大便颜色正常。

王医生　孩子出生后，有没有患过其他疾病？

母　亲　没有，一切都正常。我和他爸爸身体都很好，没有**传染病**，而且孩子的用品使用前我都**消毒**，没有感染的机会。

王医生 孩子是足月出生的吗？

母 亲 不是的，36 周就出生了。黄疸和宝宝早产有关系吗？

王医生 有关系。新生儿肝脏酶系统发育不完善，产生的**胆红素**不能及时转化，而且刚出生的新生儿肠道无菌也会影响胆红素的代谢。这些因素使新生儿的血胆红素增多而发生黄疸。由于这只是一种暂时的现象，所以又叫**生理**性黄疸。新生儿生理性黄疸有一个特点，大多在出生后 2~3 天出现，4~5 天时最严重，足月儿一般在 1~2 周消退，早产儿一般在 2~3 周消退。

母 亲 这么说我儿子是生理性黄疸？

王医生 从您的描述和孩子的体征看，生理性黄疸的可能性大，这种黄疸一般不需要治疗。先给孩子检查一下，看看属于哪一种黄疸，是否需要治疗。

母 亲 好的。

王医生 先测一下黄疸**数值**，然后抽血化验肝功能。

母 亲 化验要抽很多血吗？ 这么小的孩子受得了吗？

王医生 没问题的。医院有专门的仪器，通过接触孩子的皮肤检测黄疸值。在小孩的脸部、胸部和后背测一下，取其**平均值**就可以了，不会**伤害**孩子的。化验需要抽血，但不会抽很多，放心吧。

（检查结果出来后）

王医生 从检查结果看，孩子的肝功能正常，黄疸数值略高，结合孩子早产的情况来考虑，应该是生理性黄疸还没有消退，不要紧张。

母 亲 大夫，这种情况需要治疗吗？

王医生 暂时不用，先回去观察几天。回家后，除了给孩子好好喂奶，还要适当补充水分，使黄疸尽早排出体外。光照有助于黄疸消退。如果室内温度适宜，每天给孩子脱了衣服，隔着玻璃窗，阳光**照射**半小时。

母 亲 谢谢大夫，这我就放心了，回去让孩子多接触阳光。

王医生 回家还要多观察孩子黄疸消退、体温、吃奶、睡眠和大小便情况。有需要就给我打电话，这是我的电话号码。

Neonatal Jaundice

SITE: Pediatric Out-patient Department

CHARACTERS Doctor Wang (Pediatrician)

Baby (Patient, male, a 21-day newborn, is taken by his mother to the hospital.)

Mother: Doctor, my baby looks very yellow and I'm worried to death!

Dr.Wang: Don't worry. How long has been this?

Mother: His skin looked normal at birth. Since the third day after being born, the baby's cheek and body have looked yellow and then become more and more yellow. At the beginning, I searched for relevant information online and learned that it might be physiological jaundice in newborns, which needs no treatment and naturally tends to recover completely; therefore I didn't bring him to the hospital. Now it is the 21st day after birth and the jaundice still exists and I'm a little anxious, so I rush to the hospital lest the disease is delayed.

Dr.Wang: Is the baby breast-fed or bottle-fed?

Mother: Bottle-fed.

Dr.Wang: Does the baby have other symptoms?

Mother: The baby feeds poorly, vomiting after drinking milk, the urine color is particularly yellow and the color of bowel movement is right.

Dr.Wang: Your baby has any other diseases after birth?

Mother: No, everything is all right. His father and I are healthy without any infectious diseases, and all the articles are not used for him until they are disinfected. It's impossible to make him infected.

Dr.Wang: Was the baby born at term or not?

Mother: No, he was born at 36 weeks' gestation. Is jaundice related to it?

Dr.Wang: Yes, it is. The development of neonatal liver enzyme system is not perfect that bilirubin can't be timely transformed. In addition, the intestinal tract of the newborn without bacteria also influences the metabolism of bilirubin. These factors cause the bilirubin increase in the newborn's blood and then jaundice appears. It is known as physiological jaundice because it is only a temporary phenomenon, characterized by occurrence during 2~3 days after birth and culmination during 4~5 days. It is resolved during 1~2 weeks in the full-term infants and 2~3 weeks in the preterm infants.

Mother: Is it physiological jaundice that my son's got?

Dr.Wang: From your description and the baby's physical signs, it is likely to be physiological jaundice. First let your baby have tests to see which kind of jaundice he's developed and whether the treatment is needed, all right?

Mother: Yea, that's right.

Dr.Wang: It is needed to measure the jaundice index and then have blood tests for liver function.

Mother: How much blood will be drawn out for the tests? Can such a little baby bear it?

Dr.Wang: No problem. There is a special instrument in the hospital to irradiate the baby's face, chest and back to take the average that tells the jaundice index. This won't cause any harm to him. Laboratory tests really need to take blood but it is not much, so you can rest assured.

(After the examination)

Dr.Wang: From the results of the examination, the baby's liver function is normal, but the jaundice index is slightly higher than normal. Combined with the baby's premature situation, it is the delay of neonatal jaundice remission. Take it easy.

Mother: Does it need treatments, doctor?

Dr.Wang: No, it doesn't need for the time being. Take the baby home and observe him these days. You do not only feed him with milk but also feed him with water at home in order to discharge bilirubin. In addition, let the natural light come in as much as possible, which is beneficial to the jaundice remission. If the indoor temperature is appropriate, take off the baby's clothes and expose him to the sun through the glass window for half an hour every day.

Mother: Doctor, I can rest assured. I'll let the baby expose to sunlight at home.

Dr.Wang: Closely observe the baby's jaundice remission, body temperature, feeding, sleep and urination as well as defecation. This is my phone number. Please call me if needed.

疾病介绍

xīnshēngérhuángdǎn
新生儿黄疸

xīnshēngérhuángdǎn huò gāodǎnhóngsùxuèzhèng shì yìzhǒng xīnshēngérqī chángjiànbìng duì zúyuè huò zǎochǎn yīngér dōu huì yǒu
新生儿黄疸（或 高胆红素血症）是 一种 新生儿期 常见病 ，对 足月 或 早产 婴儿 都 会 有
yǐngxiǎng tōngcháng chūxiàn zài yīngér chūshēng de dìyīzhōu yǒuxiē huángdǎn zài yìzhōu huò liǎngzhōu jiù xiāoshī wúxū zhìliáo
影响 ， 通常 出现 在 婴儿 出生 的 第一周 。 有些 黄疸 在 一周 或 两周 就 消失 ，无需 治疗 。
gēnjù chūxiàn huángdǎn de yánzhòng chéngdù bìngyīn huò yīngér chūshēng shíjiān de chángduǎn yìxiē yīngér xūyào zhìliáo
根据 出现 黄疸 的 严重 程度 、病因 或 婴儿 出生 时间 的 长短 ，一些 婴儿 需要 治疗 。

guāngzhào liáofǎ shì zuì chángjiàn de zhìliáo huángdǎn fāngfǎ　　guāngliáo shí　　pífū zài guāngzhào xià huì zēngjiā tǐyè de liúshī
光照 疗法 是 最 常见 的治疗 黄疸 方法。 光疗 时，皮肤 在 光照 下 会 增加 体液 的 流失，
suǒyǐ zhùyì bǔchōng yètǐ　　tóngshí　xūyào zhēzhù yǎnjing bìmiǎn búshì
所以 注意 补充 液体。 同时，需要 遮住 眼睛 避免 不适。

Neonatal Jaundice

Neonatal jaundice（or hyperbilirubinemia）is a common condition in newborn infants. It affects both full-term and premature babies and usually appears during the first week of the baby's life. Some jaundice will disappear within a week or two without treatment while others need to be treated according to its severity, its cause or the length of time the baby was born. Phototherapy is the most common treatment for jaundice. The eyes are covered to prevent discomfort and additional fluids are given to counteract the increased fluid losses from skin when exposed to the light during treatment.

语言点

1. 结合……（来）考虑

意思是从……考虑。

Something is considered from…e.g. 结合实际情况来考虑，她当时的做法是对的。

2. 隔着

表示两者之间相隔。

It means "across", e.g. 他们隔着桌子相互看着。

3. 受得了

表示能够忍受，常用在陈述句或问句里。

It means to be able to endure something, e.g. 他很坚强，受得了任何委屈和磨难。

化脓性脑膜炎

词汇

化脓	huànóng	动	suppurate
脑膜炎	nǎomóyán	名	meningitis
事先	shìxiān	名	in advance
征兆	zhēngzhào	名	sign
中耳炎	zhōngěryán	名	otitis media
乳突炎	rǔtūyán	名	mastoiditis
耳道	ěrdào	名	auditory canal
流感	liúgǎn	名	influenza
颈强直	jǐngqiángzhí	词	neck stiffness
脑脊液	nǎojǐyè	名	cerebrospinal fluid

腰椎	yāozhuī	名	lumbar
穿刺	chuāncì	动	puncture
粒细胞	lìxìbāo	名	granulocyte
痊愈	quányù	动	heal
颅压	lúyā	名	intracranial pressure
膨胀	péngzhàng	动	expand;swell;dilate

地点：儿科门诊
人物：赵医生(儿科大夫)
　　　茜茜(患儿,女,3岁,由母亲带来就诊)

母　亲　赵大夫,孩子说头痛得厉害,还恶心。

赵医生　这种情况多长时间了?

母　亲　两天了,她吐了两次,呕吐好像和吃东西没关系,突然就吐,**事先**没有任何**征兆**,人总是昏沉沉的。

赵医生　发烧吗?

母　亲　是的,昨儿和今儿都发烧。

赵医生　体温多少? 吃退热药了吗?

母　亲　最高39℃,吃了美林退热,可是过几小时又烧起来了。

赵医生　以前有过这种情况吗? 得没得过**中耳炎**或**乳突炎**?

母　亲　没有。只是以前外**耳道**流过脓,经过治疗就好了。

赵医生　最近接触过传染病人没有? 比如说**流感**病人。

母　亲　没有。现在是春天,我们就怕流感什么的,特别注意不带孩子到密闭的公共场所。我想起来了,我前天到幼儿园接孩子时,她班上有一个小朋友咳嗽、打喷嚏,会不会在幼儿园感染了流感?

赵医生　有这种可能。你们有没有按时进行疫苗的预防接种?

母　亲　都按时接种了。每到接种日期,社区就会通知我们去。

赵医生　好的,请您把孩子衣服解开我看看。孩子皮肤没有淤点或淤斑,外耳道也没有分泌物,但是**颈强直**,看上去像是脑膜炎。之前有没有看过大夫?

母　亲　看了。昨天我就带她去了社区医院,医生给她化验,白细胞总数一万多,说是像化脓性脑膜炎,建议我们到大医院来。

赵医生　脑膜炎是一种感染性疾病,在婴幼儿中多见。现在需要给孩子查血常规,还要做血培养和**脑脊液**检查,根据检查结果才能确诊。

母　亲　血常规我知道,就是抽血化验。脑脊液怎么查?

赵医生　需要做**腰椎穿刺**。

母　亲　腰椎穿刺? 那么小的孩子能受得了吗? 我听说腰椎穿刺会落下后遗症,阴天下雨都会腰痛。大夫,有没有别的办法? 只要不是腰椎穿刺就行。

赵医生　腰椎穿刺是检查脑膜炎的必要方法,对孩子没有什么太大影响,请放心。

母　亲　好吧,我们听您的。

(检查结果出来后)

赵医生　血液检查结果显示,白细胞和中性**粒细胞**计数明显增加。脑脊液检查显示外观混浊,白细胞增多,中性粒细胞为主,蛋白增高,糖降低。从检查结果和孩子的临床表现看,可以确诊为化脓性脑膜炎。

母　亲　天啊! 孩子怎么会得这种病?

赵医生　极有可能是孩子在幼儿园接触了病原菌,由于孩子的血-脑屏障发育不完善,这些病菌侵入到颅内,导致了化脓性脑膜炎。

母　亲　这可怎么办呢? 我听说这种病很危险。

赵医生　是有一定的危险性。您别急,只要及时治疗,好好护理,很快就会**痊愈**的。我们马上让孩子住院,静脉点滴抗生素杀菌。

母　亲　好的。到病房就可以开始点滴了吗?

赵医生　不行。得先做皮试,看她是否抗生素过敏,没有过敏才能用药。另外还需要联合应用其他药物减轻炎症,降低**颅压**并改善细胞代谢。

母　亲　治疗中,除了用药之外,有没有其他需要注意的事项?

赵医生　饮食上选择易消化的食物,少吃多餐,可以减轻胃的**膨胀**,防止呕吐发生。另外,要注意多休息,保证充足的睡眠。

Purulent Meningitis

SITE:　Paediatric Outpatient Clinic

CHARACTERS:　Doctor Zhao (Pediatrician)

　　　　　　　Cissy (Patient, female, 3 years old, is taken by her mother to the hospital.)

Mother: Doctor, my daughter told me she'd got a bad headache and nausea.

Dr. Zhao: How long has it been?

Mother: About two days. She vomited two times. It seemed there was no relation to her diet. There was not any sign in advance. She threw up with a befuddled mind.

Dr. Zhao: Did she have any fever?

Mother: Yes, she got a fever today and yesterday.

Dr. Zhao: What was the temperature? Did she take antifebrile medicine?

Mother: A maximum of 39℃. She took ibuprofen but had a fever again after a few hours.

Dr. Zhao: Did it happen before? Had she otitis media and mastoiditis?

Mother: No, but pus discharged from her external auditory canal. She felt well after treatment.

Dr. Zhao: Has she exposed to infected patients such as the people with flu?

Mother: No. In spring, for fear of the flu we do not take her to public places. Oh, I remember, when I came to the kindergarten to pick her up the day before yesterday, I saw a child in the class coughing and sneezing. Was she infected by the influenza in the kindergarten?

Dr. Zhao: It might be. Does she have the vaccination on time?

Mother: Of course. The community staff called us upon vaccination.

Dr. Zhao: Please open your baby's clothes and let me examine her skin. There are not petechiae or ecchymoses on the skin and secretion in her external auditory canal but neck stiffness. Based on the latter, it looks like meningitis. Did you go and see a doctor before?

Mother: Yes. I took her to a community hospital yesterday. She had a blood test that showed her white blood cells more than ten thousand. She was thought to have purulent meningitis and the doctor suggested us to go to the big hospital.

Dr. Zhao: Meningitis is a kind of infectious disease which threatens the health of infants and young children. Hence a blood test, blood culture, and examination of the cerebrospinal fluid are needed. Your baby will be diagnosed based on test results.

Mother:　I know that blood test. How is cerebrospinal fluid done?

Dr. Zhao:　A lumbar puncture.

Mother:　Lumbar puncture? Can the kid stand it? I was told that the lumbar puncture resulted in severe side effects that caused the pain in the lower back in rainy days. Is there any other way? Anything is good except puncture.

Dr. Zhao:　Lumbar puncture is the necessary examination of meningitis. It will not cause harm to her. Don't worry.

Mother:　Ok. I follow your advice.

（After the test results turned out）

Dr. Zhao:　The blood test shows that white blood cells and neutrophils granulocyte have risen obviously and the examination of the cerebrospinal fluid indicates that it looks turbid, neutrophils have remained predominantly while white blood cells and protein have increased and sugar has decreased. Based on the results and the child's symptoms, purulent meningitis is diagnosed.

Mother:　My god! Why has she got such a disease?

Dr. Zhao:　It is very likely that she was exposed to pathogens in the kindergarten and the development of children's blood brain barrier is imperfect, then bacteria invade the brain to cause purulent meningitis.

Mother:　What can I do for it? I know the disease is very dangerous.

Dr. Zhao:　Yes, it is but don't worry. Good nursing and timely medical treatment will bring her round. I accept her to the hospital at once. Antibiotics will be given intravenously to kill bacteria.

Mother:　All right. Is she going to be treated with intravenous antibiotics as soon as she is in the ward ?

Dr. Zhao:　No, we'll take a skin test to see if she has any allergic reaction. They'll be taken if she is not allergic to them. What's more, other medicines are used to reduce inflammation and intracranial pressure, and improve cell metabolism.

Mother:　Are there any do's and don'ts in addition to medication during treatment?

Dr. Zhao:　Provide her with easily-digested food and let her eat less and more times in order to reduce gastric distention and prevent the occurrence of vomit. In addition, enough sleep and a good rest will restore her to health.

疾病介绍

化脓性脑膜炎

化脓性脑膜炎 是 蛛网膜下腔 的 细菌 感染，约 80% 以上 是由 肺炎 链球菌(肺炎 双球菌)、流感 嗜血 杆菌 及 脑膜炎 双球菌 引起 的，与 年龄 、季节 、地区 、机体 免疫 功能 、有无 头颅 外伤 以及 是否 有 先天性 的 神经 或 皮肤 缺陷 有关，以婴幼儿 发病 居多 并 危及 到 其 生命 。 典型 的 临床 症状 是发热 、呕吐 、头痛 、脑脊液 改变 和 脑膜 刺激，这种 病 需要 快速 诊断 和 及时 治疗，其 预后 取决于 治疗 的 速度 和 充分性 。

Purulent Meningitis

Purulent meningitis is a bacterial infection of the subarachnoid space, over 80% of which are caused by streptococcus pneumoniae (diplococcus pneumoniae), haemophilus influenza and diplococcus intracellularis, concerning various factors such as age, reason, region, immune function of organism, head trauma, and congenital defect of nerve or skin. It commonly takes place in infants and children and threatens their lives. The typical symptoms are fever, vomiting, headaches, cerebrospinal fluids (CSF) changes and meningeal irritation. It constitutes a diagnostic and therapeutic emergency. The prognosis depends on the rapidity and the adequacy of management.

语言点

1. 比如说

举例说明。

It means "for instance, for example, such as", e.g. 他确实很聪明, 比如说他学东西很快。

2. 每到……时(候)

一到……时候。

It refers to "when…", e.g. 每到下课时, 老师微笑着跟我们说再见。

3. 对……(有)影响

对人或事物起的作用。

It means to have an effect on…, e.g. 古典音乐对他的作品影响很大。

➤ 听力练习

一、听录音, 选择你听到的词语

( ) 1. A. 肌肤　　　　B. 美肤　　　　C. 皮肤　　　　D. 润肤

( ) 2. A. 耽误　　　　B. 错误　　　　C. 笔误　　　　D. 口误

( ) 3. A. 教育　　　　B. 发育　　　　C. 体育　　　　D. 养育

( ) 4. A. 生活　　　　B. 生命　　　　C. 生理　　　　D. 生病

( ) 5. A. 照相　　　　B. 照耀　　　　C. 照办　　　　D. 照射

( ) 6. A. 征召　　　　B. 征兆　　　　C. 征文　　　　D. 征兵

( ) 7. A. 耳目　　　　B. 耳机　　　　C. 耳朵　　　　D. 耳道

( ) 8. A. 穿线　　　　B. 穿衣　　　　C. 穿刺　　　　D. 穿孔

( ) 9. A. 腰椎　　　　B. 颈椎　　　　C. 胸椎　　　　D. 脊椎

( ) 10. A. 膨胀　　　　B. 肿胀　　　　C. 发胀　　　　D. 头胀

二、请选出与所听录音相符的答案

( ) 1. A. 新生儿黄疸病因和体征　　　　B. 新生儿黄疸值和特点

　　　　C. 新生儿黄疸病因和特点　　　　D. 新生儿黄疸值和体征

( ) 2. A. 医生与病人　　B. 丈夫与妻子　　C. 老师与学生　　D. 母亲与孩子

( ) 3. A. 在书上　　B. 在家里　　C. 在学校　　D. 在网上

( ) 4. A. 检查脑膜炎　　B. 检查脊髓病　　C. 检查脑血管病　　D. 检查胃肠道疾病

( ) 5. A. 治疗效果不好　　B. 治疗效果好　　C. 治疗有误　　D. 对症治疗

三、听录音,完成下面的练习

1. 根据所听到的录音判断对错

1)让患儿多喝水或葡萄糖水。(　　)

2)太阳光强烈的时候让新生儿黄疸患儿晒太阳。(　　)

3)患儿无论什么时候都不能断了母乳。(　　)

4)患儿消化道通畅有利于排出胆红素。(　　)

5)如果新生儿黄疸不是生理性的,就要用药治疗。(　　)

6)只要是新生儿生理性黄疸就不需要用药治疗。(　　)

7)给出现黄疸的新生儿用药要在医生的指导下进行。(　　)

8)蓝光照射治疗是主要的新生儿黄疸治疗方法。(　　)

2. 听录音,选择正确答案回答问题

1)新生儿化脓性脑膜炎由下列哪一项引起的?(　　)

    A. 食用菌　　　　　B. 病毒　　　　　C. 化脓菌　　　　　D. 支原体

2)下列哪一项**不**属于化脓性脑膜炎预防的范围?(　　)

    A. 情绪感染　　　B. 呼吸道感染　　　C. 胃肠道感染　　　D. 皮肤感染

3)为预防化脓性脑膜炎,产妇产前保健重点预防哪一类疾病?(　　)

    A. 心病　　　　　B. 肠炎　　　　　C. 头痛　　　　　D. 发热

4)为避免感染,新生儿皮肤护理需要防止什么?(　　)

    A. 皮肤损伤　　　　　　　　　B. 脐部被水或尿液浸湿

    C. 泪水流入外耳道　　　　　　D. ABC

5)发现新生儿有感染灶怎么办?(　　)

    A. 用抗生素　　　　　　　　　B. 用抗生素并处理局部感染

    C. 局部消毒　　　　　　　　　D. 用维生素并局部消毒

➤ 词汇和语法练习

一、给下列词语标注拼音

1. 喂养_____　　　　2. 传染_____

3. 消毒_____　　　　4. 征兆_____

5. 接种_____　　　　6. 化脓_____

7. 胆红素_____　　　8. 粒细胞_____

9. 中耳炎_____　　　10. 后遗症_____

二、选词填空

事先	颅压	黄疸	脑脊液	照蓝光	数值	膨胀	咳嗽	消毒	生理性

1. 孩子刚出生三天肤色就发黄,医生说是_____黄疸。

2. 如果孩子黄疸严重,就需要到医院去_____。

3. 医生告诉我回去要密切观察孩子_____情况,暂时不需要治疗。

4. 医院有专门的仪器来测量患儿的黄疸_____。

5. 如果婴幼儿的皮肤受到感染,应该立即_____处理。

6. 我们_____不知道去社区医院给孩子打疫苗。

7. 贝贝可能感冒了,从幼儿园回来后就开始_____不止。

8. 大夫给孩子做了腰椎穿刺,结果是_____混浊。

9. 不仅要给化脓性脑膜炎患儿用抗生素杀菌,还要用其他药物减轻炎症和降_____。

10. 病人腹腔积液很严重,肚子_____得像一个皮球。

三、用指定的词语或结构完成句子或对话

1. _____,所以孩子没有受到传染。(由于)

2. 我们_____,同意他去进修。(结合……来考虑)

3. 孩子_____晒太阳。(隔着)

4. 有些小毛病不一定要去医院,_____。(比如说)

5. _____,我们就特别高兴。(每到……时候)

6. 孩子的脑膜炎已经治好了,_____。(对……有影响)

四、把下列词语排列成句子

1. 肠道无菌 代谢 新生儿 的 也会影响 胆红素

2. 治疗 常见的 光照疗法 方法 是 新生儿黄疸

3. 主要 患儿 通过 胆红素 大便 体内的 排出

4. 传染病人 远离 应该 其他 婴幼儿 传染源 和

5. 脑膜炎 治疗 快速 化脓性 及时 和 需要 诊断

> 阅读与应用练习

一、根据课文内容补全对话

主治医师: 脑脊液检查结果显示外观混浊,白细胞增多,中性粒细胞为主,蛋白增高,糖减低。从检查结果和孩子临床表现看,可以__1__为化脓性脑膜炎。

患儿母亲: 天啊!孩子怎么会得这种病?

主治医师: 极有可能是孩子在幼儿园接触到病原菌,再加上孩子血-脑屏障__2__不完善,这些病菌进入颅内,__3__化脓性脑膜炎。

患儿母亲: 这可怎么办呢?我听说这种病很危险。

主治医师: 是的,有一定的危险性,但你别急,只要及时治疗,好好护理,很快就会痊愈的。我们马上让孩子住院,__4__抗生素杀菌。

患儿母亲: 好的。到病房就开始打点滴吗?

主治医师: 不行。得先做个皮试,看她是否有__5__过敏现象,没有过敏才能用药。另外还要用其他药__6__炎症,降低颅压并改善细胞代谢。

患儿母亲: 治疗中,除了用药之外,有没有其他__7__注意的事项?

主治医师: 让孩子饮食上吃些好消化的,少吃多餐,以减轻胃的膨胀,防止呕吐发生。另外,要注意多__8__,保证充足睡眠。

二、根据课文内容回答问题

1. 为什么贝贝母亲在他出现黄疸21天后才带他到医院看病?

2. 医生为什么说新生儿容易发生黄疸?

3. 医生给茜茜确诊为化脓性脑膜炎的依据是什么?

4. 给茜茜静脉点滴抗生素之前必须先做什么?

5. 根据课文,谈一谈如何护理化脓性脑膜炎患儿?

三、写作练习

根据第二篇会话内容,写出一篇字数不少于60个字的概述,简单介绍患儿临床表现和诊断治疗情况。

四、交际练习

参考括号里的词语进行情景对话。

情景:一位患儿在母亲的陪伴下前来就诊,医生和患儿母亲进行对话。

(感冒,咳嗽,发热,化脓性脑膜炎,药物治疗,抗生素,皮试)

第二十章　口腔内科

龋　齿

词汇

龋齿	qǔchǐ	名	dental caries
倒牙	dǎoyá	动	set one's teeth on edge
稍微	shāowēi	副	slightly
倒数	dàoshǔ	动	count backward
咬合面	yǎohémiàn	名	occlusal surface
龋洞	qǔdòng	名	caries cavity
嵌塞	qiànsāi	动	get stuck between
俗称	súchēng	动 / 名	commonly known
虫牙	chóngyá	名	rotten tooth
蛀牙	zhùyá	名	decayed tooth
牙神经	yáshénjīng	名	dental nerve
牙本质	yáběnzhì	名	dentine
中龋	zhōngqǔ	名	moderate caries
腐质	fǔzhì	名	detritus
垫底	diàndǐ	动	rebase
聚羧酸锌	jùsuōsuānxīn	名	zinc polycarboxylate
树脂	shùzhī	名	resin
充填	chōngtián	动	fill
深龋	shēnqǔ	名	deep caries
牙髓	yásuǐ	名	dental pulp

地点：口腔科门诊
人物：杨医生（主治医师）
　　　王力（病人，男，46岁）

王　力　杨医生，我发现我右侧下面大牙上有个黑色的小洞，吃饭的时候，总会塞东西，咬硬的食物时也不敢使劲儿，所以我想过来做个检查，看看究竟是怎么一回事儿。

杨医生　这种症状出现多长时间了？还有什么不舒服的感觉？

王　力　大概半个多月了。嗯，还有就是遇到冷、热、酸、甜刺激时，牙齿也会觉得不舒服，有时有"**倒牙**"的感觉。

杨医生　好的。我现在为您检查一下，请您坐到这边的治疗椅上。用器械检查时可能比较敏感，请您**稍微忍耐**一下。

　　　　（5分钟后）

杨医生　您的牙齿检查发现，右侧下面**倒数**第二颗大牙的**咬合面**上有一个**龋洞**，所以经常**嵌塞**食物。另外，当龋洞受到刺激时也会比较敏感。

王　力　杨医生，您说的"龋洞"是咱们**俗称**的"**虫牙**"吗？

杨医生　是的。"龋齿"俗称"**蛀牙**"或者"虫牙"。细菌是导致龋齿的主要原因，因此平时要注意口腔卫生和饮食习惯。

王　力　杨医生，我的龋齿严重吗？

杨医生　不算严重，您龋洞的深度离**牙神经**还有一段距离，没有发展到**牙本质**深层，属于"**中龋**"。

王　力　那我需要怎么治疗？

杨医生　您现在的情况，只需把龋洞里的**腐质**完全清理掉，然后用**垫底**材料**聚羧酸锌**垫底，再用**树脂充填**材料把龋洞**充填**好就可以了。

王　力　那我就放心了。我一直担心需要抽牙神经呢！

杨医生　您多虑了。"中龋"不需要抽牙神经。当"**深龋**"发展到一定程度，损害到**牙髓**时才需要抽牙神经呢！

王　力　那我真是幸运呢！杨医生，龋齿不治疗行吗？

杨医生　龋齿是不可能自行愈合的。它对人类的危害很大，不及时治疗，最终会导致牙齿丧失，甚至会引起身体其他部位的病变。

王　力　哎呀！杨医生，我听着都害怕了，您赶快给我治疗吧！

　　　　（半小时后）

杨医生　牙齿补好了，您感觉一下有没有什么不舒服的地方？

王　力　（上下咬了咬牙）谢谢杨医生，挺好的，没有什么不舒服的感觉。我回家以后需要特别注意什么吗？

杨医生　没有什么需要注意的，正常吃饭没有问题。

王　力　好的，我知道了，谢谢您，杨医生！

Dental Caries

SITE:　　　Outpatient Service of Stomatological Department
CHARACTERS:　Doctor Yang (Attending physician)
　　　　　　　Wang Li (Patient, male, 46 years old)

Wang Li:　Doctor Yang, I've found a black hole in my big tooth at the bottom of the right. Food always gets stuck between the teeth and I dare not to chew hard in case of tough food, so I come here for inspection to know what's wrong with it.

Dr.Yang: How long has this symptom lasted? And do you have any other uncomfortable feelings?

Wang Li: About half a month. Hum, I feel uncomfortable in it when I eat something cold, hot, sour or sweet, and sometime that sets my teeth on edge.

Dr.Yang: I see. I'll check it for you now. Please sit at the treatment chair here. When I check with device, you may feel sensitive, and endure the pain slightly, please.

(5 minutes later)

Dr.Yang: I've checked your teeth. There is a caries cavity on the occlusal surface at the second big tooth counted backward from the right lower side, so the food always gets stuck between your teeth. Additionally, the caries cavity will be sensitive in case of any stimulation.

Wang Li: Doctor Yang is, the caries cavity you said commonly known as rotten tooth?

Dr.Yang: Yes, it is. The dental caries is also called "decayed tooth" or "rotten tooth". The bacteria are a necessary occurring condition, so you should pay attention to the oral hygiene and dietary habits at ordinary times.

Wang Li: Is my dental caries serious, Doctor Yang?

Dr.Yang: No, it isn't. You are lucky that there is the distance between the depth of caries cavity and dental nerve. It has not developed to the deep layer of dentine, belonging to "moderate caries".

Wang Li: How to treat it?

Dr. Yang: As for your condition, the detritus in your caries cavity should be cleaned up, and then rebase is performed with zinc polycarboxylate before the cavity is filled with resin material.

Wang Li: What you said put my mind at rest. I'm always worried that I need to take out tooth nerve!

Dr.Yang: You're worried too much. The "moderate caries" is not required to be treated by taking out the tooth nerve that'll be taken out when the "deep caries" develop to certain degree and damage the dental pulp!

Wang Li: How lucky I am! What would happen if the dental caries were not treated, Dr. Yang?

Dr. Yang: Dental caries will not heal on its own without treatment. The dental caries will cause the great damage to human beings. It will eventually lead to the loss of teeth, and even cause the lesions on other parts of the body if it has not been treated on time.

Wang Li: Ah! Doctor Yang, I'm scared of listening to it. Let's get started.

(30 minutes later)

Dr.Yang: Your tooth has been filled. Is there anything you feel uncomfortable?

Wang Li: (Grind the teeth up and down). Thank you, Doctor Yang. I feel very well and comfortable. Well, is there anything else I should pay particular attention to when I get back home?

Dr.Yang: No, you can eat normally.

Wang Li: All right. Thank you, Doctor Yang.

龋齿

龋齿 俗称 虫牙、蛀牙，是 在 以 细菌 为主 的 多种 因素 影响 下，牙齿 发生 慢性 进行性 破坏 的 一种 疾病，不 经 治疗 不会 自行 愈合。龋病 是 人类 常见、多发病 之一，发病率 位居

qiánliè   qǔbìng gěi rénlèi zàochéng de wēihài jídà   bù jíshí zhìliáo   zuìzhōng huì dǎozhì yáchǐ sàngshī   shènzhì huì yǐnqǐ
前列 。 龋病 给 人类 造成 的 危害 极大 ， 不 及时 治疗 ， 最终 会 导致 牙齿 丧失 ， 甚至 会 引起
shēntǐ qítā bùwèi de bìngbiàn   ànzhào qǔbìng de fāzhǎn chéngdù kěyǐ fēn wèi qiǎnqǔ   zhōngqǔ hé shēnqǔ   yátǐ zài sè
身体 其他 部位 的 病变 。 按照 龋病 的 发展 程度 可以 分 为 浅龋 、 中龋 和 深龋 ， 牙体 在 色 、
xíng   zhì gèfāngmiàn jūn fāshēng biànhuà   zài gègè jiēduàn de línchuáng biǎoxiàn yě bù xiāngtóng   qiǎnqǔ búyì bèi fāxiàn
形 、 质 各方面 均 发生 变化 ， 在 各个 阶段 的 临床 表现 也 不 相同 。 浅龋 不易 被 发现 ，
méiyou míngxiǎn zìjué zhèngzhuàng   yámiàn qīngwēi fāhēi huò chéng báisè   zhōngqǔyá shàng yǐyǒu míngxiǎn qǔdòng   yáchǐ
没有 明显 自觉 症状 ， 牙面 轻微 发黑 或 呈 白垩色 ； 中龋牙 上 已有 明显 龋洞 ， 牙齿
shòudào cìjī shí huìyǒu suāntòng de gǎnjué bìng yǒu shíwù qiànsāi   shēnqǔ zìjué zhèngzhuàng míngxiǎn   yù lěng rè cìjī huì
受到 刺激 时 会有 酸痛 的 感觉 并 有 食物 嵌塞 ； 深龋 自觉 症状 明显 ， 遇 冷 热 刺激 会
yǐnqǐ téngtòng   qǔdòng yǐ fāzhǎn dào yáběnzhì shēncéng   yǒu chángshíjiān shíwù qiànsāishǐ   línchuáng jīngcháng cǎiyòng qùchú
引起 疼痛 ， 龋洞 已 发展 到 牙本质 深层 ， 有 长时间 食物 嵌塞史 。 临床 经常 采用 去除
fǔzhì   diàndǐ chōngtián de zhìliáo fāngfǎ lái zhìliáo qǔbìng   qǔbìng zhìliáo de mùdì shì zhōngzhǐ bìngbiàn guòchéng   bǎohù
腐质 、 垫底 充填 的 治疗 方法 来 治疗 龋病 。 龋病 治疗 的 目的 是 终止 病变 过程 ， 保护
yásuǐ   huīfù yá de xíngtài   gōngnéng hé měiguān
牙髓 ， 恢复 牙的 形态 、 功能 和 美观 。

Dental Caries

The dental caries, commonly known as decayed tooth or rotten tooth, is a kind of disease that the tooth is under the chronic progressive damage with the effect of bacteria and other several minor factors, which will not heal on its own without treatment. The dental caries is one of the common and frequently-occurring diseases among people, and its incidence ranks in the top list. The dental caries will cause the great damage to human beings. It will eventually lead to the loss of teeth, and even cause the lesions from other parts of the body if it has not been treated on time. According to the development degree, the detail caries can be divided into the superficial caries, moderate caries, and deep caries. The tooth will change in its color, shape and quality, and its clinical manifestations vary in different stages. The superficial caries is undetectable without obvious subjective symptoms, and the tooth presents black or chalky slightly; as for the moderate caries, the tooth has obvious caries on it and aches in case of any stimulation and food gets stuck between the teeth; for deep caries, the patient can have obvious subjective symptoms and the tooth will pain if stimulated by cold and heat. The caries cavity has already developed to the deep layer of dentine with long-time food impaction history. Clinically, cleaning up the detritus, rebasing and filling are often adopted to treat the dental caries. The treatment aims to terminate the lesion process, protect the dental pulp, and recover the shape, function and beauty of the tooth.

语言点

1. ……多虑了

想得多，考虑得多。

It means "think or consider too much", e.g. 您多虑了。

2. 算是……

"算"在这里是一个动词，当做，算做。后面常用"是"，可加名词、动词、形容词或者小句。

It is a verb, meaning "serve and count", used with "是", usually followed by noun, verb, adjective or clause, e.g. 您来得算是早的了。

3. 导致……

引起、造成(不好的结果)。

It means "cause, result in or lead to" (bad consequences), e.g. 龋齿对人类的危害很大，不及时治疗，最终会导致牙齿丧失。

牙 髓 炎

牙髓炎	yásuǐyán	名	pulpitis
解决	jiějué	动	solve
根管治疗	gēnguǎnzhìliáo	名	root canal therapy
质地	zhìdì	名	quality
邻接	línjiē	动	be adjacent to
缝	fèng	名	gap
X线牙片	X xiànyápiàn	名	X-ray tooth film
牙根	yágēn	名	tooth root
范围	fànwéi	名	range
牙髓腔	yásuǐqiāng	名	dental pulp cavity
过氧化氢溶液	guòyǎnghuàqīngróngyè	名	hydrogen peroxide
生理盐水	shēnglǐyánshuǐ	名	normal saline
交替	jiāotì	动	in turn
拔髓针	básuǐzhēn	名	nerve broach
樟脑酚	zhāngnǎofēn	名	camphor phenol
缓解	huǎnjiě	动	relieve
罗红霉素	luóhóngméisù	名	roxithromycin

地点:口腔科门诊
人物:杨医生(主治医师)
　　　张华(病人,男,45岁)

张　华　大夫,我最近几天牙疼得厉害。

杨医生　您牙疼多长时间了?

张　华　一周左右了,前几天还行,这两天明显加重了。白天还可以忍受,但是一到晚上就疼得受不了,真是"牙疼不是病,疼起来真要命"啊!

杨医生　您除了牙疼,还有什么其他不舒服的吗?

张　华　没有了,就是不能吃太凉或太热的东西,还有吃饭时也会牙疼。

杨医生　根据现在的情况判断,这是典型牙髓炎的症状,也就是俗话说的牙神经疼。如果您想**解决**疼痛,需要做**根管治疗**,也就是俗话说的抽牙神经。

张　华　我听说抽牙神经以后,牙齿的**质地**就没有以前好了,有没有好的保守治疗方法呢?

杨医生　保守治疗可以选择口服用药,但是也只能解决短期内的疼痛。如果牙疼再次发作的话,肯定会比这次疼得更加厉害。

张　华　这样啊！那还是听您的,抽牙神经吧。

杨医生　好的,请您坐到这边来,我先给您做初步的口腔检查。

（10分钟后检查结束）

杨医生　您现在感觉疼痛的牙齿是右侧上边的倒数第二颗牙,这颗牙有长期嵌塞食物的问题,并且与前一颗牙齿相**邻接**的**缝**里有龋洞,牙疼应该就是这个原因。您现在需要拍一张 **X 线牙片**,看一下这颗牙齿的**牙根**情况和龋洞的大小**范围**。

张　华　好的,医生。

（5分钟后）

杨医生　您的 X 线牙片显示,您这颗牙齿的牙根正常,但是龋洞的面积不小,已经发展到了**牙髓腔**。像我们当初说的那样,如果您想保留这颗牙齿,就要考虑根管治疗。

张　华　好的,听您的。我想问一下做这个治疗大概需要多长时间,需要吃药吗？

杨医生　整个治疗下来大概需要半个月左右的时间。治疗过程中会根据您的具体情况来决定是否需要用消炎药。

张　华　好的,那咱们现在就开始治疗吧！

杨医生　好。您之前用过麻药吗？有没有药物过敏史？您平时身体怎么样？是否有高血压、糖尿病、心脏病？

张　华　以前做手术时用过麻药,没有什么反应。平时身体还行,没有什么慢性病,就是对青霉素和花粉过敏。

杨医生　好的,我现在先给您打麻药。

（打麻药5分钟后）

张　华　杨医生,我感觉脸好像肿了,有些发热、发胀。

杨医生　没事,这是麻药起作用的正常现象,放松,不要紧张。

张　华　好的。

杨医生　治疗过程中,您有什么不适的话,请用您的左手示意。记住,不要用您的手去碰我的右手,否则我手里的机器会对您造成伤害。

张　华　好的,明白了。您尽快给我治疗吧！

杨医生　我会把龋洞内的腐质完全清除直至髓腔完全暴露,然后用**过氧化氢溶液**、**生理盐水交替**冲洗髓腔,并用**拔髓针**将已坏死的神经完全抽出并再次冲洗。最后把**樟脑酚**小药球放入龋洞内消毒。现在,我们开始治疗。

（20分钟后）

杨医生　今天的治疗到此结束。

张　华　谢谢您,杨医生。回家后我需要吃药吗？平时要注意些什么？

杨医生　您最近吃东西时尽量不要使用右边的牙齿,可以正常刷牙。如果牙齿有轻微的不适,不用担心,那是治疗后的正常炎症反应,您可以吃些消炎药,**缓解**症状。

张　华　什么消炎药？

杨医生　**罗红霉素**就可以。一天两次,一次一粒,饭后服用,连续吃三天。服药期间,要避免食用带有刺激性的食物。三天后,您再过来继续后面的根管清理消毒和根管充填治疗。

张　华　好的,谢谢您。再见！

Pulpitis

SITE:　Outpatient Service of Stomatological Department

CHARACTERS:　Doctor Yang (Attending physician)

Zhang Hua (Patient, male, 45 years old)

Zhang Hua: Doctor, I've got a terrible toothache in recent days.

Dr. Yang: How long has it lasted?

Zhang Hua: About one week. It was not too bad a few days before, but it's got worse these two days. It is not too severe in the daytime, but I can't stand it in the evening. It is really like the saying, "the toothache is not a disease in deed, but it will torment you as long as it happens"!

Dr. Yang: Hum, any more symptoms besides your toothache?

Zhang Hua: No, nothing else but the fact that I can't eat too cold or hot food. It will be hurt when eating.

Dr. Yang: According to your current condition, this is the typical pulpitis symptom, that is, dental nerve pain we commonly call. If you want to solve the pain, you need to receive the root canal therapy, or "taking out the dental nerve" as the saying goes.

Zhang Hua: But I was told that the tooth quality would not be as good as before if the dental nerve was taken out. Is there any more conservative treatment?

Dr. Yang: Only oral medication as the conservative treatment, but it can just solve the short-term pain. If the toothache flares up again, you'll feel much more painful than this time.

Zhang Hua: Ah! I'd better listen to you, taking out the dental nerve.

Dr. Yang: Ok. Please sit on the chair here. Firstly, I'll perform a preliminary oral examination.

(10 minutes later after the examination)

Dr. Yang: The tooth you feel painful is the second tooth counted downward from the right upper side. It must have a long-term food impaction issue, and the caries cavity exists in the gap adjacent to the front tooth. The toothache can be caused by it. Now, you need to take an X-ray tooth film to check out the tooth root condition and the size of its caries cavity.

Zhang Hua: Ok, doctor.

(5 minutes later after)

Dr. Yang: Your X-ray tooth film shows that the tooth root is good, but the caries cavity area on the tooth is big, and it has developed to dental pulp cavity. It is just like what I said at the beginning. If you want to save the tooth, you should consider the root canal therapy.

Zhang Hua: Ok, I'll listen to you. I am wondering that how long the treatment takes, and if I need to take any medicine.

Dr. Yang: The whole treatment will roughly take half a month. If needed, you are required to take some anti-inflammatory drugs for several days during the treatment.

Zhang Hua: Ok. Let's start the treatment now!

Dr. Yang: Did you use any anesthetic before? Do you have allergy history? How is your health? Do you have hypertension, diabetes or cardiopathy?

Zhang Hua: There was no adverse effect on me when I was given anesthetic in the operation before. I am healthy except allergy to penicillin and pollen.

Dr. Yang: I see. Now I will give you anesthetic first.

(5 minutes later after the anesthetic given)

Zhang Hua: Doctor, I feel my face swollen, hot and swelling.

Dr. Yang: It doesn't matter. The anesthetic is working. Just relax, and don't be nervous.

Zhang Hua: Ok.

Dr. Yang: If you feel uncomfortable during the treatment, signal for me with your left hand, please. Be sure not to touch my right hand, otherwise the instrument in it may hurt you.

Zhang Hua: I have got it. Let's start now.

Dr. Yang: I'll clean up the detritus in your caries cavity till the pulp cavity exposes completely, and then I'll flush the pulp cavity in turn with hydrogen peroxide and normal saline. After that, I'll take out the necrotic nerve absolutely with the nerve broach and then flush it again. Finally, I'll put the small camphor phenol medicine ball into the caries cavity for disinfection. Now, the treatment begins.

(20 minutes later)

Dr. Yang: Today's treatment is over.

Zhang Hua: Thank you, Doctor Yang. Do I need to take any medicine after I go home? Is there anything else I should pay particular attention to?

Dr. Yang: You'd better not use the right side teeth when eating. The tooth brushing will not be affected. Don't worry if you feel uncomfortable in it; it's the normal inflammatory response. You can take anti-inflammatory tablets to relieve the symptom.

Zhang Hua: What anti-inflammatory tablets shall I take?

Dr. Yang: The roxithromycin is ok, twice a day, taken after meal, one tablet a time, for three consecutive days. Please avoid eating irritating food during medication and come back in three days to continue the treatment of root canal cleaning, disinfection and root canal filling.

Zhang Hua: Ok, thank you. See you!

疾病介绍

牙髓炎

牙髓炎是指发生在牙髓组织的炎性病变。细菌是引起牙髓病最重要的因素，此外还有物理因素、化学因素和免疫因素等。牙髓炎是比较常见的牙齿疾病，以疼痛为主要症状，并且对冷热刺激的敏感性加强，俗话说"牙疼不是病，疼起来真要命"指的就是这一病程。牙髓病可以根据牙髓受损的程度进行治疗，如果牙髓病变是局限的或是可逆的，选择以保留活髓为目的的治疗方法，如盖髓术等；如果牙髓病变是全部的或是不可逆的，选择以去除牙髓、保存患牙为目的的治疗方法，如根管治疗等。牙髓炎通常需要拍牙片来帮助确诊。急性牙髓炎的感染源主要来自深龋，临床主要表现为剧烈疼痛，病人通常会疼痛难忍前来就医；慢性牙髓炎也多由深龋感染引起，但是因为临床症状不典型，所以经常不被病人重视，耽误治疗。

Pulpitis

The pulpitis refers to the inflammatory lesion occurring in the pulp tissue. The bacteria are the most important factor of pulp disease, and others include the physical factor, chemical factor and immune factor. The pulpitis is a relatively common tooth disease. The cardinal symptom is pain and higher sensitivity to cold and heat. The saying "the toothache is not a disease actually, but it will torment you as long as it happens" just describes its course. The pulp disease can be treated according to the damage degree of dental pulp. If the lesion of dental pulp is partial and reversible, the treatment method of the reservation of vital pulp will be selected, such as pulp capping; if it is entire and irreversible, the treatment method of pulp removal and diseased tooth reservation will be preferred, such as root canal therapy. Generally, the pulpitis needs to be confirmed by taking the dental film. The infection source for acute pulpitis is mainly from the deep caries with main clinical manifestation of severe pain, and the patient will generally come to the doctor due to it; the chronic pulpitis is also mostly caused by the infection of deep caries, but it often goes ignored by the patients due to its non-typical clinical symptoms, thus delaying the treatment.

语言点

1. ……就是……

"不过"的意思。前半句常为积极义，后半句为消极义。

It means "but", connecting two clauses. The former always has the positive meaning and the latter has the negative meaning, e.g. 这件衣服很好看，就是有点儿贵。

2. 直至……

"至"到的意思。"直至"一直到。

"至" means "to". "直至" means "until", e.g. 直至写完作业，我才去睡觉。

3. 将

"将"在这里是介词，"把"的意思。常用于书面语。

It means "把" here, a preposition, commonly used as a written word, e.g. 他将处方交给了我。

练习

➤ 听力练习

一、听录音，选择你听到的词语

( ) 1. A. 症状   B. 敏感   C. 刺激   D. 倒牙

( ) 2. A. 牙神经   B. 牙本质   C. 咬合面   D. 牙髓炎

( ) 3. A. 中龋   B. 龋齿   C. 龋洞   D. 蛀牙

( ) 4. A. 复诊   B. 暴露   C. 丧失   D. 愈合

( ) 5. A. 病变   B. 质地   C. 材料   D. 充填

( ) 6. A. 避免   B. 导致   C. 过敏   D. 交替

( ) 7. A. 发作   B. 判断   C. 缓解   D. 解决

( ) 8. A. 消炎药   B. 青霉素   C. 牙髓腔   D. 拔髓针

( ) 9. A. 范围   B. 面积   C. 邻接   D. 典型

( ) 10. A. 根管治疗   B. 生理盐水   C. 聚羧酸锌   D. 罗红霉素

二、请选出与所听录音相符的答案

( ) 1. A. 医生和病人家属   B. 病人和病人   C. 医生和实习生   D. 医生和病人

( ) 2. A. 深龋   B. 牙髓炎   C. 中龋   D. 浅龋

( ) 3. A. 孩子每天早晚刷牙   B. 孩子长了一颗蛀牙

     C. 吃很多甜食对牙齿不好   D. 刷牙方法不正确对牙齿不好

( ) 4. A. 补牙很便宜   B. 补牙很贵

     C. 补牙费用根据补牙材料而定   D. 补牙费用根据补牙材料和龋洞面积而定

( ) 5. A. 洗牙很贵   B. 洗牙是为了让牙齿变白

     C. 洗牙可以洗掉牙齿上的脏东西   D. 最好经常洗牙

三、听录音,完成下面的练习

1. 根据所听到的录音判断对错

1) 刷牙的正确方法是从左往右刷。(　　)

2) 每天刷一次牙就可以了。(　　)

3) 刷牙时间太短会没有效果。(　　)

4) 养成良好的生活习惯对预防蛀牙没有帮助。(　　)

5) 这段录音介绍了和蛀牙说再见的方法。(　　)

2. 听录音,选择正确答案回答问题

1) 以下说法和原文**不**一致的是:(　　)

    A. 老王就医及时　　　　　　　　B. 没有办法了老王才去医院

    C. 老王对麻药过敏　　　　　　　　D. 老王需要做根管治疗

2) 老王牙疼的时候经常吃什么药? (　　)

    A. 止疼药　　　　B. 消炎药　　　　C. 罗红霉素　　　　D. 麻药

3) 老王得了什么病? (　　)

    A. 牙髓炎　　　　B. 深龋　　　　C. 中龋　　　　D. 根管治疗

➤ 词汇和语法练习

一、给下列词语标注拼音

1. 垫底＿＿＿＿＿＿＿＿＿＿＿　　2. 牙神经＿＿＿＿＿＿＿＿＿＿＿

3. 拔髓针＿＿＿＿＿＿＿＿＿＿＿　　4. 腐质＿＿＿＿＿＿＿＿＿＿＿

5. 牙髓腔＿＿＿＿＿＿＿＿＿＿＿　　6. 生理盐水＿＿＿＿＿＿＿＿＿＿＿

7. 罗红霉素＿＿＿＿＿＿＿＿＿＿＿　　8. 根管治疗＿＿＿＿＿＿＿＿＿＿＿

9. 咬合面＿＿＿＿＿＿＿＿＿＿＿　　10. 嵌塞＿＿＿＿＿＿＿＿＿＿＿

二、选词填空

| 清理消毒　　抽牙神经　　发作　　加重　　中龋　　典型症状 |
| 俗称　　X线牙片　　消炎药　　过敏史 |

1. 请您拍一张＿＿＿＿＿＿＿＿,我好确定您牙齿的牙根情况和龋洞的大小范围。

2. 在做根管充填治疗以前,我需要对您根管内部进行＿＿＿＿＿＿＿＿＿。

3. ＿＿＿＿＿＿＿＿＿需及时治疗,否则龋齿会继续发展。

4. 当深龋损害到牙髓时,就要考虑＿＿＿＿＿＿＿＿了。

5. 根管治疗＿＿＿＿＿＿＿＿抽牙神经。

6. 牙髓炎的＿＿＿＿＿＿＿＿是牙齿疼痛,并且对冷热刺激的敏感性加强。

7. 做完治疗后如果牙齿有不适,可以吃些＿＿＿＿＿＿＿＿缓解症状。

8. 做手术前医生会问病人的药物＿＿＿＿＿＿＿＿。

9. 避免牙疼反复＿＿＿＿＿＿＿＿睡不着应该及时看医生。

10. 龋齿不治疗会继续＿＿＿＿＿＿＿＿,甚至会影响全身健康。

三、用指定的词语或结构完成句子或对话

1. 龋齿不及时治疗＿＿＿＿＿＿＿＿。(导致)

2. 病情还没发展,＿＿＿＿＿＿＿＿。(算是)

3. 我感觉好多了,＿＿＿＿＿＿＿＿。(就是)

4. 要注意口腔卫生,＿＿＿＿＿＿＿＿。(尽量)

5. 医生加班到深夜,＿＿＿＿＿＿＿＿。(直至)

四、把下列词语排列成句子

1. 大概　多长时间　治疗　需要　这个
2. 受不了　牙　得　疼　晚上
3. 这是　已经　表现　麻药　的　显效
4. 我　上　大牙　有　右上面　小洞　个
5. 器械　比较　可能　用　检查　敏感　时

➤ **阅读与应用练习**

一、根据课文内容补全对话

医生：　您的牙齿我已经为您检查过了,您右侧下面倒数第二__1__大牙的咬合面上有一个龋洞,
　　　　__2__经常会嵌塞食物。__3__,当龋洞遇到刺激时也会比较敏感。

病人：　杨医生,您说的"龋洞"是咱们__4__的"虫牙"吗?

医生：　是的。"龋齿"俗称"蛀牙"__5__"虫牙"。细菌就是龋病发生的__6__条件,__7__平时要注
　　　　意口腔卫生和饮食习惯。

病人：　杨医生,我的龋齿严重吗?

医生：　__8__严重,幸运的是您龋洞的深度离牙神经还有一段距离,没有发展到牙本质深层,属于
　　　　"中龋"。

病人：　那我现在的情况该怎么治疗呢?

医生：　__9__您现在的情况,只需把您牙齿上龋洞里的腐质__10__清理掉,__11__用垫底材料聚羧
　　　　酸锌垫底,__12__用树脂充填材料把龋洞充填起来就可以了。

病人：　那我就放心了。我还__13__担心我需要抽牙神经呢!

医生：　您__14__。"中龋"是不需要抽牙神经治疗的。当"深龋"发展到一定程度损害到牙髓
　　　　时__15__会抽牙神经呢!

病人：　那我__16__幸运的呢! 杨医生,龋齿不治疗会怎么样呢?

医生：　龋齿不经治疗是不会__17__愈合的。龋齿对人类的危害很大,不__18__治疗,最终
　　　　会__19__牙齿丧失,甚至会__20__身体其他部位的病变。

病人：　哎呀! 杨医生,我听着都害怕了,您快点给我治疗吧!

二、根据课文内容回答问题

1. 王力有哪些症状?
2. 医生给王力的诊断是什么? 如何治疗?
3. 如果龋齿不及时治疗会怎么样?
4. 张华为什么不选择保守治疗?
5. 张华 X 线牙片的诊断结果是什么?
6. 罗红霉素怎么服用?

三、写作练习

请简单写出会话二中病人张华的主要临床表现。

四、交际练习

参考括号里的词语进行情景对话。

情景:病人反复牙疼,加重一周后来医院就诊,医生和实习生对病人治疗方案进行讨论。

(症状,深龋,牙髓,X 线牙片,麻药,根管治疗)

第二十一章 口腔外科

牙齿矫形

词汇

矫形	jiǎoxíng	形	orthopaedic
咬合	yǎohé	动	bite
嚼	jiáo	动	chew
智齿	zhìchǐ	名	opsigenes
牙松动	yásōngdòng	名	gomphiasis
牙周	yázhōu	形	periodontal
牙龈炎	yáyínyán	名	gingivitis
牙列	yáliè	名	denture
正畸	zhèngjī	形	orthodontic
龈上洁治	yínshàngjiézhì	名	supragingival scaling
漱口	shùkǒu	动	gargle
头影正侧位	tóuyǐngzhèngcèwèi	名	lateral cephalometrics
全口曲面平展	quánkǒuqūmiànpíngzhǎn	名	full mouth surface flat
错殆	cuòhé	名	malocclusion
支抗	zhīkàng	名	anchorage
矫形力	jiǎoxínglì	名	orthopedic force
牵引	qiānyǐn	动	tow
牙间隙	yájiànxì	名	diastema
上颌	shànghé	名	maxillary
下颌	xiàhé	名	underjaw
托槽	tuōcáo	名	bracket
弓丝	gōngsī	名	arch wire

地点:口腔外科门诊
人物:邹医生(主治医师)
　　　邵鑫(病人,男,31 岁)

邹医生　邵先生,您好! 我是邹医生。请坐! 请问有什么可以帮助您的?

邵 鑫 邹医生,您好!我的牙齿排列不整齐,影响了我的脸型。听说能进行牙齿**矫形**,所以过来看一下。

邹医生 哦,还有其他不舒服的吗?

邵 鑫 有。吃饭的时候,我的前牙**咬合**不上,感觉嚼东西很费劲。

邹医生 前牙咬合不好有多长时间了?

邵 鑫 五年前就发现了,一直都没有治疗。

邹医生 当时的症状和现在一样吗?

邵 鑫 小的时候,我的牙齿排列还可以,随着年龄的增长,我发现牙齿紊乱情况逐渐严重。五年前,前牙开始咬合不上,但不影响日常生活。现在,这个问题已经影响到我的容貌和吃饭了。

邹医生 您的**智齿**长出来了吗?

邵 鑫 上下四颗智齿都已经长出来了。

邹医生 您平时刷牙或者吃硬东西的时候,有没有牙龈出血的情况?

邵 鑫 嗯,有这种情况。

邹医生 有没有**牙松动**的情况?

邵 鑫 没有。

邹医生 以前看过医生吗?

邵 鑫 看过一次。

邹医生 上次看病的时候,您都做了哪些检查?

邵 鑫 上次医生只给我做了**牙周检查**。

邹医生 医生告诉您是什么问题吗?

邵 鑫 医生说我有**牙龈炎**。

邹医生 好的,明白了!现在我给您做一下检查,请躺到检查床上,头后仰并向左偏。
（10 分钟后,检查结束。）

邹医生 根据您的病史和牙齿检查,您的情况属于**牙列拥挤**,伴有牙龈炎。牙列拥挤需要进行牙齿**正畸**矫形治疗,但是必须要等牙龈的炎症消退了以后才能进行治疗。

邵 鑫 哦,是这样呀!

邹医生 今天,我先给您开一些药物治疗牙龈炎。平时,请多注意休息,饮食规律,而且要戒烟、戒酒。另外,您还要去牙周科进行**龈上洁治**。

邵 鑫 还有其他需要注意的问题吗?

邹医生 您还需要注意刷牙的方法,饭前饭后要**漱口**,保持口腔清洁。牙龈炎治疗好以后,过一个月再来复诊。
（一个月后,病人复诊。）

邹医生 邵先生,您好。请坐。这一个月感觉如何?

邵 鑫 感觉好多了,牙龈已经不出血了。我能进行牙齿矫形了吗?

邹医生 您先躺在检查床上,我需要为您检查一下。
（5 分钟后,检查结束。）

邹医生 您的牙龈炎现在已经得到了控制,可以进行牙齿矫形治疗。

邵 鑫 那接下来应该怎样治疗呢?

邹医生 我先给您开个 X 线**头影正侧位**和**全口曲面平展**的检查,看一下您的具体情况。
（15 分钟后,检查结束。）

邹医生 邵先生,根据您牙齿的情况,现在可以进行正畸治疗了。正畸也就是矫形牙齿、解除**错殆**畸形。我们会在您的牙齿或者面部设置一个支抗工具,通过**支抗**产生的**矫形力**来**牵引**牙齿,以增大**牙间隙**来缓解牙列拥挤的问题。

邵 鑫 请问具体的治疗方案是什么呢?

邹医生	我建议首先拔除上下颌智齿，这样会增加您的部分牙间隙，然后在**上颌**、**下颌**的牙齿黏接正畸**托槽**，再用**弓丝**固定，观察牙齿的移动程度。通过牙列情况来调整牵引的力量，直到您的牙齿达到正常的咬合标准。期间需要您每个月来医院复查。
邵　鑫	医生，整个治疗大概需要多长时间？
邹医生	每个人的情况不同，治疗时间也不同。根据您的情况，大概需要两年时间，期间还需结合龈上洁治，进行治疗。
邵　鑫	好的，知道了，我再考虑一下。谢谢邹医生。
邹医生	不用谢！有什么问题随时来找我沟通。再见！

Dental Orthodontics

SITE:　Oral Surgery Clinic

CHARACTERS:　Doctor Zou (Attending physician)

　　　　　　　Shao Xin (Patient, male, 31 years old).

Dr. Zou:　Hello, Mr. Shao! I'm Doctor Zou. Sit down, please! What's the matter with you?

Shao Xin:　Doctor, I found that my upper and lower teeth are not neatly arranged, which affect my face, and I heard that can be orthopaediced, so I want to have a check.

Dr. Zou:　Is there any other discomfort?

Shao Xin:　My anterior tooth region don't bite during dinner. It's hard for me to chew my food when eating.

Dr. Zou:　How long have you found this symptom?

Shao Xin:　Five years ago, and it has not been treated.

Dr. Zou:　Is the symptom the same as that today?

Shao Xin:　When I was a child, my teeth were aligned. As I grew older, I found that the tooth condition was getting worse. Five years ago, I had a malocclusion of anterior tooth region, but it did not affect everyday life. Now the problem has affected my looks and eating.

Dr. Zou:　May I ask you that your opsigenes appear?

Shao Xin:　Yes, the four wisdom teeth have grown.

Dr. Zou:　Do you usually have a gum bleeding when you eat something hard or brush teeth?

Shao Xin:　Yes, I do.

Dr. Zou:　Do any other gomphiasis?

Shao Xin:　No, other teeth are good.

Dr. Zou:　Did you come to the hospital?

Shao Xin:　Yes, it was once.

Dr. Zou:　What check did you have when you saw a doctor last time?

Shao Xin:　The doctor gave me a periodontal examination.

Dr. Zou:　Did the doctor tell you the diagnosis?

Shao Xin:　Gingivitis.

Dr. Zou:　I see. Now I want to give you a check. Please lie down on the bed and head up and turn left.

　　　　　　(10 minutes later, the physical examination finished.)

Dr. Zou:　According to your medical history and physical examination, I consider your diagnosis is dental crowding, while suffering from gingivitis. Orthodontic treatment is needed for the dental crowding, but you have to wait till the inflammation subsides and gingivitis fades away.

Shao Xin:　Oh, that's it!

Dr. Zou:　Today, I'll give you some medicine for a couple of days. You should not only pay attention to rest, diet, but also give up smoking and drinking. Then go to the periodontal department for supragingival scaling.

Shao Xin:　Are there any other issues to note?

Dr. Zou:　You also need to pay attention to the method of brushing teeth, gargling before and after meals and keeping mouth clean. When the treatment of gingivitis has been completed, visit again after a month.

（After a month, Shao Xin returns.）

Dr. Zou:　Sit down, please! How do you feel this month?

Shao Xin:　The gum is not bleeding, and I can carry out the correction of the teeth.

Dr. Zou:　Lie on the bed and I'll check it out first.

（After 5 minutes, the check is over.）

Dr. Zou:　You have controlled the gingivitis, and then dental orthopedic treatment can be carried out.

Shao Xin:　And what shall we do next?

Dr. Zou:　I have prepared the X-ray examination form of lateral cephalometrics and full mouth surface falt to examine your situation.

（After 15 minutes, the check is over.）

Dr. Zou:　Mr. Shao, it can be treated according to the situation of your teeth. Orthodontic is orthodontic teeth, lifting the wrong malocclusion. Orthodontic is to relieve the crowding of teeth by means of the establishment of a anchorage tool in your teeth or face, increasing the diastema between the teeth by orthopedic force and tow power.

Shao Xin:　Oh, what is my specific treatment plan?

Dr. Zou:　According to your examination result, I suggest your mandibular wisdom teeth should be extracted, which will partly increase the diastema between your maxillary and underjaw's teeth that'll be adhered to the orthodontic bracket and fixed by the arch wire, and then the traction force be adjusted based on the dentition before your teeth reach the normal occlusal standard. You have to review every month.

Shao Xin:　Doctor, how long will it take for the whole treatment?

Dr. Zou:　Each person's situation is different. The course is also different. According to your situation, it'll be about two years, while combining with supragingival scaling.

Shao Xin:　All right, I've got it and I'll think about it. Thanks.

Dr. Zou:　You're welcome.! Communicate with me anytime you have problems. Bye!

疾病介绍

牙齿矫形

牙齿矫形是指通过正畸治疗或正颌手术等相关治疗方法来矫正牙齿、解除错𬌗畸形并改善美观。错𬌗畸形是指在生长发育的过程中由各种原因导致的牙齿、颌骨、颅面的畸形。主要治疗方案是正畸治疗和外科正颌手术治疗。正畸治疗是指通过矫正装置来调整上下颌骨、牙齿及牙齿与颌骨之间不正常的关系，使牙齿咬合达到平衡、稳定和美观。对于同时伴有颌骨关系异常或者难以通过正畸治疗达到理想效果的病人则需要行正颌手术。正颌手术术前需要正畸基础治疗，通过手术

tiáozhěng hégǔ de wèizhi lái jiànlì liánghǎo de yáhé guānxi　shùhòu xūyào zhèngjī wéichí zhìliáo
调整 颌骨 的 位置 来 建立 良好 的 牙颌 关系 。 术后 需要 正畸 维持 治疗 。

Dental Orthodontics

Dental orthopedics aims at rectifying the teeth and removing the wrong and deformed teeth by orthodontic treatment or orthognathic surgery. Malocclusion deformity refers to tooth, jaw, craniofacial deformity caused by all kinds of reasons in the process of human growth and development. The main method of treatment is orthodontic treatment and orthognathic surgery of the surgical department. Orthodontic treatment refers to adjusting the abnormal relationship between the mandible, teeth and jaw and teeth by correction device in order to achieve the balance, stability and beauty of the teeth. But patients with abnormal jaw at the same time and those who are difficult to achieve the ideal effect through orthodontic treatment will need orthognathic surgery, which can adjust the position of the jaw in order to establish better occlusal relationship between teeth and jaw. Orthodontic treatment will be needed as its preoperative treatment and postoperative maintenance.

1. 随着……

用在句子或动词的前面,表示伴随的状况。

It is used at the beginning of a sentence or a verb, meaning "with…", e.g. 随着时间的推移,他们的关系越来越好。

2. 听说

插入语,用在句首或句中。

This is a parenthesis used at the beginning or in the middle of a sentence, e.g. 听说老刘这个人很能干。

3. 或者

表示两种事物中选择一种,或同时存在。

It means "or", e.g. 你周三或者周四来取包裹。

 # 腮腺囊肿

腮腺	sāixiàn	名	parotid
囊肿	nángzhǒng	名	cyst
肿物	zhǒngwù	名	goiter
界限	jièxiàn	名	boundary
形态	xíngtài	形	shape
包膜	bāomó	名	envelope
鳃裂囊肿	sāiliènángzhǒng	名	branchial cleft cyst
病理	bìnglǐ	名	pathology

耳屏	ěrpíng	名	tragus
弧形	húxíng	名	arc
拐杖	guǎizhàng	名	crutch
解剖	jiěpōu	动	anatomy
面神经	miànshénjīng	名	facial nerve
评估	pínggū	动	evaluate

地点:口腔外科门诊
人物:周医生(主治医师)
　　　赵立(病人,男,35岁)

赵　立　周医生,您好! 我发现右耳朵下方有一个包块,这一周长得很快。
周医生　还有其他不舒服吗?
赵　立　没有了。
周医生　您发现包块有多长时间了? 有多大? 活动吗?
赵　立　一个月前发现的。当时有一个花生米大小,最近一周长得很快,现在大约有鸡蛋黄大小,可以活动。
周医生　最近有没有感冒?
赵　立　一个月前因为季节变换早晚温差大,感冒发烧了。后来就发现右边耳朵下面长了一个包块。
周医生　除了感冒发烧,最近休息怎么样?
赵　立　我是出租车司机,经常夜间开车,休息也不好。
周医生　出租车司机确实挺辛苦的! 生活没有规律。最近是不是压力大,容易焦虑呢?
赵　立　是的,上周我父亲生病了,我很担心他。
周医生　休息不好、焦虑、压力过大都容易导致免疫力下降进而生病。包块现在疼吗?
赵　立　疼,是那种隐隐约约的疼。
周医生　这一个月来医院看过吗?
赵　立　来过一次。
周医生　在医院做了什么检查? 报告单带了没有?
赵　立　做了一个彩超,这是报告单,医生告诉我是右**腮腺肿物**。
周医生　(仔细看了报告单后)知道了! 我先给您检查一下,请躺到检查床上,头后仰并朝左偏。
　　　　(10分钟后,检查结束。)
周医生　根据您的病史和体格检查,初步考虑您是右腮腺**囊肿**合并感染。我给您开一个腮腺CT,进一步检查一下。
赵　立　好的!
周医生　我暂时先给您开三天的药,治疗感染。这几天要注意休息,饮食要规律,还要戒烟、戒酒。等CT检查结果出来后,您再来找我进行下一步的治疗。
　　　　(三天后,病人CT检查已经完成。)
周医生　您好,请坐! 这几天感觉如何?
赵　立　右耳下的包块现在不疼了,好像变小了! 周医生,我的检查结果怎么样?
周医生　您的检查结果已经出来了,CT检查发现右腮腺有一个占位性病变,说明确实是右腮腺肿物。
赵　立　能确诊是什么病吗?
周医生　CT结果显示右腮腺肿物**界限**清楚,**形态**规则,有一层**包膜**。CT值为-23,内容物是液性的。考虑是右腮腺**鳃裂囊肿**的可能性比较大。

赵　立　那应该怎么治疗?

周医生　目前这种疾病的有效治疗方式是手术切除,并将切除肿物进行**病理**检查,看是否与临床诊断相符,明确诊断。

赵　立　医生,这个手术是怎么做的?

周医生　传统的手术方式是从右**耳屏**前中点做切口,延伸至耳下后向后**弧形**地切开,直到右下颌角前,像**拐杖**一样,翻开皮肤后**解剖面神经**,明确面神经与囊肿的关系后切除囊肿。

赵　立　这种手术有没有风险?

周医生　手术会有一定的风险,但是手术前我们会为您安排相关检查,**评估**全身情况后,再进行手术。

赵　立　好的,我知道了,我再考虑一下。谢谢周医生!

Parotid Cyst

SETE:　　　　Oral surgery clinic

CHARACTERS:　Doctor Zhou (Attending physician)

　　　　　　　Zhao Li (Patient, male, 35 years old.)

Zhao Li:　Hello, Doctor Zhou. I found there was an enclosed mass under my right ear and it increased rapidly this week.

Dr. Zhou:　Any more you feel uncomfortable?

Zhao Li:　No, there isn't.

Dr. Zhou:　When did you find it and how big is it? Does it move?

Zhao Li:　It was discovered a month ago. At that time it was as big as a peanut, but it increased rapidly to the size of an egg yolk. And it can be active.

Dr. Zhou:　Have you caught a cold recently?

Zhao Li:　Yes, I have. It was a month ago when I caught a cold and had a fever before I found it because of the seasonal changes combined with the large temperature difference between morning and evening. It was found that there was a packet under the right ear later.

Dr. Zhou:　How about your break in addition to a fever?

Zhao Li:　I am a taxi driver, often driving at night, so the rest is not good.

Dr. Zhou:　Being a taxi driver is really hard and there is no regularity of life. Is there anything else that happened recently?

Zhao Li:　Yes, my father was sick last week and I was worried about him.

Dr. Zhou:　Bad rest, anxiety and excessive pressure can lead to decreased immunity easily, and then sick. Is the enclosed mass painful now?

Zhao Li:　Yes, it is an indistinct pain.

Dr. Zhou:　Did you come to the hospital during the month?

Zhao Li:　Once a time.

Dr. Zhou:　Were you examined in the hospital? Did you take the report?

Zhao Li:　Yes, I was checked by color Doppler ultrasound. The doctor told me it was a right parotid goiter.

Dr. Zhou:　(After reading the report carefully.) Got it! Now I'll examine you. Please lie down on the bed, keep your head back and turn left.

　　　　　(After 10 minutes, the check is over.)

Dr. Zhou:　Based on your medical history and physical examination, my primary diagnosis is the right parotid cyst associated with infection. I'll give you a form of a parotid gland CT for further check.

Zhao Li: Okay！

Dr. Zhou: In addition, I'll prescribe three-day anti-inflammatory drugs to treat the infection. These days you have to take a good rest, keep a proper diet, stop smoking and drinking. After the CT test results come out, you will come back for the next treatment.

           （Three days later, the patient's CT examination was over.）

Dr. Zhou: Sit down, please. How about these days, Mr. Zhao?

Zhao Li: I haven't felt a pain under my right ear and it seems that the mass has become smaller. What about my test results, Doctor Zhou?

Dr. Zhou: Here are your examination results. CT examination reveals that there is a space-occupying lesion in the right parotid gland, which indicates that there is a right parotid tumor.

Zhao Li: Can you diagnose what the disease is?

Dr. Zhou: The results of CT examination showed that the right parotid gland had clear boundaries, regular shape, and a layer of envelope. The CT value is -23 and the content is liquid. The preliminary diagnosis is branchial cleft cyst.

Zhao Li: How to treat it?

Dr. Zhou: At present, the effective treatment for the disease is surgery, with resection of tumor for pathological diagnosis, to see whether it is consistent with the clinical diagnosis.

Zhao Li: How to do the operation, doctor?

Dr. Zhou: The traditional operation method is to make an arc incision from the front midpoint of the right tragus to the ear back and till the front of the right mandibular angle, like a crutch, open the skin after the anatomy of the facial nerve in order to be aware of the relationship between facial nerve and cyst, the latter of which will be removed.

Zhao Li: Does the operation place me at risk, Doctor?

Dr. Zhou: Don't worry about it first. We'll examine you and evaluate your whole body condition before the operation.

Zhao Li: I see. I'll think about it. Thank you, Dr. Zhou.

腮腺囊肿

腮腺囊肿表现为腮腺区无痛性肿块，生长缓慢，无功能障碍，一般长到相当体积后才被发现。扪诊肿物，质地柔软，有时可扪及波动感，边界清楚，与皮下组织无粘连，可活动。B超检查和腮腺CT可用于辅助诊断。囊肿以皮样囊肿和鳃裂囊肿两类多见。皮样囊肿可位于深部或浅表部位。位于浅表者可扪及如皮样囊肿的柔韧感，位于深部者与一般良性肿瘤难以区别。腮腺部位的鳃裂囊肿来自第一腮弓发育异常，鳃裂囊肿易继发感染，经抗感染治疗后，可消退。若病人免疫力低下或抗感染不及时，可形成瘘口。腮腺囊肿的治疗以手术为主，因囊肿与周围腺体常有粘连，为避免复发可切除部分腮腺组织。继发感染者需先消炎治疗，待急性

yánzhèng xiāotuì hòu jìnxíng shǒushù
炎症 消退 后 进行 手术 。

Parotid Cyst

The parotid cyst is a painless mass, growing slowly without functional disorder and it cannot be found till it grows to a considerable volume. The palpation shows a soft mass with the sensation of fluctuation occasionally and with clear boundaries without adhesion to the subcutaneous tissue. B ultrasound and CT of parotid gland can be used for the auxiliary diagnosis. The two most common cysts are dermoid cyst and branchial cleft cyst. Dermoid cyst can be located in the superficial or deep parts. The former one can be touched with general dough kneading sensation, while the latter is difficult to distinguish from benign tumors. The branchial cyst from the parotid gland is derived from the abnormal development of the first gill arch, which is prone to infections and will be dissipated after anti-infection treatment. However, the fistula will come into being if patients have low immunity or fail to get the timely anti-infection treatment. The main treatment for branchial cyst is surgery and it is necessary to remove partial parotid gland tissue to avoid recurrence because the cyst and the surrounding glands often have adhesions. Patients with complication of infection should receive anti-inflammatory treatment first and then be operated after the acute inflammation subsided.

语言点

1. 合并
指结合、归并、统一到一起。
It means "combine" or "get together", e.g. 我们医药公司与另一个公司合并了。

2. 等……再……
连接两个有从属关系的分句,表示先后顺序。
It connects two clauses to show their order of occurrence, e.g. 等你的炎症消退后再进行手术治疗。

3. 另外……
常用于一个句子中的附加解释或补充。
It means "in addition", e.g. 你可以过两天再来复诊,另外把以前的检查结果带来。

 **练习**

➤ **听力练习**

一、听录音,选择你听到的词语

( )1. A. 牙冠　　　　B. 智齿　　　　C. 牙床　　　　D. 牙齿

( )2. A. 咬紧　　　　B. 咬合　　　　C. 闭合　　　　D. 咬牙

( )3. A. 紊烦　　　　B. 混乱　　　　C. 紊乱　　　　D. 稳定

( )4. A. 畸形　　　　B. 矫形　　　　C. 矫正　　　　D. 矫情

( )5. A. 感冒药　　　B. 保肝药　　　C. 降压药　　　D. 降糖药

( )6. A. 牙龈炎　　　B. 乳腺炎　　　C. 筋膜炎　　　D. 腮腺炎

( )7. A. 包被　　　　B. 包膜　　　　C. 包块　　　　D. 肿块

( )8. A. 发烧　　　　B. 发热　　　　C. 发炎　　　　D. 火烧

( )9. A. 囊肿　　　　B. 囊块　　　　C. 红肿　　　　D. 囊变

（　　）10. A. 液性　　　　　　B. 液体　　　　　　C. 变性　　　　　　D. 血性

二、请选出与所听录音相符的答案

（　　）1. A. 不出血　　　　B. 出血　　　　　C. 有时还出　　　D. 不知道

（　　）2. A. 尖牙　　　　　B. 智齿　　　　　C. 切牙　　　　　D. 后磨牙

（　　）3. A. 病人需要马上矫形　　　　　　　　B. 病人没有口腔疾病

　　　　　C. 病人需要马上休息　　　　　　　　D. 需要治疗后再矫形

（　　）4. A. 患者吃了硬的食物　　　　　　　　B. 患者没吃硬的食物

　　　　　C. 患者一开始吃了硬的食物　　　　　D. 患者后期没吃硬的食物

（　　）5. A. 病人不需要住院治疗　　　　　　　B. 病人需要住院治疗

　　　　　C. 病人不能住院治疗　　　　　　　　D. 病人可以简单治疗

三、听录音，完成下面的练习

1. 根据所听到的录音判断对错

1）成年人的牙齿矫正需要时间长。（　　　　）

2）成年人的牙槽生长已经完成。（　　　　）

3）成年人牙齿矫正需要及早解决。（　　　　）

4）成年人牙齿矫正时间缩短不会带来不良后果。（　　　　）

5）牙齿矫正前要做好矫正规划。（　　　　）

6）矫正时要避免工作调动、怀孕。（　　　　）

2. 听录音，选择正确答案回答问题

1）病人一共看了几家医院？（　　　　）

　　A. 1 家　　　　　B. 2 家　　　　　C. 3 家　　　　　D. 4 家

2）病人第一次住院治疗是什么时候？（　　　　）

　　A. 2 年前　　　　B. 3 个月前　　　C. 半年前　　　　D. 1 年前

3）病人第一次住院的原因是？（　　　　）

　　A. 左侧腮腺包块　　B. 包块增大　　　C. 包块明显增大　　D. 肿胀

4）这次住院病人做了哪些检查？（　　　　）

　　A. CT　　　　　　B. 彩超　　　　　C. 磁共振　　　　　D. 穿刺

5）病人可能得的疾病是？（　　　　）

　　A. 淋巴结炎　　　B. 腮腺炎　　　　C. 腮腺囊肿　　　　D. 面瘫

➤ **词汇和语法练习**

一、给下列词语标注拼音

1. 牙齿＿＿＿＿＿＿＿＿＿＿＿＿　　　2. 牙龈＿＿＿＿＿＿＿＿＿＿＿＿

3. 牙槽＿＿＿＿＿＿＿＿＿＿＿＿　　　4. 感冒发烧＿＿＿＿＿＿＿＿＿＿＿

5. 腮腺囊肿＿＿＿＿＿＿＿＿＿＿　　　6. 界限清楚＿＿＿＿＿＿＿＿＿＿＿

7. 鳃裂＿＿＿＿＿＿＿＿＿＿＿＿　　　8. 解剖＿＿＿＿＿＿＿＿＿＿＿＿＿

9. 正畸治疗＿＿＿＿＿＿＿＿＿＿　　　10. 龈上洁治＿＿＿＿＿＿＿＿＿＿＿

二、选词填空

咬合无力　　感冒发烧　　彩超　　排列不齐　　难受　　规律　　口腔清洁
报告单　　病理　　牙龈炎　　矫形术

1. 昨天，邵鑫吃饭后出现牙疼、出血，到医院检查结果是＿＿＿＿＿＿＿＿。

2. 口腔科医生说我的牙齿＿＿＿＿＿＿＿＿。

3. 吃东西费力，是因为牙齿＿＿＿＿＿＿＿＿。

4. 你要保持＿＿＿＿＿＿＿＿＿＿＿＿,牙龈炎才能好起来。

5. 牙齿畸形、不齐,可以通过＿＿＿＿＿＿＿＿＿＿来解决。

6. 这两天天气变凉,别＿＿＿＿＿＿＿＿＿＿＿。

7. 公司任务多,压力大,我最近生活没有＿＿＿＿＿＿＿＿＿。

8. 你要及时去医院复查,别忘了把上次检查的＿＿＿＿＿＿＿＿＿带上。

9. 你的腮腺区肿大,要做＿＿＿＿＿＿＿＿＿检查。

10. 腮腺肿物需要手术治疗,术中需＿＿＿＿＿＿＿＿＿检查明确诊断。

三、用指定的词语或结构完成句子或对话

1. 因为牙齿不齐,影响美观,＿＿＿＿＿＿＿＿。(所以)

2. 你的牙龈炎需要治疗,＿＿＿＿＿＿＿＿。(另外)

3. 等腮腺肿胀消退后,＿＿＿＿＿＿＿＿。(再)

4. ＿＿＿＿＿＿＿＿＿,牙齿排列紊乱越来越严重。(随着)

5. ＿＿＿＿＿＿＿＿＿,而且话也说不出来了。(不但)

四、把下列词语排列成句子

1. 牙齿 排列不齐 并且 病人 牙龈出血 的

2. 咬合 牙齿 避免 您 硬东西 吃 的 不好

3. 腮腺囊肿 考虑 的 诊断 现在 您 是

4. B超 诊断 先做 需要 检查 明确 您

5. 看起来 治疗方案 不错 这种

➤ 阅读与应用练习

一、根据课文内容补全对话。

病人: 医生,我发现右 __1__ 下方有一个 __2__ ,这一周长得很快。

医生: 什么时间发现的?

病人: 大概 __3__ 月前。

医生: 有什么变化呢?

病人: 开始只有 __4__ 大小,现在已经长到 __5__ 大小了。

医生: 您最近 __6__ 了吗?

病人: 是的,换季有些着凉了。

医生: 还有其他原因吗?

病人: 最近爸爸生病,我有些 __7__ 他。

医生: 肿块现在疼吗?

病人: 是的,有一些 __8__ 的疼。

医生: 根据您的情况,我的初步诊断是腮腺囊肿伴感染。先给您开一些 __9__ ,等感染控制以后再进行下一步治疗。

二、根据课文内容回答问题

1. 邵鑫为什么来医院就诊?

2. 邵鑫牙齿排列不整齐,生活上哪些方面受到了影响?

3. 医生建议邵鑫怎样治疗牙列拥挤?

4. 诱发赵立右下颌包块的原因有哪些?

5. 医生给赵立的诊断及治疗方法是什么?

三、写作练习

简单描述会话一中病人邵鑫的主要症状及表现。(不少于40字)

四、交际练习

参考括号里的词语进行情景对话。

情景:病人的 CT 检查报告出来了,医生和病人进行对话。

(腮腺,包块,囊肿,手术,病理)

练习答案

第一章

➤ 听力练习

一、听录音,选择你听到的词语

1. D 2. A 3. C 4. D 5. A 6. A 7. A 8. A 9. D 10. B

二、请选出与所听录音相符的答案

1. D 2. B 3. A 4. A

三、听录音,完成下面的练习

1. 根据所听到的录音判断对错

1) √ 2) × 3) √ 4) × 5) × 6) ×

2. 听录音,选择正确答案回答问题

1) B 2) A 3) B

➤ 词汇和语法练习

一、给下列词语标注拼音

1. ménzhěn 2. guàhàochù 3. nèikē 4. xiōngpiàn 5. xuèchángguī

6. zhùyuàn 7. fèiyán 8. gǔkē 9. xīnzàngwàikē 10. fùchǎnkē

11. yǎnkē 12. shénjīngwàikē 13. mìniàowàikē

二、选词填空

1. 肺炎 2. 内科 3. 发烧 4. 胸部 X 线片 5. 头痛

三、用指定的词语或结构完成句子或对话

1. 而且发烧,寒战

2. 请问怎么去放射科

四、把下列词语排列成句子

1. 请问门诊在哪里?

2. 内科病房在六楼。

3. 请去二楼查胸部 X 线片。

4. 医务处主要负责管理医疗相关事务。

5. 门诊主要接收普通病人。

6. 医生根据病人病情开一些相关检查。

➤ 阅读与应用练习

一、根据课文内容补全对话

会话一

1. 办公室 2. 医务处 3. 护理部 4. 教学处 5. 科研处

6. 人力资源处 7. 财务处 8. 实习 9. 管理医疗相关事务

10. 医疗相关制度

会话二

11. 头疼、发烧　　　　12. 呼吸内科　　13. 肺炎　　　14. 胸部 X 线片　　　　15. 抽血检查

16. 住院治疗　　17. 住院登记处

二、根据课文内容回答问题

1. 呼吸内科

2. 肺炎

3. 一楼放射科做胸部 X 线片,二楼检验科抽血检查

4. 要住院

5. 医院行政部门,医院临床科室和诊断相关科室

6. 急诊外科

第二章

➤ 听力练习

一、听录音,选择你听到的词语

1. A　　2. D　　3. A　　4. B　　5. A　　6. A　　7. A　　8. B　　9. D　　10. C

二、请选出与所听录音相符的答案

1. A　　2. D　　3. B　　4. A　　5. C

三、听录音,完成下面的练习

1. 根据所听到的录音判断对错

1) ×　　2) √　　3) ×　　4) ×　　5) √

2. 听录音,选择正确答案回答问题

1) D　　2) A　　3) B

➤ 词汇和语法练习

一、给下列词语标注拼音

1. késòu　　　2. tǐwēn　　　3. bítì　　　　4. gǎnrǎn　　　5. hūxī kùnnán

6. dǎ pēntì　　7. qìchuǎn　　8. xiàomíngyīn　　9. fāshāo　　　10. fèigōngnéng

二、选词填空

1. 发烧　　　2. 体温　　　3. 阿奇霉素　　　4. 胸部 X 线　　5. 花粉

6. 哮鸣音　　7. 复诊　　　8. 预防

三、用指定的词语或结构完成句子或对话

1. 请问你要找哪位大夫

2. 只是急性上呼吸道感染

3. 主要是哪里不舒服

4. 除了咳嗽之外,还有其他症状吗

5. 根据您的病史、症状、体征与各项检查结果

四、把下列词语排列成句子

1. 昨天我在路上淋了雨。

2. 这次感冒后总是流清鼻涕。

3. 一闻到花粉气味我就气喘。

4. 医生给我开了些药。

5. 多数病人病情可以缓解。

➢ **阅读与应用练习**

一、根据课文内容补全对话

1. 咳嗽   2. 体温   3. 大约   4. 咽痛

5. 感冒   6. 难受   7. 口服液   8. 抗生素

二、根据课文内容回答问题

1. 发烧、咳嗽、脓痰、咽痛、流鼻涕

2. 腹泻

3. 花粉

4. 赵易伟闻到花粉气味以后,出现气急和呼吸困难的症状,两肺闻及哮鸣音,肺功能提示阻塞性通气功能障碍,支气管舒张试验阳性。

5. 不能根治,但可以预防和控制。

三、写作练习

参考答案:赵易伟的主要临床表现是闻到花粉气味后,鼻子痒,打喷嚏,咳嗽,后来就胸闷、气喘。晚上气喘得厉害,根本没有办法睡觉。

四、交际练习

答案略。

第三章

➢ **听力练习**

一、听录音,选择你听到的词语

1. C   2. A   3. D   4. B   5. A   6. B   7. D   8. C   9. B   10. D

二、请选出与所听录音相符的答案

1. C   2. A   3. D   4. B   5. A

三、听录音,完成下面的练习

1. 根据所听到的录音判断对错

1) ×   2) ×   3) √   4) √   5) ×   6) √   7) √   8) √

2. 听录音,选择正确答案回答问题

1) A   2) D   3) B   4) A   5) C

➢ **词汇和语法练习**

一、给下列词语标注拼音

1. gāoxuèyā   2. jiǎzhuàngxiàn   3. shìwǎngmó   4. xīnzàngbìng   5. xīndiàntú

6. xīnjiǎotòng   7. nàyán   8. fǎnyìng   9. xūhàn   10. piānhào

二、选词填空

1. 血压   2. 症状   3. 遗传   4. 副作用   5. 虚汗

6. 降压片   7. 高血压   8. 狭窄   9. 血栓   10. 复诊

三、用指定的词语或结构完成句子或对话

1. 而且恶心   2. 和他吃得太咸有关

3. 也没去医院,也没吃药   4. 边用药边观察

5. 因为有家族遗传史   6. 除了有冠心病

四、把下列词语排列成句子

1. 高血压病人要坚持按时服药。
2. 肥胖容易导致心血管疾病。
3. 冠心病病人应常备急救药物。
4. 医生建议病人改变生活方式。
5. 男性心血管病发病率高于女性。

➢ **阅读与应用练习**

一、根据课文内容补全对话

1. 发生	2. 偶尔	3. 症状	4. 明显	5. 每次
6. 眼睛	7. 清楚	8. 躺着		

二、根据课文内容回答问题

1. 刘阳刚开始没在意,因为平时血压高对他的生活和工作没有影响。
2. 因为刘阳的母亲有高血压,而且他经常喝酒,熬夜,所以这些都是导致他得高血压的因素。
3. 她觉得疲倦无力,呼吸短促,心跳加快,前胸后背疼痛难忍。
4. 根据张兰的描述和临床症状,这是典型的稳定型心绞痛,而且心电图、心超和冠状动脉造影检查结果表明她的冠状动脉狭窄,心肌缺血。
5. 开放答案。

三、写作练习

参考答案:我建议你服用三种药物,一个是硝酸甘油,缓解心肌缺血;再有就是阿司匹林,它的作用是抗凝,防止血栓;第三个是辛伐他汀,用来降血脂。要改变不良生活习惯,少吃盐和油腻的东西,睡眠充足,保持良好情绪。

四、交际练习

答案略。

第四章

➢ **听力练习**

一、听录音,选择你听到的词语

1. D 2. A 3. C 4. D 5. B 6. C 7. B 8. A 9. B 10. D

二、请选出与所听录音相符的答案

1. B 2. D 3. D 4. A 5. D

三、听录音,完成下面的练习

1. 根据所听到的录音判断对错

1) ✕ 2) ✓ 3) ✕ 4) ✓ 5) ✓

2. 听录音,选择正确答案回答问题

1) C 2) A 3) D

➢ **词汇和语法练习**

一、给下列词语标注拼音

1. shūyè	2. shíyù	3. shuǐzhǒng	4. shèngōngnéng
5. jìngmài qūzhāng	6. yídòngxìng zhuóyīn	7. xiāohuàxìng kuìyáng	8. yōumén luógǎnjūn
9. zhīzhūzhì	10. gǒngmó huǎngrǎn		

二、选词填空

1. 消化道出血　　2. 挂号单　　3. 高热　　4. 排放腹水　　5. 乙型肝炎

6. 隐隐约约　　7. 难受　　8. 诱发　　9. 胃镜　　10. 电解质

三、用指定的词语或结构完成句子或对话

1. 要尽快住院治疗　　2. 是否还有其他的治疗方法？

3. 以免产生更严重的后果　　4. 他被诊断为脂肪肝

5. 考虑他的病可能是消化性溃疡

四、把下列词语排列成句子

1. 有些病人的转氨酶高。

2. 病人的左手背上有五六颗蜘蛛痣。

3. 还要考虑肝肾综合征的可能性。

4. 医生让我住进了急诊观察室。

5. 通过这种药物治疗感染效果很好。

➢ 阅读与应用练习

一、根据课文内容补全对话

1. 胃疼　　2. 哪个　　3. 多数时间　　4. 也有　　5. 原因

6. 什么　　7. 喜欢　　8. 药

二、根据课文内容回答问题

1. 上腹疼痛、反酸和嗳气，近来加重了。

2. 吃饭不及时，有时喝点酒，天气变凉，再加上他家里的事让他上火，拼命抽烟。

3. 消化性溃疡。医生建议住院治疗并给赵哲开了一些缓解疼痛的药物。

4. 由于工作忙，忘了治疗。

5. 十五年前被诊断为乙型肝炎，但他没治，渐渐地没食欲、无力，一查是肝硬化，接着又腹部膨隆，双下肢水肿，出现典型的肝腹水症状。

三、写作练习

参考答案：赵子宇的主要临床表现有腹胀，少尿，双下肢水肿，疲乏无力，食欲减退，牙龈出血，面色晦暗，巩膜黄染，结膜苍白，蜘蛛痣，肝掌，腹部膨隆，腹壁静脉曲张，移动性浊音阳性。

四、交际练习

答案略。

第五章

➢ 听力练习

一、听录音，选择你听到的词语

1. B　　2. C　　3. D　　4. A　　5. C　　6. B　　7. D　　8. C　　9. A　　10. B

二、请选出与所听录音相符的答案

1. C　　2. C　　3. C　　4. B　　5. A

三、听录音，完成下面的练习

1. 根据所听到的录音判断对错

1）×　2）√　3）√　4）×　5）×　6）√　7）×　8）√

2. 听录音，选择正确答案回答问题

1）D　2）B　3）C　4）A　5）D

➤ **词汇和语法练习**

一、给下列词语标注拼音

1. xiāoshòu
2. duōniào
3. diǎnxíngde
4. niàoliàng
5. yǎndǐjiǎnchá
6. jiǎzhuàngxiàn
7. zhènchàn
8. mímànxìng bìngbiàn
9. yàowù zhìliáo
10. jìnjì

二、选词填空

1. 怎么样
2. 糖尿病
3. 确诊
4. 并发症
5. 临床表现
6. 甲状腺功能亢进
7. 易激动
8. 还要

三、用指定的词语或结构完成句子或对话

1. 最近两个月我瘦了将近 7 公斤
2. 就是体重下降了
3. 尿量有变化吗
4. 但我父亲有糖尿病很多年了
5. 有典型的"三多一少"症状,初步诊断是糖尿病
6. 只能采取对症治疗
7. 提示这个病人可能是甲亢

四、把下列词语排列成句子

1. 小便的次数增多了。
2. 检查病人有没有合并糖尿病慢性并发症。
3. 这些症状听起来很像是甲状腺功能亢进。
4. 甲亢是一种自身免疫性疾病。
5. 甲状腺彩超提示双侧甲状腺弥漫性病变。

➤ **阅读与应用练习**

一、根据课文内容补全对话

1. 初步诊断
2. 多饮、多尿、多食和消瘦症状
3. 家族史
4. 进一步确诊
5. 糖耐量试验
6. 血糖情况和胰岛功能
7. 慢性并发症
8. 尿常规、血生化和眼底检查

二、根据课文内容回答问题

1. "三多一少"即:多饮、多尿、多食和消瘦。
2. 糖耐量试验、胰岛素释放试验和 C 肽释放试验。
3. 糖尿病肾脏、脑血管、心脏、眼部及神经系统损害。
4. 症状体征、甲状腺功能异常、甲状腺彩超。
5. A 健康教育:情绪控制、饮食禁忌;B 药物治疗、放射性碘治疗和手术治疗

三、写作练习

参考答案:

1) 临床表现:脾气大,易激动,易发火,怕热、多汗,多食、消瘦。

2) 体征:身高 160 厘米,体重 40 公斤;甲状腺弥漫性 Ⅱ 度肿大,眼球轻微突出。心率 118 次 / 分,双手震颤明显。甲状腺听诊有杂音。

3) 检查结果:甲状腺功能检查:FT_3 和 FT_4 升高,TSH 降低;甲状腺彩超也提示双侧甲状腺弥漫性病变。

四、交际练习

答案略。

第六章

➤ 听力练习

一、听录音,选择你听到的词语

1. C   2. A   3. D   4. B   5. A   6. D   7. B   8. C   9. C   10. B

二、请选出与所听录音相符的答案

1. C   2. C   3. D   4. D   5. B

三、听录音,完成下面的练习

1. 根据所听到的录音判断对错

1) √   2) ×   3) √   4) √   5) ×   6) ×   7) √

2. 听录音,选择正确答案回答问题

1) C   2) C   3) A   4) D   5) B

➤ 词汇和语法练习

一、给下列词语标注拼音

1. pángguāng   2. géngzǔ   3. wěisuō   4. mìniàodào

5. shūniàoguǎn   6. niàosùdàn   7. fùmó tòuxī   8. jīngpílìjìn

9. tóuhūn yǎnhuā   10. shènxiǎoqiú shènyán

二、选词填空

1. 混浊   2. 体检   3. 中段尿培养   4. 过敏

5. 胃口   6. 胃液   7. 肌酐   8. 抗生素

三、用指定的词语或结构完成句子或对话

1. 我就觉得头晕、无力   2. 水都来不及喝一口

3. 以便于明确是否有梗阻情况   4. 除了腿部浮肿

5. 通过血液流通达到清洗血液的作用   6. 意味着您的肾功能受到损害

四、把下列词语排列成句子

1. 我还发现小便颜色很混浊。

2. 您的问题可能是泌尿道感染。

3. 泌尿系超声提示急性膀胱炎。

4. 我有时候觉得眼睛有点肿。

5. 您需要进行肾功能检查。

➤ 阅读与应用练习

一、根据课文内容补全对话。

1. 我的肾有什么问题吗   2. 两肾萎缩   3. 24小时尿蛋白

4. 慢性肾小球肾炎   5. 肾功能不全   6. 肾功能受到损害

7. 严重   8. 针对   9. 治疗方法

10. 住院进行治疗   11. 跟踪您的病情   12. 腹部

13. 腹膜透析   14. 清洗血液   15. 毒素排出

16. 住院多长时间   17. 停止工作   18. 您提醒我

19. 从事什么职业   20. 建议您休息2个月

二、根据课文内容回答问题

1. 血尿,尿频、尿急、尿痛,精疲力尽,发热。

2. 白细胞 3526/μl,红细胞 2585/μl。

3. 急性膀胱炎。

4. 下尿路(膀胱)大肠埃希菌感染。

5. 休息、多喝水,不要憋尿。

6. 夜尿增多、体重下降、尿色深、食欲缺乏、恶心、呕吐、腿肿胀、头昏眼花、高血压。

7. 两肾萎缩。

8. 尿素氮 21.5mmol/L,肌酐 480μmol/L。

9. 慢性肾小球肾炎,肾功能不全。

10. 腹膜透析。

三、写作练习

参考答案:张丽的主要临床表现有尿中带血、尿色混浊、尿频、尿急、尿痛、精疲力尽、发热等症状 2 天。

四、交际练习

答案略。

第七章

➢ 听力练习

一、听录音,选择你听到的词语

1. C　　2. A　　3. D　　4. B　　5. A　　6. D　　7.B　　8. C　　9. C　　10. B

二、请选出与所听录音相符的答案

1. B　　2. B　　3. C　　4. C　　5. D

三、听录音,完成下面的练习

1. 根据短文 1 回答第 1~4 题

1) 节食　　　　2) 头晕乏力　　　3) 工作压力大　　　　4) 病人情绪激动后,突然晕倒

2. 根据短文 2 回答第 5~7 题

1) 乏力,牙龈出血　　　2) 白血病是不治之症　　　3) 白血病虽然难治,但是可以治好的

➢ 词汇和语法练习

一、给下列词语标注拼音

1. yáyín　　　　　2. huàliáo　　　　　3. xuèqīngtiě　　　　4. wèinián mó

5. gǔsuǐxiàng　　　6. xuèxiǎobǎn　　　7. línbājié　　　　　8. búzhì zhīzhèng

9. zàoxuè gānxìbāo　　10. yuányòu línbā xìbāo

二、选词填空

1. 偏食　　　　2. 根治　　　　3. 子宫肌瘤　　　4. 痛经

5. 耳鸣　　　　6. 淤斑　　　　7. 血小板　　　　8. 遗传

三、用指定的词语或结构完成句子或对话。

1. 一旦活动量过大　　　　　　2. 有几次差点儿吐出来

3. 就是月经天数比较长　　　　4. 否则您的病难以根治

5. 没想到是肺炎　　　　　　　6. 等检查结果出来

7. 你的病并非不治之症

四、把下列词语排列成句子

1. 我感觉心都要跳出来了。

2. 贫血的程度已经接近重度。

3. 节食应该不是主要原因。

4. 白血病的确切原因还不太清楚。

5. 白血病细胞也有可能侵犯其他脏器。

➢ **阅读与应用练习**

一、根据课文内容补全对话

1. 有异常吗?

2. 白细胞

3. 血小板

4. 血红蛋白

5. 增生明显活跃,原幼淋巴细胞占 90%

6. 急性淋巴细胞白血病

7. 白血病是什么原因导致的?

8. 遗传因素或者某些特定化学物质的影响可能是其病因。

9. 造血干细胞

10. 产生了癌变

11. 无节制地增长

12. 占据骨髓

13. 肝、脾、淋巴结、肾脏

14. 不治之症

15. 常用的化疗方法

二、根据课文内容回答问题

1. 血红蛋白、血清铁和血清铁蛋白都比较低。

2. 缺铁性贫血。

3. 与她长期月经量多有直接关系。

4. 一般 38℃左右,下午或晚上发热。

5. 骨髓象检查结果显示增生明显活跃,原幼淋巴细胞占 90%。

6. 化疗。

三、写作练习

参考答案:病人林晓 5 个月前开始感觉头昏、乏力,快速走路时感觉气喘,两天前爬楼差点晕倒,伴有耳鸣。病人节食,爱喝浓茶,记忆力下降,月经量多,持续 9 到 10 天,不痛经。

四、交际练习

答案略。

第八章

➢ **听力练习**

一、听录音,选择你听到的词语

1. B　　2. D　　3. D　　4. A　　5. C　　6. A　　7. B　　8. D　　9. A　　10. B

二、请选出与所听录音相符的答案

1. D　　2. B　　3. D　　4. C　　5. B

三、听录音,完成下面的练习

1. 根据所听到的录音判断对错

1）×　　2）√　　3）√　　4）×　　5）√

2. 听录音,选择正确答案回答问题

1）B　　2）A　　3）D

➤ 词汇和语法练习

一、给下列词语标注拼音

1. lánwěiyán　　2. dǎnnángyán　　3. fùmó　　4. yánzhèng　　5. fùqiāngjìng

6. màishìdiǎn　　7. chángmíngyīn　　8. yùfáng　　9. qiēchúshù　　10. mòfēizhēng

二、选词填空

1. 绞痛　　2. 阑尾炎　　3. 触诊,麦氏点　　4. 直径

5. 转移　　6. 含量　　7. 减弱　　8. 尽快

9. 加强

三、用指定的词语或结构完成句子或对话。

1. 到后来肩背部也跟着痛　　2. 以免胆结石再复发

3. 不但有压痛,还有反跳痛　　4. 不努力学习的话

5. 从目前的症状、体征和检查结果来看

四、把下列词语排列成句子

1. 你还需要做一些辅助检查以便进一步确诊。

2. 我怀疑您得了胆结石,可能还伴有胆囊炎。

3. 他的腹部不但有压痛还有反跳痛。

4. 我的右肩部和腰背部也很疼。

5. 不做手术的话治疗效果不好。

➤ 阅读与应用练习

一、根据课文内容补全对话。

1. 转移性　　2. 发热　　3. 急性阑尾炎　　4. 触诊　　5. 麦氏点

6. 腹膜刺激征　　7. 白细胞　　8. 炎症　　9. 确诊　　10. 阑尾切除术

二、根据课文内容回答问题。

1. 大约 7 到 8 个小时。

2. 尿常规,血常规,血淀粉酶,B 超

3. 2 年

4. 有复发的可能

5. 平时要少吃鸡蛋黄、鱼籽和动物内脏等胆固醇含量高的食物,多喝水,减少盐、糖的摄入,多吃富含维生素的水果和蔬菜。

三、写作练习

参考答案:陈明的主要临床表现有右上腹持续剧痛,左肩部腰背部放射痛,低烧,呕吐;胆囊肿大,有触痛,还有实性感,墨菲征阳性。

四、交际练习

答案略。

第九章

➢ 听力练习

一、听录音,选择你听到的词语

1. A　　2. A　　3. B　　4. C　　5. B　　6. A　　7. D　　8. B　　9. A　　10. A

二、请选出与所听录音相符的答案

1. A　　2. A　　3. C　　4. D　　5. D

三、听录音,完成下面的练习

1. 根据所听到的录音判断对错

1) ×　　2) ×　　3) √　　4) ×　　5) ×

2. 听录音,选择正确答案回答问题

1) A　　2) A　　3) C

➢ 词汇和语法练习

一、给下列词语标注拼音

1. xiāntiānxìng　　2. dūnjù　　　　3. xīndiàntú　　4. shǒushù　　　　5. xiōngtòng

6. zhuǎnyí　　　　7. gēnzhìxìngshǒushù　　8. qīngméisù　　9. línchuáng biǎoxiàn　　10. yízhí

二、选词填空

1. 非青紫型　　　2. 分钟　　　3. 心脏移植　　　4. 痰　　　5. 也就是

6. 法洛四联症

三、用指定的词语或结构完成句子或对话。

1. 手术是唯一根治性方式　　　2. 内科治疗仅是对症治疗

3. 几乎所有的肺癌病人　　　4. 在男性恶性肿瘤中

四、把下列词语排列成句子

1. 先天性心脏病是出生前就已有的心脏病。

2. 手术使病人心脏解剖结构回到正常。

3. 遗传是主要的内因。

4. 女性发病率也迅速增高。

5. 肺癌成为危害生命健康的主要疾病。

➢ 阅读与应用练习

一、根据课文内容补全对话

1. 胸痛　　　2. 位置　　　3. 剧烈　　　4. 咳嗽

5. 时间　　　6. 发现　　　7. 检查　　　8. 抗生素

二、根据课文内容回答问题

1. 先天性心脏病的种类有很多,由于发生的部位和程度不同而分为各式各样的类型。但先天性心脏病种类大体上可分为非青紫型和青紫型两类。

2. 发绀型心脏病有轻度的畸形,可以没有任何症状,严重心脏病者,常常表现为手足和颜面发紫,特别以口唇、鼻尖和耳廓、手指尖为显著,在哭闹时更为明显。另外发绀型心脏病的病人,活动或行走后可出现蹲踞。

3. 先天性心脏病选择何种治疗方法以及选择正确的手术时机,主要取决于先天性心脏畸形的范围及程度。严重的先天性心脏病在出生后必须立即手术,否则患儿将无法生存。

4. 肺癌的临床表现,取决于肿瘤发生部位、病理类型、有无转移及有无并发症,咳嗽是最常见的症状,痰中带血或咯血亦是肺癌的常见症状。

三、写作练习

参考答案:肺癌是发病率和死亡率增长最快,对人群健康和生命威胁最大的恶性肿瘤之一。近 50 年来许多国家都报道肺癌的发病率和死亡率均明显增高,男性肺癌发病率和死亡率均占所有恶性肿瘤的第一位,女性发病率占第二位,死亡率占第二位。

四、交际练习

答案略。

第十章

➢ 听力练习

一、听录音,选择你听到的词语

1. A　　2. B　　3. C　　4. A　　5. B　　6. D　　7. A　　8. B　　9. B　　10. C

二、请根据录音判断正误,对的写"T",错的写"F"

1. F　　2. F　　3. F　　4. T　　5. F

三、听录音,完成下面的练习

1. 根据所听到的录音判断对错

1) ×　　2) ×　　3) √　　4) √　　5) ×

2. 听录音,选择正确答案回答问题

1) C　　2) D　　3) B　　4) A

➢ 词汇和语法练习

一、给下列词语标注拼音

1. ráogǔ　　　2. yuǎnduān　　　3. yāpò　　　4. yùhé　　　5. wěisuō

6. shuāidǎo　　7. cígòngzhèn　　8. yìngmónáng　　9. zhuījiānpán　　10. wànguānjié

二、选词填空

1. 不对劲儿　　2. 防止　　3. 风险　　4. 压迫　　5. 可能性

6. 喷　　　　　7. 固定　　8. 增强　　9. 尽量　　10. 采取

三、用指定的词语或结构完成句子或对话

1. 我们考虑他得的是腰椎间盘突出　　　2. 手术存在很大的风险

3. 不能排除癌症的可能性　　　　　　　4. 在紧急的情况下

5. 不会受到太大的影响

四、把下列词语排列成句子

1. MRI 的图像比 CT 的更清晰。

2. 腿部麻痛是腰椎间盘突出引起的。

3. 我们还不能排除骨折的可能性。

4. 要经常活动指关节防止肌肉萎缩。

5. 病人手腕的活动没有受到太大影响。

➢ 阅读与应用练习

一、根据课文内容补全对话。

1. 桡骨远端　　2. 复位　　3. 打　　4. 有点儿疼　　5. 绷带

6. 拆石膏　　　7. 三个月　　　　　8. 不要用力　　　　　9. 发生移位　　10. 复查

11. 定期　　　12. 你骨骼愈合的情况　13. 拆石膏的时间。

二、根据课文内容回答问题

1. 半年前就觉得腰痛了,最近一两个月,疼得越来越厉害了。疼起来,像针刺一样,一直疼。

2. 刚开始,睡觉的时候觉得有点麻。后来,觉得越来越麻了,走路也有点困难了。

3. 医生建议病人做磁共振检查,因为磁共振检查的图像比 CT 的清晰。

4. 检查结果显示病人的 L_{1-2} 和 L_{2-3} 椎间盘向后突出,$L_5{\sim}S_1$ 椎间盘向四周膨出,硬膜囊受压,确诊是腰椎间盘突出。

5. 目前,医生建议病人采取保守治疗,因为手术治疗存在一定的风险。

三、写作练习

参考答案:这个病人的 X 线片显示是桡骨远端骨折,但是骨折的情况不是特别严重。因此,医生建议采取保守治疗。也就是先把病人骨折处进行复位,然后再用石膏固定。

四、交际练习

答案略。

第十一章

➤ 听力练习

一、听录音,选择你听到的词语

1. C　　2. B　　3. D　　4. A　　5. C　　6. B　　7. D　　8. A　　9. D　　10. D

二、请根据录音判断正误,对的写"T",错的写"F"

1. F　　2. T　　3. F　　4.T　　5. F

三、听录音,完成下面的练习

1. 根据所听到的录音判断对错

1) ×　　2) ×　　3) ×　　4) √　　5) ×

2. 听录音,选择正确答案回答问题

1) B　　2) D　　3) A　　4) B

➤ 词汇和语法练习

一、给下列词语标注拼音

1. éyè　　　2. guānchá　　3. chēhuò　　4. yìshí　　5. lúnèi

6. xuèzhǒng　7. fàngshèkē　8. qiǎngjiùshì　9. dòngmàiliú　10. shénzhì bùqīng

二、选词填空

1. 控制　　2. 呈　　　3. 配合　　4. 清除　　5. 脱离;密切

6. 伴　　　7. 尽力　　8. 撞　　　9. 偏

三、用指定的词语或结构完成句子或对话

1. 憋不住了　　　　　　　2. 呈阳性

3. 是畸形血管破裂造成的　4. 连脑中线都移位了

5. 还是存在术后复发的风险

四、把下列词语排列成句子

1. 病人右颞有脑挫伤,还伴有脑出血。

2. 畸形血管破裂会引起自发性脑出血。

3. 病人的颅内出血量随时可能增加。

4. 他的偏瘫是脑卒中造成的。

5. 病人出现了喷射状呕吐。

➤ 阅读与应用练习

一、根据会话二补全对话

1. 模糊	2. 烦躁	3. 瞳孔反应	4. 脑动脉瘤或血管畸形
5. 颅内出血	6. 脑室	7. 中线	8. 发生移位了
9. 风险	10. 偏瘫、长期昏迷	11. 不做手术	12. 手术同意书

二、根据会话一内容回答问题

1. 头部有外伤,意识比较清楚。

2. CT 检查是右颞多发散在的脑挫伤,伴有脑出血,但出血量不大。

3. 医生建议继续观察,暂时不手术。

4. 病人意识开始模糊,出现了喷射性呕吐。

5. 第二次 CT 发现脑出血面积增大。医生建议马上手术。

三、写作练习

参考答案:开颅手术发现这个病人颅内存在血管畸形。畸形血管破裂引起了自发性脑出血。病人颅内出血量较大,出血已进入脑室,造成了脑中线移位,从而出现了颅内血肿。

四、交际练习

答案略。

第十二章

➤ 听力练习

一、听录音,选择你听到的词语

1. B 2. D 3. A 4. A 5. B 6. B 7. D 8. B 9. A 10. A

二、请选出与所听录音相符的答案

1. D 2. B 3. D 4. D

三、听录音,完成下面的练习

1. 根据所听到的录音判断对错

1) √ 2) × 3) √ 4) √ 5) √

2. 听录音,选择正确答案回答问题

1) B 2) D 3) D

➤ 词汇和语法练习

一、给下列词语标注拼音

1. xiázhǎi	2. kòuzhěn	3. géngzǔ	4. xuèniào
5. xìngbìng	6. yīzhǔ	7. jiǎotòng	8. shènyùjīshuǐ
9. qiánlièxiàn	10. shènshuāijié	11. shēngzhíqì	12. zhícángzhǐjiǎn
13. yàomínshìyàn	14. xìjūnpéiyǎng	15. bìngyuántǐ	

二、选词填空

1. 医嘱	2. 尿频	3. 直肠指检	4. 中段尿
5. 尿不尽	6. 狭窄	7. 排石冲剂	8. 药物敏感性试验
9. 绞痛	10. 叩诊		

三、用指定的词语或结构完成句子或对话

1. 根据你的临床症状和实验室检查结果

2. 预防结石的形成

3. 引起剧烈疼痛

4. 只要没有引起长期严重的肾盂积水

5. 该大肠埃希菌对大环内酯类药物敏感

四、把下列词语排列成句子

1. 严重的肾盂积水会导致肾衰竭。

2. 请问你有憋不住尿的感觉吗?

3. 可以确诊你患有肾结石。

4. 你要耐心等待药物敏感性试验结果。

5. 心理因素可能会引起前列腺炎。

➢ 阅读与应用练习

一、根据课文内容补全对话。

1. 隐隐疼痛	2. 坠胀感	3. 大约	4. 异常	5. 影响
6. 尿不尽	7. 得过	8. 直肠指检	9. 常规检查	10. 细菌培养

二、根据课文内容回答问题

1. 田华除了有肾绞痛的症状之外,还有恶心、呕吐并伴有血尿。

2. 因为结石卡在了输尿管狭窄处,引起梗阻性疼痛。

3. 医生诊断田华患有肾结石,治疗方法:输液解痉止痛,排石冲剂,并叮嘱病人多喝水,多运动,少食用含钙高的食物。

4. 他觉得不好意思,所以拖延了半年。

5. 确诊依据是临床症状和前列腺液细菌培养结果。

三、写作练习

参考答案:前列腺炎常见的临床症状包括下腹部隐痛,并可放射到生殖器和肛门,导致尿频、尿急和夜尿增多。严重的病人可出现发烧等全身症状。体征包括前列腺增大,并有压痛。前列腺液检查可能有细菌感染,并伴有白细胞增高。

四、交际练习

答案略。

第十三章

➢ 听力练习

一、听录音,选择你听到的词语

1. A　2. D　3. B　4. A　5. B　6. D　7. A　8. C　9. B　10. C

二、请选出与所听录音相符的答案

1. C　2. A　3. C　4. A　5. B

三、听录音,完成下面的练习

1. 根据所听到的录音判断对错

1) √　2) ×　3) ×　4) ×　5) √　6) ×

2. 听录音,选择正确答案回答问题

1) B　2) B　3) B

➢ **词汇和语法练习**

一、给下列词语标注拼音

1. shāoshāng 2. miànjī 3. shēndù 4. shǒushù 5. zhòngdù
6. shuǐpào 7. pǔzhuàngbānhén 8. téngtòng 9. bāozāzhìliáo 10. bānhén

二、选词填空

1. 烧伤 2. 冷疗 3. 包扎 4. 浅Ⅱ度 5. 特重度烧伤
6. Z成形术 7. 蹼状瘢痕 8. 皮瓣 9. 瘢痕增生

三、用指定的词语或结构完成句子或对话

1. 当时烫伤后给予正确治疗 2. 就会使创面深度变浅
3. 与创面深度有关 4. 而且也影响外观
5. 还是到正规医院救治好

四、把下列词语排列成句子

1. 影响烧伤愈合的主要因素是创面深度。
2. 烧伤Ⅱ度创面可见水疱。
3. 蹼状瘢痕常需要Z成形手术治疗。
4. 一般住院2周可以出院。
5. 在门诊可行局部麻醉下的小手术治疗。

➢ **阅读与应用练习**

一、根据课文内容补全对话。

1. 手术 2. 麻醉 3. 禁忌证 4. 植皮
5. 蹼状 6. 皮瓣 7. 锻炼

二、根据课文内容回答问题

1. 李晓亮烫伤后,主要是疼痛,胳膊活动不便。
2. 属于轻度烫伤。
3. 腋窝处的瘢痕呈蹼状,需要手术治疗,可采取Z成形术。
4. 烫伤后需要立即给予冷水冲洗或冰块湿敷,大面积烫伤后需要给予干净的布料或被褥暂时覆盖。
5. 当时烫伤深度为Ⅲ度,现在腋窝处的瘢痕切除直接缝合,还会形成直线瘢痕,需要采取皮瓣修复。

三、写作练习

参考答案:右前臂热水烫伤,散在多个大水疱,疼痛,去除水疱液,大部分表皮游离,少许表皮剥脱,基底红润,渗出多,前臂屈伸受限,不灵活,下垂右下肢疼痛感及胀感加重。

四、交际练习

答案略。

第十四章

➢ **听力练习**

一、听录音,选择你听到的词语

1. A 2. B 3. B 4. D 5. B 6. C 7. C 8. D 9. A 10. A

二、请选出与所听录音相符的答案

1. D   2. D   3. A   4. A   5. A

三、听录音,完成下面的练习

1. 根据所听到的录音判断对错

1) ×   2) ×   3) ×   4) √   5) ×

2. 听录音,选择正确答案回答问题

1) A   2) B   3) C   4) A   5) A

➢ **词汇和语法练习**

一、给下列词语标注拼音

1. báidài chángguī   2. sàoyǎng   3. wèishēngjīn   4. yīndào yánzhèng

5. wàiyīn yīndào jiǎsījiàomǔjūn bìng   6. tíngjīng   7. huáiyùn

8. huángtǐtóng   9. chūchǎnfù   10. yìwèi rènshēn

二、选词填空

1. 阴道炎   2. 性生活   3. 尿频尿痛   4. 豆渣

5. 妇科检查   6. 先兆流产   7. 黄体酮   8. 隐隐地

9. 早日康复   10. 急诊室

三、用指定的词语或结构完成句子或对话

1. 今天感觉阴道瘙痒越来越厉害了

2. 我现在肚子痛得很

3. 真是美极了

4. 根据病人的临床表现,初步诊断为阑尾炎

5. 口服每天两次,每次两片,一共服用1周

6. 我的肚子痛好多了

7. 除了发烧,还拉肚子

8. 还需要与异位妊娠进行鉴别

9. 你已经停经60多天了

10. 没有阴道流血,也没有肚子痛

四、选择句子完成对话

1. C   2. B   3. A   4. D   5. E

五、排列下列句子的顺序

1. D   2. E   3. A   4. C   5. B

六、把下列词语排列成句子

1. 病人阴道瘙痒得越来越厉害。

2. 根据检查结果初步诊断为阴道炎。

3. 病人以前出现过类似的情况。

4. 最近有没有更换过卫生巾。

5. 病人阴道黏膜充血很明显。

6. 您的末次月经是什么时候?

7. 您都做了哪些检查?

8. 医生给我用黄体酮保胎。

9. 通过辅助检查来鉴别异位妊娠。

10. 劳累后出现阴道流血伴随下腹痛。或劳累后出现下腹痛伴随阴道流血。

➢ 阅读与应用练习

一、根据课文内容补全对话。

（一）1. 阴道　　　　2. 性生活或"在一起"　　　3. 白带

　　4. 豆渣　　　　5. 检查或治疗　　　　6. 阴道炎

（二）7. 阴道流血　　8. 先兆流产　　　　9. 住院

　　10. 超声　　　　11. 黄体酮针　　　　12. 早日康复

二、根据课文内容回答问题

1. 张洁患阴道炎的主要临床表现是阴道瘙痒伴随有白带异常。发病原因是和老公性生活。

2. 张洁患阴道炎后白带的性状是白带量多，白色的，稠厚，像豆渣，没有臭味。

3. 外阴阴道假丝酵母菌病的治疗方案是口服和阴道用药的联合药物治疗。氟康唑片，口服，每天两次，每次两片，仅服用一天。克霉唑阴道栓，每天塞阴道一粒，一共塞 7 天。

4. 在阴道炎治疗方面的注意事项有：①按时按量用药；②用药 2 周后复查；③建议丈夫同时检查。

5. 先兆流产的症状有：①停经；②腹痛；③阴道流血。

6. 诊断先兆流产前，医生一般需要做妇科检查，验血，超声检查。

7. 先兆流产的治疗方案有卧床休息，药物（黄体酮针）保胎治疗。

8. 先兆流产主要要与异位妊娠相鉴别。

三、写作练习

参考答案：病人性生活后感到阴道瘙痒，同时发现白带增多，白色、稠厚像豆渣样。病人到医院就诊，妇科检查发现阴道黏膜充血明显，结合白带常规的检查结果，诊断为外阴阴道假丝酵母菌病。医生为她开了氟康唑片口服及克霉唑阴道栓塞阴道治疗，并建议两周后回医院复查。

四、交际练习

答案略。

第十五章

➢ 听力练习

一、听录音，选择你听到的词语

1. B　　2. A　　3. C　　4. A　　5. D　　6. C　　7. A　　8. D　　9. B　　10. A

二、请选出与所听录音相符的答案

1. C　　2. D　　3. B　　4. A　　5. B

三、听录音，完成下面的练习

1. 根据所听到的录音判断对错

1）√　　2）×　　3）×　　4）×　　5）√

2. 听录音，选择正确答案回答问题

1）C　　2）D　　3）A

➢ 词汇和语法练习

一、给下列词语标注拼音

1. yuèjīng　　　　2. wěisuō　　　　3. gōngjǐng　　　　4. xiàfùtòng

5. pénqiāngyán　　6. shuāngfùjiàn　　7. fǎnfùfāzuò　　8. yīndào fēnmìwù

9. gōngqiāngnèi cánliú　　10. wēichuàng shǒushù

二、选词填空

1. 月经 2. 乏力 3. 残留 4. 肌瘤切除术 5. 妇科 B 超

6. 后遗症 7. 妇科检查 8. 缩短 9. 抗生素 10. 持续性的

三、用指定的词语或结构完成句子或对话

1. 你最好到医院检查一下

2. 后遗症有不孕、异位妊娠、慢性盆腔痛等

3. 是间歇性的还是持续性的

4. 除了吃些药物控制症状以外,还应做子宫和宫颈检查

5. 如果能及时、恰当地使用抗生素治疗就能彻底治愈

四、把下列词语排列成句子

1. 我害怕做肌瘤切除术,可以保守治疗吗?

2. 子宫肌瘤有复发的可能性。

3. 你可以口服一些铁剂纠正贫血。

4. 盆腔炎能彻底治愈吗?

5. 这个病人最近两天下腹持续性疼痛。

➤ **阅读与应用练习**

一、根据课文内容补全对话

1. 月经不规律 2. 经期 3. 月经周期 4. 贫血

5. 症状 6. 妇科 B 超 7. 子宫肌瘤 8. 雌激素

二、根据课文内容回答问题

1. 王婷月经不规律,经量增多,经期较长,头晕,乏力。

2. 医生让王婷做妇科 B 超和血常规检查。

3. 医生给王婷的初步诊断是子宫肌瘤。医生让王婷做肌瘤切除术。

4. 李玟做了无痛人流术,术后未用消炎药,术后有过一次性生活。

5. 盆腔炎的后遗症有不孕、异位妊娠、慢性盆腔痛、盆腔炎反复发作等。

三、写作练习

参考答案:李玟症状表现为下腹部持续性疼痛伴发热;体征表现为下腹压痛、反跳痛;妇科检查宫颈举痛、子宫体有压痛、双侧附件稍增厚、有压痛。医生诊断为急性盆腔炎。医生建议口服抗生素,并加强营养,保持体位引流,防止炎症波及上腹部,预防再次感染。

四、交际练习

答案略。

第十六章

➤ **听力练习**

一、听录音,选择你听到的词语

1. C 2. A 3. C 4. B 5. A 6. D 7. C 8. B 9. D 10. A

二、请选出与所听录音相符的答案

1. C 2. A 3. C 4. D 5. B

三、听录音,完成下面的练习

1. 根据所听到的录音判断对错

1) √ 2) × 3) √ 4) × 5) ×

2. 听录音,选择正确答案回答问题

1) C 　2) A 　3) D 　4) B 　5) A

> 词汇和语法练习

一、给下列词语标注拼音

1. zǎi 　　2. línchǎn 　　3. shuízhǒng 　　4. pòshuǐ 　　5. yángshuǐ

6. fēnmiǎn 　　7. gōngsuō 　　8. yùchǎnqī 　　9. sīliè 　　10. réngōng pòmó

二、选词填空

1. 妊娠 　　2. 水肿 　　3. 左侧卧位 　　4. 食补 　　5. 待产

6. 预产期;破水 　7. 扩张;枕后位 　8. 撕裂

三、用指定的词语或结构完成句子或对话

1. 由新的感冒病毒导致的 　　2. 只要在家吃药就行了 　　3. 和他本人相符

4. 对莉莉来说 　　5. 在网络上面试

四、把下列词语排列成句子

1. 最近这一周我的脚踝肿了。

2. 您还需要做一个胎心监护。

3. 宫颈口扩张完全就可以生了。

4. 医生把她送进了分娩室。

5. 您的丈夫已经在同意书上签字了。

> 阅读与应用练习

一、根据课文内容补全对话

1. 水肿 　　2. 便秘 　　3. 纤维 　　4. 粗粮 　　5. 规律

6. 假临产 　　7. 见红 　　8. 破水 　　9. 胎头下降感

二、根据课文内容回答问题

1. 测量血压,腹部检查,彩色超声,胎心监护及血常规和尿常规。

2. 出现规律的肚子疼,见红、破水和胎头下降感

3. 破水,肚子疼。

4. 1) 宫缩力量不够; 　　2) 胎位不正。

5. 注意休息,加强营养。建议母乳喂养。产后42天内禁房事、免盆浴,保持外阴清洁。如果有腹痛、异常阴道流血及发热等情况马上找医生。

三、写作练习

参考答案:张欣是初产妇,较预产期提前4天破水,未见红,有规律宫缩。人工破膜后进入分娩室。宫口开全后,打催产素增加产力;因胎位不正(持续性枕后位)行手转胎头术后顺利分娩一女婴。

四、交际练习

答案略。

第十七章

> 听力练习

一、听录音,选择你听到的词语

1. B 　2. A 　3. A 　4. D 　5. D 　6. A 　7. B 　8. B 　9. C 　10. A

二、请选出与所听录音相符的答案

1. C   2. A   3. D   4. D   5. C

三、听录音,完成下面的练习

1. 根据所听到的录音判断对错

1) √   2) ×   3) ×   4) √   5) √

2. 听录音,选择正确答案回答问题

1) B   2) B   3) A   4) C

➢ **词汇和语法练习**

一、给下列词语标注拼音

1. tāimó   2. gōngdǐ   3. shīmián   4. zǐxián

5. rènshēn   6. zhuǎnān méi   7. pínxuèmào   8. gōngnèi jiǒngpò

9. gōngsuō fálì   10. níngxuè gōngnéng zhàngài

二、选词填空

1. 缓解   2. 产妇纸   3. 按摩子宫   4. 动静脉比

5. 指标   6. 裂伤   7. 排除   8. 断断续续

三、用指定的词语或结构完成句子或对话

1. 疼得不得了 / 晕得不得了

2. 排除了凝血功能异常

3. 有助于帮助子宫收缩 / 有助于控制子宫出血

4. 根据您的体征和检查结果

5. 否则会影响胎儿的发育 / 否则会危及生命

四、把下列词语排列成句子

1. 实习生注意一下病人的中毒反应。

2. 生产后症状会逐渐减轻。

3. 产后出血会让您的贫血症状更加恶化。

4. 请帮我把她扶到产检床上。

5. 症状好转一些后再口服琥珀酸亚铁片。

➢ **阅读与应用练习**

一、根据课文内容补全对话

1. 你有什么不舒服?   2. 食欲

3. 看东西不清楚   4. 您的产前检查一直在做吗?

5. 头晕得不得了   6. 腿也肿得厉害

7. 躺了好几天也没好转   8. 缓解

9. 您家里有人有高血压吗?   10. 失眠

二、根据课文内容回答问题

1. 全身乏力,心慌头晕,阴道流血,色暗红,有凝血块。

2. 产后出血的原因主要是子宫收缩乏力、胎盘胎膜残留、凝血功能异常等。

3. 主要是按摩子宫,同时静脉滴注缩宫素。

4. 眼底检查可以反映病人的全身小动脉痉挛程度,有助于医生对病情的估计和处理。

5. 妊娠期高血压如果治疗不及时,会影响胎儿的发育,甚至造成宫内窒迫,危及生命。

三、写作练习

参考答案:病人吴菲菲主诉头晕浮肿、胃胀,没有食欲,眼睛视物不清,经常失眠。根据病人的体征

和各项检查结果,医生诊断为子痫前期。医生的治疗方案如下:

1. 开镇静药帮助睡眠。

2. 测 24 小时尿量,血压每天测四到六次。

3. 静滴尼卡地平控制血压。

4. 输人体白蛋白,注意利尿。

5. 使用解痉药硫酸镁并注意病人的毒性反应,随时检查。

四、交际练习

答案略。

第十八章

➤ 听力练习

一、听录音,选择你听到的词语

1. B   2. C   3. D   4. C   5.A   6. C   7. D   8.A   9.B   10. A

二、请选出与所听录音相符的答案

1. D   2. B   3. A   4. C   5. A

三、听录音,完成下面的练习

1. 根据所听到的录音判断对错

1) ×   2) √   3) ×   4) ×   5) √   6) √

2. 听录音,选择正确答案回答问题

1) C   2) D   3) A

➤ 词汇和语法练习

一、给下列词语标注拼音

1. chuǎnxī   2. xiūkè   3. rèxìng jīngjué   4. bíyì shāndòng

5. tīngzhěnqì   6. zhǐké huàtán   7. jìngmài bǔyè   8. mǔrǔ wèiyǎng

9. lúnzhuàng bìngdú 10. qiánxìn āoxiàn

二、选词填空

1. 不舒服   2. 发烧   3. 退烧药   4. 便常规

5. 雾化   6. 脱水   7. 治疗室   8. 诊疗计划

9. 及时   10. 酸中毒

三、用指定的词语或结构完成句子或对话

1. 是静脉补液还是口服补液   2. 我没有当回事儿

3. 症状没有见好   4. 又吐又拉

5. 轻易不带孩子来医院   6. 怕宝宝受罪

四、把下列词语排列成句子

1. 交费取药后,到治疗室找护士输液。

2. 脱水的孩子需要尽快补液治疗。

3. 医生给患儿做体格检查。

4. 妈妈不知道孩子能不能配合治疗。

5. 找医生看一下化验结果。

➤ **阅读与应用练习**

一、根据课文内容补全对话

1. 流鼻涕	2. 厉害	3. 当回事儿	4. 见好
5. 埋怨	6. 呼吸困难	7. 小儿肺炎	8. 血常规
9. C 反应蛋白	10. 胸部 X 线		

二、根据课文内容回答问题

1. 乐乐的主要症状有流鼻涕、咳嗽、发烧、喘气快,而且没精神,不爱吃饭。

2. 肺里有广泛的湿啰音。

3. 医生的诊断是细菌感染引起的小儿肺炎,建议静脉点滴头孢呋辛治疗。

4. 壮壮的大便是稀水样,黄绿色,大便一天大约十次。

5. 医生建议暂停喂辅食,继续母乳喂养,待腹泻好转后,由少到多,由稀到稠逐渐恢复正常饮食。

三、写作练习

参考答案:壮壮呕吐 2 天,腹泻 1 天,大便稀水样,黄绿色,一天大约十次,尿量少。护士测体温 38℃,体格检查发现壮壮略有口唇干燥,前囟凹陷,肠鸣音活跃。

四、交际练习

答案略。

第十九章

➤ **听力练习**

一、听录音,选择你听到的词语

1. C 2. A 3. B 4. C 5. D 6. B 7. D 8. C 9. A 10. A

二、请选出与所听录音相符的答案

1. C 2. B 3. D 4. A 5. B

三、听录音,完成下面的练习

1. 根据所听到的录音判断对错

1)√ 2)× 3)× 4)√ 5)√ 6)× 7)√ 8)×

2. 听录音,选择正确答案回答问题

1)C 2)A 3)D 4)D 5)B

➤ **词汇和语法练习**

一、给下列词语标注拼音

1. wèiyǎng	2. chuánrǎn	3. xiāodú	4. zhēngzhào
5. jiēzhòng	6. huànóng	7. dǎnhóngsù	8. lìxìbāo
9. zhōngěryán	10. hòuyízhèng		

二、选词填空

1. 生理性	2. 照蓝光	3. 黄疸	4. 数值
5. 消毒	6. 事先	7. 咳嗽	8. 脑脊液
9. 颅压	10. 膨胀		

三、用指定的词语或结构完成句子或对话

1. 由于预防措施得当   2. 结合工作需要来考虑

3. 隔着玻璃窗   4. 比如说感冒

5. 每到放假的时候　　　　6. 不会对他的大脑发育有影响

四、把下列词语排列成句子

1. 新生儿肠道无菌也会影响胆红素的代谢。

2. 光照疗法是常见的新生儿黄疸治疗方法。

3. 患儿体内的胆红素主要通过大便排出。

4. 婴幼儿应该远离传染病人和其他传染源。

5. 化脓性脑膜炎需要快速诊断和及时治疗。

➤ **阅读与应用练习**

一、根据课文内容补全对话。

1. 确诊	2. 发育	3. 导致	4. 静脉点滴
5. 抗生素	6. 减轻	7. 需要	8. 休息

二、根据课文内容回答问题

1. 贝贝的母亲在网上看到,一般新生儿黄疸是生理性的,不用治,自然消退,可是二十多天过去,贝贝的黄疸还没有消退,所以才来医院。

2. 新生儿肝脏酶系统发育不完善,产生的胆红素不能及时转化。此外,刚出生的新生儿肠道无菌也会影响胆红素的代谢。

3. 孩子有头痛、发热、呕吐和颈强直等临床表现。验血发现白细胞和中性粒细胞明显增加,脑脊液外观混浊,白细胞增多,中性粒细胞为主,蛋白增高,糖减低。

4. 给予抗生素皮试,确定茜茜没有对抗生素过敏,才能用药。

5. 让孩子饮食上吃些好消化的,少吃多餐,以减轻胃的膨胀,防止呕吐发生。另外,要注意多休息,睡眠要足。

三、写作练习

参考答案:患儿茜茜发热、头痛和呕吐,母亲带她来就诊。医生查体发现她颈强直,马上为她抽血化验和腰椎穿刺,确诊为化脓性脑膜炎。医生立即让她入院,给她静点抗生素来治疗。

四、交际练习

答案略。

第二十章

➤ **听力练习**

一、听录音,选择你听到的词语

1. C　　2. A　　3. C　　4. D　　5. C　　6. A　　7. C　　8. B　　9. A　　10. A

二、请选出与所听录音相符的答案

1. C　　2. D　　3. B　　4. D　　5. C

三、听录音,完成下面的练习

1. 根据所听到的录音判断对错

1) ×　　2) ×　　3) √　　4) ×　　5) √

2. 听录音,选择正确答案回答问题

1) A　　2) A　　3) A

➤ 词汇和语法练习

一、给下列词语标注拼音

1. diàndǐ
2. yáshénjīng
3. básuǐzhēn
4. fǔzhì
5. yásuǐqiāng
6. shēnglǐ yánshuǐ
7. luóhóngméisù
8. gēnguǎn zhìliáo
9. yǎohémiàn
10. qiànsāi

二、选词填空

1. X 线牙片
2. 清理消毒
3. 中龋
4. 抽牙神经
5. 俗称
6. 典型症状
7. 消炎药
8. 过敏史
9. 发作
10. 加重

三、用指定的词语或结构完成句子或对话

1. 会导致其他疾病
2. 他来得算是早的了
3. 就是有点儿累
4. 尽量少吃甜食
5. 直至病人病情稳定了才回家

四、把下列词语排列成句子

1. 这个治疗大概需要多长时间?
2. 晚上牙疼得受不了。
3. 这是麻药已经显效的表现。
4. 我右上面大牙上有个小洞。
5. 用器械检查时可能比较敏感。

➤ 阅读与应用练习

一、根据课文内容补全对话

1. 颗
2. 所以
3. 另外
4. 俗称
5. 或者
6. 必要
7. 因此
8. 不算
9. 根据
10. 完全
11. 然后
12. 再
13. 一直
14. 多虑了
15. 才
16. 算是
17. 自行
18. 及时
19. 导致
20. 引起

二、根据课文内容回答问题

1. 王力吃饭的时候,总会塞东西,咬硬的食物时也不敢使劲儿。另外,遇到冷、热、酸、甜刺激时,牙齿也会觉得不舒服,有时有"倒牙"的感觉。

2. 医生给王力的诊断是右侧下面倒数第二颗大牙的咬合面上有一个龋洞,属于"中龋"。治疗方案:将牙齿上龋洞里的腐质完全清理掉,然后用垫底材料聚羧酸锌垫底,再用树脂充填材料把龋洞充填好。

3. 如果龋齿不及时治疗会导致牙齿丧失,甚至会引起身体其他部位的病变。

4. 张华不选择保守治疗的原因是保守治疗只能解决短期内的疼痛。如果牙齿疼痛再次发作的话,会疼得更加厉害。

5. 张华 X 线牙片的诊断结果是牙髓炎。

6. 一天两次,饭后服用,一次一粒。服药期间,避免食用带有刺激性的食物。

三、写作练习

参考答案:牙疼难忍,晚上牙疼加重,不能吃太凉或太热的东西。

四、交际练习

答案略。

第二十一章

➤ 听力练习

一、听录音,选择你听到的词语

1. D　　2. B　　3. C　　4. B　　5. A　　6. A　　7. C　　8. A　　9. A　　10. A

二、请选出与所听录音相符的答案

1. A　　2. B　　3. D　　4. A　　5. B

三、听录音,完成下面的练习

1. 根据所听到的录音判断对错

1) √　　2) √　　3) ×　　4) ×　　5) √　　6) √

2. 听录音,选择正确答案回答问题

1) B　　2) D　　3) B　　4) B　　5) C

➤ 词汇和语法练习

一、给下面的词语标准拼音

1. yáchǐ	2. yáyín	3. yácáo	4. gǎnmào fāshāo
5. sāixiàn nángzhǒng	6. jièxiàn qīngchǔ	7. sāiliè	8. jiěpōu
9. zhèngjī zhìliáo	10. yínshàng jiézhì		

二、选词填空

1. 牙龈炎	2. 排列不齐	3. 咬合无力	4. 口腔清洁
5. 矫形术	6. 感冒发烧	7. 规律	8. 报告单
9. 彩超	10. 病理		

三、用指定的词语或结构完成句子或对话

1. 所以要做牙齿矫形　　　　　　2. 另外要保持口腔清洁

3. 再行手术治疗　　　　　　　　4. 随着年龄的增长

5. 不但鼻子不通气

四、把下列词语排列成句子

1. 病人的牙齿排列不齐并且牙龈出血。

2. 您的牙齿咬合不好,避免吃硬东西。

3. 现在考虑您的诊断是腮腺囊肿。

4. 您需要先做 B 超检查明确诊断。

5. 这种治疗方案看起来不错。

➤ 阅读与应用练习

一、根据课文内容补全对话

1. 耳朵　　2. 包块　　3. 一个　　4. 花生米　　5. 鸡蛋黄

6. 感冒　　7. 担心　　8. 隐隐约约　　9. 药物

二、根据课文内容回答问题

1. 上下牙齿排列不整齐,影响脸型。

2. 容貌和吃饭。

3. 先消炎后再手术治疗。

4. 休息不好,生活没有规律,担心父亲的病情。

5. 鳃裂囊肿,先控制感染后再进行手术治疗。

三、写作练习

参考答案:邵鑫的牙齿排列不整齐,影响到了他的脸型和外貌。同时牙齿排列不齐导致牙齿咬合不上,吃东西很费劲。这样的情况随着他年龄增长越来越严重,他担心未来会更重。

四、交际练习

答案略。